D1594774

Alcohol

ROD PHILLIPS

Alcohol

a history

THE UNIVERSITY OF NORTH CAROLINA PRESS | CHAPEL HILL

The paper in this book meets the guidelines for permanence and durability
of the Committee on Production Guidelines for Book Longevity of the Council
on Library Resources. The University of North Carolina Press has been a
member of the Green Press Initiative since 2003.

Jacket illustration © benidio/Stockphoto.com

Library of Congress Cataloging-in-Publication Data
Phillips, Roderick.
Alcohol : a history / Rod Phillips.
pages cm
Includes bibliographical references and index.
ISBN 978-1-4696-1760-2 (cloth : alk. paper) — ISBN 978-1-4696-1761-9 (ebook)
1. Alcohol—Social aspects—History. 2. Drinking of alcoholic beverages—
Social aspects—History. 3. Alcoholic beverage industry—History. I. Title.
GT2884.P45 2014
394.1'3—dc23
2014013124

18 17 16 15 14 5 4 3 2 1

TO RUTH

Companion to many archives, companion in many glasses

Contents

Alcohol

Introduction

Ever since humans began to consume alcohol, they have had a difficult relationship with it. Alcohol is a colorless liquid that has, in itself, no material, cultural, or moral value. But like many other commodities, it has been ascribed complicated and often contradictory sets of values that have varied over time and place, and that are interwoven with the complexities of power, gender, class, ethnicity, and age in the societies in which it is consumed.

All these values derive fundamentally from the action of alcohol on the human nervous system. Readers who have consumed alcohol will recognize one or more of the stages of intoxication that begin with the first sip of alcohol, whether it is beer, whiskey, wine, a cocktail, or a beverage made from the myriad commodities used to produce alcohol. A small volume of alcohol generally gives the drinker a sense of well-being, and further drinking can lead, in turn, to feelings of euphoria, relaxation of social inhibitions, loss of balance and coordination, slurred speech, vomiting, and loss of consciousness. Severe cases of alcoholic poisoning can be fatal.

Needless to say, not all consumers of alcohol drink so much that that they experience anything more than a pleasant and uplifting sense of well-being. Not only did that sense became highly valued and much sought-after, but the state of euphoric otherworldliness that came with further drinking has been, in some cultures, thought of as spiritual and as bringing the consumer closer to the gods. In other cultures, the potential of alcohol to harm its consumer produced dire warnings about excessive consumption and various punishments for becoming perceptibly intoxicated.

The result was a polarity of views toward alcohol. On one hand, alcoholic beverages have been widely employed as a social lubricant and adhesive in daily interactions, as varied as Russian workers drinking in their factories in the nineteenth century to women gathering at an all-female dramshop in London to drink gin in the early 1700s. Alcohol has historically played a role at marriages and funerals, and it has commonly marked commercial, political, and other events. Madeira was used to launch one of the U.S. Navy's first frigates in 1797, while some East African peoples celebrated marriages with banana beer. Alcohol has often been provided to pay for work, and it was widely used as currency when Europeans extended their economic activities to the wider world; whiskey, gin, and rum bought slaves and commodities as varied as beaver pelts and copra, influence, and land.

Alcohol helps people relax and sometimes to forget their cares. Alcoholic beverages, especially beer and wine, have often been associated with divinity, and they have historically been credited with having medicinal or therapeutic properties; it is hard to think of an illness, disease, or physical pathology that has not, at some time, been treated by some form of alcohol. It has been credited with ridding the body of worms and cancer, aiding digestion, fighting heart disease, and turning back old age and extending life itself.

On the other hand, alcohol has been described as a menace, not only to the individual consumer but to the society in which it is consumed. It has been described as evil, as the gift of a devil rather than of any god. Some nineteenth-century Christian theologians were so horrified at the thought that their god might have approved of alcohol that they reinterpreted the Bible to show that Jesus's first miracle was to turn water into grape juice, not wine. Islam and some other religions banned the consumption of alcohol and other intoxicants. Alcohol has been blamed for illnesses, insanity, accidents, immorality, impiety, social disorder, catastrophes, crime, and death. From the Middle Ages to the present, it has been a convention for some commentators to see alcohol as the core problem from which all other problems flow.

Many critics of alcohol have acknowledged that, consumed in moderation, alcohol need not have dire consequences. Reflecting this position, most authorities have historically tried to mitigate the worst effects of alcohol by surrounding its production, distribution, and consumption by regulations. They have included controlling the alcohol content of beverages, forbidding drinking by children, and limiting the hours of taverns and bars. Other authorities have shown little confidence that men and women can voluntarily limit their intake of alcohol and have deemed it better for everyone to abstain from alcohol completely. Such prohibition rules have been implemented at various times among small Jewish and Christian sects, over vast stretches of the Muslim world, in countries as varied as the United States, Belgium, India, and Russia, and among numerically significant denominations such as the Church of Jesus Christ of Latter-day Saints (Mormons).

A key theme in the history of alcohol, then, is its regulation, for there are few societies where alcohol has not been restricted in some way. These regulations have taken many forms, such as banning the consumption of alcohol for sections of populations defined by age (children), gender (women), or ethnicity/race (such as Native Americans). In some cases, patterns of alcohol consumption have been regulated informally by social pressure that might be reinforced by social ostracism. In other cases, regulation has taken the form of legislation backed by punishments for disobedience. Drinking by children was for thousands of years discouraged by physicians who warned of the dangers of alcohol on children's bodies. Only in the nineteenth and twentieth centuries were minimum legal drinking ages defined by law and enforced by the courts.

The other attributes ascribed to alcohol form other themes in its history. Alcohol was positively associated with gods in ancient cultures, and wine was embraced by mainstream Christianity, which incorporated wine into its most important rituals. But religious organizations have also been prominent critics of the personal and social effects of immoderate alcohol consumption. Similarly, while physicians have for thousands of years considered some alcoholic beverages as having medicinal value (during prohibition in the 1920s, half of American doctors thought whiskey was therapeutic, and a quarter thought the same of beer), they have also warned of the dangers to health of excessive consumption.

An important dimension of the history of alcohol, then, is its contested status and the struggle to find a way to realize its benefits while minimizing its dangers. It might be argued that prohibitionists simply gave up and advocated the position that it was better to deprive moderate drinkers of their alcohol than to allow irresponsible drinkers to misuse it and to place themselves and social order at risk. On the other hand, few people, even the most ardent opponents of prohibition, have ever adopted the opposite position, that all restrictions ought to be removed from alcohol.

These debates on alcohol did not take place in a material or cultural vacuum. Alcohol was a potent signifier of status and power in almost all societies. In many early societies, such as ancient Egypt, beer was consumed by all classes, but wine was also consumed only by the elites. In Greece, only wine was consumed, but it varied hugely in quality; the wine consumed by the elites bore little resemblance, in flavor, texture, and alcohol content, to that consumed by the lower classes. In some cases, alcohol was (in theory, at least) reserved for dominant, colonizing populations: some British administrations in Africa imposed prohibition policies on the indigenous peoples while themselves drinking alcohol, and white governments did the same to native populations in the United States and Canada.

At the material level, until the nineteenth century, alcohol (mainly beer and wine) was widely consumed by Europeans and North Americans for hydration because so many sources of water were unsafe to drink. Within centuries of being founded, Rome had to be supplied with potable water from aqueducts because the River Tiber was polluted. Major waterways and wells in urban centers in Europe (from the Middle Ages) and the Americas (from the eighteenth century) were too contaminated to be sources of safe drinking water. Fermented alcoholic beverages were safer to drink because the process of fermentation killed many harmful bacteria, as did distilled alcohol when it was added to water. Alcohol seems to have become a default beverage to the point that "alcohol" and "drink" became synonymous: the debate on alcohol was called "the drink question," and "heavy drinking" did not refer to water or tea.

The usefulness of alcohol as a safe form of hydration was a compelling argument for its availability, and no government could adopt prohibition policies unless there was an alternative in the form of reliable supplies of potable water or other nonalcoholic beverages. It is no coincidence that the temperance and prohibition movements arose at the same time that municipal governments in Europe and North America began massive projects to provide urban populations with supplies of safe drinking water, and as coffee, tea, and other nonalcoholic beverages became widely consumed.

At the same time, even though "drinking" generally refers to drinking alcohol, we must be careful not to assume that, before safe water was available, everybody drank alcohol for hydration purposes. Water, potable or not, was free, but alcohol was not. The poor must have consumed any water that was available, a practice that undoubtedly contributed to their low life expectancy. Nor did children often drink alcohol, and in many societies, women were either forbidden or strongly discouraged from doing so. The commonly accepted generalization that everyone in earlier societies consumed alcoholic beverages must surely be wrong, and that is one of the issues addressed in this book.

This is a survey of the ways that alcohol was situated in the various cultures within which it was consumed, and a description and explanation of how alcohol related to structures and processes of power and to issues of gender, class, race/ethnicity, and generation. The focus of the book is Europe, and there is extensive treatment of North America, too. The justification is that, even though alcoholic beverages might have originated elsewhere, and were certainly consumed throughout most of the world, Europeans integrated alcohol more extensively, and in greater volumes, into their cultures than people of any other region. In time, they extended their alcoholic beverages and, to some extent, their alcohol cultures to the wider world. Alcohol became one of the fields of contact, cooperation, and conflict that engaged Europeans and others in the processes of imperialism, colonization, and eventually, decolonization. I have tried for a global perspective in this book, but in doing so I have given priority to the story of the expansion of European alcohol, rather than to analyzing drinking cultures in regions such as Asia and the Pacific, in their own right. I think that approach makes the book thematically more coherent.

I wish to acknowledge the authors of all the material I have used and to thank the staffs of the various libraries and archives I have used. They include the British Library and the Wellcome Institute for the History of Medicine, London, and a number of Archives Départementales in France. My colleagues Matthew McKean and Michel Hogue gave useful advice, Dr. Rob El-Maraghi helped with some medical issues, and I am very grateful to David Fahey and Thomas Brennan, who made innumerable helpful comments and suggestions on the text. Of course, any errors and omissions are all my own work. Finally, it was a great pleasure to work with the helpful, friendly, and efficient people at the University of North Carolina Press. Chuck Grench, who signed me on for this book many years ago, deserves a medal for his patience.

A Note on Usage

ALE AND BEER

I have referred to grain-based fermented drinks as "beer" in all periods, apart from the Middle Ages. There, I make a distinction between "ale" (which was made without hops) and "beer" (which was made with hops), so as to highlight the transition from ale to beer in many parts of Europe in the late Middle Ages. It would be more consistent to refer to these beverages as "ale" in earlier periods (such as Ancient Mesopotamia and Egypt, and early medieval Gaul) and in cultures (such as many in sub-Saharan Africa) where hops were not used. But historians have consistently used "beer" as the generic term, and I have followed suit.

WHISKEY AND WHISKY

Although it is common to use "whiskey" to refer to certain spirits from some regions (such as Ireland and the United States) and "whisky" for other regions (such as Scotland and Japan), there are no hard rules. I have used "whiskey" as a generic term throughout the book.

Alcohol in Ancient Worlds

NATURE AND THE HUMAN HAND

We can trace alcoholic beverages made by humans to about 7000 BC, nine millennia ago, but it is almost certain that prehistoric humans consumed alcohol in fruits and berries many thousands of years earlier than that. When fruits and berries pass the point of optimum ripeness and sweetness and start to decay, wild yeasts begin to consume the sugars they naturally contain and to produce alcohol by a spontaneous process of fermentation. The alcohol thus produced in the flesh and juice of rotting fruits often reaches levels of 3 or 4 percent and sometimes goes higher than 5 percent, giving them an alcoholic strength similar to that of many modern beers.[1] Any fruit or berry is capable of going through this kind of fermentation, as long as two conditions are satisfied. First, the fruit must have a reasonable sugar level, and one that will attract yeasts. Sugar levels rise as fruit ripens, making it sweeter, and ripe fruits typically have sugar concentrations of between 5 and 15 percent of their mass.[2] Second, there must be ambient wild yeasts (on the skin of the fruit or in nearby trees and bushes) that can gain access to the sugars in the flesh of the fruit once its skin splits.

Various mammals, birds, and butterflies are known to eat decayed and fermented fruit and to experience varying degrees of intoxication. The Malaysian tree shrew, the poster animal for alcohol consumption, often feeds on fermented flower nectar, which can reach an alcohol level of almost 4 percent. This animal probably has an interesting perception of the world. Yet its agility as it leaps from tree to tree seems unimpaired by its alcohol intake, and there is no evidence that it engages in the risky behavior often associated with intoxication. Other creatures consume alcohol only periodically and opportunistically. A New Orleans newspaper reported in 1954 that thousands of migrating robins were getting drunk on the overripe berries on the bushes in city parks. A local birdwatcher noted that the blackbirds that followed could hold their alcohol better than the robins: "The blackbirds fall off into the grass and then wallow around to sober up. But the robins! I saw three big fat robins topple into the gutter and just lie there."[3]

Videos of supposedly intoxicated animals have become popular viewing on the internet, and although many seem to be authentic examples, scientists are skeptical about widespread and long-standing reports of African elephants getting tipsy on the rotting fruit of the marula tree. The scenario is somewhat improbable because elephants prefer their marula fruit ripe, rather than overripe or rotting. But even more unlikely, an adult elephant would have to avoid water and eat marula fruit with a minimum alcohol level of 3 percent at more than 400 times its normal maximum food intake in order to achieve a blood-alcohol level that would make it perceptibly inebriated.[4] Simply because of their body size, smaller creatures are more likely to feel the intoxicating effects of eating fermented fruit. In prehistoric times, primates and humans were almost certainly among them.

As long as 20 million years ago, our primate forebears lived primarily on a diet of fruit and berries: early human tooth structure was similar to that of modern apes, which gain almost all their calories from fruit, and the modern human genome is close to that of chimpanzees, which feed almost exclusively on plants, mostly fruit. Like other mammals and birds, humans might well have preferred fruit that was optimally ripe, when it was brightly colored and eye-catching, rather than when it was either underripe or beginning to rot. Yet they might also have gathered the more easily accessible overripe—and possibly fermenting—fruit from the ground where it had fallen and have thus consumed alcohol on an occasional or regular basis at the end of each ripening season. If they made the connection between eating overripe fruit or berries and feeling a pleasant sense of light-headedness, they might well have made it a regular practice and looked forward to each year's vintage.

But although we are talking of the prehistory of alcohol, it is important to stress that before there was any beer or wine, there was water. Water is a requirement of life on earth, and humans need to consume water regularly to compensate for what they lose daily, mainly in the form of perspiration, urine, and feces. The volume of water humans need to rehydrate themselves varies according to the climate, their diet, and their patterns of physical activity, but water is always needed—about 2 liters a day for adults in modern Western societies. Until methods of delivering drinking water over long distances were devised, humans lived only where there was regular access to fresh water in the form of rivers, streams, lakes, springs, wells, or precipitation as rain or snow. For hundreds of thousands of years, humans relied on water, both for individual rehydration and to support the supplies of fruit, vegetables, berries, meat, fish, and other items in their diet, all of which not only required water but also contained water. If alcoholic beverages became part of the prehistoric diet, they must have made a negligible contribution to rehydration at first (and for tens of thousands of years), because nomadic populations would not have been able to produce significant volumes of alcohol while constantly on the move.

Everything changed in the Neolithic period (about 10,000 to 4000 BC), when humans began to build permanent settlements, cultivate cereals and other crops, and keep livestock. Domesticated varieties of many kinds of crops began to appear, including cereals that were suitable for making beer and grape varieties that were selected for wine production because they were easier to propagate and had a higher ratio of flesh to seeds than many wild grapes. In this period we find the earliest evidence of beer and wine, partly because Neolithic cultures also began to produce pottery; it is in clay pots and jars that archaeologists have found some of the oldest evidence of alcoholic drinks, in the form of seeds, grains, yeasts, acids, and other residues. These discoveries raise the question of whether evidence of wine and beer dating to pre-Neolithic times (further back than about 10,000 BC) will ever be found, simply because the vessels used to hold the liquids—perhaps made from wood or leather—have totally disintegrated.

So at least 9,000 years ago—but almost certainly much earlier—a human history of alcohol was added to the natural history of spontaneous fermentations in rotting fruits and berries. It began when the first winemaker or brewer crushed grapes or other fruit, or processed barley or another cereal, and let the liquid stand until it fermented. Fermentation was not explained as a biological process until the middle of the nineteenth century, when French scientist Louis Pasteur carried out his experiments with wine. Yet thousands of years earlier, someone, somewhere—northeastern China and western Asia are currently considered the most likely locations—seems to have made a historic observation: if the juice of fruit or berries (or a mixture of water and honey or processed cereal) were left for a short time in warm enough conditions, it began to bubble or froth. Once the bubbling subsided, the resulting beverage produced a pleasant feeling when consumed in small volumes and a sense of otherworldliness when those initial small volumes were followed by more.

The world has not been quite the same since. For some people, the discovery of alcohol and methods of producing it created new opportunities for health and pleasure: alcoholic beverages were found to be generally more nutritious than the produce they were made from; they were for centuries safer than the polluted water that was available for drinking in many parts of the world; they gave their consumers a feeling of well-being; and they were quickly associated with positive qualities like conviviality, fertility, and spirituality. In contrast, other people have found history since the advent of alcohol resembling one long hangover for humanity: alcohol has long been ascribed negative associations such as social disruption, violence, crime, sin, immorality, physical and mental illness, and death.

We will never know who gave birth to these contested histories by intentionally producing the first alcohol, and the further back we take the history of alcohol, the more speculative it becomes. It might well have begun with an unplanned yet observed fermentation. If the first alcohol was wine, the history of alcohol might have started when wild grapes collected by prehistoric humans for consumption as fresh fruit were placed for safekeeping in a wooden or leather container or in a bowl-shaped indentation in a rock. The grapes at the bottom of the pile would have been squashed by the weight of those on top, producing juice that fermented when it attracted the wild yeasts living on the skins of the grapes or in nearby trees or bushes. Or it might have started with another fruit, like pomegranates or haws (the fruit of the hawthorn tree). Or it might have begun with something entirely different, such as honey, treasured as a food because of its sweetness, that was liquefied and diluted by rain and then fermented into the alcoholic beverage that later became known as mead. (Honey needs to be diluted by about 30 percent water before it ferments.)

All these products, as well as many grains (such as barley and rice), were used in some of the earliest alcoholic beverages that have been identified by archaeologists. As long as the product possessed sugars, was liquefied, and was left long enough in warm enough conditions for wild yeasts to do their work, fermentation would take place and an alcohol-bearing liquid would result. This liquid might have had a low level of alcohol and its flavor and texture might have been quite unrecognizable to us as beer, wine, or other common alcohol, but it would have been an alcoholic beverage.

The next step in the story of the earliest alcohol takes us from this unintended fermentation to a process engineered by a human. After having one or two tastes of this fermented liquid and experiencing its pleasing effects, our accidental winemaker who had gathered and stored the grapes, the fruit, or the berries might have tried to replicate fermentation, even though he or she was completely unaware of the biological process involved. After piling grapes or other fruit into a container several times to produce the juice that turned into this pleasing beverage, he or she might have shortened the process by simply squashing *all* the fruit or berries—maybe by hand, maybe by foot—thus increasing the volume of wine produced.

Making beer would have been more complicated, as the cereals it is made from contain very little fermentable sugar. They do have sugars and starches, but these are almost completely insoluble and must be made soluble before yeasts can turn them into alcohol. (A beverage with traces of alcohol can be made from unprocessed grain, but it would not have had the impact on the drinker that made beer and wine so attractive.) The sugars in cereal can be converted if one chews the grains: an enzyme in human saliva is effective, and chewing grain and spitting it out was one way alcoholic beverages were made in various Caribbean, Latin American, and Pacific cultures before European contact. The more common process is to malt the grain (soak it in water until it germinates, then dry it) and mash it (soak it in warm water) to produce a liquid containing soluble sugars that can be fermented.

This is clearly a much more complex process than fermenting fruit, berries, or honey. Although beer might have been produced spontaneously—if grains successively fell from or were blown off the stalk, were rained on, then sprouted, were dried by the sun, were rained on again, and finally were fermented by wild yeasts—and was consumed, it is difficult to see how drinkers would have known how to replicate the process. Eventually, of course, the process was mastered, but the relative simplicity of fruit and honey fermentation argues for fruit- or berry-based wine, or perhaps mead, to have been made before beer.

The human history of alcoholic beverages might have begun by these various accidental fermentations. Or perhaps not, because such scenarios, suggesting that the first deliberate production of alcohol followed upon the observation of unintended fermentations, are entirely speculative. We can no more know the circumstances in which the first beer, mead, or wine was made than we can know who first baked bread or first boiled an egg. Yet there has been some compelling need to explain the inexplicable, and many cultures have produced stories that set out the origins of alcoholic drinks. Some attribute the advent of wine and beer to gods rather than humans. A song (dating to about 1800 BC) to Ninkasi, the Sumerian goddess of beer, describes how beer is made and the pleasures of drinking it. In Egypt, Osiris, the god of the underworld and also the source of all life on earth, was credited with bestowing wine and beer on humans. In Greece, wine was associated with Dionysus, and in Rome, with Bacchus. Jews and Christians, on the other hand, traced wine to a mortal, Noah, who was said to have planted vines on the slopes of Mount Ararat, where his animal-laden ark came to rest once the Great Flood had subsided: "Noah, the tiller of the soil, was the first to plant a vineyard," says the Old Testament.[5] In the Babylonian version of the flood story, in contrast, wine and beer were provided to the workers building the boat *before* the flood occurred.

Although Noah seemed to know intuitively (or by divine revelation or guidance) how to make wine from his grapes, other accounts stress the accidental character of the first fermentation. One narrative sets it in the court of the Persian king Jamsheed, who was so fond of fresh grapes that he kept jars of them in order to have supplies out of season. When he found one lot no longer sweet because, unknown to him, the grapes had fermented, he had the jar labeled "poison." Soon after, a woman from the royal harem, suffering from a terrible headache, drank some of this "poison" in order to kill herself and end her misery. Overcome by the alcohol, she fell asleep, and when she woke and (counterintuitively) found her headache gone, she told the king of the magical cure. He promptly ensured that more of his grapes were allowed to ferment.[6]

In contrast, a Chinese account suggests that the first product to be fermented was rice, and that it occurred "when discarded rice was fermented and it accumulated a rich fragrance after a long period of time in an empty trunk." But an eleventh-century Chinese treatise on wine takes a more pragmatic view: "As for who was the first one who invented wine, I can only say that it was a certain wise person."[7]

Accounts like these often point us to some of the enduring cultural associations of wine—such as its religious and medicinal properties—but they do not bring us much closer to an understanding of the historical origins of alcohol more generally. For that, we look to archaeologists, some of whom have turned the quest for the earliest alcohol into a small industry. They search for evidence of alcohol, generally in the form of remains of the fruit, berries, or cereals used or the chemical residues of liquids that had been absorbed into the interior walls of pottery jars and vats. The residues of grape wine generally take the form of grape seeds, tartaric acid (which occurs naturally in grapes and some other fruit), yeasts, and malvidin, a pigment that black grapes share with few other fruits. Although unfermented grape juice and even fresh grapes might leave the same evidence as wine, grape juice would almost certainly have quickly fermented in the warm climatic conditions that prevailed in China and the Middle East, where most of this sort of evidence has been collected. Other evidence of alcoholic beverages that can last for

thousands of years includes calcium oxalate (or "beerstone," which often ac-
cumulates in vessels that have been used for brewing); grains of cereals used
in brewing (such as rice, barley, millet, and emmer); wax from honey; and tree
resin, which was often used to seal the inside of pottery jars and to preserve
the alcoholic beverages they held.

The findings that make up the earliest known history of alcohol—from
about 7000 BC to the beginning of the Christian era, a little more than 2,000
years ago—produce a continually changing narrative. Archaeologists, historians, linguists, chemists, and other scholars regularly report finding evidence
they claim to be the earliest example of this or that aspect of alcohol. The earliest evidence of any form of alcoholic beverage has been found in northern
China, while the earliest known wine production facility is claimed for Armenia. There is evidence that of one of the earliest commercial breweries was
located in Peru[8] and a suggestion that the first evidence of distilling alcohol is
to be found in the regions now occupied by Pakistan and northern India.[9] The
earliest known alcohol in liquid form, preserved in airtight bronze vessels and
dating back an astonishing 4,000 years, was found in central China. Many of
these findings have shifted some attention from the Middle East, which was
long assumed to be the birthplace of beer, wine, and distillation—and which
gave us the Arabic origin of our word "alcohol"—even though there is an important concentration of evidence of ancient alcohol in that region.

Yet although we should expect to see the history of ancient alcohol continually revised, as researchers develop new analytical techniques and investigate new sites, there is probably a practical limit to the historical depth of our
knowledge. As most of the evidence of the earliest alcoholic beverages takes
the form of residue in pottery jars, we should not expect to find evidence
before the widespread use of pottery in the Neolithic period. Before clay was
used to make vessels for holding liquids, alcoholic beverages would have been
stored in containers made from wood or leather, or perhaps from textiles, all
materials that have long rotted away and taken their all-important residues
with them.

It is not surprising, then, that the earliest evidence of an alcoholic beverage was found in a dozen pottery jars from the early Neolithic village (about
7000–5600 BC) of Jiahu, in Henan province of northern China. Judging by
the residue, the beverage in question was wine made from a combination
of rice, honey, and fruit—probably grapes or haws because both have high
levels of tartaric acid. The rice might have been exposed to a fungus that
made its sugars suitable for fermentation. As for the honey, it might have
been added last to sweeten the beverage, but it might also have been added

before fermentation to attract wild yeasts to the unfermented liquid; although grapes and haw berries can play host to yeasts, rice does not.[10]

There is no way of knowing the social context in which this beverage might have been drunk, but later evidence of Chinese wine was found in a large number of bronze vessels, suggesting that alcohol in ancient China was particularly associated with the wealthy. Dating from about 1900 BC (4,000 years ago), these vessels had not only held fermented beverages, but some still contained liquid after thousands of years; they were initially well sealed and later corrosion made them perfectly airtight. One vessel gave up 26 liters (equivalent to about three dozen standard wine bottles) of what was described as a liquid with "a fragrant aroma," but the sensory evidence was short-lived because the compounds that convey aromas and flavors volatilized within seconds of being exposed to air.[11]

In China, as in contemporary Egypt, wine was buried with the high-ranking dead for consumption in the afterlife. There were also ceremonies in which people drank wine to achieve a mind-altered state that would enable them to communicate with their ancestors.[12] More evidence of the funerary purposes of wine-drinking emerges from the later Shang dynasty (1750–1100 BC). Excavations of thousands of tombs show that wine vessels were often buried with the dead, not only with the powerful (70 percent of the bronze vessels buried with the queen of King Wu-ting are wine containers) but even with some of the poor.[13] In the Chou dynasty (1100–221 BC), there is less evidence of wine being used for funerary purposes but a strong emphasis on drinking at festive occasions, if not on an everyday basis. Poems describe drinking "sweet wine" at parties after hunting for boar and rhinoceros, and the number of different names for wine—or the number of names for different wines—proliferated. Although the earliest evidence of alcohol in China suggests that it was made from rice, honey, and fruit, later references to production commonly refer to cereals (wheat and millet), and the process—malting, cooking, and fermenting grain—indicates that it was beer rather than wine that was being produced.

Our present knowledge suggests that China has had the longest continuous evidence of alcohol production, starting with the residues of a 9,000-year-old fermented beverage made from several products and continuing unbroken to the burgeoning Chinese wine industry of the early twenty-first century. Yet there is also widespread evidence of early alcohol production (although beginning three or four thousand years after the earliest known alcohol in China) in western Asia, in regions occupied by modern Iraq, Iran, Turkey, Armenia, and Georgia. In some of these areas, alcohol has had a discontinuous history because of the Islamic prohibition of alcohol in the seventh century and the alcohol policies enacted by successive Muslim administrations. At the present time, for example, alcohol consumption is forbidden in Iran and by citizens in Saudi Arabia (some allowance is made for foreigners), while Turkey has a significant wine industry.

The earliest western Asian evidence of alcohol dates from 5400 to 5000 BC (about 7,000 years ago) in Hajji Firuz, a community in the Zagros Mountains, which run along the frontier between modern Iraq and Iran. Telltale residues in the pottery vessels found there indicate both beer and wine. Beer can be deduced by the presence of oxalate ion, a common residue from brewing, on the inside of a jar and the presence of some carbonized barley at the same location. Wine, on the other hand, left grape seeds, tartaric acid, and tree resin inside pottery jars. While it is possible that the jars contained unfermented grape juice rather than wine, in the warm conditions of the region, the sugar-rich juice would almost certainly have attracted yeasts and quickly started fermenting. The traces of resin also support the conclusion that the jars held wine, as tree resin was widely used in wine as a preservative—a practice that continues today (but for flavoring, not conservation purposes) in resinated wines of the eastern Mediterranean, such as Greek retsina. The beverages these jars contained were thus made from single products, rather than from several fermented fruits and cereals, as in the earliest Chinese finding, although they might well have been mixed with other beverages or additives before they were consumed.

The total volume of the Hajji Firuz wine jars was 54 liters (the equivalent of 72 standard bottles of wine). This would not have gone far, given that wine had to last a year (until the next vintage), although we do not know if the community had access to a little or a lot more wine than these six jars represent. The fact that the wine jars were found close to jewelry and other luxury artifacts suggests that the wine was owned by a well-off household.[14] More earthenware wine vessels containing tartaric acid from wine, this time dating from 3500 to 3000 BC, were found in Godin Tepe, a trading post and military center to the south of Hajji Firuz. These jars held between 30 and 60 liters each, and the vertical patterns of the internal staining showed that, after being sealed with clay stoppers, the jars had been stored on their sides, just like modern bottles with cork closures. In the same community, archaeologists also found a large basin that might have been used for fermenting grape juice and a funnel that might have been used in winemaking.

However, an earlier and much more complete winemaking facility, dating from 4100 to 4000 BC, was found near the village of Areni, in the Little

Caucasus Mountains of southern Armenia, not far from the Zagros range where Hajji Firuz and Godin Tepe were located. It consists of a shallow basin in which grapes would have been crushed (probably by foot), with a hole allowing the juice to flow into an underground vat, where it fermented. These vessels, along with cups and bowls, showed evidence of malvidin, and grape seeds, pressed grapes, and dried grapevines at the site further support the belief that this was a winemaking facility. The scale of production suggests that by this time, 6,000 years ago, grapes suitable for wine might well have been domesticated.[15]

As we can see, two regions in Asia—an area of northeastern China and a relatively small area of western Asia bounded by the Caucasus Mountains, eastern Turkey, eastern Iraq, and northwestern Iran—have surrendered the very earliest signs of alcohol. This is not to say that alcohol was not produced as early in other places, for societies in most parts of the world fermented some of their local resources into alcohol. The Nahua of Central America fermented the juice of a variety of agave, and many African societies fermented the sap of palm trees. Apart from the anomaly of most of North America, where there is no evidence of native peoples making alcohol despite the availability of suitable raw materials, the cultures that did not acquire the knowledge and technique of making alcohol lived in environments—such as the Arctic and the Australian desert—where no suitable fruit or cereals grew.

That said, it has proved impossible, in many of these cases, to determine how far back alcohol production went. Although alcoholic fermentation might have been practiced first in Africa or the Americas, the greatest certainty lies with the Chinese and western Asian evidence that dates back to the period between 7000 and 3000 BC, some 5,000 to 9,000 years ago. The regions involved lie many thousands of kilometers apart, but they were connected by the Silk Road and by other trade networks for thousands of years before that. It is possible, then, that knowledge of fermentation was developed in one region and transferred to the other. Alternatively, each region might have started to practice fermentation independently, or the process of making alcohol might have been discovered in a third, as yet unidentified, region of Asia and then transferred to other parts of the continent.

Brewing and winemaking, the processes that produced the two most common alcoholic beverages in the ancient world, seem to have followed different paths of diffusion and development. The transfer of winemaking knowledge and technology seems fairly linear, as it moved from western Asia to the eastern Mediterranean and Egypt, and from there to Crete, Greece, and southern Italy, before reaching the rest of Europe about 2,000 years ago.

Winemaking knowledge seems to have reached the Etruscans of northern Italy by a different route, as they were producing wine at the same time as the Greeks, and it is possible that the Phoenicians transferred the same knowledge directly to Spain.

Brewing, in contrast, was being practiced at a number of locations at about the same time. In addition to the early evidence of millet beer in China and barley beer in Godin Tepe, which dates from 3500 to 3000 BC, there are signs of brewing in Upper Egypt (3500–3400 BC) and in Scotland (about 3000 BC), where honey and herbs were added to the beverage.[16] This wide but contemporaneous dispersal suggests that brewing was discovered by a number of cultures independently; but the evidence is scattered and uneven, and drawing firm conclusions from it is risky.[17]

Much more reliable evidence of the production of alcohol and of cultures of alcohol consumption emerges from about 3000 BC onward. There is detailed pictorial evidence of wine production in Egypt by 3000–2500 BC, and an Egyptian census from 1000 BC lists 513 vineyards owned by temples. Most were located in the Nile Delta, but there were also scattered vineyards at oases farther south. Everywhere, grapevines tended to share space with other plants and trees (which provided habitat for the yeasts needed for fermentation), as in a two-and-a-half-acre block that belonged to a high official of Saqqara in 2550 BC: "200 cubits long and 200 cubits wide . . . very plentiful trees and vines were set out, a great quantity of wine was made there."[18]

The grapes in Egyptian vineyards were grown on trellises or up trees, and when they were ripe, they were picked and taken in baskets to be crushed by foot in large vats. Wall paintings show four to six men treading the grapes, each holding on to straps hanging from overhead poles so as not to slip on the skins and fall into the juice. Sometimes the workers trod grapes to a cadence set by women singing songs, such as one dedicated to the goddess of the harvest: "May she remain with us in this work. . . . May our lord drink [the wine] as one who is repeatedly favoured by his king." Wine is invariably shown as red or a dark color in Egyptian wall paintings, which suggests (unless it is an artistic device) that black grapes were used and that there was skin contact before or during fermentation, because red wine gets its color from pigments in the skins of dark grapes.

Fermentation might have begun in the crushing vat, but it continued and ended in the large clay jars used to store wine. Once each jar was full, it was sealed with a pottery cap and made airtight with a lump of Nile clay. Small holes were made near the top of the jar to enable the carbon dioxide (along with alcohol, a product of fermentation) to escape while the fermentation was in progress, so that the jars did not crack or explode under pressure of the gas. The holes were later closed to protect the wine from air, which would oxidize and spoil the wine. Finally a clay seal—a forerunner of the modern wine label—was fixed to the cap. It was etched with information that might include the vineyard the wine came from, the name of the winemaker, the year of vintage, and even the quality or style of the wine. One such seal on a jar in the tomb of King Tutankhamun reads, "Year 4. Sweet wine of the house-of-Aton—Life, Prosperity, Health!—of the Western River. Chief wine-maker Aperershop." Seals on jars in other locations read variously, "Wine for merry-making," "Very good wine," "Wine for offerings," and even "Wine for taxes."[19] It is not clear whether wine used to pay taxes in kind was superior or mediocre in quality; perhaps its quality determined its value as a tax payment in kind.

Wine was drunk only by the elites in Egypt, as it was in many ancient cultures. The scarcity of wine probably gave it cultural value everywhere because it was made only once a year, unlike beer, which could be made continually, year-round, in small batches using stored-up grain. Moreover, suitable grapes—grapes with a high flesh-to-seeds ratio that yielded plenty of juice—ripened successfully in fewer regions than cereals could be cultivated. Made in few places and produced in small volumes that had to last for a whole year until the following vintage, wine was far less likely than beer to be readily available, and its scarcity must have made it more expensive, even when it did not have to be transported to consumers in places where grapes did not grow. These two related qualities, scarcity and cost, contributed to the social cachet of wine and perhaps to its eventual associations with religion and spirituality. Unlike beer, wine was sometimes traded over long distances (down the Tigris and Euphrates Rivers in Mesopotamia, for example), and it was drunk by the elites and used in festivities and ceremonies. Thus wine was more likely to enter the historical record, with the result that we know more about ancient wine than about ancient beer, even though beer was far more commonly consumed.

The Code of Hammurabi, issued in Babylon about 1770 BC and one of the earliest known codifications of law, regulated the price and strength of beer. Although these laws refer to "wine-shops," it is clear that, for the most part, these establishments sold beer. There is an implication here and elsewhere that public drinking places in Mesopotamia were generally run by women and were often associated with prostitution.[20] This is an early expression of themes that run through the longer-term history of alcohol: the production of alcoholic beverages by women and the association of alcohol with sexuality.

Not only did beer become relatively plentiful in the ancient world, but (unlike most modern beers) it was remarkably nutritious. The malting process raised the caloric value of the base cereal, giving beer more calories than bread made with an equivalent amount of grain. In addition, beer was rich in carbohydrates, vitamins, and proteins. It also gave its drinker a pleasant feeling. Although we cannot know for certain the alcohol level in ancient beer, it was probably high enough to make an impact but not so high that drinking a liter or two a day—making it excellent for hydration—would prevent anyone from getting on efficiently and safely with daily life. It was probably tasty, even though it was not filtered, and would have been cloudy, with bits of husk and stalks floating on its surface. But ancient alcohol producers and consumers were no purists. Not only did they co-ferment various fruits, berries, cereals, and honey, but when they did make straight beer, they regularly flavored it with coriander, juniper, and other additives. In Egypt, beer was made from barley, although wheat, millet, and rye were occasionally used. It was provided to workers and slaves (such as those constructing the pyramids) as part of their salary and was also attributed medicinal properties, especially as a laxative and purgative.[21]

Beer, then, was a smart drink from almost every perspective—health, nutrition, hydration, and pleasure—and it soon became the universal drink, despite the common belief that the masses drank only beer and the elites drank only wine. In fact, everyone who drank alcohol drank beer, but whereas the wealthy supplemented their beer with wine, the bulk of the population did not. Wall paintings from Egypt in the second century BC show scenes of banquets where members of the royal family and their entourage are drinking two beverages. One, probably beer, was drunk from large jars through straws or tubes, probably to prevent the drinkers from ingesting the husks and stalks that floated on the surface. The other beverage, probably wine, was sipped from cups.[22] These different modes of drinking suggest that beer was consumed in greater volumes than wine, even though both beverages were consumed on these occasions.

One reason why wine was monopolized by the wealthy and powerful in ancient societies was simple cost. It cost more to produce, and its relative scarcity raised the price further. In Mesopotamia the price of wine was inflated by the need to ship it to the towns where the elites were concentrated. Although beer was readily produced from barley grown on the plains near southern cities such as Babylon, Ur, and Lagash, wine was produced in the mountains to the northeast and then shipped downstream along the Tigris and Euphrates. This is the first known example of a long-distance wine trade, but its extent was limited by small production and its high cost structure. Wine and other goods were easily sent to market on the south-flowing rivers, but the purpose-built wine barges were broken up after each trip because they could not return north against the current. The end price of goods thus included the capital cost of the barge. But wine was clearly a lucrative trade for merchants, for in 1750 BC a merchant of Babylon named Belânu showed frustration at the absence of wine from a shipment of goods that had arrived on the Euphrates. He wrote to his agent, "The boats have arrived here at the end of their journey at Sippar [50 kilometers north of Babylon], but why have you not bought and sent me some good wine? Send me some and bring it to me in person within ten days!"[23]

Given the price of wine, only people such as the ruler of Lagash could purchase it in big volumes. It was reported in 2340 BC that he had established a wine cellar, "into which wine is brought in great vases from the mountains." These vases were the forerunners of amphoras, the clay jars later used by Greek and Roman merchants to ship millions of liters of wine throughout the Mediterranean and Europe. The mass of the population drank only beer, and the place of beer in the diet of Mesopotamians is denoted by the description of basic daily fare as "bread and beer." The hymn to Ninkasi celebrated the brew that exhilarates the drinker, "makes the liver happy and fills the heart with joy."[24]

Beer and wine were similarly consumed in Egypt, where grapes were far more difficult to cultivate than cereals. At first, wine was imported from the east. Hundreds of wine jars found in the burial chamber of one of the Egyptian kings, Scorpion I (about 3150 BC), contain deposits and resin identical to those found at Godin Tepe in the Zagros Mountains, and the jars themselves were made from clay that seems to have come from the area now occupied by Israel and Palestine. This suggests the existence of a complex wine industry where jars were imported, filled with wine, then re-exported farther afield.

Wine was not only consumed as part of the elites' diet in ancient Egypt; it was also employed in ceremonies, often being poured as a libation as prayers were said. Beer, oil, honey, and water were also used in libations, but wine tended to have more religious or spiritual associations throughout the ancient world. Planting vines might have been perceived as a religious obligation, as the pharaoh Ramses III suggested when he addressed the god Amon-Ra: "I made for thee wine-gardens on the Southern oasis, and Northern oasis likewise without number." Ramses claimed to have presented 59,588 jars of wine to gods in his lifetime.[25] And if the lifetime was important, so was the afterlife, for supplies of wine were buried with eminent Egyptians, as vessels of alcohol were with the dead in China. When Tutankhamun died at the age of nineteen (at or below the legal drinking age in most countries today), three dozen jars of wine were buried with him, most from the fourth, fifth, and ninth years of his reign. Although the pharaohs drank beer while they were living, beer would not have been buried with them, not because it was unworthy, but because it was known not to last more than a week or two.

It is worth noting that until the wine-rich heydays of the Greeks and Romans, there is no evidence of a negative attitude toward beer. The Greeks and Romans thought beer was utterly inferior to wine. Wine, they said, was a manly and civilized beverage; beer, which made men effeminate and was fit only for barbarians, was to be avoided by peoples who aspired to greatness and civilization. These views (explored in more detail in the next chapter) contributed to a belief, which still has some currency, that wine possesses intrinsic civilizing qualities and is culturally superior to beer. A lot of nonsense has been written about wine's being a sign of "civilization," a statement predicated on the assumption that the life of the elites was civilized and the life of the masses was worth little in any cultural sense. It ignores the reality that in most ancient societies, until Greece and Rome came into their own, the elites themselves must have drunk far more beer than wine. If they produced longer-lasting artifacts and ideas than the masses, they did it with the aid of beer, at least as much as of wine.

So far was beer from being considered an inferior beverage that Mesopotamia's classic piece of literature, the *Epic of Gilgamesh*, identified beer-drinking as essential to being human, as the process of humanizing Enkidu, the wild man, shows: "Enkidu does not know of eating food; of beer to drink he has not been taught. The prostitute opened her mouth. She said to Enkidu, 'eat the food Enkidu, it is the luster of life. Drink the beer as is done in this land.' Enkidu ate the food until he was sated; of the beer he drank seven cups. His soul became free and cheerful, his heart rejoiced, his face glowed. He rubbed . . . his hairy body. He anointed himself with oil. He became human."[26]

Both beer and wine were served at the funeral banquet of a person thought to have been King Midas, in about 700 BC.[27] Evidence of the banquet was found in a five-by-six-meter burial room deep in a human-built earthen mound that looks, from the outside, like a natural hillock. It is located in Gordion, now in central Turkey but formerly the capital of the Phrygian empire over which Midas ruled. The burial chamber contained the skeleton of a sixty- to sixty-five-year-old male laid out on dyed textiles in a log coffin surrounded by 150 bronze vessels. More than 100 drinking bowls littered the chamber, and there were also three 150-liter vats, which probably held the beverage that was poured into bronze jugs and from there into individual bowls. (There were also some larger, two-handled bowls, perhaps for the thirstier guests.) The crowd of mourners implied by the number of pieces in this drinking set could not possibly have fitted into the burial chamber, so the wooden furniture and the bronze bowls, plates, and vats must have been placed around the body after the banquet (probably held outdoors) was over.

As for what was consumed at King Midas's funeral banquet, both the food and drink were combinations of ingredients. The meal was a stew of goat or sheep meat that was marinated in oil, honey, and wine before being grilled, mixed with lentils and cereals, and flavored with herbs and spices. It was accompanied by a beverage that was no less complex: a mixture—"blend" is probably a more positive term—of grape wine, barley beer, and mead. If the three 150-liter vats were only half full, there would have been more than 200 liters of this beverage available for the 100 guests, which would have made for a convivial gathering.

Was the banquet of King Midas a kind of ancient wake, and did the eating and drinking have religious associations? There were strong links between wine and religion (stronger links than between beer and religion) in the ancient world and later, and several explanations have been advanced. One is that mild or more advanced intoxication gave drinkers a sense of lightheadedness that felt like slipping from the mundane world and approaching the gods. Yet this would not necessarily differentiate wine from any other alcoholic beverage. What was different was the higher alcohol level of wine than, say, beer, so that consuming the same volume of wine would get the drinker closer to the gods more rapidly. Another explanation is that wine gained spiritual value from the apparent miracle of fermentation, when grape juice rose in temperature and bubbled without any external stimulus, such as fire. But again, this is common to all fermented beverages, although the roiling fermentation of wine might have been more impressive than the foaming of fermenting beer. A third suggestion is that the life cycle of the grapevine— which flourishes in spring, bears fruit during summer and autumn, then appears to die during the winter, only to sprout leaves and flowers again in the spring—appeared to ancient peoples like a recurring miracle of death and resurrection. But many other plants and trees—though not the cereals used for brewing—go through the same annual cycle. Perhaps the spiritual associations of wine reflected all these properties.

The strong association of alcohol with feasting indicates its high status at these times; banquets, whether celebrating life events or death, were often important political events, used for purposes such as forming and cementing social alliances, creating social debt, and demonstrating social distinctions.[28] All the alcoholic beverages in the ancient world had some religious connotations that might well have reflected the perceived wonder of fermentation and the feelings of other-worldliness that even mild alcoholic intoxication produces. If wine had stronger religious associations, which it did in many ancient cultures, it might well have been more because of its scarcity than of any intrinsic quality. It is not surprising that the social elites in Mesopotamia, Egypt, and elsewhere stressed the godly associations of the beverage to which they had virtually sole access; it gave them a proximity to and an intimacy with the divine that was greater than any the masses had access to. Some cultures treated mead as divine, too—perhaps a measure of its scarcity, perhaps reflecting a widespread belief that bees were divine, perhaps because honey was the sweetest commodity known in the ancient world. Intense sweetness was a treasured quality, and Christians would later adapt this notion to the idea of the "sweetness" of Jesus.[29]

Alcohol occupied not only a religious position in ancient cultures; it was regularly employed as a medicine, either in its own right or as a medium for plants, herbs, and other produce that were believed to have therapeutic properties. Many of the Neolithic alcoholic beverages identified in China and the Middle East contained plant material that was not used for the production of the alcohol, and although it might well have been used to add flavor, it might also have been added because of its perceived medicinal value.

Ancient Egypt provides comprehensive information, even though most of the plants named in hieroglyphics have not been identified. Coriander is an exception, and a common remedy for stomach problems was beer infused with coriander, bryony (a flowering plant), flax, and dates. Grated and mixed with chaste-tree and an unidentified fruit, then infused into beer, strained and drunk, coriander was also prescribed as a cure for blood in the feces.[30] In general, wine was considered a particularly good aid to digestion, and it was prescribed to increase the appetite, purge the body of worms, regulate the flow of urine, and act as an enema. It was often mixed with *kyphi*, a concoction of gum, resin, herbs, spices, and even the hair of asses, animal dung, and bird droppings. Alcohol dissolves solids more effectively than water, and its higher concentration in wine made it a very good medium for many medicines. Wine was also applied externally as a salve to reduce swelling, and recognition that alcohol was a disinfectant led to wine being applied to bandages to treat wounds.[31]

Wine was highly valued in Chinese medicine, too; the character for "medical treatment" contains the elements of the character for wine, indicating the close relationship between wine and medicine.[32] The earliest Chinese medical and pharmaceutical works cite wine as an important drug and antiseptic and as a means of circulating medicines in the body. Among its specific uses, wine was employed as an antiseptic, an anesthetic, and a diuretic, and in the Taoist period it was an ingredient in longevity elixirs.[33]

For all these positive qualities attributed to alcoholic beverages, they were also recognized as having a darker side. There was, first of all, the matter of simple overconsumption. It is argued that heavy drinking became so widespread, at least in the royal court, that it brought about the collapse of the Shang dynasty in China (1750–1100 BC). In reaction, subsequent rulers not only warned against excessive drinking but made it punishable by death.[34]

The general tolerance and even encouragement of drinking during festivities is suggested by a scene from the Egyptian tomb of Nakhet, where a girl is shown offering her parents wine and saying, "To your health! Drink this good wine, celebrate a festive day with what your lord has given you."[35] Although light intoxication at celebrations, like drinking to achieve a spiritual lightheadedness, might be tolerated, heavy drinking at festivals and other occasions sometimes got out of hand. One Egyptian sage, Ani, said of the drunk person, "When you speak, nonsense comes out of your mouth; if you fall down and break your limb, no one will come to your assistance."[36] Another sage advised, "Do not get drunk, lest you go mad." Egyptian artists were not shy about showing the seedier side of alcohol-charged festivities, and wall drawings depict men and women vomiting and being carried unconscious from banquet rooms. There is no explicit suggestion of moral disapproval here, but some writings suggest that public intoxication was more frowned upon than excessive drinking in private.

What began to emerge in the ancient world is a theme that runs through the history of alcohol to the present: that moderate consumption was not only acceptable, but a good thing for reasons of health and pleasure. But drinking too much alcohol, either on specific occasions (what is now called binge-drinking) or as a regular pattern, was bad. It was detrimental to the drinker's health and morals, harmful to those immediately affected by his or her behavior, and damaging to society more generally. It led to a debate, which continues today, about how to define the line between moderation and excess, and how to ensure that no one crossed the line. Historically, some commentators have identified the line by the unruly behavior of the drinker, but this meant that it was defined only after it had been crossed. Others have prescribed specific volumes of alcohol as moderate and safe, as modern public health policy-makers recommend a maximum of so many standard servings of alcohol a day. Attempts to prevent excessive drinking constitute an important strand in the history of regulation, as one society after another has variously tried to control the production, distribution, and consumption of alcohol. Some later societies attempted to prohibit alcohol entirely, and in those cases the distinction between moderate and excessive consumption was moot. The distinction might have been less of an issue in ancient societies where alcohol was produced and consumed in relatively small volumes, but it became much more important as alcohol production increased and alcoholic beverages became central to the daily diet, as they did in Ancient Greece and Rome.

2

Greece and Rome

THE SUPERIORITY OF WINE

Beer was the drink of the masses throughout much of the ancient world, but it was not consumed at all in Greece and Roman Italy, the only societies to produce cereals without using them to brew beer. Climatic conditions on the two peninsulas (and their associated islands) were far more suitable for the cultivation of grapes than in any regions where wine had been produced to that time. Instead of drinking beer and wine, as Egyptians and Mesopotamians did, Romans and Greeks of all social classes consumed only wine, although there were significant class- and gender-specific distinctions in patterns of consumption. Not only did they drink wine exclusively, but Greeks and Romans constructed ideological and medical arguments that beer had harmful properties in general and was particularly unfit for civilized peoples like themselves. As part of their respective civilizing missions, they exported wine to predominantly beer-drinking societies throughout the Mediterranean region and beyond, and later they transferred knowledge of vine cultivation and winemaking to western and central Europe. Within the remarkably short period between 500 BC and AD 100, wine production had spread throughout Europe, to regions ranging from Spain and Portugal in the west to modern Hungary in the east, and from England in the north to Crete in the south.

Knowledge of grape cultivation and winemaking reached Greece from Egypt, by way of Crete. A wine trade between Egypt and Crete began as early as 2500 BC, and by 1500 BC grapes were being grown and wine made on the island itself. There is also some evidence, in the form of jars and jugs that seem to have held a barley-based liquid, that the Minoan inhabitants of Crete produced and consumed beer. Thus Crete was similar to Egypt and Mesopotamia in having an alcohol culture that encompassed both major fermented beverages. In this respect Greece stood out: there is no reliable evidence that the Greeks themselves drank beer before the introduction of viticulture and wine production, and they did not adopt brewing as a parallel activity to wine-making. It is probable that Greeks drank mead before wine entered their diet, as the Greek word for "intoxicant," *methu*, is very similar to the word for mead in other languages. But they eschewed beer and, as we shall see, constructed elaborate arguments that beer was a beverage unfit for their civilization. The Greeks (known then as Mycenaeans) ruled beer- and wine-drinking Crete for about two centuries from 1420 BC, and there is plenty of evidence of wine-drinking in their palaces, as well as a reference to Dionysus (the Greek god of wine) on one of the Linear B tablets from that period. But there is no evidence that the Greeks drank beer while they occupied the island, even though it is possible that the indigenous Cretans continued to do so.[1]

If the Greeks did have contact with beer while on Crete, it must not have been a good experience, and they left the knowledge and technology of brewing behind when they left; they even apparently forgot it, for later Greek writers described beer in other societies as if they had never come across such a beverage before. The Greeks did, however, learn how to grow vines and make wine, and they transferred this knowledge to the mainland. Until this period, the cultivation of grapevines in western Asia and the Middle East had been largely restricted to the limited cooler areas of predominantly hot regions, such as the mountains to the north and west of Mesopotamia, the valleys on the eastern shore of the Mediterranean, and the Nile Delta in Egypt. But many regions throughout the Greek mainland were hospitable to vines, and by about 1000 BC, hundreds of vineyards had been planted close to cities such as Athens, Sparta, Thebes, and Argos, which were the main markets for wine. Five hundred years later, the demand for wine had grown such that vineyards had to be established much farther afield, especially on the more distant islands. Some, like Thasos, Lesbos, and Chios, earned reputations for the quality of their wines. By 400–300 BC, a true wine industry, on a scale never seen before, had been established in Greece, and wine soon became, with olive oil and grain, one of the three main products of economy and commerce in the Mediterranean region.

Not only did Greeks export their own wine, but they extended viticulture under Greek ownership to new regions and expanded existing production elsewhere. As early as the fifth century BC, Greek wine was found in various regions of France and Egypt, around the Black Sea, and in central Europe. When they colonized Egypt from about 300 BC, the Greeks planted many new vineyards, and they also introduced vines to southern France (near

Marseilles), Sicily, and southern regions of the Italian mainland. Southern Italy proved such a successful location for viticulture that the Greeks called it *Oenotria*, "the land of trained vines." Viticulture became so important there that, in one southern Italian site dating from 400–300 BC, grapevine remains made up a full third of vegetation recovered by archaeologists.[2]

Yet the movement of viticulture and wine production was not unilinear. It is possible that viticulture was introduced to Spain not by the Greeks, as was once thought, but by the Phoenicians, or even that it was established independently of outside influences. Similarly, the Etruscans of northern Italy seem to have received winemaking knowledge from the Phoenicians, and Etruscan amphoras, the large ceramic jars used for shipping wine, were modeled on the Phoenician form.[3] At the time Greeks were introducing vineyards to southern Italy, Etruscans were making wine and exporting it across the Alps as far as Burgundy, in France.

Even so, it was the Greeks who established the first major long-distance wine trade routes in the ancient world, and thousands of Greek amphoras—the clay jars used for transporting wine and other products until the first century of the Christian era—can be found throughout Europe. Ungainly looking objects, amphoras came in a variety of shapes and sizes, each typical of a producer or region of production, so that the origins of most can be fairly easily identified. Most amphoras held between 25 and 30 liters, and all had pointed bases, bodies that broadened toward the top, and two handles. Their design enabled them to be carried at both ends, because a full amphora was too heavy for one person to carry: an average amphora held about 30kg of wine, to which was added the weight of the amphora itself. The pointed ends made it possible to pivot an amphora, but they also made storage difficult, as amphoras could not stand upright without support. In wine cellars they generally leaned against one another, like so many drunks with bellies full of wine. When they were shipped, the ends were planted in a wooden framework or in a bed of sand. Amphoras were eventually replaced by wooden barrels, which had significant advantages in that they held more wine and could be rolled and pivoted by one person. But the adoption of barrels did historians no favors; unlike amphoras, which have survived for centuries as evidence of the early wine trade, the wooden barrels have rotted away.

Most ancient wine was transported on water, throughout the Mediterranean and its seas and along Europe's rivers, because water was by far the cheapest medium for shipping anything. But it was a high-risk venture, and hundreds of thousands of Greek amphoras lie at the bottom of the waterways across which the Greeks traded. These are cargoes lost when ships sank during storms or were blown onto rocks, and heavy concentrations lie along the southern coast of France. One site includes as many as 10,000 amphoras, which would have contained about 300,000 liters of wine, the equivalent of 400,000 modern bottles. It is estimated that as much as 10 million liters of wine were shipped to Gaul each year through Massilia (Marseilles), the Greeks' main trade gateway to Gaul. There is also evidence of the transfer of Greek wine-drinking culture, in the form of cups and bowls. At Châtillon-sur-Seine, in northern Burgundy, a massive *krater* (a vessel used for mixing wine with water) was located. It was clearly intended for decorative use, as it stands two meters high and has a volume of a thousand liters, but it speaks to the status of wine in Celtic Gaul.[4]

At home, wine was consumed among all levels of Greek society, but there were important differences in the quality of the wine consumed and the circumstances in which it was drunk. The most famous Greek wine institution was the symposium; the modern meaning of the word—a conference or meeting—is much diluted from the original. The Greek word *symposion* means "drinking together," and it referred to a get-together of upper-class Greek men (usually between twelve and twenty-four of them) for a long night of wine consumption, discussion, and entertainment. Symposiums could also be rites of passage, occasions for the induction of young men into adult male society. A number of representations of the symposium have come down to us, and it is vividly portrayed on the ornate pottery jars and cups that were used as the night progressed. They show men wearing garlands on their heads, leaning on couches, drinking wine from shallow goblets (called *kylixes*), talking, and listening to singers and musicians. Some symposiums were serious affairs, as the men discussed politics and the arts through the night. Others seem to have been boisterous drinking parties where drinking as well as sex with prostitutes and boy servers took priority. Many symposiums were probably a blend of all these activities.

Although the format of symposiums varied, there were some standard features. The first cup of wine might be drunk straight, without any added water, but the rest was diluted. Greeks generally thought that drinking wine straight was barbaric (some writers argued that drinking wine straight, or even diluting it by half, could make the drinker insane), and they commonly added water (sometimes seawater) to their wine, as well as herbs and spices for flavoring. The host (*symposiarch*) of each symposium decided on the ratio of wine to water, but the water was always dominant. Ratios of 3:1, 5:3, and 3:2 seem to have been common, meaning that the participants drank a beverage that was between 25 and 40 percent wine. Because much of the wine favored by better-off Greeks was made from dried grapes, whose higher sugar concentration produces wine with higher levels of alcohol than wine made from fresh grapes, the diluted wines might well have had alcohol levels of between 4 and 7 percent, about the same as modern beer. Very likely the aim was to produce a drink strong enough to induce mild intoxication and a convivial atmosphere but not so strong that the participants became too intoxicated or fell asleep too soon. Clearly the intended strength or consumption sometimes went wrong, and the images on some vases and kylixes show men keeling over, holding on to one another for balance, and vomiting.

A number of contemporary works on the symposium suggest that the ideal was for participants not to drink to the point of serious intoxication. The Greeks prided themselves on drinking moderately and contrasted this virtue with the tendency of other cultures (such as the Scythians and Thracians) to drink to excess. The comic poet Alexis praised the Greek way of drinking moderately and described the practices of others as "drenching, not drinking," probably because they downed their drink so greedily that they spilled it all over themselves.[5] Of course, diluting wine with water (which was portrayed as mixing wisdom with pleasure) helped keep intoxication in the moderate range. Greeks criticized other drinking cultures for drinking their wine (and their beer) undiluted.

As the quintessentially civilized institution for drinking wine, the symposium was expected to be a relaxed but fairly sober occasion. A play attributed to the poet Eubulus sets out the effects of drinking successive kraters of wine. Just how much each member of the symposium consumed would have depended on the size of the krater and the number of participants. Eubulus's argument need not be read literally but as a demonstration of the progressive effects as the participants moved from moderate to excessive consumption. He has the host of the symposium say,

> I mix three kraters only for those who are wise.
> One is for good health, which they drink first.
> The second is for love and pleasure.
> The third is for sleep, and when they have drunk it, the wise wander homewards.
> The fourth is no longer ours, but belongs to arrogance.
> The fifth leads to shouting.
> The sixth to a drunken revel.
> The seventh to black eyes.
> The eighth to a summons.

The ninth to bile.

The tenth to madness, in that it makes people throw things.[6]

Quite clearly, the advice was that participants should stop drinking and go home after three kraters of wine had been consumed, for nothing good results from drinking more. "Hubris," the result of the fourth krater of wine, was a civic offense in Greece, and it was a term that could encompass acts as serious as rape and adultery.[7] By the eighth krater, the participants were in real danger of running into the law, while drinking all ten kraters drove men to madness. Here was a graphic portrayal of the way a pleasurable activity could degenerate into a violent one, simply through the consumption of too much wine, even when it was well diluted. It is a graphic reminder of the historic tension between the positive and negative perceptions of alcohol.

Wine was not merely the medium used for lubricating the sociability inherent to symposiums; its centrality to the occasion is suggested by the games the participants played. Some involved inflated wineskins, and in one game a skin was smeared with grease and players had to try to balance on it. In another game, called *kottabos*, players tossed small quantities of wine or wine dregs from their bowl at a bronze disc balanced on the top of a pole. The aim was to knock the disc off so that it fell and struck a larger disc fixed halfway down the pole, making it ring like a bell.[8] In yet another game, a saucer floated in a bowl of water, and wine and dregs had to be thrown so as to fill the saucer and sink it—a reminder that ancient wine was not the clear liquid it is today but contained bits and pieces of solid matter from the grapes and vines themselves, as well as from the additives, such as herbs. Games like these involved various motor skills, balance, and aiming accuracy, all of which were likely to be impaired by alcohol and increasingly impaired as the night wore on. Perhaps winning such games demonstrated the victor's ability to hold his wine. As simple as they were, they underlined the centrality of wine to the symposium, and some also demonstrated that the participants and host were wealthy enough literally to throw wine away.

By convention, symposiums were confined to males, and any women present were musicians, servers, or prostitutes or sometimes looked after men who had drunk themselves sick. Women of the Greek upper classes also drank wine, but this practice was not looked upon favorably. A number of Greek writers—all male—alleged that while men drank their wine diluted, women preferred to drink it straight, with predictably unfortunate consequences. Whether or not this was true, the idea placed women on the same level as barbarians. One aspect of this belief was the often-expressed fear that women who drank wine lost their moral bearings and were prone to become sexually promiscuous. The association of drinking women and sexual activity is common in Western cultures and an excellent example of the double standard of sexual morality, which holds women to different standards of behavior from those permitted to men.

To men of the Greek elite, wine was clearly a special beverage, and while this can be said of elites in other societies where wine was consumed, none regarded wine so highly that they eventually vilified beer and the people who drank it. As the Greeks came into contact with the regions around them, they encountered peoples who drank solely beer or beer and other alcoholic beverages. Greek soldiers did drink beer and date wine when they were in regions where they were produced, but the first Greek reference to beer, specifically to beer-drinking by Thracians in the seventh century BC, is what one historian has called "infelicitous": it likened their practice of drinking beer through a straw (to avoid the chaff and other debris that floated on top) to a woman performing fellatio.[9]

However, when the Greek general Xenophon traveled through Armenia about 400 BC and encountered beer drunk through reeds, he wrote about it in a fairly noncommittal way. "There was also some wheat, barley, pulse, and barley wine in mixing bowls. . . . And it was very strong unless one poured in water. And the drink was very good to the one used to it."[10] Armenian beer was strong enough that it could be diluted with water, as wine was in Greece, and Xenophon admits that it was very good, although the qualification "to the one used to it" might suggest that he himself didn't like it.

This dispassionate description of beer contrasts with what became the common Greek attitude, for starting from the fifth century BC, Greeks began to denounce beer as making men "effeminate." It is possible that the association of beer and effeminacy resulted from the humoral understanding of the body, where men were considered to be warm and dry and women to be cold and moist. Within the same conceptual framework, wine was considered to be a hot beverage (there were some exceptions), so that it aligned with men. Hippocrates considered cereal to be a cold substance, although hot when it was processed as bread. But when later medical writers wrote about beer (Hippocrates did not), they designated it as a cold beverage and therefore more like a woman than a man. In short, wine was considered a manly drink and beer a womanly or effeminate one.[11] Beyond that, the Greeks thought that beer and wine were different beverages, as they were not aware that alcohol was the active ingredient in both. Aristotle classified wine with opium and other drugs but put beer in a separate category, and he thought that drinking them produced different effects. Anyone who drank wine to the point of intoxication fell flat on his face, because wine made one "heavy-headed." In contrast, a man intoxicated by beer fell backward, because beer was "stupefying."[12] Statements like these might not make much sense, but they do show that the two beverages were considered to be quite different from each other.

Not only did they fault foreigners for drinking beer, but Greeks also deplored their drinking habits. As we have seen, barbarian peoples such as the Thracians and Scythians were portrayed as drinkers to excess; as messy, noisy drinkers; and as generally given to intoxication. To some extent, these drinking customs were attributed to climate. People who lived in cool climates, Greek philosophers argued, might be courageous in war, but they were also excitable and passionate, which led them to drink immoderately. If this were not bad enough, barbarians were promiscuous when it came to using intoxicating commodities, unlike the Greeks who drank only wine, the beverage of the civilized. The Scythians were perhaps the worst of the lot, for they not only drank wine and beer undiluted but also drank mead and fermented milk and used cannabis and other plants that seemed to have psychoactive ingredients.[13]

Moreover, belligerence and excessive drinking, which Greek writers thought resulted from living in cool climates, could be a toxic combination, and the Macedonian leaders Alexander the Great and his father, Philip II, made excellent examples. Philip was said to drink like a sponge and become intoxicated every day, including days when he led his troops into battle. He was also said to have forced Greek captives to labor in shackles in his vineyards.[14] As for Alexander, he was said to be given to bouts of drinking that left him unpredictable, violent, and even homicidal. A later Roman commentator reported that Alexander "often left a banquet stained with the blood of his companions" and that he had killed his friend Clitus (who had once saved his life) during a drunken quarrel.[15]

The Romans carried on what was by then the Greek tradition of thinking of wine as a superior beverage. Like the Greeks, the Romans eschewed beer for wine and judged other cultures partly by what they drank and how they drank it. At first, one historian argues, the Romans were caught between wanting to be part of "the civilized symposiastic world" and resisting "the libidinous associations of vinous excess" cataloged by writers like Pliny the Elder.[16] To resolve the tension, Romans stressed the role of wine in making life possible and highlighted the excellence of wine from their peninsula, and as they later extended their institutions throughout their empire, they transferred wine consumption to foreign elites in other societies. At first wine was traded, and there was, for example, a substantial wine trade between Roman Gaul and London about AD 70–80.[17] The Romans not only exported their own wine but extended viticulture and wine production throughout Europe. In this respect, they built on the earlier activities of Etruscans, who were actively trading with the French port of Lattara (near modern Lattes) as early as 500 BC. Excavations have revealed Etruscan amphoras from that period and a grape-pressing platform from about 400 BC. The latter suggests not only the earliest commercial wine production in France but also the transplantation of the Eurasian grapevine (*Vitis vinifera*), the main genus of grapes used in modern winemaking.[18]

But the Romans took their wine imperialism much further. By the beginning of the Christian era, Romans had sponsored the planting of vineyards in many of the best-known modern wine regions in France (including Bordeaux, the Rhône Valley, and Burgundy), as well as in England and many parts of central and eastern Europe. At first, vineyards were owned by Romans, but in time, non-Roman inhabitants of the empire were given rights of ownership. With due recognition to Greek influence in the south and Etruscan winemakers in the north of Italy, the modern European wine industry was kick-started by the growth of Rome and its enormous demand for wine.

It is possible that what became a massive wine market in Rome resulted from a shift in diet. For centuries, Romans consumed cereal in the form of gruel or porridge, known as *puls*, and bread was a relative latecomer to the Roman diet. Bread might have been baked in private homes, but the first public bakeries were set up between 171 and 168 BC.[19] The shift from a wet food (puls) to a dry one (bread) required liquid to wash it down, and wine was the chosen beverage. Swelling from about 100,000 inhabitants in 300 BC to more than a million only three centuries later, Rome demonstrated an impressive thirst for wine, especially for cheap wine that the masses could afford. It is estimated that Rome imported some 1.8 million hectoliters of wine a year, almost half a liter of wine a day for every man, woman, and child in the city.[20] Most came from vineyards around the city and from the coastal regions to the south, where vineyards had expanded rapidly during the second century BC.

We should note at this point that historical estimates of per capita consumption of wine or any alcohol, not only in ancient and classical times but right up to the present, must be treated cautiously. In most cases, until the twentieth century, they are based on estimates of both population size and the volume of alcoholic beverages available, and the margins of error in both are sizeable. In some places and periods, for example, wine was taxed when it entered a locality or a town, so we have fiscal records that document wine entering a community. But in such cases we have no idea how much escaped the tax records by being smuggled in, or whether the inhabitants went outside the city to drink less-expensive, tax-free wine. As for estimates of population, they are just that—estimates—until reliable censuses were taken. When both the base population and the volume of alcohol consumed are uncertain, per capita calculations are highly suspect.

But even if a figure of per capita consumption is statistically correct, it is not very useful, because it ignores the wide variations in alcohol consumption among different sections of the population. Historically, children have drunk less alcohol than adults, and men have drunk more alcohol than women. And among adult men, some—as individuals or as members of particular social classes—have historically drunk more than others. The result is that expressing consumption in broad per capita terms is as useful as describing a population that is composed in equal numbers of eighty-year-olds and one-year-olds as having an average age of forty-one years. It is true, but misleading and useless as a portrayal of the population.

Then there is the question of the alcohol content of the beverages in question. One reason to calculate per capita consumption of alcoholic beverages in the past is to get a sense of the volume of pure alcohol people were taking in; it makes a difference if someone drinks a liter of wine, a liter of beer, or a liter of distilled spirits each day. But we often have little reliable information on the alcohol content of alcoholic beverages in the past. Small errors in any estimates of probable alcohol content are amplified when they are generalized as per capita volumes on an annual basis.

All of these problems confront us in the case of Rome, where we can calculate that every member of the population had access to half a liter of wine a day by the first century of the Christian era. Yet we cannot be sure how widely wine was consumed, even though it seems to have been drunk from one end of the social spectrum to another. Romans had their own version of the Greek symposium, the convivium, but over time it gave way to a more formalized banquet model, which placed more attention on food and thereby diluted the primacy of wine.[21] Women were occasionally permitted to participate in conviviums; but their inclusion was much debated, and the drinking of wine by married women was denounced by some men on the grounds that it led them into adultery. It is a reminder of the historical link between women drinking alcohol and sexual promiscuity, based on the assumption that women were essentially sexual and that alcohol dissolved the restraints that society had constructed to contain and channel sexual expression.

The poet Juvenal wrote, "When she is drunk, what matters to the Goddess of Love? She cannot tell her groin from her head." At various times, Roman women were banned from any association with wine—including pouring wine libations at religious ceremonies—and in some periods, Roman law allowed a man to divorce his wife if she were caught drinking wine. (The last divorce on this ground was granted in 194 BC.) A more severe penalty was death. One story tells of a woman condemned by her family to starve to death simply because she was found in possession of the keys to the wine cellar.[22] In *Memorable Deeds and Words* (first century AD), Valerius Maximus relates the story of Egnatius Mecenius, "who beat his wife to death with a club because she had drunk some wine. And not only did no one bring him to court because of his deed, but no one even reproached him, for all the best men thought she deserved her punishment for her example of intemperance. For assuredly any woman who desires to drink immoderately closes the door to all virtues and opens it to all vices."[23]

So there must be some uncertainty about the consumption of wine by women in Rome, and if it were true that women were generally cut off from wine, males would have access to twice as much, a liter each day. But did all males drink wine? It is true that wine was consumed in all social strata; the well-off and the comfortable seem to have drunk wine regularly, and wine was also part of a soldier's rations and a slave's entitlement. Archaeologists have discovered hundreds of bars in Roman cities, and some 200 have been excavated in Pompeii, the major wine-shipping port buried when Mount Vesuvius erupted in AD 79. There were no fewer than eight bars in one seventy-five-meter-long stretch of one street.[24]

However much Romans drank, they deplored (publicly, at least) drinking to excess and intoxication, and allegations of drunkenness were harmful to anyone's reputation. Cicero was especially fond of labeling his opponents drunkards. He alleged that Mark Anthony, his main rival, led a dissolute life at home and started drinking early each morning. To illustrate the point, Cicero cited the occasion when, supposedly as a result of drinking too much wine, Mark Anthony had vomited in the senate. Not only could excessive consumption lead to disgraceful scenes like this, but habitually heavy drinking, according to Roman commentators, could produce all manner of physical and mental ailments. Lucretius warned that wine's fury disturbed the soul, weakened the body, and provoked quarrels, while Seneca wrote that wine revealed and magnified defects in the character of the drinker. Pliny the Elder, while praising quality wines, warned that many of the truths revealed under the influence of wine were better unspoken.[25]

But "wine" referred to many beverages in Roman Italy.[26] The wine that Cato the Elder provided for his slaves was undoubtedly of poor quality, and for three months of the year they were given a concoction of which only a fifth of the volume was grape juice. Perhaps its quality explains Cato's apparent generosity, as he allowed his slaves seven amphoras of wine (about 250 liters) each per year—the equivalent of about a modern bottle a day. We do not know the alcoholic strength of the wine, of course, nor was the ration distributed evenly throughout the year, as some was saved for major festivals.[27]

Many poorer Romans drank wine-based beverages such as *posca*, a mixture of water and sour wine (wine that had spoiled but had not turned into vinegar). Technically it was as much "wine" as the diluted wine served at a convivium or symposium; quality is not an issue here. Posca was much cheaper than unspoiled wine, and it was this that soldiers, too, were provided as part of their rations. Only when they were sick or wounded were soldiers given what we might think of as wine: made from fresh grapes, in good condition, and with higher alcohol content. Roman soldiers must have preferred it to the thin posca that was part of their daily rations, and it is reported that, in one case, troops stationed in northern Africa pillaged their locality in order to get slaves and livestock to exchange for wine. In 38 BC, Herod provided wine and other foodstuffs to Roman soldiers after they threatened to mutiny because of the lack of supplies.[28] Another winelike beverage available in Rome was *lora*, which was made from soaking in water the solids (skins, seeds, vine matter) that were left over from winemaking. The result must have been pale and thin and barely alcoholic, but it was different enough from water to be viable. Cato reported providing his slaves with lora for three months after the grape harvest, while Varro gave it to his farmworkers during the winter.

So although it can be said that Roman men of all social classes consumed wine, this clearly meant one thing at the top of the social scale, where wine was full of flavor, color, and alcohol (even if it was diluted with water before consumption), and another thing entirely lower down, where wine was a thin, watery beverage that was all but bereft of alcohol. Sensory and aesthetic considerations aside, better-off Roman men consumed a lot more pure alcohol than those beneath them, although it is almost certain that all men, taken as a whole, consumed more alcohol than all women.

Although Romans did not consume beer, they encountered plenty of it as they advanced into Europe, and many of them commented on its qualities. Repeating the Greek refrain about the effects of not diluting beer, Pliny the Elder noted, "There is a particular intoxication too among western people, with soaked grains, [made] in many ways among Gauls and Hispanians. . . . The Hispanians have even taught the aging of such types [of drinks]. Egypt has also devised similar drinks for themselves from cereal, and intoxication is absent in no part of the world, since they drink such juices [from cereal] pure, not weakening it through dilution as with wine."[29] This was more a comment on the way beer was consumed than on beer itself; Pliny was quite positive, writing that as milk was good for the bones and water for the flesh, beer nourished the sinews.[30] It was an argument for the inclusion of various beverages in the diet, and in general, the Romans took a more balanced view than the Greeks of wine. Although they reported and deplored the drunkenness they saw among beer-drinking peoples, they did not condemn beer itself as the Greeks did.

On the other hand, the Romans clearly thought wine was superior to beer. Not only did they not incorporate beer into their own diets, but they were influential in having foreign elites adopt wine as their drink of choice. When they occupied Egypt in the first century BC, they seem to have extended wine-drinking to a somewhat wider social group of Egyptians. Even so, the mass of the population must have continued to drink beer, because domestic wine production could not have supplied the whole Egyptian population, and imported Italian wine would have been too expensive for most Egyptians. We get a sense of the differential cost of beer and wine from the AD 301 edict that fixed maximum prices for various products throughout the Roman Empire. Beer made by the Celts cost 4 *denarii* for about a pint, compared with only 2 *denarii* for the same volume of Egyptian beer and 8 for the cheapest wine. For Egyptians, then, the cheapest wine was four times, and for others in the empire two times, the price of beer.[31] It is a moot point whether the price differences reflected the respective costs of production and distribution (long-distance transportation, in the case of some wine) or whether there was a premium on wine because of its relative scarcity or its cultural cachet.

Part of the cachet resulted from wine's religious associations. In Greece, the wine god was Dionysus, the son of Zeus and a mortal woman, Semele. According to the story of Dionysus, Zeus was tricked into burning Semele while Dionysus was still in her womb, but Zeus rescued him and implanted him in his own thigh until he was born. Later, Dionysus was expelled from his home on Crete and fled to Egypt, where he learned to make the wine with which he was identified. This account parallels the transfer of winemaking knowledge from Egypt to Crete and then to Greece, and in fact Dionysus appears to have been a wine god in Crete as far back as the second millennium BC.[32] The Greeks acknowledged Dionysus as having bestowed all the goodness of wine on them and frequently poured libations of wine in his honor. A cult that developed around him was initially opposed by the authorities; but it was eventually sanctioned, and Dionysus entered the Greek establishment, to the extent that his likeness appeared on some coins.

In Rome, the wine god Bacchus was widely celebrated, and by the third century BC, a cult that centered on him had emerged in central and southern Italy. It is not clear how extensive its membership was; but most of its adherents were said to be women, and they held festivals (called bacchanalia) that were often portrayed as sexual orgies fueled by wine and punctuated by animal sacrifices. In 186 BC the Roman senate banned the cult, but although the senate might have done so because of the cult's supposed immoral activities, it is also possible that the cult of Bacchus was a form of protest against Roman authority. The structure of the Bacchic cells, with their oaths of secrecy, their hierarchical structure, and their funding and property holdings, cut across officially approved patterns of family and political authority. It is very likely that this, rather than any putative drunkenness, provoked the ban—although inebriation would also have been deplored, especially if women were involved.[33]

Despite some differences between the Greek and Roman wine cultures, they shared a number of common features, including production methods. Grapes for wine were often dried in the sun so that they lost water and shriveled, giving their juice the more intense flavor and higher sugar level that translated into wines with more concentrated flavor and higher alcohol content. This was ideal for wines intended to be consumed diluted, as the final beverage had good levels of both flavor and alcohol. Not only was the base wine high in alcohol, but it was often sweetened by unfermented grape juice (which would have reduced the alcohol level somewhat) and sometimes by honey. *Apicius*, the collection of recipes compiled in the late fourth or early fifth century, provided guidance for making spiced wine (with ingredients such as honey, pepper, laurel leaves, and saffron) and wine infused with rose petals and violets.[34]

One recipe that called for as much honey as wine must have produced a sweet, viscous beverage quite unlike any wine known today. But if attempts were made to appeal to the sweet tooth, there were also methods of reducing sweetness. Salt water was sometimes added in order, as the Roman poet Pliny said, "to enliven a wine's sweetness," perhaps meaning that the salinity counteracted it to some extent. Other additives included herbs and spices and also lead, which contributes some sweetness. Some recipes recommended boiling the grape juice in lead vessels, while others specified the addition of lead compounds to wine. Lead is a preservative that might have slowed the spoiling of wine, but it is also toxic and must have made many drinkers sick, if it failed to kill them.

It is impossible to reconstruct the flavor of ancient wine. For the most part, the contemporary writers describing them tended to locate wines on the two spectrums of sweetness and strength: wines were more or less sweet and more or less strong. The point of reference for sweetness was honey, and some wines were described as "honey-sweet." Depth of color was appreciated, and it is possible that an association was made between color and strength. Few writers mentioned aromas, although Cato provided a recipe for imparting a "sweet aroma" to wine: add to the fermenting wine a tile that had been smeared with pitch and covered with warm ashes, aromatic herbs, rush (a flower), and "the palm that the perfumers keep."[35]

Aroma was perhaps less important aesthetically than as an indicator that a wine was spoiling, and Cato also gave a recipe for removing a bad odor from wine. This is a reminder that, despite the use of preservatives such as resin, the wines of Greece and Rome were not stable enough to last a long time. Often the aim—which is very modest by modern standards—was simply to make a wine that would last the year before the next vintage was available. When Ulpian asked, "What is old wine?" he answered that it is wine that came from the previous vintage.[36] The Greek writer Athenaeus gave the optimum age for the best wines as between five and twenty-five years, but the higher end appears entirely unrealistic for the period, and even five years seems an unlikely goal if we are talking about wine in good condition. Still, aged quality wines commanded higher prices than young, ordinary wines—although it is not clear whether the quality or age alone was the criterion. In AD 301, the Roman emperor Diocletian set the price of ordinary wine at between a half and a third the price of older wine.[37]

Preferences in color, strength, and flavor led to some wines winning accolades, and a number of Greek and Roman writers produced annotated lists of their preferred wines. In Greece, Mareotic wine from Egypt was widely praised, despite one suggestion that Cleopatra had become crazed under its influence. Athenaeus thought that Taeniotic wine, produced southwest of Alexandria, was even better than Mareotic; it was, he said, pale, pleasant, aromatic, and slightly astringent, with an oily quality that dissolved when gradually diluted with water. For his part, Pliny praised the wine of Sebennys in the central Nile Delta. As for the Greeks' own wines, those from the Aegean island of Thasos won frequent praise. The rulers of Thasos might have produced one of the earliest wine laws when they set down regulations to govern the winemaking process, quality, and even sale: wine could be sold only in Thasian amphoras of a specified size and could not be diluted before it was sold. The prescribed winemaking process included drying the grapes and boiling the must, both of which would have increased the alcohol and sugar content. Thasos prospered for some time, but by the second century BC, its wines had faded in popularity and were overtaken by wines from the islands of Rhodes, Cos, Lesbos, and Skiathos.[38]

Roman writers, too, rated wine. As far as Italian wines were concerned, those from the south were preferred, especially from Latium and Campania, coastal regions south of Rome that supplied wine to the imperial capital. When wine production began to expand, there was some concern that quality might be sacrificed to quantity. Columnella, for one, wrote that while supplying wine to the population was important, producers should never compromise on quality, even to the point of retaining valued but relatively low-yielding grape varieties instead of planting new varieties that gave higher yields.[39] One wine that stood out was from the Falernium vineyard, which lay on the border of those two regions. There are a number of references to the exquisite character of the wine and of the legendary 121 BC vintage, known as Opimian, after Opimius, who was consul that year. In his play *Satyricon*, Petronius has a banquet host bring out bottles labeled "Falernian. Consul Opimius. One hundred years old." Clearly, Petronius expected his audience to understand the reference. As we would expect, Falernian wine commanded a premium price: in one of the many taverns of Pompeii that were destroyed by the eruption of Mount Vesuvius, a measure of Falernian cost four times as much as ordinary wine and twice as much as "the best wine."[40]

It was not only wine from their peninsula that Romans appreciated, for the selection available in the city was truly imperial in scope. When Pliny the Elder prepared a catalog of wines in the first century of the Christian era, he included 91 varieties of wine, 50 quality wines, and 38 kinds of foreign wines, as well as salted, sweet, and artificial wines.[41] He was notable in ranking wines by grape variety as well as their region of production. Perhaps wine critics like Pliny the Elder were the Robert Parkers of their day, awarding Caecuban wine LXXXIX points and Falernian XCVI points out of C, recommending certain regions and vintages and perhaps driving up the prices of some wines in the process.

Flavor and strength were not the only criteria by which wine was judged, for many classical writers assessed wines as much for their supposed health benefits and medicinal properties as for the sensory pleasure they gave. Athenaeus described a Mareotic white wine as "excellent, white, pleasant, fragrant, easily assimilated, thin, not likely to go to the head, and diuretic."

Wine was generally seen as healthy when consumed in moderation, and Hippocrates, whose writings are fundamental to the Western medical tradition, recommended wine as an aid to digestion. But not all wines had the same effects. Echoing Egyptian beliefs in the laxative properties of wine, Hippocrates noted that "dark and harsh wines are drier, and they pass neither well by stool nor by urine, nor by spittle." More productive were "soft dark wines . . . [which] are flatulent and pass better by stool."[42]

The relationship between wine and digestion became a principle of Western medicine, as did the notion that wine was a "hot" substance. This was important when the body was understood as containing hot and cold elements that needed to be balanced. Wine was not recommended for bodies that were considered very hot by nature, as children's bodies were thought to be, or hot through illness, as when a patient had a fever. In these cases, wine would add to the hotness and aggravate the imbalance, and this was one reason parents were advised not give wine to children. In contrast, wine was recommended for bodies that were naturally cold, as old people's bodies were believed to be, as they approached the final coldness of death.

Physicians also warned against the dangers of wine, usually when it was consumed to excess. Among the wine-related ailments enumerated by Seneca and Pliny were memory loss, identity confusion, impaired speech and vision, narcissistic self-indulgence, antisocial behavior, a distended stomach, halitosis, quivering, vertigo, insomnia, and sudden death.[43] Nor was substantial wine consumption recommended for athletes. Epictetus noted that successful Olympic competitors avoided desserts and cold water and drank wine only sparingly, rather than when they felt like it. Philostratus noted that athletes who drank too much wine "have an excessive paunch . . . and too much drinking is discovered by a fast pulse."[44]

Like wine, beer was attributed both positive and negative medicinal qualities. As we have seen, Pliny thought beer was good for the sinews, and in the first century AD the medical writer Celsus ranked beer above milk and wine in nutritional value. On the other hand, most classical physicians wrote negatively about the physical effects of drinking beer. The Greek herbalist Dioscorides, who wrote soon after Celsus, thought that beer was a diuretic and variously affected the kidneys and sinews, was harmful to the membranes, and caused flatulence, headaches, bad humors, and elephantiasis. But beer, like wine, could be used as a medium for herbal and other remedies. One physician advised women who wanted good and plentiful breast milk to drink a mixture of beer with either the crushed unripe fruit of the sesame plant or five to seven earthworms of the type used by fishermen, along with palm dates. Another recommended using a suppository soaked in beer and herbs to deal with intestinal worms.[45]

Alcoholic beverages became a healthy choice in another respect, too: as a potable alternative to unsafe or polluted water. This is a common explanation for the apparent ubiquity of alcohol in parts of the world where available water supplies were, for one reason or another, either not safe to drink or believed to have been not safe to drink. Humans settled only where potable water was available, but the freshwater lakes, rivers, streams, and artesian wells that delivered this essential water often became, over time, contaminated by human, animal, and industrial waste. Eventually there seems to have emerged some awareness that while drinking the local water made people ill and sometimes killed them, those who drank beer or wine generally remained healthy. As far back as the classical period, there were warnings about the dangers of drinking water that had been exposed to lead, and by the early modern period (from about AD 1500 to 1800) most European doctors recommended that people abstain from water entirely.

The argument that alcoholic beverages became a staple of the European diet because they were safer than water is logical and persuasive, but it must be qualified. First, there were variations among alcohols. In the process of making wine, grape juice is exposed to a hot fermentation process that eliminates some bacteria, and to this extent it is safer than untreated water. If it were diluted with water, as it commonly was in Greece and Rome, it would be less safe, even though the alcohol and acid in the wine would neutralize some of the bacteria in the water that was added. Variants on wine, like the Romans' posca, made by mixing sour wine and water, would also have had the alcohol and acidity to make it safer to drink—even if only marginally so—than untreated water alone. As for beer, water was used in brewing, and the warmth of the fermentation, plus the alcohol, rendered beer safer than the water used in its production. Overall, we can conclude that alcoholic beverages were safer than water, if not absolutely safe. (Distilled beverages, such as gin and whiskey, which were not widely produced until the sixteenth century, were even safer: distillation required heating the base fermented liquids until the alcohol vaporized, and the finished product was much higher in alcohol than any fermented beverage.)

It is one thing to drink alcohol for its medicinal properties, such as curing constipation or aiding digestion. It is quite another to drink alcohol because it was the safest beverage available. The first behavior treated alcohol as a beverage that might be drunk occasionally in addition to water. The second would lead one to drink alcohol exclusively. It is possible, then, to think of alcohol consumption as having gone through three stages in the ancient world:

first, as a beverage consumed only rarely, and then mainly on ceremonial or festive occasions; second, as a beverage more generally consumed, partly because it was believed to have general health benefits; and third, as the only beverage consumed, because it was believed to be safer than water. The first two stages could easily overlap, but the third gave alcoholic beverages a quite different status: that of a staple element in the daily diet.

When might people have shifted from treating alcohol as a discretionary beverage to a necessary one? By the sixteenth and seventeenth centuries, European doctors were almost unanimous in their belief that drinking water was dangerous, but it is difficult to know how far back that view went. Clearly, the quality of water must have varied from place to place, although it is possible that enough examples of localized or periodic pollution led to a cultural aversion to water that was geographically broader than the regions affected by poor water. It is also possible that, given a choice, people simply preferred beer, wine, or any alcoholic beverage—even miserable posca—to water, even when the available water was safe. Beer was certainly nutritious, and wine provided some nutrients, if not as many as beer. Both gave drinkers a sense of well-being and sometimes the pleasure of mild inebriation or the temporary enjoyment of severe intoxication.

We do know that water was frequently unsafe, but we are not sure where and when this happened. Did Mesopotamians turn to beer because the Tigris and the Euphrates were polluted? Did most Egyptians embrace beer because of the quality of Nile water? Or did they do so because beer provided everything they could reasonably ask for: it hydrated and nourished the body, it tasted good, and it delivered a pleasurable sensation that river water simply could not match. Water hydrated, but that was all. Why would anyone drink water if they could drink beer?

Romans certainly had problems supplying water to their burgeoning population, and the River Tiber, along whose banks the original city was built, was soon polluted—a process probably accelerated by the practice of throwing the bodies of executed people into it. To provide Romans with potable water (as well as water for public baths, fountains, and industries), eleven aqueducts were built in the 500 years between 312 BC and AD 226. Collectively, they delivered enough water for each of Rome's million inhabitants to have about a liter a day. If that were all consumed, and the wine and food in the Roman diet contained the same volume of water, it might well have been enough for rehydration.

Another qualification to the assumption that Europeans began, en masse, to avoid water in favor of alcoholic beverages is that substantial numbers of them almost certainly, for cultural or financial reasons, did not drink alcohol. Children might have drunk some beer or wine; but there is no evidence that they consumed enough for rehydration, and parents were often advised not to give any alcohol to children. Women were often discouraged from drinking alcohol or were actually forbidden to do so, as they were at times in Rome. If children and women did not drink enough beer or wine to rehydrate, what did they drink, if not water? Milk was not produced in commercial volumes, fruit juices were rare, and hot water-based beverages such as coffee and tea did not reach Europe until more than a millennium later. As for the poor, they must have had no alternative but to drink water if alcohol was beyond their financial means.

We should conclude that consuming bad water contributed (along with poor nutrition and housing) to lower life expectancy among the poor and among women of all classes. It is reasonable to see water consumption implicated in the high historic levels of childhood mortality. Put another way, alcohol must have contributed to lower mortality and higher life expectancy among those who consumed it. But we can only speculate, and we certainly cannot isolate alcohol from the many variables that produced historic levels of morbidity and mortality. What is equally certain is that we cannot generalize about alcohol consumption and its effects without taking into account gender, age, and social position.

It is clear, nonetheless, that Greece and Rome developed cultures of alcohol consumption that were more extensive and elaborate than any before them. Not only did people from almost all social classes consume alcohol, but alcoholic beverages—especially wine and, to a lesser extent, beer—became important topics of discussion and analysis. The ways in which wine and beer were consumed became significant markers of social distinction within and between cultures. Moreover, Greek and Roman patterns of alcohol consumption and attitudes toward specific alcoholic beverages both informed the influential Christian doctrines of drinking and were the foundation for medieval drinking ideologies and practices.

3

Religion and Alcohol

THE PATHS OF CHRISTIANITY AND ISLAM

The relationship between alcohol and religion began thousands of years ago. As we have seen, much of the earliest evidence of alcohol, whether in China or the Middle East, has been found in contexts suggesting it was used in religious ceremonies of various kinds. In many ancient and classical cultures, gods were associated with various alcoholic beverages, especially beer, wine, and mead; Bacchus and Dionysus are only the best known. Alcohol was not the only commodity to have dedicated deities—in Greece, Demeter was the goddess of bread, fruit, and vegetables—yet wine and beer were more consistently linked to religion. Why that was so is a matter of speculation. According to one common argument, the feelings of relaxation, light-headedness, and disorientation that result from drinking increasing volumes of alcohol (a progression that is prosaically called mild to severe intoxication) were sensations so different from drinkers' quotidian experience that they were thought of as "otherworldly." Alcohol elevated the drinker to sensory dimensions that were understood as having spiritual or religious significance.

Positively or negatively, the association between alcohol and religion may be thought of as a historical constant, but Christianity and Islam—two religions that emerged in the same millennium—forged unique, divergent, and persistent relationships with alcohol. Christianity elevated one alcoholic beverage—wine—to a position of centrality in its symbolism and rituals, while Islam is the first major religion known to have rejected alcohol entirely and to have forbidden its followers to drink alcoholic beverages. There were precedents for both. On one hand, wine was central to the ceremonies of the cult centered on Bacchus, the Roman god of wine, and integral to Jewish doctrine and ceremonies; on the other hand, some pre-Christian Jewish sects and secular laws (such as Sparta's) prohibited the consumption of alcohol.

But these latter were marginal or short-lived bans. In contrast, Christian and Muslim doctrines on alcohol have had long-term meaning for their millions of followers and have endowed alcohol with much of the religious freight it carries to this day.

The direct background of the Christian position on alcohol was the Jewish Torah (the first five books of the Old Testament of the Christian Bible), which contains many references to wine and the effects of drinking, as well as a reference to beer in a Greek version (but not in the Hebrew and later translations).[1] In the New Testament, however, the grapevine is the most frequently mentioned plant, and there are many references to wine; but beer is not mentioned at all, even though it was widely consumed in the eastern Mediterranean in the first centuries of the Christian era.

There is a debate among some biblical scholars and commentators about the meaning of various terms and how biblical references to alcohol should be interpreted. Although some biblical texts can be read as treating the consumption of wine in a positive light, others are neutral, and yet others are indisputably negative. One text in Genesis treats wine in a matter-of-fact way, as integral to dining: "And Melchizedek king of Salem brought forth bread and wine."[2] Another text celebrates wine: "Go thy way, eat thy bread with joy, and drink thy wine with a merry heart; for God now accepteth thy works."[3] The therapeutic uses of wine were also recognized. Timothy advises, "Drink no longer water, but use a little wine for thy stomach's sake and thine other infirmities,"[4] while Luke alludes to wine's antiseptic qualities: "And went to him, and bound up his wounds, pouring in oil and wine."[5]

Yet other biblical texts appear to warn against any drinking, such as, "For he shall be great in the sight of the Lord, and shall drink neither wine nor strong drink."[6] Many of the biblical texts dealing with wine make a clear distinction between moderate and excessive drinking and condemn the latter: "Be not among winebibbers [drunkards]; among riotous eaters of flesh"[7] and "Likewise must the deacons be grave, not double-tongued, not given to much wine, not greedy of filthy lucre."[8] In these cases, excessive drinking was condemned alongside other forms of excess, such as gluttony and money-grubbing. It is likely that the abuse of wine, not wine itself, was the specific target of condemnation, just as food and money were not, in themselves, subjects of criticism.

These ambiguities were not a major issue for religious commentators until the nineteenth century. Until then, alcohol was widely consumed—not least because it was a safer alternative to the water then available for drinking—and the moderate consumption of beer and wine was viewed in a positive light. There was an assumption that any negative message about alcohol in the Bible was aimed at excessive consumption or some other form of misuse, not at consumption itself. When the Bible was quoted, it was almost always to warn against drunkenness and its associated sins. But in the 1800s, supplies of safe drinking water and other nonalcoholic beverages became much more widely available in Europe and North America, and alcohol ceased to be necessary as an alternative to the water many populations had access to. Put simply and briefly (the issues are explored in more detail in Chapter 9), the availability of alternatives to alcohol made total abstinence from alcohol the viable option it had not been until that time. One result was that much of the attention and criticism that had been directed at drunkenness and at the negative effects of habitual heavy drinking shifted to the consumption of any alcohol at all.

Nineteenth-century biblical scholars, working in a cultural climate increasingly receptive to temperance and prohibitionist ideas, began to reinterpret the treatment of alcohol in the Bible in light of the widespread acceptance of the notion that the consumption of even the smallest volume of alcohol led to sin and social disorder. If drinking alcohol led to immorality, they asked, why did Jesus turn water into wine at the wedding feast at Cana? Why did Jesus drink wine? And why would wine symbolize the blood of Christ in communion? Seizing on the existence and apparent ambiguity of many different Hebrew words used to refer to alcoholic beverages, they adopted a "two-wine" theory: that the positive, approving references to "wine" in the Bible referred not to wine—the beverage resulting from fermentation—but to unfermented grape juice, whereas the negative references referred to actual wine. For them, the miracle at the marriage at Cana was that Jesus turned water not into wine but into grape juice. (Cynics might see this as a more modest miracle.) In contrast, they argued that negative examples of wine involved the real thing, as when Noah drank so much wine that he stripped naked, and when Lot's daughters so befuddled their father with wine that he was not aware he was having sex with them. In these and other cases, supporters of the two-wine theory argued, alcohol was clearly at work, erasing the line between moral and immoral behavior.

Many of the Christian denominations founded in the 1800s (such as the Church of Jesus Christ of Latter-day Saints and the Salvation Army) forbade their adherents to drink alcohol and rallied to the two-wine interpretation of the Bible. There was also a movement to celebrate communion in mainstream denominations with grape juice, or what they designated by the oxymoron "unfermented wine." The place of alcohol in the Old and New Testaments is still a subject of lively debate. Some commentators have added up the positive, negative, and neutral references to beer and wine in the Bible and concluded that they are predominantly negative; whether that is true, and whether it means anything if it is, is a matter of interpretation and individual decision.

What is clear is that wine was of great importance to both Jews and Christians. The book of Genesis reports that when the Great Flood had receded and the earth needed to be replanted and repopulated, the first plant cultivated by Noah was not cereal for making bread but a grapevine to provide wine. Having cultivated his grapes, Noah proceeded to make wine, and this was apparently a good thing. But the narrative ended badly when Noah drank too much, stripped off all his clothes, and fell into an intoxicated stupor in his tent. His youngest son, Ham, came in and saw his father naked, and for this offense Noah cursed Ham's son, Canaan.[9] This is a complicated story (commentators suggest there was some form of sexual violation by Ham of his father), and there are several explanations why Canaan, rather than Ham, bore the punishment. But what is important, in this context, is that what appeared to start out as the unproblematic consumption of inherently good wine led to breaking God's laws and a family tragedy that is emblematic of human life in the new world after the flood.[10]

The tragedy was prefigured in some Jewish commentaries on the story of Noah and wine that set out the problems of excessive alcohol consumption more explicitly. According to one, Noah was about to plant his vineyard on the slopes of Mount Ararat when Satan offered to help in exchange for a share of the produce. Noah agreed, and Satan promptly slaughtered, in turn, a sheep, a lion, an ape, and a hog (presumably taken from the ark's passengers, which would have made the reproduction of these species problematic) and fertilized the vineyard with their blood. This was meant to demonstrate to Noah that after the first cup of wine, a drinker's behavior is as mild as a sheep's, but that after a second cup, the drinker becomes as courageous as a lion. The third cup of wine makes one behave like an ape, and after the fourth, the drinker acts like a hog that wallows in mud.[11]

Other Old Testament texts associated drunkenness not so much with bad, crude, or bestial behavior but explicitly with sin. In the case of Lot's daughters, the offense was incest, when they plied their father with wine so that he would sleep with them in order "to preserve seed of our father." They appear to have calibrated the amount of wine well so that Lot was not so drunk that he could not perform sexually yet was sufficiently intoxicated that when each daughter slept with him on consecutive nights, "he perceived not when she lay down, nor when she arose."[12] We might add, "nor who she was."

Coexisting with such examples of the abuse of wine are clearly positive statements. When Moses led the Hebrews from Egypt into Israel, he dispatched scouts, and they returned with a bunch of grapes so big and heavy that it took two men to carry it on a rod on their shoulders. While the Jews might well have valued eating juicy, fresh grapes after their trek, it is as likely that they relished the thought of drinking wine, the highly valued beverage of the Egyptian elite that had enslaved them. The Hebrews' god enjoined them to enjoy wine (and bread, oil, and meat) at annual festivals[13] and ordered priests to make offerings of bread and wine: "And the meat offering shall be two tenth deals of fine flour mingled with oil, an offering made by fire unto the Lord for a sweet savour: and the drink offering thereof shall be of wine, the fourth part of an hin."[14] Perhaps the most positive statement about wine was the affirmation, "Wine maketh glad the heart of man, and oil to make his face to shine, and bread which strengtheneth man's heart."[15]

The importance of wine to the Hebrews is also strongly suggested by the threats that God made to those who disobeyed his laws: they would not suffer eternal roasting in some far-off hell but the much more immediate penalty of having no wine. That, at least, seems to be implied in threats to make the vineyards barren: "The new wine mourneth, the vine languisheth, all the merryhearted do sigh. . . . There is a crying for wine in the streets; all joy is darkened, the mirth of the land is gone,"[16] and "I will surely consume them, saith the Lord: there shall be no grapes on the vine, nor figs on the fig tree, and the leaf shall fade."[17]

Beer was far from neglected, as we should expect from a society where beer was widely consumed.[18] Yahweh is said to consume the equivalent of 2 liters a day (and more on the Sabbath), and there are other positive references to beer. There is one suggestion that beer should be given to "him that is ready to perish, and wine unto those that be of heavy hearts. Let him drink and forget his poverty, and remember his misery no more."[19]

In their overall positions on alcohol, the Old and New Testaments can be read as representing fairly conventional restatements of the attitudes adopted by ancient and classical writers: wine and beer had the potential for either good or evil, and their effects depended on how they were consumed; as beverages, they were to be judged on their effects, not on any quality intrinsic to the beverages themselves. This is not surprising, as alcohol consumption was common among Jews (including the authors of the New Testament). Wine was integrated into festivities such as Purim, it had a place at Passover seders (including the Last Supper), and like their Greek and Roman colleagues, Jewish physicians employed wine as both internal and external therapies for a wide range of physical and emotional ailments.[20]

While among Jews wine had banal, therapeutic, and symbolic presences, among Christians it took on a more intensely critical meaning. The doctrine of transubstantiation, which was articulated in the first centuries of Christianity, holds that at the Eucharist the substance of the bread and wine become the body and blood of Christ, even though they keep their outward appearances. In the fourth century, St. Augustine quoted Cyprian as saying, "For as Christ says 'I am the true vine,' it follows that the blood of Christ is wine, not water; and the cup cannot appear to contain His blood by which we are redeemed and quickened, if the wine be absent; for by the wine is the blood of Christ."[21] Although this referred only to wine blessed for the Eucharist, and not to the wine consumed on a daily basis, it would not be surprising to find Christian doctrine taking a more stern view than other religions of the abuse of wine. Excessive drinking not only had the common range of personal and social consequences, but for Christians it involved the misuse of a substance charged with religious meaning. Perhaps it is for this reason that, under Christianity, we see the emergence of more systematic regulations governing the drinking of wine and other alcoholic beverages.

Christianity introduced Christ as a figure who, in many respects, resembled a new wine god. Christianity adopted many of the symbols of existing beliefs, and there were many similarities between Christ and other wine gods who were still venerated in the first centuries of Christianity. Dionysus, for one, was born of a god and a human woman, and he, too, performed the miracle of turning water into wine—although Dionysus filled only three jars with wine, not six, as Christ did. In the early centuries of Christianity there was a complex interplay between Christ and wine gods. A fifth-century mosaic from Paphos, in Cyprus, depicts the infant Dionysus in a tableau that echoes representations of the adoration of the magi in Christian iconography.[22]

So important was wine to the image of Christ that the first miracle performed by Jesus was the transformation of water into wine at the celebration of a marriage. When Mary, his mother, observed that the wine had run out before the festivities were over, Jesus called servants to fill six jars with the water that would normally be used for washing and then instructed one servant to give a bowl of the water to the man leading the festivities. Miraculously (and apparently without any words or gestures on Jesus's part) the water had become wine. There is a sense in which the miracle partially prefigured transubstantiation: when Jesus presented the bowl to the host, it appeared still to contain water, and he had to taste it before he recognized it as wine. (We might infer from this that it was white wine.) As with transubstantiation, the appearance had not changed, although its essential properties had.

In addition to the basic miracle, Jesus had turned bad water (intended for washing, not drinking) into high-quality wine; the host observed that while the best wine was usually served first, before the guests became too intoxicated to appreciate its quality, the wine Jesus provided was better than the wine that had been served first and had run out.[23] Was it wine? The word used might be open to several meanings, but the context—a marriage celebration—is the kind of occasion at which wine was typically served. It is worth noting that water, whether or not it was intended for washing, was not considered appropriate for the festivities.

For many centuries, until the 1800s, religious scholars and the clergy did not question that the wine referred to in the Bible was the alcoholic beverage made by fermenting grape juice. This is demonstrated by the use of wine in communion and by the way Christ was represented for hundreds of years. One genre of religious painting was "Christ in the wine-press," in which he is shown standing in a vat where grapes are crushed and pressed for their juice. Christ is usually depicted bearing a cross and wearing a crown of thorns, with blood running from the wounds on his head and body into the grapes that he is pressing with his feet. The red liquid running from the vat is thus a blend of Christ's blood and the grape juice, showing the essential convergence of the two. There can have been no doubt in the mind of the artist or of the audience of these works that what was in play here was what we know as wine.

Such was the centrality of wine to Christianity that it became associated with the religion. In fact, in the first few centuries of the Christian era, some Christian writers echoed the prejudices of the Greeks and Romans and portrayed beer as an inferior and harmful beverage. Eusebius, the fourth-century Christian historian, wrote that Egyptian beer "was both adulterated and cloudy. The Egyptians used it as a drink, before the Lord lived among them." (There is a hint here of the common notion, contested by some historians, that converts to Christianity shifted their drinking preferences from beer to wine.) About the same time, St. Cyril wrote that beer was "a cold and cloudy drink of Egyptians which could cause incurable illnesses," whereas wine "gladdened the heart." In turn, the fifth-century Christian thinker Theodoret wrote that Egyptian beer "is an invented beverage, not a natural one. It is vinegary and foul-smelling and harmful, nor does it produce any enjoyment. Such are the lessons of impiety, not like wine which 'gladdens man's heart.'"[24] Such characterizations of beer seem to have died away by the sixth century, and later Christian criticisms of beer referred to its consumption in pagan festivals or to simple excessive consumption. The way was clear for the Christians to embrace beer and for the church's religious houses to produce beer as well as wine.

Over time, the importance of having wine for communion led the Christian church and its institutions, such as religious houses, to became significant sponsors of an extensive wine industry. Many vineyards were planted on monastic lands, and monasteries became important commercial producers of wine. Only small volumes of wine were needed for communion, and wine was an integral part of the diet in some religious orders and for the church hierarchy; but many monasteries also produced wine for sale to the better-off strata of secular society. By the time the Roman Empire had reached its farthest extent about AD 400, the church had helped extend viticulture and winemaking to many parts of France (including now-famous regions like Bordeaux, Burgundy, and the Rhône Valley), as well as to present-day England, Portugal, Spain, Germany, Austria, Hungary, and Poland.

Thanks largely to the church, viticulture and wine production were well established throughout much of the Romans' western empire when Germanic populations (Franks, Burgundians, and others) from central and eastern Europe began to invade during the fifth century. By about AD 500, each major Germanic group had settled and established political control over parts of what had been the western Roman empire. It was the Romans who designated them "barbarians," and the word was soon given its meaning of "culturally inferior." The names of some individual populations—in particular the Vandals and Huns—later took on more specific but equally negative connotations. As we have seen, the Romans objected not only to their languages but also to their drinking customs: for the most part, the Germans (like every other group, apart from the Greeks and Romans) drank beer and were reputed to drink it to excess on a regular basis. Julius Caesar wrote that the Germans were suspicious of wine and that they initially opposed its importation into their regions because they feared it would make men effeminate.

If they were opposed to wine when they first encountered it, the Germans quickly overcame their qualms, and their elites were soon consuming wine as well as beer and mead. In the second century, the Greek philosopher Posidonius described their morning meal as consisting of roasted meat, milk, and undiluted wine.[25] By the late ninth century, King Alfred the Great referred to beer as one of the basic necessities of life (along with weapons, meat, and clothes) in Britain, but in the following century, the English abbot Aelfric laid out the hierarchy of beverages: wine for the rich, ale for the poor, and water for the poorest.[26] Among the Celts, who inhabited Gaul, the situation was similar, and beer was also widely consumed. In the sixth century, one physician wrote that "it is on the whole extremely suitable for all to drink beer or mead or spiced mead, since beer which has been well made is excellent in terms of benefits and is reasonable. . . . Similarly also mead made well, as long as the honey it has is good, helps a lot."[27]

Although Germans and Celts drank a range of alcoholic beverages, Edward Gibbon, the eighteenth-century historian of the fall of the Roman Empire, echoed the worst Roman prejudices (and amplified them with his own) when he described the "barbarians." They were, he wrote, "immoderately addicted" to "strong beer, a liquor extracted with very little art from wheat or barley, and corrupted . . . into a certain semblance of wine." But, he added, some of the barbarians who had "tasted the rich wines of Italy, and afterwards of Gaul, sighed for that one delicious species of intoxication." He added that "the intemperate thirst for strong liquors often urged the barbarians into the provinces on which art or nature had bestowed those much envied presents."[28] In short, Gibbon thought the barbarians invaded some regions of western Europe primarily to get their hands on wine, not for its sensory pleasures, but purely for its ability to intoxicate more rapidly than beer.

Were Edward Gibbon's views of these beer-guzzling, wine-hankering tribes shared by west Europeans as they faced the incursions by the peoples from the east? If so, they must have feared for the vineyards that had been initially planted under Roman sponsorship, then extended by Christian missionaries and religious houses, and for the wine that was increasingly regarded as a symbol of civilization and Christian piety. If it were true that the barbarians lived in crude disorder but loved wine, they could easily be imagined consuming the existing stocks in one drunken binge before letting the vineyards fall into ruin.

Yet when the German peoples invaded western Europe, they did not so much interfere with the production of wine as dislocate the established patterns of commerce. Trade declined as the Roman commercial system broke down and as the empire fragmented and was replaced by the smaller political units that were established throughout the region. The process did not affect ale, as it was consumed where it was made, but the wine trade was one of the casualties. We can only imagine the impact of political instability on Bordeaux's young wine industry. In the fifth century alone, the Bordeaux region was invaded successively by Goths, Vandals, Visigoths, and Franks. Then the Gascons from Spain arrived in the seventh century (giving the region the name Gascony), and in the eighth century the Franks were back. Such dramatic changes in political power and the shifting alliances that went with them were hardly conducive to the continuity of existing commercial links or the development of stable new ones.

This does not mean that the newcomers were hostile to wine. Even if they did not expand existing vineyards, and even if the wine trade was disrupted when the Roman Empire collapsed, the various German tribes maintained wine production more or less intact. Visigothic legal codes set out heavy penalties for damage to vineyards, and the Vikings, whose name has become a byword for theft and pillage and whom historians long treated as an early medieval chapter of the Hell's Angels, became active participants in the wine trade of northern Europe. Many of the rulers of the new political entities transferred vineyards to monastic orders. Ordono, the Gothic king of Portugal, did so in the ninth century, and a hundred years later the English kings Eadwig and Edgar granted vineyards to the monks of several abbeys.[29] Wine was clearly a valued commodity in the diets and medical preparations of these peoples, not simply something to be quaffed until the drinker fell into an intoxicated stupor, as Edward Gibbon suggested. Contemporary recipes called for wine in the preparation of stewed meat and fruit, and elite attitudes toward wine after the collapse of the empire were little different from the advice of Roman and Greek commentators. A seventh-century Anglo-Saxon text, for example, advised that "wine is not the drink for children or the foolish, but for the older and wiser."[30]

The promotion of wine by the Christian church reinforced the cultural status of wine and its consumption by the German and Celtic elites. Most lived in northern Europe, where cereals were easily cultivated but where the climate made viticulture either marginal or impossible. Wine had to be imported, sometimes over short but sometimes over longer distances, and transportation costs made wine more expensive than beer. Even where wine could be made, producers of the middling classes likely did not drink it on a daily basis because of its value as an exchange commodity. Beer, then, remained the drink of the masses outside the major wine-producing regions. It was a nutritious beverage (a given amount of grain provided more nutrients as beer than as bread) and safer than much of the water available for drinking. Both these considerations help explain why there were no attempts to restrict the production of ale so as to conserve stocks of grain for bread. At various times, authorities tried to limit the area of land under viticulture in order to preserve land for cereals (and, later, to restrict distilling of cereal-based spirits so as to reserve grain for bread). But until the early twentieth century, when temperance ideas influenced government policy and beer no longer had the nutritional value of earlier styles, no one tried to restrict beer production so as to conserve cereals for baking.

At various times in the early Middle Ages, climatic and other factors led to poor grain harvests. Drought reduced crops across much of Europe in the 860s, and in the following decade, locusts devoured the ripening grain throughout much of Germany. For lack of grain reserves, poor harvests led to shortages and famines, local or regional, throughout the Middle Ages and beyond. Although it is unlikely that many deaths can be attributed solely to starvation, many people died of disease as malnutrition weakened their immune systems. Warfare, too, could result in grain shortages, often because outside armies deliberately destroyed crops in the field. In any period when grain was in short supply, ale production must have declined, and populations must have been forced to drink the only alternative: water. It is probable that polluted drinking water contributed to the diseases and mortality that attended periods of famine.

It is impossible to know how much ale Europeans drank on a daily basis in the early Middle Ages. Consumption must have varied broadly on a regional basis, as well as by class, gender, and age. One calculation suggests that, in the eighth and ninth centuries, monks drank 1.55 liters of ale, while nuns drank 1.38 liters. Among lay consumers, the volume of ale was calculated as varying between 0.6 and 2.3 liters of beer (and 0.6 to 1.45 liters of wine), a wide range.[31] In all cases, the volume of alcohol would have increased during festivities, though perhaps it decreased during periods of penance and fasting, and it would certainly have decreased in years when grain harvests were poor.

In the early medieval period, ale was made to be consumed within days of being brewed, not to be kept for any extended length of time. It was generally brewed in small quantities in each household, usually by women as part of their responsibilities for baking bread and preparing food more generally. There are scattered references to brewing from all parts of Europe at this time—from England, Iceland, Spain, France, and elsewhere—but few provide much detail, probably because brewing was such a commonplace activity. In the eighth century, the emperor Charlemagne appointed a brewer to his court to maintain the quality of the ale, and he also enjoyed ale to celebrate military victories. Several English and Irish scholars complained about the poor quality of ale on the Continent, compared to what was available at home.[32]

The first large-scale brewing operations were set up in monasteries from the eighth century. Not only were monasteries wealthy enough to buy the equipment for commercial production, but they also owned the land that would provide the necessary supplies of grain. Beyond that, larger religious houses needed to produce more than a family household because they had to meet the dietary requirements of more people: the scores of monks in residence and the various travelers who might stay at a monastery. In contrast, a typical family household in much of western Europe comprised only four or five members, including women and children who did not drink as much ale as adult males.

One of the first religious houses to embrace brewing was the monastery of St. Gall (in what is now Switzerland). The buildings included three breweries—one for making ale for the monks; another, for distinguished guests; and a third, for pilgrims and paupers—but it is not clear if there was a quality distinction among the three ales. In general, monks were free to choose to produce wine or ale, and many seem to have made both, as well as other alcoholic beverages. In 843, the abbot of a monastery near Paris wrote that produce of all kinds was in such short supply that beverage production was difficult. There was a scarcity of grapes for wine, pears for making perry were unavailable, and a shortage of grain all but ruled out ale, so all that was left for the monks to drink was water. It is as clear a statement of the hierarchy of beverages as we could wish for.[33]

Many religious orders and houses prescribed daily allotments of wine and/or beer, but despite some attempts to standardize rules in the eighth century, there were many variations in what and how much was permitted. For some orders, the higher alcohol content of wine was problematic, as a ninth-century account of the founding of the monastery at Fulda, in Germany, makes clear: "Whilst he was explaining the Holy Rule to the brethren [the abbot] read out the passage which states that the drinking of wine does not befit the vocation of a monk, and so they decided by common consent not to take any strong drink that might lead to drunkenness but only to drink weak beer. Much later this rule was relaxed at a council held in the name of King Pippin, when, owing to the increasing numbers in the community, there were many sick and ailing among them. Only a handful of the brethren abstained from wine and strong drink until the end of their lives."[34] The synod of Aachen in 816 decided that the daily ration of alcohol in religious houses should be about half a pint of wine and a pint of ale. Examples such as these show that ale was considered fit for the Christian clergy. This policy marked a significant departure from the anti-ale positions that Christianity inherited from the Greeks and Romans, and it is even more significant in light of the centrality of wine to Christian doctrine and rituals.

There is some debate as to who produced the wine that seems to have flowed through Europe in quite generous volumes during the Middle Ages up to about AD 1000. Many historians have argued that the church, for which wine was symbolically so important and which needed regular supplies for communion, had almost single-handedly protected vines from the ravages of the easterners who invaded Rome's western empire. But a more nuanced and positive view of the Germans themselves has undermined the facile contrast between images of pious monks tending vines and harvesting the grapes for the glory of God, on one hand, and scenarios of brutish pagans carousing drunkenly until they exhausted the supply of wine, on the other.

But did monks and priests really contribute more than secular landowners to the survival of viticulture during the early Middle Ages? Records of landownership by the church were kept more systematically and have survived better than those of individual secular owners, because the clergy were more literate and there was more continuity in ecclesiastical establishments and archives. In fact, we often know about many secular holdings only from church records that record that lay proprietors gave or bequeathed vineyards to the church. In the sixth or seventh century, for example, Ementrud, a Paris aristocrat, left property including vineyards to her entourage and to several Paris churches.[35] In 764, when the monastery of St. Nazarius of Lauresham, near Heidelberg, was founded, it was given vineyards by two secular landowners. In the next century it accumulated many more from secular donors, and by 864 it owned more than 100 vineyards near Deinheim alone.[36] We do not know what percentage of vineyards was owned by the church and religious orders and what percentage was in secular hands, but it is clear that the church was far from solely responsible for viticulture and wine production in this period—and perhaps not nearly as responsible for innovations in winemaking as many commentaries suggest.

Yet while we can recognize the probable significance of secular vine owners in this period, we must give full credit to the church for its role in extending wine production up to and beyond the end of the first Christian millennium. The importance of wine to the church ensured that, among other things, viticulture spread wherever Christianity extended its influence. As missions were established throughout central Europe, each planted vines for the production of sacramental wine—a pattern that would be repeated when Catholic missionaries extended their faith throughout Latin America and California from the fifteenth to the eighteenth centuries.

Some of the monastic vineyards were extensive. In the early ninth century the abbey of St.-Germain-des-Prés, near Paris, owned a total of 20,000 hectares of land, of which 300 to 400 hectares were in vines. The vineyards were scattered throughout the total estate, but they were located close to the Rivers Marne and Seine so that the wine could be easily transported to Paris, the single most important market in France. Each year the abbey's vineyards, mostly cultivated by peasants who leased the land, produced about 1.3 million liters of wine, equivalent to 1.7 million modern bottles.[37] This was production on a substantial scale.

Most church vineyards were much smaller, though, and were cultivated to provide what was needed for ritual purposes, to supply a priest or religious house with a daily ration of wine and enough for special occasions, and perhaps to allow some extra for the market. The only churches that did not have vineyards were located in regions where grapes would not grow or perhaps where viticulture was extensive enough that there was no difficulty obtaining supplies of wine. In more isolated areas that could sustain vines, priests were not only encouraged but sometimes ordered to plant them. The Council of Aachen decreed in 814 that every cathedral should have a college of canons, one of whose obligations was to cultivate vines.[38]

Between about AD 500 and 1000, various monastic orders were responsible for planting vines, and the number of vineyards in Europe rose substantially. Because the volume of wine needed for communion was very small, most of the wine produced directly by the medieval church was consumed on nonreligious occasions and became an integral part of the diet of the clergy. As we have seen, monks might have had about a liter and a half of alcohol (ale and/or wine) each day, and nuns had a little less. The rule of St. Benedict, which became the most influential model in western Europe, allowed a daily measure of wine for each monk, but in contrast with the strong positive association of wine with monks, St. Benedict conceded the ration only reluctantly: "Wine is no drink for monks; but since nowadays monks cannot be persuaded of this, let us at least agree upon this, that we drink temperately and not to satiety. . . . We believe that a *hemina* [about half a liter] of wine a day is sufficient for each. But those upon whom God bestows the gift of abstinence, they should know that they have a special reward." In recognition of the medicinal value of wine, however, the prior could allow a sick monk to have a larger ration. The Benedictines drank ale when they did not drink wine.[39]

It is clear that wine and ale were firmly entrenched in the culture and diets of Europeans in the first millennium of the Christian era. The collapse of the Roman Empire did not diminish the popularity of wine, and the spread of Christianity extended viticulture. Even the so-called barbarians turned out to be defenders, rather than the ravagers, of Europe's nascent wine industry. But if these great changes were no threat to alcohol, Islam was. Beginning in what is now Saudi Arabia, Islam quickly gained support throughout the Middle East and then began a journey of spiritual and military conquest much farther afield. Moving westward, it took in much of the northern fringe of Africa along the Mediterranean and by the eighth century had expanded to Sicily, to the Iberian Peninsula, and for a brief time, into southwestern France—areas where wine and beer (depending on the region) were integral to the diet.

The rise and spread of Islam is important for the history of alcohol because Islam represented the first example of a comprehensive prohibition policy that banned the production, distribution, and even consumption of alcohol. (More recent prohibition policies, such as the well-known national prohibition in the United States from 1920 to 1933, criminalized the production and sale of alcohol, but not its consumption.) Moreover, Islam's prohibition policies proved to be remarkably successful, having lasted in many parts of the Muslim world for nearly 1,500 years. While it is true that alcohol is explicitly or implicitly permitted in some modern countries that are officially or predominantly Islamic, such as Turkey, there is very little alcohol consumption in many others, including Iran and Saudi Arabia. For their populations, drinking alcohol is simply out of the question, as it is for adherents of other religions that ban alcohol, such as the Church of Jesus Christ of Latter-day Saints (Mormons) in the United States. A key difference between Mormons in the United States and Muslims in countries that prohibit the consumption of alcohol is that Mormons choose to abstain from alcohol, whereas Muslims in countries like Iran and Saudi Arabia are forbidden by law to drink alcohol and can be punished if they do so.

Islam was first implanted in regions of the Middle East where alcoholic beverages were widely consumed in pre-Islamic times and where some of the earliest evidence of wine and beer has been found. Initially, the Prophet Muhammad was no more hostile to alcohol than Jews and Christians were, but after a short time he forbade his followers to drink wine and any other fermented beverages. The reason was not because these drinks were evil in themselves—a position adopted by later advocates of abstinence—but because the weakness of humans led to excessive drinking and then to blasphemy, sin, immorality, and antisocial behavior.

The Qur'an contains a number of references, both positive and negative, to wine, and one scholar notes that a critical analysis of all references reveals that the Qur'an treats wine "with great ambivalence; the potent liquid that constitutes an abomination in one verse becomes a source of 'good food' in another."[40] But it is important to note that the texts of the Qur'an were "revealed" gradually over time, not as a completed corpus, and that later texts could abrogate earlier ones. Read in this way, the references to the Qur'an are less contradictory than when read in an achronological manner, and they are more consistent in their condemnation of alcohol than they might at first appear. Wine might be described as both an intoxicant and a wholesome food, but one text in particular has been understood as representing the final Muslim doctrine on wine: "Believers, wine and games of chance, idols and divining arrows are abominations, devised by Satan. Avoid them so you may prosper. Satan seeks to stir up enmity and hatred among you by means of wine and gambling, and to keep you from the remembrance of Allah and from your prayers."[41]

This verse is thought to have been a response to conflicts within the Muslim community that were exacerbated by alcohol. One account explains Muhammad's ban on alcohol as the result of his experience at a wedding. When he saw the guests drinking wine and joyfully celebrating the marriage, Muhammad praised wine as a gift from God. But when he returned to the house the next day, he saw that the guests had drunk too much, that their joy had turned to anger, and that the celebration had turned violent. Surveying the wreckage and the injuries, Muhammad cursed wine and thenceforth advised Muslims against drinking alcohol in any form. Such a narrative accords with a developmental model of the alcohol doctrine of the Qur'an, with one position being abrogated by another in the light of new information, insights, or guidance. Muslims who abstained from intoxicating beverages on earth would, however, have access to them in Paradise, which is depicted as flowing with rivers of delicious wine. But nowhere in the Qur'an are these two wines, the earthly and the heavenly, or the implications of consuming them, actually brought into a direct relationship.

The Qu'ran did not expressly forbid the consumption of alcohol, although it strongly advised against it. Later commentaries and the *hadith* (sayings attributed to Muhammad) promoted the prohibition of wine consumption perhaps, according to some scholars, to strengthen Muslim identity and to allow Muslim leaders to control their populations more easily.[42] Even so, there are two major lines of thought about alcohol in Islam. The dominant one is that any intoxicating drink, known as *khamr*, is forbidden to the faithful. They are liable to be punished if they drink it in any quantity or buy, sell, or serve it, but no one who spoiled or destroyed alcohol would suffer any punishment. In contrast, a minority school holds that khamr is made only from grapes, and only it is banned absolutely; other fermented beverages, made from ingredients such as honey and dates, are permissible, but intoxication from drinking these beverages is prohibited and punishable.[43] There is a similar division over whether alcohol may be used for medical purposes. Most Islamic scholars agree that it may not, but others believe that it may be used under certain circumstances, notably when a patient's life is endangered if he or she does not take alcohol in some form, such as in a medicine.[44]

Muhammad appears to have deterred wine production by limiting the kinds of vessels in which fruit juice could be made or stored. Only vessels made from skin were permitted, and gourds, glazed jars, and earthenware vessels coated with pitch were forbidden, although it is hard to see how any fruit or grape juice, whatever it was contained in, could be prevented from fermenting into wine, given the warm temperatures of late summer when fruit and berries were ripe, and the ambient yeasts that must have been present if there had been alcohol production before the ban was imposed. Muhammad's wives made a potentially alcoholic drink called *nabidh* (traditionally made from raisins or dates and which may be alcoholic or nonalcoholic) for him in a vessel made of skin. "We prepared the Nabidh in the morning and he drank it in the evening and we prepared the Nabidh in the night and he drank it in the morning."[45]

The twelve hours between preparation and consumption might or might not have been long enough for fermentation to begin, but it is unlikely that the resulting beverage would have enough alcohol in it to be classified as alcoholic today. The Qur'an not only forbade the consumption of fermented beverages but dealt with the situation where a Muslim did not know whether or not a liquid had fermented. Faced with nabidh on one occasion, Muhammad diluted it three times before he believed he was able to consume it.[46] The implication might be that the Qur'an did not insist on absolutely alcohol-free beverages—perhaps a recognition of the likelihood that any fruit-based beverage would begin to ferment in a short period—but that, sufficiently diluted, an alcohol-bearing beverage could be consumed, as long as the drinker was sincerely uncertain whether any fermentation had taken place.

The Islamic prohibition of alcohol affected broad swaths of the Middle East, northern Africa, and southwestern Europe, regions where ale, wine, and other alcoholic beverages (such as date and pomegranate wine) were commonly consumed. Early Islam did not extend the ban on alcohol consumption to non-Muslims of Muslim-governed territory, and wine presses and other evidence of wine production have been found in many parts of the early Muslim world.[47] Over time, the prohibition was enforced with varying degrees of rigor in different regions of the Muslim empire. It was probably more rigidly enforced in areas closest to the origins of the religion, but less so at the fringes of the Muslim world. In Spain, Portugal, Sicily, Sardinia, and Crete, for example, a number of policies succeeded one another or even coexisted, as some caliphs prohibited wine production in law but allowed it to continue in practice, even to the point of acknowledging the fact by taxing wine. Arab sources suggest that vineyards for wine production were widespread in southern Spain (especially in Andalusia) and in Portugal under Muslim rule. Islamic horticulture was so advanced that the number of recognized grape varieties increased, and some Muslim texts on agriculture included instructions on taking care of fermentation vats. Yet for all that some caliphs tolerated or turned a blind eye to drinking in parts of the Muslim world in the first centuries, others did not. In the tenth century, Caliph Ozman ordered the destruction of two-thirds of the vineyards of Valencia, in Spain; presumably the grapes of the surviving vines were to be eaten fresh or as raisins.

It was also in Spain, however, that Muslim legal scholars interpreted the prohibition on alcohol consumption in such a way as to permit it. They argued that the beverage referred to in the Qur'an was wine made from grapes and that it referred exclusively to that kind of wine. (The vineyards closest to Mecca were a thousand miles away, but wine from Syria and other places had been imported for consumption there before the ban on alcohol.) Therefore, they argued, wine made from dates was permitted. But if date wine was permitted, so was any wine (including grape wine) as long as it was no more intoxicating than (that is, had an alcohol level no higher than) date wine.[48] Needless to say, this interpretation, which effectively undermined what seems like an unambiguous prohibition on alcohol, was not accepted by all Muslim scholars. It failed to answer the objection that even if drinking did not lead to drunkenness, it was certainly a distraction from pious thoughts.

Over the long term, there are many examples of Muslims accommodating the production and consumption of alcohol. In sixteenth-century Ottoman Crimea, for example, wine production was extensive, and vineyards were owned by members of both the majority Christian and minority Muslim populations. The Muslim state benefited from the taxes it imposed on these activities, but in order to maintain the fiction that Muslims had nothing to do with intoxicants, the tax was imposed on wine produced by Christians and on the grape juice produced by Muslims.[49]

Later experiences of prohibition—in twentieth-century Russia and the United States, for example—would lead us to think that the initial ban on alcohol in Muslim societies generated some resistance. Only the most determined efforts, combined with the adoption of the new faith, could have curtailed private, domestic production and brought about such a dramatic change in drinking habits. Yet some Muslim writers assert that whole populations rapidly gave up drinking: "In a matter of hours a whole city-state [Madina] had become abstinent and the most successful campaign that had ever been launched by man against alcohol dependence was miraculously achieved."[50]

Within decades of the birth of Islam, the poet Abu Jilda al-Yaskuri wrote of his repentance of the old ways:

I was once made rich by a choice wine,
[I was] noble, one of the illustrious men of Yaskur.
That [was] a Time whose pleasures have passed—
I have exchanged this now for a lasting respectability.[51]

The possibility of drinking seems to have been embraced by some Muslims in Spain, although it is thought that wine consumption was lower among them than among Christians.[52] Muslims drank on occasions reminiscent of Greek symposiums: men gathered after the evening meal to drink wine, diluted with water, while relaxing on cushions. Wine was poured by serving boys, and the participants talked, recited poetry, and were entertained by female singers and dancers. Similar occasions were common among Jews in Muslim Spain, and they gave rise to a particular genre of poetry that celebrated the ability of wine to banish cares and bring joy.[53] Later poems in the genre included Omar Khayyam's *Ruba'iyat*, a long poem in praise of wine and love that included sentiments such as "I cannot live without the sparkling vintage / Cannot bear the body's burden without wine." More to the point, he cynically implied that illegal drinking (and sexual relationships) were common:

They say lovers and drunkards go to hell,
A controversial dictum not easy to accept;
If the lover and drunkard are for hell,
Tomorrow Paradise will be empty.[54]

Compliance with the Muslim prohibition on alcohol must often have fallen short. As easy as it was to decree an end to production and consumption of alcoholic beverages, the raw materials needed to make them were in plentiful supply. Cereals that could be used for brewing ale were needed for baking bread, and grapes cultivated to be eaten fresh or as raisins could be crushed and fermented. If table grapes are not ideal for wine, they can still be fermented, and grapes that have begun to shrivel to raisins make wine with a higher alcohol content than grapes that are merely ripe. It is certain that alcoholic beverages were made and consumed clandestinely in the Muslim world despite the prohibition on them, although we cannot know how extensive resistance to the policy was.

However successful it was—and it seems to have been remarkably successful over the longer term—the Islamic ban on alcohol represented a radical break with historic and prevailing attitudes toward drinking. Although a few marginal Christian and Jewish sects had required abstinence from alcohol, the mainstream Jewish and Christian faiths not only tolerated but even encouraged drinking for reasons of nutrition, health, and conviviality. They were at one in condemning excessive consumption and drunkenness and in arguing that humans should resist the temptation to drink too much, and they provided penalties for those who proved too weak. But they did not consider the option of removing the temptation from the table, as Muslim doctrine did so effectively.

To make it clear that Christians should not consume alcohol to excess or to the point of intoxication, penitentials (guides to the penances that Christians should do if they acted immorally) included drunkenness among the various sins and offenses against God. Penances for this offense were generally light, such as spending three days without consuming wine or meat. This is a mild enough penalty when we think that wine or ale might be easily forgone for a couple of days after a bout of drunkenness, especially when it took the form described in one penitential: "It changes the state of the mind and the tongue babbles and the eyes are wild and there is dizziness and distention of the stomach and pain follows." Yet if the penitentials treated ordinary drunkenness with relative lenience, they came down hard in some circumstances. Following a general pattern, the same penitential prescribed much more severe penances for the clergy than for laypeople, because priests were held to a higher standard of behavior. If a layperson spent three days without wine or bread, a priest spent seven days, a monk spent two weeks, a deacon spent three weeks, a presbyter four weeks, and a bishop five weeks.[55]

A Spanish penitential made further distinctions. A cleric who got drunk was to perform a penance of 20 days, but if he vomited, his penance was extended to 40 days; if he aggravated the offense by vomiting up the Eucharist (the communion bread), an additional 20 days were added. The penance for a layperson in these circumstances was less severe and set at 10, 20, and 40 days, respectively.[56]

The frequent references to drunkenness in the penitentials do not necessarily mean that drunkenness was common in the early Middle Ages, but they do show us that the church frowned on it, no doubt because intoxication was frequently associated with other proscribed activities, such as illicit sexual activity and blasphemy. From this point of view, it is easy to see why the writers of the penitentials regarded drunkenness by the clergy as especially horrifying. Perhaps, too, that is why the clergy figure so prominently in contemporary accounts of drunkenness. The bishop of Tours was said to be "often so completely fuddled with wine that it would take four men to carry him from the table." The bishop of Soissons was said to have been "out of his mind . . . for nearly four years, through drinking to excess," to the point that he had to be locked behind bars whenever royalty visited his city. Gregory of Tours complained that monks regularly spent more time drinking in taverns than praying in their cells.[57] In 847, perhaps because of perceptions of widespread clerical drunkenness, the Council of Prelates ordered that any person in religious orders who habitually drank to the point of drunkenness should abstain from fat, beer, and wine for forty days. The council signaled its seriousness by including both beer and wine in the ban, effectively forcing an offending monk to drink nothing but water for more than a month.

Such penalties were part of the continuing battle that the authorities, religious and secular, continued to wage against excessive alcohol consumption. But it is notable that until the brief period from about 1914 to 1935, when several national governments experimented with prohibition policies, no non-Muslim authorities took the radical step of banning alcohol altogether. If anything, the rise of Christianity elevated one form of alcohol, wine, to unprecedented status, and it might be argued that in doing so, the church implicitly gave a nod to alcohol consumption more generally. Europeans did not need the blessing of the church before they drank, of course, and ale and wine became increasingly integral to their diets as the second Christian millennium opened.

4

The Middle Ages
1000–1500

THE BIRTH OF AN INDUSTRY

From about AD 1000, changes in the political, economic, and cultural land-
scapes of Europe brought about significant shifts in the social position of
alcohol and in drinking cultures. After the four or five centuries of turmoil
that followed the migrations of easterners into western Europe and the dis-
integration of the Roman Empire, there was a period of relative peace and
political stability. Both fostered economic development and the growth of
trade. Europe's population began to increase steadily, doubling from about
40 to 80 million between 1000 and 1300, and there was a burst of urbanization in northern Europe and the north of Italy. These cities (such as Antwerp,
Bruges, Florence, and Milan) embodied new cultures and markets for alcohol,
and their merchants, professionals, and artisans developed new ways of doing
business—including the business of alcohol. Such social and economic developments, together with the arrival of a warmer phase in Europe's climate that
stimulated agriculture and made viticulture viable in more northerly regions,
had profound and lasting influences on patterns of alcohol consumption and
on the organization of the alcohol industry. It might seem inappropriate to
think of an "alcohol industry" this early, but significant changes in the organization of ale and wine production and trade appear to justify it.

Right through the Middle Ages, ale was brewed in households in rural
areas, although even in these places there was likely some commercial production. Making ale took time and required equipment, and integrating
brewing into the daily agricultural work was not always easy, especially during periods (such as harvesttime) when all hands were needed in the fields.

The result was that many peasants purchased or bartered goods and produce for ale. In addition, some religious houses in rural areas made far more ale than their members consumed, and large landowners also made ale for sale to their tenants.

The conditions in the cities that began to appear and grow from the eleventh century onward worked against small-scale ale production and made commercial brewing more practical. The single most important development was the creation of a concentrated market of urban consumers. City dwellers were less and less likely to grow or otherwise produce their own food and drink, and retailers—bakers, butchers, and vendors of fresh produce and cooked food—began to crowd urban centers. As far as brewing was concerned, most of the urban population, the poor and workers, lived in cramped conditions with no room for the equipment and barrels that were needed for brewing, even if they could have afforded them. These people, many of whom were migrants from the countryside, ceased being producers and consumers of ale and became exclusively consumers.

While brewing continued in the large urban and rural houses of the well-off, where ale was produced for family and servants, more and more common people purchased ale made in the commercial breweries that grew in number and size during the Middle Ages. These breweries appeared in response to the growing demand for ale, and their appearance, growth, and distribution were fostered by a number of other conditions, apart from the simple economies of scale from which they benefited. As city administrations became more active in regulating economic life, they began to intervene in many aspects of brewing. The risk of fire, which devastated numerous towns in this period, led some municipalities to require brewers to use wood for their fires rather than the traditional straw and stubble that tended to produce clouds of dangerous sparks. To reduce fire hazards even more, some cities stipulated that breweries should be built of stone rather than wood.[1] In the Netherlands, urban governments controlled the sale of gruit (the herbs used for bittering and flavoring ale), which they sold at inflated prices. There were savings in bulk purchases, but only commercial brewers could take advantage of them. Good ale also needed plenty of fresh, clean water, but brewers also polluted water with their refuse, to the extent that some English towns (like London, Bristol, and Coventry) forbade brewers access to sources of public drinking water.[2] Regulations such as these, many imposing considerable costs on brewers, made the survival of small-scale, domestic brewing in the medieval city increasingly difficult.

There was also a major, expensive technological innovation: the gradual replacement by copper kettles of the pottery vessels that were used for boiling the wort.[3] Copper kettles used heat more efficiently and were reputed to make better ale, and they could also be made in much larger sizes. While pottery vessels were limited to about 150 liters, copper kettles holding 1,000 liters were in use by the late 1200s, and by the 1400s, some held as much as 4,000 liters of ale. Needless to say, these new kettles, even the smaller ones, required significant capital investment and contributed to the forces that, over time, pushed small-scale urban operators out of business.

Some cities got ahead of this trend and banned domestic ale production outright—Utrecht did so by 1493—while others gradually created a network of regulations whose complexity strangled small-scale brewers. Some cities required brewers to have a license. In Hamburg, for example, the municipal government established a licensing system by 1381, demonstrating that brewing was a privilege (an activity that had to be explicitly permitted) and not a right. By the middle of the fifteenth century, Hamburg (an important brewing center) had virtually outlawed brewing in private households. Other centers set out rules governing the entire brewing process. From the early 1300s, Nuremberg's city administration regulated the composition of ale, the brewing time, the locations and hours, and in what volume ale could be served. In places as diverse as England, Austria and Nuremberg, the price of ale was fixed, first locally and then regionally.[4] In England, the first national regulations date from 1267, when the Assize of Bread and Ale set the price of beer at 2 gallons for a penny in the cities and 3 gallons for a penny in the country. Higher prices could be charged when grain prices rose, but beer was always to be less expensive in the country, close to the source of cereals and where the costs of doing business were lower. Finally, even though the retail sale of ale was not always the direct concern of brewers (although some taverns were connected to breweries), the hours and other conditions of sale often fell under municipal regulations. Taverns were licensed in London as early as 1189, and in the early 1300s their hours of business were established by law.

In these myriad ways, the organization of beer production in the city evolved as urban centers became more populous and their organizations more complex. Regulations governing production and sale were not peculiar to the brewing industry, and they reflected the spread and intensification of municipal control over many dimensions of the economy and society. In rural areas, where the great bulk of the medieval population continued to live, brewing tended to be more dispersed, the concentration of ownership and production took place more slowly, and the larger breweries did not have the same scale as their urban counterparts. In the town of Exeter, in southwest England, 75 percent of households brewed and sold ale at least once between 1365 and 1393, but only 29 percent did so ten or more times.[5] At the very most, only a quarter of these households could be called regular brewers in that they made and sold beer an average of three times a year—and brewing three times a year sets the definition of "regular" very low.

One notable effect of the shift to commercial brewing was the decline of women's participation. When brewing was a household task, it was carried out by women (called "alewives" or "brewsters") for whom it was an integral part of the domestic responsibilities of cooking, baking, and household management for which women were responsible. On the manor of Brigstock, in Northamptonshire, more than 300 women—a third of all the women who lived there—brewed ale for sale in the decades preceding the Black Death. In the early 1300s, there were about 115 brewsters in Oxford, which had a population of about 10,000, while 250 brewsters made ale for Norwich's 17,000 inhabitants.[6] Most brewsters were married, and many brewed ale occasionally rather than on a regular and full-time basis. But while most brewed in limited volumes, some brewsters operated on a more commercial basis. In 1301–2, Maud Elias of Hull, in Yorkshire, sold 100 gallons of ale to the household of King Edward I.

Yet even this, a substantial volume for a brewster, was dwarfed by the commercial operations that measured production in tens of thousands of gallons. This scale of brewing was dominated by men, and as the number and size of these breweries rose, the participation of women declined correspondingly. There were 137 brewsters in Oxford in 1311, but the number fell steadily until in 1348, just as the Black Death arrived, there were about 83.[7] Throughout England, nearly all the commercial brewing was done by brewsters before the Black Death in the late 1340s, but by the end of the 1500s scarcely any women were involved, and most of those were widows of brewers, women who were permitted to continue in the profession under their dead husband's name.

The Black Death seems to have marked a sudden change in both the brewing and consumption of ale in England. Not only were fewer women involved in production after the worst of the plague had receded, but there is some evidence that the consumption of ale rose; more people were drinking more ale,[8] such that the population losses due to plague were not reflected in demand for ale. A buoyant market, combined with the technological and commercial changes (and later the introduction of hops), made brewing increasingly profitable, and it attracted men of means who had eschewed small-scale brewing with its corresponding small-scale revenues. These men were more familiar with the urban world of commerce and its methods of investment and systems of distribution. Women were not excluded by law (although they were denied some of the privileges of membership in the English brewers' guilds), but they experienced gradual exclusion, as men progressively monopolized brewing and its institutions.

Judith Bennett, the foremost historian of this process, explains the virtual disappearance of women's brewing as the result of a culture of misogyny that took various forms.[9] Perhaps the most striking was the identification of brewsters with ale, the traditional drink flavored with gruit, and male brewers with beer, the new beverage made with hops. (This is explained below.) Although ale continued to be made (and although there is a lot of fluidity between the two words "beer" and "ale"), it was portrayed in this time of transition as a beverage that was on its way out. Moreover, new images of women brewers as dishonest, unhygienic, and immoral began to appear. In short, there emerged during the 1400s and 1500s a new culture, as well as an economy, of male commercial brewing. In the 1500s, this shift took institutional forms, as various authorities began to exclude women from all aspects of the brewing industry, whether as producers or retailers. The result was that, whether by ambient cultural forces or by explicit legal instruments, women were excluded from the new beer-brewing industry. Instead of being able to use it as a means of enriching themselves and gaining social status, they remained participants in the less prestigious occupations of the late medieval economy, although as we shall see, women did participate in the small-scale phase of distilling that emerged from the 1500s onward.

The urban production of beer for local sale was one thing, but this period also saw the beginning of a substantial beer trade, another facet of the maturing industry. Until this phase of the Middle Ages, beer (unlike wine) had generally found only local markets, whether in country or city, because beer remained in good condition for a matter of days or a few weeks at most—too short a time to be shipped to any distant market and to be sold in good condition. There was some trade in ale over relatively short distances, as between England and Flanders, but only on a limited scale. What changed the picture was the replacement of gruit, an herb mixture used for bittering and flavoring beer, by hops, a plant that had sporadically been used for making beer in some monasteries since the ninth century. Hops are a preservative; they kill certain bacteria and give beer longevity, enabling it to be transported for longer periods of time and therefore over longer distances. Before hops were used, higher levels of alcohol were sometimes used to keep bacteria at bay, so the introduction of hops meant that lower-alcohol beer could be made. Hopped beer was also less sweet than unhopped ale, so the introduction of hops involved a shift in the style and flavor of beer—a shift that was welcomed more readily in some markets than in others.

Hops began to be used regularly in brewing from about 1200 in northern Germany, and port cities like Hamburg soon became centers of a vibrant export trade in beer. Ports dominated the beer trade (and other commerce) because waterborne shipping was far less expensive than land transportation. Medieval roads were rudimentary, and liquids easily leaked from barrels when transportation across rough terrain on carts with wooden wheels dislodged the staves. Moreover, the costs of land transport, together with taxes added as goods crossed national and provincial frontiers, could increase the price of commodities to the point that they were no longer competitive on the destination market. One estimate is that the price at origin increased by 25 to 70 percent for every 100 kilometers that beer had to travel over land.[10] Coastal shipping was a far safer and cheaper means, and during the thirteenth and fourteenth centuries, German Baltic ports like Bremen, Hamburg, and Wismar established a profitable beer trade with the Low Countries. Even over shorter distances, waterborne transport was cheaper. In 1308–9, wine sent from Bristol to the bishop of Coventry and Lichfield's residence in Lichfield used both the Severn River and an overland route. The cost per barrel-mile was 0.4 pence for the water portion but 2.5 pence, six times more, for the land portion of the trip.[11]

Hamburg dominated the beer export trade along Europe's north coasts to the point that "Hamburg beer" became the generic name for beer from northern Germany. Amsterdam imposed an import duty on Hamburg beer from the early 1300s, but it did not blunt demand; annual shipments by the 1360s averaged more than 5 million liters, a volume that represented about a fifth of Hamburg's total beer production.[12] From this same period, Germany's brewers began to extend their exports throughout the Baltic area and into Scandinavia. In all these export markets, the Germans were successful not because there was no local beer, but because local brewers were technologically less advanced. To this extent, the dominance of the north German brewers on the northern European markets persisted only as long as they held the technological advantage, and that gap narrowed significantly, especially in the Low Countries, toward the end of the 1400s.

Like that of beer, the production and distribution of wine evolved in the later Middle Ages. Although there are few useful statistics on wine production in this period, it clearly increased dramatically to serve the growing markets, particularly the swelling urban markets of northern Europe. There was a burst of vine planting from 1000 to 1200, mostly stimulated by the increase in population and aided by warmer climatic conditions that created new regions where grapes could be grown. French landowners cleared forests and drained marshes to plant vines and converted poor arable land to viticulture. In Germany, vines flourished in the Rhineland, Swabia, Franconia, and Thuringia. By the early 1300s, vines were planted as far east as the farthest frontiers of Hungary, including the Tokay region, which would later produce an iconic sweet wine. In England, the *Domesday Book*, an agricultural census taken in 1086, listed only 42 vineyards, but two centuries later there were more than 1,300. In some areas, such as northern Italy, vineyards increased to provide wine for the burgeoning cities nearby: Venice, Milan, Florence, and Genoa. Similarly, the growth of Paris's population stimulated viticulture along the Rivers Seine, Marne, and Yonne. Meanwhile, expanding cities that lacked adequate sources of wine nearby, like London in England; Ghent, Bruges, and Brussels in the Low Countries; and cities on the Baltic coast, spurred growth in the vine-growing regions they imported wine from, especially the Rhine Valley in Germany and in southwestern France.

Several major wine routes were established in medieval Europe. One was anchored in present-day Bordeaux, thanks largely to a dynastic link forged between Aquitaine (the Bordeaux region) and England by the marriage of Eleanor of Aquitaine and Henry, Duke of Normandy, who became Henry II of England. With Aquitaine and England under the same crown, wine began to flow from southwestern France to the relatively prosperous merchants of England's commercial cities, and by the 1200s, Gascon wine, much of it from the modern southwestern region that lies inland from the vineyards of present-day Bordeaux, had stormed the English market. This was young wine, what today might be called "nouveau," because it was shipped only weeks after the harvest and soon after fermentation was complete. Every October, hundreds of ships set sail from Bordeaux on the minimum weeklong voyage to England. Smaller fleets would sail from Nantes and La Rochelle with wine from the Loire Valley in northwest France. At a time when wine was unstable and scarcely lasted a year, this new wine was highly prized and fetched good prices. Further shipments were made the following spring, when weather permitted; but the older wine, although only six or eight months old, was considered inferior, and it sold for less. Most of this wine was red (it was called "claret" because of its light color), but some was white: Scottish financial records from 1460 show receipt of "five pipes of Gascon wine, one white and four red."[13]

Toward the end of summer, as this French wine was starting to fade in availability or quality or both, wine arrived in England from the Mediterranean: from

Cyprus, Corfu, Greece, and Italy. These were sweeter and much higher in alcohol than the French wines, making them more durable and giving them the stamina to survive the long summer voyage across the Mediterranean, through the Straits of Gibraltar, and up the Atlantic coast to England and also to northern Europe. It was a grueling voyage that could take as long as three months, and it was accomplished sometimes by sailing ships and sometimes by galleys, with merchants themselves occasionally at the oars. But the effort was worthwhile. The more flavorsome and substantial Mediterranean wines fetched wholesale prices up to twice those of Gascon wines, and demand was further piqued because only three of London's taverns were licensed to sell them on a retail basis.

The limited Mediterranean wine trade served a small, wealthy market in England, but Bordeaux's exports were massive, especially in the early 1300s. In the three years 1305–6, 1306–7, and 1308–9, exports averaged 98,000 barrels a year, more than 900 million liters. The English kings were regular and mostly loyal clients. In 1243 alone, Henry III bought 1,445 casks, or about 1,400,000 liters, of Gascon wine. Production always depended on weather, of course— the 1310 harvest was only half that of the previous few years—and exports were also affected by political events. Exports declined dramatically when France and England went to war in 1324 and again from the 1330s when the Hundred Years War broke out.

Wine from Bordeaux was also exported to other important urban markets in northern Europe and to towns on the Baltic Sea. These population centers were also supplied by a wine trade route than ran down the Rhine to the North Sea and served northern Germany, the Low Countries, England, Scandinavia, and the Baltic Sea area. In eastern Europe, Cracow, a Polish city home to a royal court and a wealthy merchant elite, became not only a good market for wine but also an ideal transshipment point. Wine from many parts of the Mediterranean region, and often shipped by Italian merchants, arrived there for forwarding to other markets in eastern Europe, Russia, and around the Baltic Sea.[14]

Like the long-distance beer trade that emerged in northern Europe in the 1400s, the trade in wine was an important aspect of the development of Europe's alcohol industry. Institutions and codes of practice developed, with guilds of vintners (wine merchants) beginning to assume positions of importance in many cities. As early as the first decades of the thirteenth century, more than a third of London's aldermen (city councillors) were vintners, as was the mayor who represented the city at the signing of the Magna Carta in 1215. All over Europe, wine was taxed in money or kind by authorities as diverse as monarchs, dukes, and municipal authorities. English wine-shippers had to pay "prisage," the right of the king to take two barrels of wine from every shipment of more than twenty-one barrels, and one barrel from every shipment smaller than that. The authorities in Paris taxed wine as it passed through the gates in the city walls, while the municipality of Cracow taxed all wine traded by the city's merchants.[15] Such payments produced revenues that their beneficiaries were reluctant to surrender. In the 1340s, the king of England took more than 200 casks of wine (180,000 liters) as prisage. During the same period, 88 percent of the city revenues in Bruges, in Flanders, came from taxes on wine and beer.[16] The largest single source of funds to support the Dutch revolt against Spain (1566–1648) was the tax on beer, such that it might be argued that "beer created Belgium."[17]

Even granting that wine merchants must often have successfully evaded the taxes on wine, the income must have increased steadily from AD 1000, as Europe's populations grew and the better-off wine-drinking sections of the population expanded. More land was planted with vines, and production must have increased steadily to keep up with demand. There was probably a broad continuity of church and secular ownership of vineyards, but many religious houses produced only enough wine for their own needs. These varied from order to order, but consumption could be significant. At the monastery of Cluny, in Burgundy, a small meal called the *mixtum*, consisting of bread and a glass of wine, was available to start the day, and main meals (including meals during times of penance) were served with a half-pint of undiluted wine. On feast days, *pigmentum*—warm wine flavored with honey, pepper, and cinnamon—was served.[18]

If many monastic wineries produced exclusively for their own use, the general rise in production must have involved an extraordinary increase in the output of wineries owned by private individuals. However, just as in the early Middle Ages, so in this period many secular owners transferred vineyards to the church in the expectation of tangible or intangible benefits. From the twelfth century, the Crusades proved to be a real boon to monasteries because many knights gave land to the church for prayers to be said for their souls in case they died while away. Almost every house in the important Cistercian order received at least one vineyard during the 1100s. In 1157, for example, a widow and her six sons gave a Cistercian house about four acres of vines so that the monks would pray for their dead husband and father.[19]

Dozens of such gifts to the Cistercians' founding abbey in Cîteaux, in Burgundy, meant that by the mid-fourteenth century the order had accumulated hundreds of hectares of vineyards in what are now some of the most prestigious communes of the region—Beaune, Pommard, Vosne, Nuits, and Corton among them. By 1336, the Cistercians owned 50 hectares of vines in the commune of Vougeot, at the time the largest single parcel of vineyards in Burgundy. The Cistercians developed a reputation for fastidious work in the vineyards and the cellar, and they gained not only land but fame and privileges. In 1171, Pope Alexander III exempted them from paying the tithe (a church tax) on their vineyards and later threatened to excommunicate anyone who challenged the exemption, which suggests that other wine producers might have objected to the favorable treatment the Cistercians received. The same year, the Duke of Burgundy freed the Cistercians from paying any of the dues that would normally be levied on the transportation and sale of their produce.[20]

This sort of encouragement led the Cistercians to expand rapidly—there was a veritable empire of 400 abbeys within fifty years of the order's founding—and the monks planted vineyards in all their locations, even though many made only the wine they needed for their own communions and consumption. Yet others, like the founding house in Cîteaux, became significant commercial producers. Another was Kloster Eberbach, in the Rhine district, founded by monks from Burgundy who discovered that the Rhine Valley's climate was exceptionally suitable for white wine production. By 1500, Kloster Eberbach owned nearly 700 hectares of vines, the largest vineyard estate in Europe, and the entrepreneurial monks also owned a fleet of ships that ferried the wine down the Rhine to Cologne.

Examples of massive wine production, such as Kloster Eberbach's, were rare, but they reflected a broad trend: an increase in the production of wine from about 1000. Even so, the increase was anything but linear and steady. Production fell from 1350 to 1400, when the Black Death reduced the population of Europe by as much as a third. Big towns and cities that had seen their populations swell for two or three centuries saw them decline dramatically in a few years as their inhabitants died or fled from the plague. As population fell, so did the market for wine. In the vineyards, there was a shortage of skilled workers, and many vineyards in the worst-affected regions were simply abandoned.

By the Middle Ages, wine and beer were staples of the European diet, but other alcoholic beverages were also available. Mead (fermented diluted honey) was drunk in small volumes in many regions. Cider, fermented apple juice, was popular where apples grew easily, as in Normandy and Brittany. The Normans are thought to have introduced cider to England in the eleventh century, and an industry was established in the southwest. Finally, the science of distilling fermented drinks to make much stronger alcoholic beverages began to spread through Europe from the thirteenth century. But until the 1500s (see Chapter 6), distilling (usually producing brandy from wine) was largely confined to religious houses, and the spirits were used almost exclusively for medical purposes.

Although beer and ale were in plentiful supply, there must have been many poor people who could afford neither and who drank only water, much of which was polluted and unsafe to consume. This practice (together with a generally meager and unhealthy diet and poor living conditions), must have contributed to the low life expectancy of the period. There is a strong suggestion of water-drinking in the allegation, during the Black Death, that Jews had poisoned wells in order to cause the fatal outbreaks of the plague.[21] In parts of Germany and France, Jews were killed in order to eliminate the supposed source of the problem. The episode speaks not only to the virulence of anti-Semitism in medieval Europe but also to both the continuing suspicion and consumption of water. Jews, we might note, were not accused of poisoning barrels of beer or wine.

For the most part, the diets of the homeless, the transient, and even the stable working poor are lost to us, but there is occasional, if uneven, evidence for the strata above them. In the village of Montaillou, in the foothills of the Pyrenees, peasants drank wine as part of the daily diet. The 250 inhabitants supported a wine-seller who made rounds of the houses selling wine brought by mule from Tarascon and Pamiers; but shepherds drank only sour wine and some milk on a daily basis, and good wine was reserved for festive occasions.[22] Farther east and north, in wine-producing Lorraine, wine was consumed in households as grand as that of the Duke of Lorraine and as modest as those of peasants who made it for their own consumption. In the late 1400s, the duke's household went through 7,000 liters of wine a month, or the equivalent of about 300 standard bottles a day, but we do not know how many people shared them or how the volume was distributed. When the duke traveled, he provided 2 or 3 liters of wine a day for each person in his retinue. The duke's kitchen also used wine in the preparation of food, and in 1481 alone, some 468 liters were designated "for cooking his lordship's fish."[23]

The royal courts of England and Scotland also helped boost demand for wine, especially from Gascony. In 1243, Henry III of England spent more than £2,300 on 1,445 casks of wine, about a third of a million gallons. Some was poor quality, but more than two-thirds was considered high standard and cost more than £2 a barrel. When Henry's daughter Margaret married Alexander III of Scotland in 1251, the guests went through 25,000 gallons of wine.

It washed down the 1,300 deer, 7,000 hens, 170 boars, 60,000 herrings, and 68,500 loaves of bread that the wedding party and their guests consumed.[24] In one year, Alexander III had to pledge all his revenues from the port of Berwick to guarantee payment of the £2,197 he owed a Bordeaux merchant for more than 100,000 liters of wine.[25]

The medieval nobility also supported the alcohol trade. The Earl of Northumberland's household consumed 27,500 gallons of ale and 1,600 gallons of wine in one year, although we do not know the number of the earl's family and staff. In 1419, Dame Alice de Bryene's household, which brewed its own ale for domestic consumption, also took care of 262 gallons of red wine and 105 gallons of white. On the clerical side of the social ledger, the installation of the archbishop of York in 1464 was celebrated by the consumption of 100 casks of wine.[26]

Lower down the social scale, people received alcohol as gifts and as part of their wages and pensions. In 1499 the nursing sisters of Nancy were given 1,874 liters of red wine, and in 1502 the Minor Brothers received 2,342 liters of red wine "to assist them to live." Wine was included in the annuities provided by the dukes of Lorraine to reward men and women for their services in positions as varied as valets, falconers, trumpeters, and midwives. Meanwhile, all kinds of artisans—masons, carpenters, and cartwrights among them—received wine, beer, and other foodstuffs as part of their wages. Elsewhere, when the belfry of the church in Bonlieu-en-Forez was being built, the workers were provided with eggs, meat, rye bread, beans for soup, and "plenty of wine."[27] The same was true of beer, which was provided as part of the wages in many regions of Europe, as well as off the shores of Europe: beer provided a significant proportion of the daily calories of seamen while they were at sea.[28]

Ale was commonly part of the diet that harvest workers were fed in England during the Middle Ages, and it seems that, as time went on, greater volumes of ale were provided. Between 1256 and 1326, ale made up less than 20 percent of the value of meals served to harvest workers in Norfolk, but from 1341 to 1424, it was never less than 20 percent and rose as high as 41 percent. On a per capita basis, the actual volume of ale provided to harvesters more than doubled, rising from 2.83 pints (1.61 liters) in 1256 to 6.36 pints (3.61 liters) in 1424.[29] There was no tension between working and drinking alcohol, as there is today, because most workers consumed alcohol periodically throughout the day in order to hydrate themselves.

Nor was there any perceived problem in supplying soldiers with alcohol while they were on duty or in battle. The Bayeux Tapestry, depicting the

Norman conquest of England in 1066, shows a wagon loaded with a cask of wine—"carrum cum vino," explains the text—among the military and other supplies the Norman army brought ashore. We might assume that the wine was destined for consumption by Duke William or, more cynically, that it was used to bolster the fighting spirit of the soldiers (as rum was in the British army during the First World War). But we also know that rations of alcohol (wine and ale) were regularly supplied to French and other soldiers at this time. During 1406, the six men responsible for guarding the Château de Custines were supplied with 2 liters of wine a day—more than might be thought desirable, perhaps, for men whose main job was to keep a sharp lookout for intruders. In 1316, Edward II of England ordered 4,000 barrels of wine for his army in action in Scotland, and a French plan of campaign from 1327 provided about a tenth of a gallon of wine a day for ordinary soldiers.[30] Alcohol was especially useful when armies were marching and fighting and when water supplies were contaminated, as they frequently were at siege sites. At the forty-day siege of Dover Castle in 1216, the 1,000 soldiers went through 600 gallons of wine and more than 20,000 gallons of ale.[31] Adding wine to water (another way of looking at diluting wine) was a means of killing some harmful bacteria and staving off sickness among soldiers. It is known, for example, that the microbes that carry typhoid fever die when they are immersed in wine.[32]

Examples of alcohol consumption like these can be multiplied many times over from across Europe and throughout the period 1000–1500. They can only be impressionistic, as they are too scattered geographically and over time to allow us to develop any sense of patterns and trends. Nonetheless, we should expect alcohol consumption to have been higher in the upper social and political strata than the lower, and greater among men than among women. There is plenty of evidence of male anxiety about women drinking alcohol, and although this need not mean that women did drink less than men, it is reasonable to assume that, on average, women did drink less.

More generalized rates of consumption of ale and wine in the Middle Ages must remain uncertain, although in regions like England the volume of ale consumed must have been much greater, in absolute terms, than wine, which was higher in both price and alcohol content. In fourteenth-century England, ale cost a penny for 2 gallons in the city and a penny for 3 gallons in the country. The price of Gascon or Spanish wine was about 6 pence a gallon, making wine twelve to twenty-four times the price of ale per unit of volume,[33] although only about four to eight times more expensive in terms of pure alcohol delivered by each beverage. One estimate of per capita ale consumption in northern Europe from the late fourteenth to the end of the fifteenth century shows a range of 177 to 310 liters a year, a fairly modest one-half to two-thirds of a liter a day. The author's conclusion reflects the uncertainty of such figures: "A general estimate for medieval England of between four and five liters each day is reasonable but perhaps too high. More sensible and likely is an estimate of some 1.1 liters each day for each person." He goes on to propose that members of better-off farm families might have consumed as little as half a liter of ale a day, while aristocratic families consumed between 1.5 and 2 liters.[34]

As for wine, one compilation of estimates of per capita consumption in France shows a range from 183 to 781 liters a year, or from half a liter to just over 2 liters a day. The low volume was for a monk in the early fourteenth century (with an added liter on feast days), and the high figure was for the six soldiers on sentry duty at the Château de Custines, who received this very generous wine allowance even though they were expected to remain awake and alert. Between the extremes in this compilation of statistics we find such rates as 220 liters a year (half a liter a day) for students at a papal school and 365 liters a year (a liter a day) for a chambermaid in Vernines.[35] Quite clearly, there is no such thing as a general per capita consumption rate of ale or wine in medieval Europe. If the individual cases are correct, there was a very wide variation in volumes consumed, and there seems to have been no evident correlation with gender, class, occupation, or context. Although it is disappointing to reach the very vague conclusion that many medieval people drank a lot of alcohol and that per capita consumption was almost certainly much higher than it is today, it might be the best we can do.[36]

The volumes of alcohol downed on a daily basis in the Middle Ages were probably substantial, and most involved a liter of ale and/or the equivalent of a bottle or two of wine. But volumes were sometimes well below what was necessary for rehydration, especially when we consider that many people in the Middle Ages did hard physical work from sunrise to sunset. The findings raise the question of where they were getting their additional water from. The water in gruel and soups must have been an important source, but we must consider it probable that considerable numbers of Europeans drank water at this time for lack of other than alcoholic beverages. Even if they were concerned about the safety of water, the poor had no alternatives. In England, the price of beer and ale was fixed by law, and under the regulations of 1283, 4 liters of ale—a reasonable daily allowance for two adults—would have cost a craftsman a third of his daily wages and a laborer about two-thirds. Women, who were paid about two-thirds the male wage, were that much less likely to be able to buy ale or beer. This is another case where we need to draw a careful distinction between social prescription, which warned against drinking water, and practice, which reflected material conditions that must have allowed no alternative to it.

The upper classes might have drunk more alcoholic beverages, but did they drink better? One of the trends that emerged in the Middle Ages was a sense of connoisseurship, meaning that certain products began to acquire a degree of cultural cachet for their perceived quality. Applied to alcohol, this was not entirely new; we have seen that both Greek and Roman writers drew up lists of wines they considered a cut above the rest. We might expect wine to have attracted this sort of differentiation earlier than beer: until the later Middle Ages, people had a limited range of beers to choose from, as they were not transported over significant distances and people drank what was brewed locally. Even then, there were very likely preferred brewers, especially in larger towns where numerous brewers competed with one another. But the development of a longer-distance beer trade brought new products to a number of markets, and as we have seen, beer imported from Hamburg became more popular than local products in parts of the Low Countries and Scandinavia.

Better-off wine-consumers in key markets such as London, Antwerp, and Paris were even more fortunate, for they could regularly choose among wines from many parts of Europe and the Mediterranean region. Connoisseurship of wine seems to have become more systematic in the Middle Ages. English consumers gave high marks to the body and light color of the Bordeaux they consumed in such vast volumes. They called it "claret" for its color, and the name was commonly used to refer to red wine from Bordeaux until the late twentieth century. In Italy, wealthier wine consumers made a quality distinction between wines made from common grape varieties (which they called "Latin wine") and wines made from newer varieties (like white wine made from vernaccia grapes in the area around San Gimignano, in Tuscany) and from some other parts of Europe. The late thirteenth-century poet Cecco Angiolieri put it this way:

And I want only Greek and Vernaccia,
For Latin wine is more distasteful
Than my woman, when she nags me.[37]

In France, a ranking of European wines by quality resulted from a fictitious "Battle of the Wines," which was the subject of two poems in the thirteenth and fourteenth centuries. Each gave an account of a wine-tasting—essentially a forerunner of modern wine competitions—organized by King Philip Augustus of France. As if to emphasize the association between wine and the church, the king was said to have nominated an English priest to judge the wines. This priest donned his stole as he tasted the wines so that he could "excommunicate" any that he found unacceptable. The wines judged to be the best were to be given not medals, as they are today, but ecclesiastical and secular titles, ranging from pope to peers.[38]

In the earlier of the two poems, the wines were predominantly white and predominantly French (particularly from the north of France, where white wine was and is more common than red), although there were some representatives of other parts of Europe and the Mediterranean area. Of the 70 wines mentioned by name, only 2 were from the Bordeaux region, 6 from Anjou-Poitou, 2 from Burgundy, and 4 from Languedoc. The handful from outside France included wines from Alsace, Mosel, and Spain and also a wine from Cyprus, which the priest judged the best of all:

> The king crowned the wines judged good
> To each with a title he honoured
> A pope he made of the Cypriot wine
> For like a star in the heavens it shone.[39]

In all, twenty wines were honored for their quality. The runner-up was named a cardinal, while others were named kings, counts, and peers. Eight wines, all from the north of France, were "excommunicated."

As wine became more and more closely associated with its region of origin, it was subjected to tighter regulations. Some were designed to control quality at the point of production, like regulations dealing with pruning, vine care, and harvesting in Burgundy. A council of city representatives and vine-growers also decreed the date (called the *ban de vendange*) when the Burgundy harvest could begin, a measure that ensured that grapes were picked when they were ripe and also stopped vine owners from entering the vineyards and stealing grapes from vines they did not own. Other regulations tried to prevent adulteration by merchants and retailers. Bad wine was sometimes mixed with good, and multiregional blends were passed off as coming from a place whose wines commanded higher prices. In his *Canterbury Tales*, Geoffrey Chaucer had the Pardoner warn of the counterfeit wine for sale in London:

> Keep clear of wine, I tell you, white or red,
> Especially Spanish wines which they provide
> And have on sale in Fish Street and Cheapside.

That wine mysteriously finds its way
To mix itself with others—shall we say
Spontaneously?—that grow in neighboring regions.[40]

Chaucer knew what he was talking about: his family had been in the wine and tavern business for generations, and he grew up living above the cellars.

In addition to counterfeit wine, customers had to be careful they were not buying "corrected" wine—wine that had spoiled and then been treated with additives to conceal the telltale odors and flavors. Stored in barrels where it was exposed to increasing volumes of air as it was drawn off and sold, wine must often have oxidized. Moreover, the state of barrel hygiene in the Middle Ages must have meant that many casks were infected with brettanomyces, a yeast that gives wine flavors that today are described variously as "smoked meat," "mousy," and even "rotting corpses." Because wines with an unappealing smell and flavor must have been fairly common—and this at a period when a host of ambient smells were unattractive—many books gave advice on correcting wine. The frequency of such advice in the medieval and early modern periods suggests that few people were willing to throw away wine that had spoiled and would do almost anything to make it palatable again. Perhaps the wealthy and sensitive of palate would dispose of it—the Earl of Northumberland had his "brokyn" wine made into vinegar—but most people probably tried, literally, to make the best of it.

One widely distributed late fourteenth-century work, *Le Ménagier de Paris*, possibly written by a knight in the service of the Duke of Berry, purports to advise a young wife on such diverse and useful subjects as obedience to her husband, hiring servants, training dogs, and ridding hawks of lice. It also describes ways of fixing spoiled wine. Wine that had gone sour could be made drinkable by adding a basket of fresh grapes to the barrel; wine that smelled bad could be improved by the addition of elder wood and powdered cardamom; muddy wine could be clarified by hanging in it bags containing the whites of eggs that had been boiled and then fried; unwanted color in white wine could be removed by adding holly leaves to the barrel; bitter wine could be softened by adding hot boiled corn or, if that failed, a basketful of sand that had been well washed in water drawn from the River Seine.[41] Some of these remedies might have worked. Egg whites (raw, not cooked) are still sometimes used for fining (clarifying) wine. As for the rest, their effectiveness is a matter of conjecture.

Even though private individuals might have used such methods to correct their wine, retailers and merchants were not permitted to. In fact, they were not permitted to tamper with wine in any way. In London, cellars in taverns had to be visible to customers so that they could see their wine being drawn, although some tavern keepers put up curtains to conceal their illicit activities. Additives known to have been used to "improve" the smell and flavor of wine included pitch, wax, gum, and powdered bay, while turnsole (a purple dye) was used to deepen color. A 1306 statute in Frankfurt banned the addition of distilled spirits, and a 1371 Würzburg law forbade the use of spirits, alum, ground glass, chalk, and iron slag in wine.[42] When one London tavern keeper, John Penrose, was found to have adulterated some of his wine, he was condemned to drink some of the concoction and throw away the rest and was banned from selling wine for five years.[43] In 1456, when it was discovered that Lombard wine merchants had added substances to their sweet wine, the lord mayor of London ordered 150 barrels of the wine to be staved in. The wine ran through the streets, a slightly ambiguous account read, "like a stream of rainwater in the sight of all the people, from whence there issued a most loathsome savour."[44]

Regulations also controlled the quality of ale and beer. In eleventh-century England, "ale-conners" (literally, "ale-knowers") were appointed to certify that ale was properly made and priced. But they could still be deceived by brewers. A 1369 court record noted that all the brewers of Thornbury, near Bristol, "each time they brew, and before the tasters arrive, put aside the third best part of the brew and store it in a lower room. It is sold to no one outside the house but only by the mug to those frequenting the house as a tavern, the price being at least one penny per quarter-gallon. The rest is sold outside the house at two-and-a-half pence or threepence per gallon, to the grave damage of the whole neighbourhood of the town."[45]

Despite the evidently poor quality of much of the wine and ale on offer and the suspicion that adulteration was common, Europeans downed vast quantities of it. There seems to have been an increase in anxiety about drunkenness from the later 1300s, following the Black Death. This might have reflected a rise in sensibility on the part of commentators, but it is equally conceivable that it reflected an actual increase in heavy drinking, perhaps as a collective response to the widespread, catastrophic mortality. Some series of estimates of per capita alcohol consumption suggest that there was a slight increase in northern Europe, but statistics such as these are inconclusive. The relationship between drinking alcoholic beverages and drunkenness is mediated by many factors, including the volume consumed, the alcohol content of the beverage, the physical characteristics of the consumer, and the patterns of consumption—whether the alcohol was drunk in small, regular volumes or episodes of heavy consumption. Put simply, we cannot infer a higher incidence of drunkenness from nothing more than an increase in per capita consumption.

Even so, commentators on tendencies in drunkenness picked up the pace of criticism, to the level of what one historian calls "a drastic escalation in preachments" against "overindulgence in drink."[46] Some of the comments on intoxication are no more or less remarkable than those in other periods; they restate the point that drunkenness is a poor choice and that it has negative consequences for the drinker and society more broadly. In *The Canterbury Tales*, the Pardoner (who some commentators contend was drunk throughout his recitation) commented to his fellow travelers,

Witness the Bible, which is most express
That lust is bred of wine and drunkenness.
Look how the drunken and unnatural Lot
Lay with his daughters, though he knew it not;
He was too drunk to know what he was doing . . .
But seriously, my lords, attention, pray!
All the most notable acts, I dare to say,
And victories in the Old Testament,
Won under God, who is omnipotent,
Were won in abstinence, were won in prayer.
Look in the Bible, you will find it there.[47]

This might have been a call to total abstinence, but that is unlikely. It was probably a warning about drunkenness generally and advice to avoid being under the influence of alcohol when making critical decisions.

The Pardoner might well have directed his words to his clerical colleagues, for the clergy are well represented in the medieval accounts of drunkenness. On a thirteenth-century visitation to parts of northern France, church officials found many priests in breach of the rules governing alcohol. The priest in St. Rémy was said to be notorious for drunkenness and for frequenting the local tavern, where he had got into fights on several occasions; the priest at Gilemerville had occasionally lost his clothes in taverns (possibly by gambling, or perhaps in other circumstances); the priest in Pierrepoint was habitually drunk; the priest in Grandcourt was notorious for his excessive drinking; the priest in Panlieu not only was well-known as a drunk but also sold wine and often got his parishioners drunk.[48]

As these examples suggest, taverns became implicated in episodes of drunkenness (this is a long way from the modern legal requirement of refusing service to intoxicated patrons), and we see more and more condemnations of public drinking places as sites of gambling, prostitution, and other forms of poorly regarded behavior. The setting easily reinforced the historically persistent notion that drinking alcohol gave rise to all other forms of immorality. In response, authorities in many places attempted to rein in unacceptable behavior with regulations on drinking. Some tried to limit drinking hours, like the 1350 royal decree requiring Paris innkeepers not to allow new customers into their inns after the bells of Notre Dame Cathedral had rung out the curfew hour.

Yet for all the concern about heavy drinking and drunkenness, medieval doctors continued to praise the curative and health-giving properties of beer and wine, drawing on Greek and Arabic traditions that employed alcohol to treat a wide range of illnesses and conditions. Henri de Mondeville, a fourteenth-century French surgeon, stressed the benefit of wine for the blood, although he pointed out that it should be the best wine one could find—light, white, or rosé, with a good aroma and pleasant flavor. In a secular restatement of the doctrine of transubstantiation, de Mondeville wrote that wine was the best beverage for generating blood, for it entered the bloodstream directly and was immediately transformed into blood. But he added that he could also see the benefits of drinking both wine and milk: people who drank only wine had a reddish complexion, while those who drank only milk were pale. A proper balance of the two beverages made for the ideal, a pale complexion with rosy cheeks.[49]

According to some medieval advice, wine consumption could not start too soon. A German physician recommended in 1493 that children should be weaned from wine (an interesting notion in itself) at about eighteen months old and given water or honey to drink instead. But if the wet-nurse was unable to get the child off wine, "she should give him wine that is white, light, and well-diluted."[50] Although they countered classical advice not to feed children wine, various physicians in Germany, Italy, and France suggested giving babies wine along with breast milk or as part of a soft pap with bread, honey, and milk.[51]

The growth of urban administrations, the consolidation of church power, and changes in the economic and commercial structures of Europe between 1000 and 1500 combined to bring about many important changes in the place of alcohol in European society and culture. Among the most significant were the origins of what we might fairly call an alcohol industry, with the beginnings of concentration of ownership in brewing and long-distance trade in both beer and wine. Overall production increased, and the commentaries on excessive drinking might lead us to believe that consumption increased, too. But although the church seems to have adopted a more rigorous tone toward excessive drinking by the clergy and laypeople, it would be criticized in the sixteenth century for being lax and permissive where alcohol was concerned.

5

Early Modern Europe
1500-1700

ALCOHOL, RELIGION, AND CULTURE

The early modern period, from about 1500 to the eighteenth century, saw alcohol firmly entrenched in the daily diets of European populations but also witnessed immense changes in the types of alcohol available. Distilled spirits, with their much higher alcohol levels, had been made in Europe for medicinal purposes in very small volumes for a century or more, but they became much more widely available and consumed during the 1500s. (This is the subject of Chapter 6.) Brewing, as we have seen, had already undergone major organizational and technological changes: from small to large in scale, and hops were used to make beer that lasted longer and could be shipped to more distant markets. During the 1500s, the issues of conservation also began to bear on wine, which was notoriously unstable. Producers in some regions began to take advantage of the distilled spirits being made in commercial volumes to add brandy as a conservation agent. These "fortified wines," notably sherry and port, had higher alcohol levels and more lasting power than regular wine, and they quickly found eager consumers in England and other parts of Europe.

But before spirits and fortified wines began to make an impact on European drinking patterns, a religious shift, the Protestant Reformation, had important consequences for the history of alcohol in Europe. Protestantism was a cool-climate religion, more successful in northern Europe than in the south. Generally aligned with the geography of alcohol, it had more traction in beer-drinking (and, later, spirits-consuming) societies than in southern and Mediterranean regions where wine was easily produced and more commonly consumed. This correlation is intriguing, and it has been suggested that in Catholic cultures, wine was heavily symbolic of social unity, so that any threat to wine was seen and was resisted as a danger to the community.[1] Protestants might have been viewed as latter-day barbarians, sweeping into Catholic Europe with a message of moderation in alcohol consumption and critical of contemporary drinking practices. But it seems to be nothing more than coincidental that Protestantism was largely unsuccessful in the wine-producing regions of Europe. For one thing, some of the wine-producing areas of southern France, northern Germany, and Switzerland rallied to the Protestant cause. For another, the decisions as to which faith to follow were far more often made by political leaders (kings, dukes, and others) than by the mass of the population.[2]

Did the Protestants really pose a threat to wine and other alcoholic beverages? Reformers like Martin Luther and John Calvin had myriad objections to the doctrines and practices of the Church of Rome (the Catholic Church), and they accused it of having a lax attitude toward all kinds of immorality. Yet Protestant and Catholic positions on alcohol were essentially the same: everyday consumption was desirable for dietary and health purposes, but drinking beyond those needs—and, of course, drunkenness—was sinful and socially dangerous and should be punished. But if they agreed with Catholics on the basic message, Protestants argued that the Church of Rome had failed to enforce these rules and had turned a blind eye to the heavy drinking that they believed was widespread and the prime cause of the blasphemy and sinful behavior that afflicted the Christian world. They often portrayed Catholic priests and monks as lazy, alcohol-sodden fornicators who were as guilty as the sinful hordes that they were supposed to be models for. In doctrinal terms, then, Protestants were more rigorous toward alcohol consumption, and it is noteworthy that Protestants were far more active than Catholics in the temperance and prohibition movements in the nineteenth and twentieth centuries.

In the 1500s, only a few radical Protestants called for complete abstinence from alcohol—an extraordinary policy to advocate at a time when beer and wine were intrinsic parts of the daily diet for most adults and were considered far healthier alternatives to water. One would-be prohibitionist was the German reformer Sebastian Franck, who condemned alcohol for its contribution to all manner of vice and, believing that humans were too weak to resist it, called for it to be banned altogether. Anyone who drank alcohol, he wrote, should be expelled from the community of believers: "Oh misery! We are not alone drunk from wine, but drunk, drunk with the lying spirit, error and ignorance. . . . For so long as no ban [on alcohol] exists, and is in place, I recognize no Gospel or Christian community to speak of. One must remove the impure from the community of God."[3]

In contrast to such ideas, most Protestant leaders attempted the more feasible (but still daunting) task of suppressing excessive drinking, rather than alcohol itself, and various Protestant churches introduced stringent laws against unnecessary drinking. John Calvin, for one, tried to make taverns less attractive as places of sociability by prohibiting some of the practices that brought people together there. His 1547 regulations forbade any person to treat another to a drink, under penalty of a fine of 3 *sous*. In cases of drunkenness, a first offense carried a fine of 3 sous; a second offense earned a fine of 5 sous; a third offense was punished by a fine of 10 sous and a period of imprisonment.[4] Nor were these regulations, similar versions of which were applied in a number of Lutheran towns in Germany, mere threats. In the Calvinist community of Emden, in the Netherlands, during the second half of the 1500s, convictions for drunkenness made up a quarter of all breaches of social order. Among those convicted, men outnumbered women by five to one.[5]

Another reformer, Martin Bucer, also adopted rigorous alcohol policies. He believed that Christians should watch what they ate and drank (and what they wore and how they lived generally) to ensure that they behaved in a godly manner. He was opposed to the very existence of public drinking places, and while acknowledging that inns were necessary for travelers, he insisted that innkeepers should be moral, decent people who looked after the spiritual well-being of their guests as well as their physical needs.[6] Bucer was one of the influential theologians within the ranks of English Puritans, some of whom later settled in America. During the 1500s, English Puritans railed against the evils of excessive drinking and identified the tavern as the main problem. Taverns, they argued, were not only places of sin, immorality, and blasphemy but also sites of crime and social disorder. As one English Puritan colorfully put it in 1631, alehouses were "nests of Satan where the owls of impiety lurk and where all evil is hatched."[7]

The Protestants' rigor was directed toward all forms of alcohol, but they might have had a special concern that wine—which, like Catholics, they considered symbolic of Christ's blood—was not abused. The Protestants stressed the need for Christians to take communion frequently, not merely once a year as many Catholics did. Moreover, they insisted that communicants should receive both bread and wine, rather than only bread, as had been the practice in the Roman church since the twelfth century. Calvin denounced the church for "stealing" communion wine from the people and giving it "as special property to a few shaven and anointed men."[8] His personal commitment to wine is demonstrated by his receiving seven barrels of it a year as part of his salary.[9]

Controlling alcohol consumption was no less a challenge in the 1500s than it had been for political and religious authorities in earlier centuries. Sometimes—on days free of work, on feast days, and at celebrations such as marriages—alcohol was consumed mostly for pleasure and conviviality with other members of the community. But beer and wine were consumed every day of the workweek; there was no sense that working and drinking ought to be strictly segregated, even if only to the extent that workers might drink alcohol during breaks and mealtimes. The modern Western model of work discipline—observing fixed hours of work, with breaks at specified times and of closely monitored duration—emerged only in the nineteenth century; early modern workers expected to drink on the job, just as modern workers expect to have access to water as they work.

The drinking patterns of the great mass of people in preindustrial Europe are unknown. Most people lived in the country and worked in family economies, where all members of the family contributed to their collective survival. Just how regularly they drank alcohol, and how much, is not known, as they left few records. We have sporadic and uneven information on the alcohol rations of some workers in the labor market. Sailors on Dutch merchant ships in the 1600s drank 1.6 liters of beer a day in winter and 2 liters a day in summer, although we have to bear in mind that on long voyages beer was consumed only until it spoiled.[10] Fishermen from Brittany and Normandy who sailed across the Atlantic Ocean to the Canadian coast to catch cod took about 240 liters of wine or cider for each person.[11] But drinking on the job was not limited to those who worked on ships. French domestic servants drank poor quality wine called *vin de domestique* as part of their keep, while construction workers often received beer or wine (depending on where in Europe they worked) as part of their pay. The diary of an apprentice set out the pattern in an English printer's shop in the early 1700s: "My companion at the press drank every day a pint [of ale] before breakfast; a pint at breakfast with his bread and cheese; a pint between breakfast and dinner; a pint at dinner; a pint in the afternoon about six o'clock, and another when he had done his day's work."[12] That amounted to six pints of ale a day.

The most spectacular example of drinking while working was provided by the Republic of Venice, whose naval strength was underpinned by the Arsenal, a massive shipyard that employed more than 2,000 workers.[13] Like most workers at the time, the Arsenal's expected to have beer or wine for hydration and nourishment as they labored, but their high status led the authorities to provide them with unusually large volumes of wine of unusually superior quality. Wine was diluted in the ratio of two parts of water to one of wine to make a drink called *bevanda*, which probably had a final alcohol level of about 4 or 5 percent, similar to that of many modern beers. Wines from northern Italy tended to lack strength and flavor once diluted, and after complaints by workers, the Arsenal's management turned to the higher-alcohol wines of southern Italy's warm-climate regions and each year arranged for sizeable volumes to be shipped up the Adriatic coast. The managers of the Arsenal were so sensitive to the requirements of their skilled labor force that they paid almost any price for wine that would meet the workers' approval.

Once in Venice, the wine was stored in massive 2,000-liter casks, and each day staff would dilute the required volume, generally about 6,000 liters, using fresh water brought specially from the Brenta River rather than the local wells that were sometimes contaminated by salt water. Twelve men then carried the bevanda in buckets to various parts of the sixty-acre Arsenal twice a day so that workers had access to it throughout their shifts. Bevanda was more than a thirst-quencher; it was a stimulant that helped workers get through the long, ten-hour workday—extra rations were made available for workers doing overtime—and if it failed to arrive on time, gang leaders would send workers to fetch it.

Not only did workers get a wine ration as part of their regular benefits, but they also enjoyed additional wine when a ship was completed and launched: about 2 liters of undiluted wine for each worker and apprentice who had been engaged on the ship. Nor was wine confined to the workers. Senior managers at the Arsenal received barrels of wine that were the equivalent of as much as a third of their money wages—another incentive for them to order good-quality wine. The barrels were delivered directly to their houses and, depending on the recipient's rank, ranged from 450 to 1,800 liters a year. A wine ration also extended to others who worked for the Venetian state. Cattle butchers received wine when they worked in the municipal slaughterhouses, as did the sailors and free oarsmen on Venice's naval and merchant ships.

But the Arsenal has drawn attention because the thirst of its workers was astonishing. They went through more than half a million liters a year, and wine featured as the second most expensive item in the Arsenal's annual budget, second only to timber for ships and accounting for much more than was spent on such shipbuilding necessities as tar, canvas, and rope. In time, the Senate of Venice began to show concern at the cost of the Arsenal's wine, which accounted for 2 percent of the republic's total annual budget, and ordered an investigation. It found that the volume of wine consumed had increased steadily over time, from an average 3.2 liters per man each day in the period 1615–19 to 5 liters a day in the late 1630s. In the mid-1500s, consumption had been 2.5 liters a day per worker, so per capita consumption had doubled in less than a century.

The authorities seem to have abetted this increase in the mid-1630s by building a wine "fountain," a structure in an open room where bevanda flowed from three bronze tubes. A French visitor to the Arsenal, Robert de Cotte, described it as "a basin where there are three spigots an inch in diameter: a fountain running continuously, where all the workforce go to take as much wine as they please."[14] It is estimated that the fountain spewed out 10 liters of liquid a minute, or 6,000 liters during the workday. The point of the fountain is not clear, although there seems to have been some concern for the quality of the bevanda in the vats where it was diluted, as workers put their hands into the liquid while helping themselves to their rations. If hygiene was the rationale for the fountain, it reveals surprising squeamishness for a period not known for hand-washing practices. The fountain would have reduced this sort of contamination, but the continuous flowing of the bevanda cannot have improved its intrinsic quality, as the constant aeration must have oxidized the wine. Robert de Cotte noted that "this wine is not of the best,"[15] but being French, he might well have thought that of all Italian wine.

The Arsenal's workers were apparently less discriminating, as consumption rose after the fountain was built, but an investigation into the increased consumption ignored the effects of the fountain and suggested other reasons. First, workers were staying at the shipyard during their ninety-minute lunch break and consuming the state's wine, rather than their own, with their meal. Second, masses of men and women, including friends and relatives of workers, vagrants, and members of various commercial and political delegations that visited the Arsenal, were helping themselves to the wine that was so freely available from the fountain. Yet even though Venice's government was constantly looking for economies, the wine fountain was retained, perhaps because it was a powerful and conspicuous symbol of the wealth and largesse of the republic.[16] Clearly, if foreigners were as impressed by the fountain as their many references to it suggest, it was rare for workers elsewhere to have apparently unlimited access to wine like this.

As for the general level of alcohol consumption in Europe in the early modern period, we are again faced with uncertainty. The statistics are imprecise, and estimates of per capita consumption do not help us with the all-important variations in consumption by gender, class, and age. The figures from individual towns often range widely, as these annual per capita levels of beer consumption show:

Leuven (1500) 275 liters (adults only)
Antwerp (1526) 369 liters
Bruges (1550) 263 liters
Ghent (1580) 202 liters
Wismar (1600) 1,095 liters (hospital inmates).[17]

The figure for Antwerp would provide each inhabitant a liter of beer a day, but if we bear in mind that early modern European populations included a high percentage of children and young people, there is a possibility that adult males, the heaviest consumers, had much more (perhaps about 50 percent more) than the average liter. But we should remember that there was no legal minimum drinking age at this time, and that the line between adulthood and childhood was drawn at ages different from today's. Young people often began working full time in their early teens, and we do not know whether these young workers drank the same amount as workers in their twenties and older.

Ghent's 202 liters provided little more than half a liter of beer a day, which might have meant that adult males got three-quarters of a liter or more. On the other hand, the inmates of Wismar's hospital seem to have received 3 liters of beer a day. Other figures of beer consumption include 2 liters a day in a Danish children's workhouse in 1621 and 4.5 liters a day at Stockholm Castle in 1558, before the rules were revised in 1577 to give nobles 5.2 liters of beer a day and tradesmen and workers 3.9 liters a day.[18]

The variations in figures might well reflect variations in practice; there is no need to assume that there was a standard level of alcohol consumption in this period any more than there is today. But it is important to remember that most adults in this period would have needed at least 2 liters of water a day—possibly as much as twice that, given the demands of physical labor—simply for rehydration. A liter or two of beer would have gone so far to meet this requirement, but the rest must have been made up by water in food, water alone, or other alcoholic beverages.

We can only imagine the trepidation with which many poor people must have consumed water, if they were aware (as they must have been) of the dire warnings against it. Although some water (from springs or rain) was considered less harmful than other (such as from rivers and wells), water as a beverage was generally advised against. It was considered especially dangerous in England (and, we should suppose, elsewhere in northern Europe), where (according to prevailing medical opinion) the damp, cold climate demanded that people consume foods and beverages that contributed dryness and warmth. Some of the medical advice recognized, however, that the poor had no option but to drink water.

If the poor could not afford beer, they certainly could not afford wine, which tended to be more expensive, but consumption levels of wine in early modern Europe are no less certain than those of beer. As a beverage of daily consumption, wine was more common in the southern half of Europe where it was made, and again the figures—often based on the volume of wine that was taxed and on estimates of population—vary widely. One compilation proposes these examples of annual wine consumption in selected towns and cities of France:

> Paris (court apothecary and assistants, 1555) 680 liters
> Toul (cathedral worker, 1580) 456 liters
> Murol (construction worker, 1591) 365 liters
> St. Germain des Prés (monk, 17th century) 438 liters
> Paris (1637) 155 liters
> Lyon (1680) 200 liters
> Toulouse (late 17th century) 274 liters.[19]

We might well expect an apothecary and his assistants to drink more wine (and perhaps spirits, too) than the average Parisian, but perhaps not almost five times more (1.9 liters vs. 0.4 liters a day), especially when overall consumption seemed to be higher in the later period. Again, figures of individual and per capita consumption might indicate something, but it is difficult to see what, as there is no concentration within the range of volumes of wine consumed.

An unusual window into elite drinking is offered by the diets of Bishop Hugh Latimer and Archbishop Thomas Cranmer while they were confined in Oxford before being burned (in 1555 and 1556, respectively) as Protestant traitors and heretics. They were served alcohol (either ale or wine or both) at every meal, but Cranmer's superior rank gave him more of it. On average, the bread and ale Cranmer received at dinner and supper cost a shilling (a considerable sum), while Latimer's cost a quarter of that. Cranmer also received wine costing 6 pence at the two meals, while Latimer's cost less than half that sum. And while Cranmer's alcoholic drinks between meals cost 2 pence, Latimer's cost only 1. In addition to the clear hierarchy of volume, the sheer scope of expenditure on alcohol was remarkable: bread and ale (they were combined in the budgets, reinforcing the notion that ale was thought of as liquid bread), together with wine, accounted for 29 percent of the total expenditure on their prison diets, which included a wide range of fish, poultry, meat, and other food.[20]

Overall, it is impossible to describe alcohol consumption rates, and therefore trends, with any confidence. The statistical information is scattered, and even if it is reliable, it does not help us establish anything more than per capita consumption for specific populations, groups, or individuals, which is of limited use. Neither are inferences based on economic and demographic conditions always helpful; commodity prices rose dramatically during the 1500s as population increased and put pressure on resources, and we might expect consumption of beer and wine to have declined. In fact, the production of both seems to have increased steadily, and that indicates increased consumption. Moreover, the wine trade, in particular, became more complex and sophisticated, ensuring reliable and regular movement of wine from the producing to the consuming regions.[21]

But although it is difficult to form a reliable picture of drinking patterns in the early modern period, we are faced with an embarrassment of material telling us what various authorities—mainly medical and religious—thought about alcohol. With the invention of printing in the middle of the fifteenth century, books began to pour off the presses, and one of the most popular genres, at least until the mid-1600s, dealt with diet. Hundreds of books, most written by physicians, dealt with food and drink and their implications for physical and intellectual well-being. According to Ken Albala, a preeminent historian of the literature, "wine is given fanatical treatment, and is often considered a necessary nutrient."[22]

For all that both beer and wine were valued as good and nutritious, familiar warnings against excessive drinking were voiced throughout the early modern period. Too much wine, in particular, was blamed for sending vapors into the head that brutalized the spirit and provoked a desire for sensual pleasure and other passions. Popular proverbs, often vehicles for the expression and reinforcement of community values, conveyed the message of moderation. "Eat bread as long as it lasts, but drink wine moderately," advised one French saying. "Whoever surrenders to too much wine retains little wisdom," ran another, while others expressed the common male anxiety about women drinking: "A drunk woman is not the mistress of her body." But proverbs, like the people who mouthed them, were not hostile toward wine in itself. One sixteenth-century French saying, "Drink wine like a king, water like a bull," reflected the association between wine and social status, while another was simply negative toward water: "Water makes you cry, wine makes you sing." Yet another pointed to the sociability of wine-drinking: "Wine without a friend is like life without a witness."[23]

Not only levels of consumption but types of alcohol varied according to class, gender, and age. Throughout northern Europe especially, beer was the least expensive alcohol, and it was consumed at all levels of society, other than by the indigent who could not afford it. Some of the poor might have drunk some beer when it was dispensed on festive occasions and supplemented it with water in order to satisfy their needs. Above that, people drank beer and avoided water whenever possible, and many began to add small volumes of brandy and other spirits to their diet. Those at even higher social levels—the middle and upper classes—drank many types of alcohol. But in the southern, wine-producing regions of Europe, the pattern of drinking seems to have been quite different. Beer was less commonly consumed, as were spirits, and there were variations by class in the wine consumed. Peasants diluted their wine or drank wine by-products, like the pale, thin, low-alcohol beverages obtained by soaking wine residue, mainly grape skins, in water. They supplemented this with water and sometimes milk. In contrast, the better-off drank wine, its quality (and cost) rising with the consumer's status.

Although there was an established and robust international and long-distance trade in beer by this time, most of the beer consumed in Europe was locally produced. Grain grew almost everywhere, and local beer was less expensive than beer that had been shipped any distance. Wine was another matter, because most of northern Europe (with the exception of the Loire Valley in France and the lower Rhine in Germany) was sparsely planted in vines. The south of Europe provided wine for the north, and in the north lay the large, urban populations of England, the Low Countries, Germany, and the Baltic area, with their prosperous middle classes. During the early modern period, these populations were receptive to innovations in all aspects of material life, including food and drink, and they were effectively responsible for the success of several wine regions and new styles of wine-based beverages. In 1587, William Harrison listed fifty-six kinds of French wine on the London market and another thirty from places like Italy, Greece, Spain, and the Canary Islands, including such obscure styles as "vernage, cute, piment, raspis, muscatel, rumney, bastard, tyre, osey, caprice, clary and malmsey."[24] A selection like this speaks to a consumer market that supported a wide range of products.

One of the success stories in the world of wine in the 1500s was Spain, which in 1519 became (by dynastic marriage) part of the Habsburg Empire. This gave Spain an affiliation with the Netherlands, and before long Antwerp became a major destination for Spanish wine, both for consumption there and for re-export throughout northern Europe and beyond. It was especially popular in Poland from the beginning of the 1600s.[25] Given the success of Spanish wine producers in Europe, it is not surprising that they looked upon the kingdom's new colonies in Central and South America as additional markets and persistently pressed the king to halt wine production on the far side of the Atlantic. This was not to be, as many regions in South America proved to be ideal for viticulture, and wine shipped from Europe to the Americas rarely arrived in good shape. But even without the American market, Spain's vineyards and wine production grew throughout the sixteenth century, to the point that the authorities became concerned at the loss of arable land to viticulture. In 1597, King Philip II imposed regulations in the interests of ensuring good quality wine for his court and reducing the production of the poor quality wine that was believed to be causing widespread drunkenness among his subjects. Among other things, the rules forbade blending red and white wine and using harmful additives, and they required winemakers in Valladolid (where the royal court was located) to obtain a license.[26]

Spanish wine—from both the mainland and the Canary Islands—became especially popular in England after the English lost Gascony in 1453 and thus the political link that had given the English easy access to the wines of Bordeaux for three centuries. As exports to England grew, one of the Spanish wines to attract particular attention was sherry (often called "sack" or "sherry-sack" at the time) a fortified wine from the south of Spain. Sherry remained for centuries a quintessentially English (as well as Spanish) drink and entered the cultural lexicon through William Shakespeare, who in *Henry IV, Part II* had Falstaff credit sack for the virtues of Prince Henry (here called Harry). Sherry, asserts Falstaff, drives out foolishness and dullness and quickens the intellect and the wit. It warms the blood and makes the coward brave. "Hereof comes it that Prince Harry is valiant; for the cold blood he did naturally inherit from his father he hath like lean, sterile and bare land, manured, husbanded and tilled, with excellent endeavour of drinking good and good store of fertile sherries, that he has become very hot and valiant. If I had a thousand sons, the first principle I would teach them should be to forswear thin potations and to addict themselves to sack."[27]

The English stayed loyal to Spanish wines through the 1600s and beyond. In the 1590s, an average of 640 pipes (barrels) of Canary wine landed in London, but that number rose to more than 5,000 in the 1630s and to 6,500 in the 1690s.[28] By 1634 the writer James Howell declared, "I think there's more Canary brought into England than into all the World besides. When Sacks and Canaries were brought in first among us, they were us'd to be drunk in *aqua vitae* measures [i.e., small measures for distilled spirits], and 'twas held fit only for those who us'd to carry their leggs in their hands, their eyes upon their noses, and an almanack in their bones; but now they go down everyone's throat both young and old, like milk."[29] An anonymous poet penned a piece of doggerel in praise of Spanish wine:

> All you that troubled are with Melancholly,
> The *Spaniards* have a Juyce will make you jolly;
> Good wine, good wine, I say's the thing,
> That can for such distemper comfort bring:
> It comforts the heart, and quickens each vein,
> If a man be half dead, it will fetch him again.[30]

Another alcoholic beverage that emerged from the early modern period was sparkling wine. Although now made by various methods, including simply injecting wine with carbon dioxide, sparkling wine originally resulted when wine fermented in a sealed bottle. As grape juice ferments into wine, it produces both alcohol, which is retained, and carbon dioxide, which is allowed to disperse. But if fermentation takes place in a sealed bottle, the carbon dioxide cannot escape; it is dissolved in the liquid and slowly escapes as bubbles of gas when the wine is opened. In the modern "Champagne method," used widely since the nineteenth century, yeast and sugar are added to base wine, then sealed, causing a second, in-bottle fermentation that produces the potential bubbles.

The origins of sparkling wine are much debated, but a credible argument is made for the role of an English scientist, Christopher Merret, who presented a paper on wine to the Royal Society in London in the 1660s. It included a demonstration that adding sugar to wine in a bottle and then sealing the bottle produced a second fermentation that resulted in bubbles when the wine was opened. Merret's areas of scientific research and publication included glassmaking (hence a link to bottles) and tree bark (a link to cork). It is possible that Merret's was a chance finding. Sugar was just becoming popular among wealthy Europeans in the 1600s, and they began to sweeten everything—including coffee, tea, and chocolate, which had not been sweetened where they were originally consumed outside Europe. The English also began to add sugar to wine, as Fynes Moryson observed in 1617: "Gentlemen carouse only with wine, with which many mix sugar. . . . And because the taste of the English is thus delighted with sweetness, the wines in taverns (for I speak not of merchants' or gentlemen's cellars) are commonly mixed at the filling thereof, to make them pleasant."[31]

It is conceivable that, instead of putting a teaspoon of sugar in each glass of wine, as with tea and coffee, some gentlemen added sugar to the bottles they brought home from their wine merchants, then sealed them for drinking later. They might have found, when they opened the bottles, that their wine was dry and bubbly, rather than sweet and still. It is possible then, that early sparkling wines—and perhaps the earliest made by the "Champagne method"—were made not in the mysterious and romantic ambience of a monastery cellar in northern France but accidentally in the cellars of London gentlemen who were simply trying to sugar up their wines to satisfy the taste preferences of the day. The original sparkling wines (including champagne) were probably much sweeter than the dry (brut) style most popular today; "sugar-free" champagne was first made for the English market in the late 1800s.

The person once credited with inventing sparkling wine, the French monk Dom Pierre Pérignon, is surrounded by too many myths to be any longer considered the inventor. The winemaker at the abbey of Hautvilliers, near Epinay, in the 1660s, Dom Pérignon is reputed to have been blind and to have put the bubbles in his wine by accident. Tasting it for the first time, he is said to have cried, "I am drinking the stars!" But this, and most of the Dom Pérignon story, was developed in the early nineteenth century as part of a process of rehabilitating the reputation of the church in France after the French Revolution.[32] Other claimants to the title of producing the first sparkling wine are Limoux, in France, and Franciacorta, in Italy, both regions now well known for their sparkling wine. With sparkling wines, as with Bordeaux wines in the thirteenth century and sherry in the sixteenth, the relatively prosperous English market was responsible for the initial success.

Port was another wine whose initial success rested on its popularity among English consumers. Like sherry, port is wine fortified with brandy, with the difference that the brandy is added to the wine during fermentation (rather than after, as with sherry), before all the sugar in the grape juice is converted to alcohol. The addition of brandy raises the alcohol level to a point that kills the yeast, leaving port with elevated alcohol and also sweet because of the residual sugar not converted to alcohol. The port style of wine seems to have been first produced in the 1670s and was probably a variant on what had become a common practice of adding some brandy as a stabilizer and preservative to barrels of wine that were being shipped to England. English wine merchants had looked to Portugal to make up some of the deficit during one of the periodic interruptions in trade with France. Much of the Portuguese wine imported to England came from the Douro Valley (now the sole source of port) and was shipped through the town of Porto. The association gave the wine the name *porto*, which remains its name in French.

Another wine style that appeared in the sixteenth century also appealed to Europeans' sweet tooth: *Tokaji aszu*, a sweet white wine from the Tokaj region of Hungary. Made first around 1570, Tokaji aszu was (and is) made by leaving grapes on the vine after the usual harvest period until they had shriveled (*aszu* means "dried"); thus they lost water content and increased their sugar ratio. The resulting wine, which often fermented for months, was rich, sweet, and expensive, and it was a hit on many elite markets. In 1562, Pope Pius IV declared that Tokaji aszu was the wine fit for popes, and King Louis XV of France declared it to be "the king of wines and the wine of kings."[33] Tokaji aszu was widely served in Europe's royal and imperial courts through the nineteenth century, and such was the concern to protect its quality that a vineyard classification system was in place by 1730. Other regulations, governing the region and production methods (a forerunner of the "appellation" system) were added by the end of the eighteenth century.

As we can see, a number of different styles of wine became fashionable among Europe's middle and upper classes in this period, particularly in England and to varying extents elsewhere. The English lower classes had their turn with gin in the eighteenth century, but until then, the alcohol component of their diet was consistent: ale and beer, although for two decades, between 1530 and 1552, English beer was a casualty of the Reformation. Although beer (made with hops) had become sufficiently popular in England that beer brewers had achieved guild status, in 1530 King Henry VIII forbade the use of hops in brewing, thus making only ale (made with gruit) legal. This might have reflected Henry's personal taste, but there was also a religious dimension, in that most of the hops used in English brewing were imported from the Protestant Low Countries. In 1530, Henry had not yet broken with the Church of Rome and had been named Defender of the Faith by the pope. Henry VIII might well have considered beer containing hops as Protestant—an impression reinforced by the fact that Europe's major beer-producing regions had become Protestant—and this might explain his excommunication of beer from the English community.

Buttressing the ban on beer was an argument that ale was the only brewed beverage that was appropriate for the English. Andrew Boorde, an English physician, wrote in 1542 (during the ban on hopped beer), "Ale is made of malt and water . . . [and] ale for an Englishman is a natural drink. . . . Beer is made of malt, of hops and water. It is a natural drink for a Dutchman. And now in these late days it is much used in England to the detriment of many English men; especially it killeth them the which be troubled with the colic and the stone . . . ; for the drink is a cold drink yet it doth make a man fat, and doth inflate the belly; as it doth appear by the Dutch men's faces and bellies."[34] Nonetheless, small amounts of hops were cultivated in England at this time, and there was clearly some demand for hopped beer. In 1552, King Edward VI lifted the ban on using hops, and English brewers resumed their production of beer.

Henry VIII, often represented as a hearty drinker in his own right, also had an impact on England's brewing industry when he eventually broke with the Church of Rome and dissolved England's religious houses. Monasteries had long been centers of distilling and brewing, and their disappearance left the production of spirits and ale entirely in the hands of individual owners, many of whom were former monks who applied their skills in the secular world. Ale was also made in institutions like the Oxford and Cambridge colleges, each of which had its own brewery. The days of domestic ale production were coming to an end, and brewsters (women brewers) were disappearing even more quickly. Their activities within guilds were restricted and, as of 1521, although a woman was allowed to continue brewing after her brewer husband died, she had to relinquish the right as soon as she remarried.[35]

As we have seen, the shift from ale to beer had important implications for the brewing industry and for women because the durability of beer made it the choice beverage for export and for important clients such as armies. As early as 1418, Londoners had sent both ale and beer to their army besieging Rouen, but by the early sixteenth century, the English military used beer exclusively. In the first years of Henry VIII's reign, about 1512–15, an extensive brewery was constructed at Portsmouth for the sole purpose of providing beer for the English fleet.[36] The sheer scale of production needed to supply beer to early modern armies and navies and to feed the growing beer trade quickly excluded women from the most profitable sectors of brewing. Women did not have access to the capital needed, and married women were unable to sign contracts in their own right and thus could not form business partnerships. Although many women became active in the small-scale distilling industry that developed throughout northern Europe during the 1500s, they virtually disappeared from the much more extensive brewing industry.

For better-off Europeans, some alcohols were increasingly treated as commodities with cultural value, rather than as material necessities for health and hydration. The wealthy middle and upper classes could quench their thirsts with beer and wine and enjoy spirits for their flavor and impact, but these were often not generic beverages. As we have seen, more than a hundred different wines, identified by place origin or style, were imported into England by the late 1500s, and all beverages underwent this kind of (what is now called) brand differentiation. We can see a transition to it in the description of the beverages ordered for the installation of the archbishop of Canterbury in 1504: 6 pipes (a pipe holds 535 liters) of red wine, 4 pipes of claret, a pipe of choice white wine, a pipe of wine of Osey, a butt (573 liters) of malmsey, 2 tierces of Rhenish wine, 4 tuns (a tun holds 1,146 liters) of London ale, 6 tuns of Kentish ale, and 20 tuns of English beer.[37] Some of the descriptions are generic (red wine) or fairly generic (choice white wine), but the remainder are origin-specific. If there were not desirable distinctions, why would the order not be simply for 10 tuns of ale, rather than 6 from Kent and 4 from London? At the same time, they are not yet identified by individual brewer.

By the later 1600s, however, wine began to be identified by producer when Arnaud de Pontac, a noble and president of the Parlement (royal court of law) of Bordeaux and the owner of vineyards around a château called Haut-Brion, began to sell his wine on the wealthy and status-conscious London market. The English diarist Samuel Pepys, as status-conscious as anyone, recorded a visit to the Royal Oak tavern, where he "drank a sort of French wine, called Ho Brian, that had a good and most particular taste I never met with."[38] It is intriguing to imagine what the wine tasted like; for Pepys to have commented on it that way, it must have been very different from the rest of the clarets then available in London.

Englishmen traveling on the Continent started to show critical appreciation of the wines they encountered. John Raymond commented that Albano, near Rome, "deserves seeing, if not for the Antiquity, yet for the good wine; one of the best sorts in Italy." Richard Lassel's guide to the streams and fountains of Caparola noted, "Having walked these gardens about, youl [sic] deserve after so much water, a little wine, which will not be wanting to you from the rare cellar lyeing under the great terrasse before the house, and perchance youl think the wineworks here as fine as the waterworks." Richard Fleckno was complimentary about the wine of Rome, if not its winemakers: "Good meat there is, delicious wine, and excellent fruit. . . . But that is the Climat's virtue, and none of theirs."[39]

Given that beer and ale were shipped and stored in big barrels, individual consumers were not likely to keep a reserve on hand for personal use. But well-off wine-drinkers could avail themselves of developments in glassmaking and purchase wine bottles they could fill at wine merchants and taverns. Samuel Pepys noted his pleasure at going to The Mitre tavern in 1663 to watch as his wine was poured into his newly acquired bottles, each adorned with his personal crest. Pepys was fascinated by wine and wrote of the cellar of Thomas Povey, a London merchant and politician: "Upon several shelves there stood bottles of all sorts of wine, new and old, with labels pasted upon each bottle, and in order and plenty as I never saw books in a bookseller's shop." On a return visit, Pepys noted that the cellar included a well to keep the wine cool. Pepys's own cellar, in contrast, seems to have been a collection of small casks and other vessels, and he did not mention bottles, even though he owned some: "I have two tierces of Claret, two quarter casks of Canary, and a smaller vessel of Sack; a vessel of Tent [Spanish red wine], another of Malaga, and another of white wine, all in my cellar together." Pepys was very pleased with his collection (the equivalent of more than 750 modern bottles of wine), "which, I believe, none of my friends of my name now alive ever had of his owne at one time."[40] The comment suggests not only the novelty of the personal wine cellar but also the sense of status that it conveyed.

As more attention was given to the aesthetic variations in wine (a general appreciation of grape varieties followed later), more attention was paid to its finer therapeutic qualities. There was some discussion of the temperature at which wine should be consumed, in view of the widespread practice of warming it first. According to Bruyerin Champier, physician to Francis I of France, many people warmed their wine by the fire or diluted it with warm water, while others heated up iron blades that they plunged into the wine, and the poor achieved the same effect less elegantly with burning sticks taken straight from the fire. Champier disapproved of all these practices, but he also counseled against drinking wine brought directly from a cool cellar. The temperature of such wine, he wrote, damaged the throat, chest, lungs, stomach, and intestines; corrupted the liver; and brought on incurable diseases and sometimes a rapid death. He advised anyone with a cool cellar to let wine warm up to the ambient temperature before drinking it—an early expression of the notion of serving wine at "room temperature."[41] A similar discussion took place with respect to beer, although it is more surprising to read of warmed-up beer than wine.

But there was no consensus on warming wine, not least because the consideration was not the sensory experience of wine but the effects of temperature on the body. A few decades after Champier advised against drinking wine cool, another physician, Laurent Jaubert, recommended cooling wine and other drinks, especially for young people with hot blood.[42] Other physicians appealed to the warmth of wine in humoral terms, as distinct from its temperature measured by a thermometer. The Italian physician Baldassare Pisanelli recommended wine in the diet of old people because "the progressive decline of their natural heat requires a supplementary source of warmth to overcome the coldness that accompanies old age." On the other hand, Pisanelli continued, children should not drink wine because "it adds to more fire on slender kindling, and it disturbs their minds." Likewise, young people "have a warm and fervent nature," so that when they drink wine, they "run the risk of becoming powerfully impassioned in the spirit and in the body furiously excited"—presumably a warning that wine aroused sexual feelings.[43] It seems to have been a common view. Cardinal Silvio Antoniano wrote in 1584 that children, especially girls, should have little or no wine and should eat simple foods balanced between wet and dry.[44] This sort of advice runs against the common assumption, which seems often justified by historical sources, that small volumes of alcohol (beer and wine) were consumed by children and young people on a regular basis. It does raise the question (which Pisanelli and Antoniano did not address) of what children should drink, if not wine.

Some physicians, bringing biological models of the ancient world together with prevailing ideas about class-specific biological characteristics, began to develop notions of certain wines being better suited to certain classes. Olivier de Serres, a soil scientist whose expertise in viticulture did not prevent him from advancing medical views, wrote in 1605 that "good, full-bodied red and black wines" were "appropriate for working people . . . and greatly sought after by them, as much as white and claret wines by people of leisure." (The distinction between "red and black wines" is probably between medium and very dark red wines.) Jean Liebault, another agronomist but also a physician, explained the reason a few years later: "Red wine nourishes more than white or claret, and is more suitable for those who work hard; because work and vigorous exercise neutralize any of the disadvantages that red wine has." As for black (very dark) wine, "it is best for vignerons and farmers, because . . . it gives more solid and plentiful nourishment and makes the man stronger in his work."[45]

Liebault pointed out that dark wines weighed on their consumers and made their blood "thick, melancholic and slow-flowing," but that this was of no concern for manual workers, because they were known to be crude, earthy, thick, and slow anyway. But the same wine would have terrible effects on nobles, the bourgeois, and the clergy, whose work required them to be lively and spiritual. Such men would suffer obstructions of the liver and spleen, loss of appetite, and rawness in the stomach. Such theories effectively anthropomorphized wines, enabling them to be matched to consumers by the similarity of their supposed physical and personality characteristics.

Such arguments were refinements within the general medical belief that, whatever other properties they possessed, alcoholic beverages—especially wine—were therapeutic. The English physician Andrew Boorde wrote that wine "doth rejoice all the powers of man, and doth nourish them; it doth ingender good blood, it doth nourish the brain and all the body." Surgeons sold ale to their patients, women drank extra beer to help their milk flow, and 43 of the medicinal recipes in the first English handbook on gynecology contained some form of alcohol.[46]

For medical or more prosaic reasons of hydration and pleasure, wine was clearly becoming central to the diet in many parts of France. Some physicians allowed that peasants, presumably in the north of France, who could not afford wine might drink beer or cider instead, but others argued that beer was too harsh and that a weak solution of wine was far preferable. In the sixteenth century, it was alleged that cider-drinking was responsible for the leprosy that was widespread in Normandy, then known for cider (and later for calvados, an apple-based distilled spirit). Stung by the allegation, Julien le Paulmier, an aptly named Protestant physician (the pronunciation of his name is very close to *pommier*, the French word for "apple tree"), leaped to defend cider, which he believed had cured him of the heart palpitations he had experienced following the St. Bartholomew's Day Massacre of Protestants in 1572. Le Paulmier argued that wine was a dangerous drug that should be closely controlled by professionals and not left to patients who did not know which wine to consume, how to dilute it, and how to suit it to the climate, season, or individual needs. Cider, in contrast, was good for the digestion and blood, was warm but moderately so, and generally had all the benefits claimed for wine with none of its disadvantages. In short, wrote le Paulmier, "a man who drinks cider lives longer than a man who drinks wine."[47]

Le Paulmier's strictures notwithstanding, wine became ever more indispensable in the care of the ill, and when Louis XIV founded Les Invalides, the famous military hospital, in 1676, he exempted it from paying taxes on the first 55,000 liters of wine it purchased each year for the patients. Such was the hospital's expenditure on wine (there are echoes here of the Arsenal in Venice) that by 1705, only thirty years later, the exemption was raised fifteenfold, to 800,000 liters a year. Officers convalescing in Les Invalides were given a wine ration of one and a quarter liters a day, served as a quarter-liter in the morning and a half-liter each with lunch and dinner. Noncommissioned officers received a smaller allotment, and all evening servings of wine were doubled on certain feast days. So important was wine that when officers were sent from Les Invalides to a spa for treatment, they took a supply of wine with them in case none was available at their destination. On the other hand, deprivation of the wine ration was a punishment for such offenses as writing obscenities on the hospital walls; throwing refuse, urine, or water out the windows; not respecting the rules of cleanliness; and having a fire or candle lit at night after the beating of the retreat.[48]

Outside the walls of institutions like Les Invalides, people drank in the growing number of public drinking places. Each language had its own words for these places, of course: taverns and inns in England, cabarets and guinguettes in France, and Gaststätten in Germany, for example. But there were common categories based on the type or types of alcohol they served (such as alehouses and dramshops in England, serving ale and gin, respectively), whether they also offered meals (taverns), and whether they provided accommodations for travelers in addition to food and drink (inns). Various jurisdictions defined drinking places with some precision and determined what each was permitted to serve its clients. (Here all these categories will be covered by the generic term "public houses.") Although public houses can be traced back thousands of years, only in the sixteenth century did they become fixtures in both rural and urban communities in Europe and places where ordinary people gathered on a regular basis—a practice quite probably enabled by the Protestant Reformation. Throughout the Middle Ages, the most important center of community life was the church and its immediate vicinity. This was the favored location of meetings, community games, and festivities such as church-ales, occasions when parishes sold donated food and ale to raise funds, often for poor relief. When the Reformers largely restricted the use of the church to sacred purposes—and in many cases tried to suppress activities like dancing, game-playing, and communal drinking—people transferred secular functions to the local alehouse or tavern.[49]

The ubiquity of public houses in England is suggested by the fact that by 1577 there was one alehouse for every 142 inhabitants, and that fifty years later there was one for about every 100.[50] Alehouses were more densely distributed in cities and large towns than in rural villages, and when we bear in mind that half the English population was under the age of eighteen years, we can see that, overall, English adults were well provided with places to drink alcohol. Within London, there was one public house for every sixteen houses and, in poorer districts, one for every six or seven.[51] The numbers also speak to the decline of domestic brewing, because that ratio of alehouses could have survived only with the regular patronage of a substantial proportion of the adult population. In the English countryside, alehouses provided cheap drink, food, and accommodations for the growing numbers of vagrants and migrant workers, to the extent that they offered an alternative community and family.[52]

The regulations governing pubic houses varied widely across Europe, but in many Protestant regions the authorities tried to suppress the very activities that drew people to them: social drinking, gaming, and sometimes dancing. In Catholic regions, drinking places were no less regulated in the interests of maintaining public order. In France, a 1677 police order required brandy-sellers to close after 4:00 PM between November 1 and the end of May in order to stop criminals and other undesirables from drinking to the point of intoxication and then going out to cause trouble under cover of the long hours of darkness. Other regulations from this period required tavern own-ers in Paris to report any disturbances (like brawls) to the police and forbade gambling and serving undesirables such as vagabonds and prostitutes.[53]

The relationship of public houses to crime is uncertain, even though the contemporary authorities were convinced that public houses were the haunts of criminals. They probably were, as much as they were also gathering places for men not engaged in criminal or immoral activities, but taverns were sin-gled out in the "Proclamation against Debauchery" issued by England's King Charles II in 1660. Writers of the period made the easy association of drink-ing with other immoral and criminal activities. One work focused on drunk-enness as the reason a deserting soldier had shot one of the soldiers sent to find him: "All that he had to plead for himself was, that he was in Drink when he did it."[54] Another wrote that "sloth is linked with drunkenness, drunk-enness with fornication and adultery, and adultery with murder."[55] A num-ber of murders in Shakespeare's tragedies are linked to drinking: the killing of Duncan and his grooms in *Macbeth* and of Desdemona and Roderigo in *Othello* are examples that the plays' contemporary audiences might well have understood.[56]

But it is more difficult to establish the link between taverns specifically and crime, although some studies suggest that a quarter of violent crime had some kind of tavern connection.[57] Certainly, brawls in public houses seem to have been common, and taverns might have provided many opportuni-ties for crimes such as pocket-picking and other forms of theft. In 1674, one woman was convicted of stealing a silver cup from a London alehouse. She had ordered ale and spent some time drinking it, and when the proprietor went to fetch her a chamber pot, the woman left the alehouse, taking the cup with her.[58]

Although the clientele of early modern public houses often included women, women rarely had access to them on terms that were the same as men's. In Augsburg, Germany, in the 1500s, women could drink in taverns without any problem only if they were married and their husbands were drinking there at the same time.[59] Other women might enter a tavern temporarily to sell goods, buy wine and beer to take home, or carry out commercial transactions. But these occasions were rare, and for the most part, single and married women risked their reputations when they entered a tavern alone. Called "common" and "dishonorable," they were suspected of being sexually loose or of being prostitutes—a suspicion that, needless to say, reveals the presumed morals of a tavern's male clients. Such was the stigma that some married women who came to a tavern to fetch their husbands home would stand at the door and call for them rather than place even a foot inside.

The tavern could also be problematic for men. Intrinsic to the principle of male honor in Augsburg (and throughout Europe) was an ability to consume alcohol and yet maintain a family and household. It is a constant complaint throughout the history of alcohol in Western societies (and very prominent during the temperance period of the nineteenth and twentieth centuries) that too many men were unable to balance these activities and that, when forced to choose, they opted for more alcohol over their family responsibilities. In doing so, these men contributed to what was perceived as an increase in drunkenness from the mid-sixteenth century on. Perhaps this perception resulted from heightened sensitivity, as Protestant authorities cracked down on drinking because it was the right thing to do, and Catholic authorities did the same as the Counter-Reformation brought in a more rigorous view on morality. In England, drunkenness was made a civil offense (rather than an offense judged by church courts) in 1552, and the following year there was an attempt to limit the number of taverns. In 1583, the English moralist Philip Stubbs wrote evocatively of drunkenness: "I say that it is a horrible vice, and too much used in England. Every county, city, town, village, and other places hath abundance of alehouses, taverns, and inns, which are so fraught with malt-worms, night and day, that you would wonder to see them. You shall have them sitting there at the wine and good-ale all the day long, yea, all the night too, peradventure a whole week together, so long as any money is left; swilling, gulling and carousing from one to another, til never a one can speak a ready word."[60] The English church also suppressed church-ales, which were often occasions for collective intoxication.

The perception that drunkenness has never been worse is common to many periods; it is rather like the belief, which can be traced back many centuries, that the family is on the verge of disappearance. They are facets of a generalized culture of nostalgia, which would eventually be challenged by ideologies of progress and improvement. Above the monotony of continual dire warnings of the prevalence of drunkenness, we must look for the important time- and class-specific variations. In the case of early modern Europe, two sources of drunkenness proved distinctive. One, as we have seen, was the spread of public drinking houses, which was seen as giving ever-increasing opportunities for Europeans, men in particular, to drink to excess. The other was the arrival of distilled spirits into mainstream drinking cultures, and that is the subject of the next chapter.

6

Distilled Spirits
1500-1750

THREATS TO THE SOCIAL ORDER

Until the end of the Middle Ages, the alcoholic beverages consumed in Europe were produced solely by fermentation. By far the most important were beer and wine, although mead, cider, and other fruit-based wines were also consumed in the regions where they were produced. Alcoholic beverages made by distillation appeared in Europe by the twelfth century, but even as late as 1500 they were produced in very limited quantities and almost exclusively for medical purposes. Yet by the end of the 1500s, distilled spirits had entered the mainstreams of European and American drinking cultures and the bloodstreams of their populations. The first form of spirits to be produced was brandy, which is distilled from wine, but before long, other beverages (notably whiskey, gin, and vodka) were distilled from cereals. In the seventeenth century, the distillation of rum from molasses, a by-product of sugar production, began. The appearance of these new alcoholic beverages, which were much higher in alcohol by volume than beer and wine and lacked their cultural traditions, had short- and long-term implications for patterns of alcohol consumption and regulation. They make the period from 1500 to 1750 a critical one in the history of alcohol.

Distilling alcohol involves heating an alcohol-bearing liquid, usually made from grapes or cereals but also from fruits and vegetables, such as potatoes. Because alcohol boils at a lower temperature than water, it vaporizes before the water in the liquid, and the vapor is collected and then cooled, so that it condenses and produces concentrated alcohol in liquid form. Modern spirits go through one or two, and sometimes three, distillations; each distillation produces a liquid that is higher in alcohol by volume than the one before. The origins of the process are unclear, but an image in the works of the Egyptian/ Greek alchemist Zozimos of Panopolis in the early fourth century is easily recognizable as distilling equipment.[1] This does not mean that distilled alcoholic beverages were produced at that time. Distilling can be used to separate any substances having different points of volatility. It is likely that the earliest distillation was used to purify substances like mercury, water, and various oils—and to pursue the alchemists' ultimate goal of turning base metal into gold—rather than to produce a more intensely alcoholic beverage. Moreover, although classical texts contain many references to the production and consumption of fermented beverages, there are none to beverages made by distillation. Arab scientists who later advanced the work of the Greek alchemists might well have distilled alcohol, and much of the language associated with the process has Arabic roots: there is the word "alcohol," for a start, and also "alembic," the apparatus used for heating the liquid and cooling the vapor. But an argument has also been made that distilling began in the border areas of modern Pakistan and India.[2]

When Europeans learned and applied the science of distilling alcohol is not clear. It has been suggested that the first batch of spirits was produced in 1100, at the prestigious medical school at Salerno, in southern Italy,[3] but if that is so, it took a remarkably long time for alcohol distilling to catch on more widely. Although there are references to distilling throughout the rest of the twelfth century, some with the object of purifying water, none records distilling alcohol. Perhaps the few instances of alcoholic distillation were carried out only as a curiosity, or the product tasted so bad that distillers did not drink enough of it to appreciate its effects and its potential.

The first unambiguous references to distilled alcohol as a beverage date from the thirteenth century. In Spain, a Catalan scholar of Muslim science, Ramon Lull, admired the smell and flavor of his distilled spirit and presciently suggested that it might be an excellent stimulant for soldiers before they went into battle.[4] His colleague Arnaldus de Villa Nova, from Valencia, promoted distilled alcohol as having rejuvenating effects—this two centuries before his fellow countryman Ponce de Leon looked for rejuvenating waters (the Fountain of Youth) in the New World. One of Arnaldus's scientific preoccupations was identifying ways to maintain or regain youthfulness. His various recommendations included drinking a concoction of saffron, aloes, and viper juice; being cheerful and moderate; and avoiding sex and strenuous exercise.[5] Perhaps it is not surprising that he would think that, in distilled spirits, he had found yet another effective substance.

Alcohol, he enthused, "has the power to heal all infirmity and diseases, both of inflammation and debility; it turns an old man into a youth."[6] Later in the thirteenth century, in Italy, a number of scholars recommended distilled alcohol—which was by then becoming known as *aqua vitae*, or "the water of life"—for its supposed medicinal values, whether it was consumed or applied to wounds.

Yet before distilling alcohol could gain acceptance and respectability, it became a casualty of the reaction against alchemy. In the fourteenth century, alchemy was declared to be contrary to nature and akin to magic, and it was condemned by church and secular authorities alike. Pope John XXII declared aspects of alchemical theory to be heretical in the early 1320s, and in 1326 the inquisitor general of Aragon, in Spain, started a campaign to suppress it. It was forbidden in England, Venice, and elsewhere, and in 1380, Charles V of France made the ownership of distilling apparatus, which was widely associated with alchemy, a capital crime.[7]

This was not a climate that encouraged the production of distilled alcohol. But some scientists and scholars persisted, and there are occasional but sparse records of spirits production throughout the 1400s, when the pressure against alchemists was gradually relaxed. Michele Savonarola, court physician in Ferrara, published a book on distilling, *De Aqua Ardente* (*On Burning Water*, a reference to the fire used to heat the base liquid), in which he stressed the therapeutic effects of spirits and their efficacy in dealing with the plague, which continued to affect many parts of Europe. On the other hand, Leonardo da Vinci designed an improved alembic for distilling alcohol from ale or wine, but only for use as a solvent or as an incendiary for military purposes; he warned against drinking distilled spirits.

By the end of the fifteenth century, distilling alcohol for medical purposes was largely differentiated from alchemy, even though both used the same apparatus. Distilling alcohol had been appropriated by physicians and apothecaries who, in many countries, were given rights to distill, prescribe, and sell spirits. Sometimes the distillate was used in its pure form; at other times it was distilled with flowers, plants, herbs, and spices, each form being prescribed for particular ailments. In 1498, the high treasurer of Scotland recorded a payment of 9 shillings to a "barbar" (barber-surgeon) "that brocht aqua vitae to the King in Dundee by the King's command."[8] It was also made in religious houses, where monks and nuns sometimes made medicinal "waters." In one of the earliest references to distilling in Scotland—a 1494 order for "eight bolls of malt to Friar John Cor wherewith to make aqua vitae"—the producer was a member of a religious order.[9]

The health value attributed to spirits was signaled by their generic name, aqua vitae—ironic, because the process of distilling separated the alcohol from the water in the base liquid. The name was replicated in other languages, such as the French *eau-de-vie*, Scandinavian *aquavit*, and Gaelic *uisge beatha* or *usquebaugh*, which in the 1700s became "usky," "uiskie," and "whiskie." (The word "brandy," meaning "burnt wine," was coined in the seventeenth century, from the Dutch *brandewijn*.) One of the earliest printed books on aqua vitae, in this case brandy, was published in Germany in 1476 and recommended a half-spoonful every morning to prevent conditions as varied as arthritis and bad breath. Other physicians wrote of the beneficial effects of brandy for physical ailments (it cured headaches, heart disease, gout, and deafness); as an aid to appearance (it improved the bust and stopped hair graying); and as therapy for emotional and other problems (it banished melancholy and forgetfulness).[10] The inclusion of conditions commonly associated with aging (such as deafness, forgetfulness, and graying) reflects the claims that drinking brandy prolonged youth and thus life itself.

The essential property that was attributed to brandy and other spirits was heat. Aqua vitae was also known as "burning water" (*aqua ardens*) and "hot water," after the process used to heat and vaporize alcohol-bearing liquids, and distillers themselves were often called "water-burners." No doubt because of the burning sensation of concentrated alcohol in the mouth and throat, distilled spirits were believed to embody the heat of the fire that was required to make them. As heat-giving beverages, spirits played an important medical role because of the dominant medical model of the time, which understood health as a balance of the properties that coexisted within the human body: heat and cold, dryness and moistness. Aqua vitae could be used to counteract excessive cold, and it was thus ideal for old people whose bodies were cooling—but not necessarily for old widows, whose bodies were believed to be so dry that they might combust if brought into contact with such a fiery beverage. Nor was brandy advised for young people: they were considered to be naturally warm and could overheat if they consumed "hot waters." Overall, though, the health benefits of brandy, the first distilled spirit to enter the medical arsenal, seemed incontestable. Doctors readily prescribed it, and their patients happily took their medicine. Brandy became popular as a general tonic, and some wealthier people adopted the habit of starting the day with the burst of warmth and energy that distilled alcohol provides, a tradition that continues in some parts of Europe to this day.

In 1545, the German physician Walter Ryff provided a comprehensive explanation of the medicinal value of brandy, which, he wrote, was not to be drunk as a beverage but as a "powerful medication." Ryff first described all the therapeutic properties of wine—especially "thick, red wine," which increases the blood supply—and then argued that because brandy is the essence of wine, it has even more medicinal properties. "Aqua vitae," he wrote, "is especially useful in treating a cold, moist head and brain. . . . It drives out the threat of apoplexy, minor and major strokes, paralysis, dropsy, epilepsy, shaking and trembling limbs, and if the limbs have fallen asleep and become numb and without feeling because of cold, it is rubbed externally on the skin or drunk in an appropriately suitable amount."[11]

But brandy and other spirits also presented problems because of their high alcohol content. Alcohol levels could not be measured at this time, but even though spirits often contained various additives and were frequently drunk diluted and adulterated, it is quite probable that many had an alcohol content well above the 40 percent that is commonly the maximum allowable strength today. Simply by virtue of being distilled from wine, brandy had far more alcohol by volume than wine. This alone does not mean that spirits were (or are) more likely to produce intoxication, which is a function of the volume of the beverage consumed, not only of its inherent alcohol level. It is possible that when spirits first entered the market, consumers drank them with almost the same gusto as they downed wine and beer, with regrettable consequences, but it is more likely they were consumed in small measures.

If the excessive consumption of fermented beverages such as beer and wine aroused concern and had historically been subjected to regulations and penalties, we can easily understand why the even greater potential of distilled alcohol to cause intoxication, personal risk, and social disruption justified even more rigorous restrictions on its production and consumption. Because alcohol had not been identified as the agent common to spirits, beer, and wine, spirits were initially treated as a distinct class of beverage, and they became the first of many substances to be highly regulated. By the early 1700s, in a reprise of the attempts to suppress alchemy, there were calls for distilled spirits to be banned entirely. The water-burners who provided Europeans with brandy (and later with gin, vodka, and rum) had ignited a debate on alcohol, health, and social order that would simmer at varying levels of intensity for centuries.

The fundamental problem was that it was impossible to restrict consumption of brandy to the medicinal purposes that were first deemed its proper use. Indeed, it was impossible to define the conditions for which brandy might be useful, so as to specify what constituted proper consumption and what was abusive. Like wine, brandy was a medicine that was not only prescribed for specific ailments but also approved for limited consumption as a general tonic that might be consumed daily to maintain a state of physical and emotional well-being. This ambiguity, and the ambivalence about brandy-drinking to which it gave rise, was nicely encapsulated in a 1532 German book on distilling. Brandy, the author wrote, "is good for the sad and the melancholy. . . . It gives back physical strength and makes one hearty and happy."[12] Just as it was hard to distinguish medically defined physical and emotional ailments from the banal worries and troubles of daily life, so it was difficult to determine where therapeutic consumption ended and recreational drinking began.

Although spirits continued to have strong medicinal associations until the twentieth century, they began to slip from the grasp of the medical profession during the early 1500s. The town of Colmar was licensing and taxing alcohol distillers by 1506.[13] In many places, the right to distill was extended to guilds that produced food and drink, such as the victuallers and vinegar-makers; in France, these guilds had been granted distilling privileges by the 1530s.[14] On the other hand, distilling remained under the supervision of physicians in England until the 1550s, when a commission of the Royal College of Physicians was appointed to inspect distillers. Not until 1601 were the monopolies on distilling in England ended, and Elizabeth I declared that her subjects should "have all the cheap aqua vitae they wanted to warm their chill stomachs."[15]

As physicians began to lose control of aqua vitae, so did religious orders when, from the 1530s, reformers dissolved religious houses in most of the regions where Protestantism became dominant. Many former monks and nuns continued their distilling activities when they entered the secular world, and women were very prominent in the world of distilling. Half of the thirty distillers in Munich in 1564 were women; there were reports of prominent women in places as diverse as England, Hungary, and Brunswick making aqua vitae; and much of the spirits production in England was in the hands of working women. At this time, distilling was largely a domestic, small-scale operation, and women distillers were an echo of the brewsters who, by the 1500s, had almost disappeared from ale production. In 1546, Henry VIII, nearing death, appointed a woman to keep two gardens at Hampton Court for "making and stilling all manner of . . . herbs, waters and other necessaries" for his use.[16]

The distillation of alcohol not only from wine but also from cereal-based fermented liquids (essentially ale) had important implications in northern European regions. There the climate ruled out viticulture, particularly from the sixteenth century, when a phase of more severe winters destroyed many vineyards in marginal regions. Grain-based spirits gave people who could not afford imported wine access to a locally produced beverage with a higher alcohol content than beer. It is arguable that the very warming qualities of spirits produced an especially receptive market in the cooler climates and cold winters of northern Europe, and by 1600, grain-based aqua vitae was being produced in Ireland, Scotland, Germany, Scandinavia, and elsewhere. Perhaps some consumers were too receptive. Distilling in Scotland clearly accounted for a good share of barley production, and in 1579, in anticipation of a poor grain harvest, the Scottish parliament banned distilling, except by earls, lords, barons, and gentlemen. The parliament declared that "a great quantity of malt [is] consumed in the whole part of this realm by making of aqua vita, which is a great cause of the dearth."[17]

As the consumption of spirits widened socially and perhaps increased on a per capita basis, there were the predictable warnings about excessive drinking. In the Holy Roman Empire, a police ordinance of 1530 blamed drinking to one's health (which had already been banned) as a cause of increasing drunkenness: "The abuse and mischief of pledging healths has increased everywhere, becoming more and more entrenched and extensive, leading to blasphemy, murder, manslaughter, adultery and other such misdeeds."[18] By 1550, the Dutch physician Laevius Lemnius noted that aqua vitae had become so common as a beverage that people in western Germany and Flanders were drinking more than was good for them.[19] In part these warnings reflected the wish of the new Protestant churches to curb the immoral activities of all kinds that they alleged the Church of Rome had tolerated or encouraged. In Switzerland, Jean Calvin introduced rigorous laws that not only punished drunkenness but also curbed the sociability that had centered on drinking in taverns. Such regulations affected all kinds of alcohol, but spirits were regarded as potentially far more dangerous, both to health and to the social order, than fermented alcoholic beverages.

While the health benefits of spirits continued to be promoted, they were often qualified. Doctors in Nuremburg warned in 1572 that "brandy is more seriously damaging than other [drinks], especially to pregnant women and young working people, and causes many damaging illnesses and maladies on a daily basis."[20] Authorities throughout Europe began to try to regulate the production, sale, and consumption of spirits. In the interests of public health, the German city of Nuremburg in 1567 required brandy to be made only from "good, proper wine or wine lees."[21] Augsburg began to tax brandy as early as 1472, and various municipalities began to ban the sale of brandy on Sundays or during church services. Nuremberg did so in 1496 (and several times more in the 1500s, which suggests there were problems of compliance), as did Munich in 1506 and Augsburg in 1529. In Nuremberg, brandy could be sold on other days only from stalls in the marketplace, but in Augsburg it could legally be purchased from grocers or craftsmen in their shops or directly from the homes of distillers.[22]

In these and other German towns, brandy was surrounded by restrictions designed to prevent it from becoming a beverage that might be consumed daily in sociable circumstances, as wine and beer were. Laws prohibited citizens from sitting and drinking brandy where they bought it. Instead, customers could either stand and drink brandy where it was sold or take it home to consume it in private.[23] If they did drink it on the spot, they were forbidden to toast and drink to anyone's health, and the most that could be consumed on the premises was 1 *pfennig*'s (a penny's) worth.[24] Because a shot of brandy became a popular way to start the day, some German states limited brandy sales to workday mornings, unlike wine and beer, which could be sold and consumed throughout the day and evening.

The authorities were clearly anxious to limit spirits consumption, and they continually reminded consumers that it was essentially for therapeutic use rather than for recreational drinking. But officials also came under increasing pressure to relax restrictions. Distillers and brandy retailers in cities throughout Germany argued that they faced unfair competition from unregulated producers and sales in the countryside, that brandy was such a beneficial beverage that the authorities should encourage its availability rather than make it more difficult to obtain, and that as prices rose during the inflationary 1500s, 1 pfennig bought a negligible volume of brandy. The Augsburg city council responded by raising the limit to 2 pfennigs in 1580 and to 4 in 1614, and although it also agreed to permit customers to sit while drinking brandy, it perversely refused to allow them to consume food with it. The continuing special status attributed to brandy is highlighted by the 1614 warning that "brandy is not a drink to be taken immoderately, but only for strength or medicinal purposes."[25]

Attempts to limit consumption to small therapeutic doses proved futile, however, and production of spirits spread rapidly throughout Europe. The distilling industry, like religion, was one of the first beneficiaries of the invention of the printing press. From Gutenberg's marvel flowed a veritable stream of books that described the technique of distilling and lauded the value of aqua vitae. By 1525, books on distilling (and on brandy specifically) had been published in a variety of European languages, including French, German, Dutch, Italian, and English. Distilleries were constructed everywhere, and consumption undoubtedly kept pace with increasing production; but there are no useful statistics on either, because spirits were only sporadically subjected to taxation and their producers seem frequently to have evaded it.

By the seventeenth century, spirits were entrenched in European drinking cultures, and they were increasingly normalized, so that by the mid-1600s, policies on the manufacture and sale of spirits were similar to those imposed on beer and wine. Guilds of distillers had been established, and duties were levied on their products. In Augsburg the last prosecution for illicitly producing spirits for sale (in this case it was distilled rye) was brought in 1643, even though the law remained on the books for some decades afterward. The English distilling industry took off, and by 1621, when the London Company of Distillers was founded, some 200 distillers were producing "Aqua Vitae, Aqua Composita and other strong and hott waters." Other stills made alcohol from substances as varied as wine lees (an early grappa), beer dregs, and rotten fruit.[26]

One of the most important developments in the history of distilling was the birth of major concentrations in the southwest of France. The first was Armagnac, which began to develop as early as the 1300s, but the second, in the Charente region north of Bordeaux, became far more important in commercial terms. Still the center of French brandy production (and the region that includes Cognac, the district that gave its name to a premium brandy), Charente possessed two vital resources: vineyards that produced large volumes of white wine and forests that provided fuel for the distillery fires. Dutch entrepreneurs began to establish stills in the 1620s, and before long they were turning out unprecedented volumes of brandy. In the mid-1640s, England was importing about 200,000 gallons of brandy from Charente each year; by 1675, imports had risen to a million gallons, and by 1689 that figure had doubled.[27]

Figures like these suggest that the volume of spirits on European markets must have risen markedly during the seventeenth century. In 1677 the Paris police claimed that "crooks, vagabonds and other evil people" were using brandy to commit the "evil deeds," thefts, and other crimes that supported their lives of "libertinage and debauchery." They would "make their way every evening at dusk to whatever quarters they desire at some brandy seller's as a meeting place from which after having drunk an excess of brandy . . . they depart furious at all hours of the night causing great disorder and obstructing public safety." The police forbade brandy- and liquor-sellers to admit anyone after 4:00 PM between October 1 and the end of May, when the days were short and darkness fell early.[28]

But the reservations expressed about brandy paled against the anxiety provoked by grain-based spirits when they began to enter mainstream European drinking cultures in the early 1600s. These spirits included gin, a Dutch beverage distilled from grain and flavored with juniper berries, and whiskey, which was made from barley.[29] Gin and whiskey attracted suspicion because even though they were made by the now-familiar process of distillation, they were relative newcomers to the range of commercial beverages, and their merits and dangers were unknown. In 1609, King James VI of Scotland blamed the state of his rebellious subjects on the Southern Isles on whiskey and wine: "One of the chief causes of the great poverty of the Isles, and of the cruelty and inhuman barbarity practiced in their feuds, was their inordinate love of strong wines and aquavite."[30] But whiskey was clearly more problematic, as James allowed them to make as much whiskey as they needed for use by their families but banned the importation of any more. (Lords and "wealthy gentlemen" were exempted.)

As different as they were from each other, grain spirits and brandy traveled similar paths in terms of regulation from 1500 to 1700. They were first defined as prescribed medicines. In 1505, for example, the Scottish whiskey trade was placed under the control of the Royal College of Surgeons in Edinburgh.[31] Next they were retailed under restrictive conditions, on the understanding that they were beneficial to health but that their consumption for pleasure alone needed to be controlled. Finally, as the spirits entered the world of recreational consumption, the restrictive regulations were repealed or simply fell into disuse, and the authorities realized that greater benefits were to be gained by taxing them. The Dutch imposed taxes on spirits in the early 1600s; they were followed by the English in 1643 and by the Scots a year later. When Scotland and England formed a union in 1707, the common excise rate was 1 penny per gallon of spirits.[32]

Rum had a different history. Made by distilling fermented molasses and the waste products from sugar-making, it was first produced in British and French colonies in the Caribbean in early seventeenth century, although there are ambiguous references as early as 1552.[33] (There are also earlier examples of fermented sugarcane juice in China and India.) Rum quickly became a popular drink among European colonists and indigenous populations in the Caribbean region. It was attributed a wide range of medicinal properties—such as relieving fevers by using "fire to drive out fire"—and was valued for its calories.[34] It also found a niche market in European navies and merchant fleets. Rum was added to barrels of water as a preservative, and it was the only alcohol that could be taken onboard ships on the American side of the

Atlantic. The Royal (British) Navy began to provide sailors with a daily measure of rum as early as 1655 (the practice continued until 1970), and rum soon became identified as a seaman's drink. Although rum was imported in small volumes to England (where it was popular among seamen in port towns), it remained marginal because the costs of shipping it across the Atlantic generally made it much more expensive than brandy and locally made grain spirits. It did, however, became an important part of the drinking culture of North Americans in the seventeenth and eighteenth centuries, to the point that a number of rum distilleries (using molasses imported from the Caribbean) were founded in the American colonies.

The other main distilled alcoholic beverage was vodka, which was first produced in the broad region now occupied by Russia, Poland, Belarus, and Ukraine. The first producers were probably monks who distilled cereal-based beverages (usually from rye) for medicinal uses (as in the rest of Europe), either to be consumed by patients or applied externally. By the sixteenth century, however, improvements that included adding flavorings (such as honey, spices, and herbs) made vodka a popular beverage. It is a matter of contention whether Poles or Russians first developed vodka; the word, which means "little water," could be derived from either language. There are references to a distilled spirit (called *gorzalka*, derived from the Polish word for "to burn") in Poland in the eleventh century, but it is not clear whether this can be thought of as vodka.[35] Whether or not Poland was the birthplace of vodka, a Polish vodka industry was in place by the end of the seventeenth century. By 1620, a number of cities were licensing distillers, and in that year Gdansk alone issued sixty-eight licenses. In 1693, a Cracow distiller published recipes for vodka and also showed that it could be made from potatoes as well as cereals.

In Russia, however, the tsars established a series of monopolies over vodka as early as the 1470s and used it as a source of revenue and as a means of political and social control.[36] In the 1500s, Ivan IV created a new privileged class and gave its members exclusive access to vodka in return for their loyalty. Peter the Great continued to dole out vodka to his supporters and used it to manipulate diplomats and guests. In 1695, he created the Drunken Council of Fools and Jesters, which required its members (including himself) "to get drunk every day and never go to bed sober."[37] This early participation of the Russian state in vodka production set the tone for centuries, as successive imperial administrations and their successor Soviet regimes relied on revenues from alcohol.

The reception of distilled alcoholic beverages in seventeenth-century Europe led to a debate on their merits, relative not only to one another but also to beer and wine, the fermented drinks of long standing. Commentators also discussed tea, coffee, and chocolate—which were introduced to the diets of better-off Europeans in the 1600s—in these contexts, and it is worth noting that they made no sharp distinction between alcoholic and nonalcoholic beverages. Although caffeine was not identified by name as the active ingredient in the new hot drinks, they were recognized as having stimulating effects that were not dissimilar to alcohol's. Tea, wine, coffee, and beer do not seem easily interchangeable as beverages now, but some seventeenth-century writers saw nothing incongruous in arguing that tea was preferable to wine because it conveyed all the benefits of wine without the disadvantages of intoxication and a hangover. As for coffee, many writers roundly condemned its consumption as vehemently as they did abuse of alcohol. One French doctor pointed out that coffee and chocolate were "at first us'd only as Medicines while they continued unpleasant, but since they were made delicious with Sugar they are become Poison." He pointed out that coffee caused insomnia, reduced the appetite, stunted children's growth, and "renders both Sexes less fruitful." In the last context he reported that one woman who saw a horse being gelded commented, "They need only give him Coffee to moderate the Passion he had for Mares."[38]

The discussion on alcoholic and nonalcoholic drinks encompassed the most widely available beverage of all: water. There was disagreement on the value of water, in itself and in comparison to the other beverages. A French doctor proclaimed water "the wholesomest of all Drinks . . . a curb to the excessive Heat that consumes us" and argued that "those who drink nothing but Water, are ordinarily more healthful and live longer, than those that drink wine. Since Noah, who was the first that drank . . . [wine], the Life of Man is become more short, and Diseases more frequent than before."[39]

This minority voice was drowned out by most others, among them that of Richard Short, one of England's noted seventeenth-century physicians. Short agreed that water was appropriate for people who lived in hot climates (such as "Africa and Libya"), but he insisted that it was dangerous for the inhabitants of cool-climate countries like England, where "many have endangered themselves, many have lost their lives by drinking of water." Water destroyed their natural heat and caused all kinds of ailments, especially in old men whose bodies were already growing cold and needed to be heated. Dr. Short was alarmed at "the new mode of drinking it" and described drinking water after dinner as "growne much in use now a dayes."

Short's comment might have exaggerated the trend, but it raises the possibility that water was being added more frequently to the range of beverages on the seventeenth-century table. While it is almost certainly the case that the poor drank water, much of it undoubtedly of poor quality, Short seems to have been thinking more of the middle and upper classes. He conceded that one might take a little water after having wine with dinner because the effect was simply to dilute the wine, but he described water after beer as "madnesse."

Short did not suggest that spirits were the best drinks but recommended wine ("absolutely better than water") and beer ("sweet and healthful and affords good nourishment"). While he gave sound medical reasons why wine and beer were more beneficial and more easily digested, Short buttressed the case against water by appealing to gastronomic tradition: "We are not accustomed to drink water in our country. . . . We ought not to change custom when 'tis ancient. . . . A National custom in diet is rational." Short left his readers in no doubt as to his opinion of water-drinking: "I see no reason but that we may as well give Narcoticks, that is, stupefying things, as poppy, and opium, as well as water in our country."[40]

The debate on water reminds us that alcohol was frequently a safer beverage than the available water. Short did not discuss pollution as such, although he wrote that water from wells was worse than water taken from rivers. But his contemporaries did express concern about drinking water. One seventeenth-century proposal for supplying London with "good and cleare strong water" noted that the prevailing supply was foul and muddy and "not fit for many uses." It called for the construction of a closed aqueduct to provide the city with "excellent good water, fit for any use, either for dressing of meate, for washing, baking, brewing, or drinking."[41] Maybe it is significant that drinking was placed last in this list of purposes to which clean water would be put.

The same period also threw up proposals for desalinizing (removing the salt from) seawater, a process that would have been invaluable for the navy and merchant marine. Long voyages at sea were becoming more and more common as Europeans explored the rest of the world; established settlements in the Americas, Africa, and Asia; and fished as far from Europe as the cod-rich seas off the coast of Newfoundland. Such voyages raised problems of carrying enough drinking water for crews and ensuring that the water did not foul in the wooden barrels used for holding it. As spirits became more widely available, they were often added to barrels of water to slow spoilage, but desalinization was a more attractive alternative.

One invention that was widely advertised in the seventeenth century promised to produce 90 gallons of fresh water from salt water every twenty-four hours. Its backers argued that this would be not only a boon to sailors but also a great help to communities "that lye near the Sea, and either want [lack] good, or have Brackish Water." The proposal to desalinize had the support of twenty-three doctors, including Richard Short, whose strictures against water-drinking we have already noted. Presumably, although water was dangerous to the English in England, it could be safely consumed by English seamen when they sailed in the warmer climates off Africa and in the West Indies. The doctors who endorsed the desalinization process pointed out that the "brackish Waters of the Sea-coast, and the putrifying Waters made use of at Sea, might probably have afforded them a great number of Patients, which may hereafter be lessened by the use of the wholesome Water."[42]

Proposals such as this, designed to provide safe drinking water, are reminders that it is wrong to think that Europeans drank only alcoholic beverages. Yet if there was concern about the quality of water, there was a lot more anxiety about the availability and consumption of vast volumes of alcohol. Drunkenness was said to be commonplace in England in the late seventeenth and early eighteenth centuries. Beer production appears to have peaked in England in this period, and one commentator predicted that before long the whole kingdom would be "nothing but a Brewery or Distillery, and the Inhabitants all Drunkards."[43]

But spirits caused the greatest headaches—not only to many consumers but also to those worried by what they saw as rising consumption. Gin was said to be much stronger than brandy and to be, as such, a much "hotter" beverage that could "overheat" its consumers. If excessive brandy-drinking in the morning led to the abuse of wine and beer in the afternoon, the risk was that much greater when grain spirits were involved. Warnings about the potential dangers of spirits seemed to be justified by a number of moral panics in the early eighteenth century, the most dramatic and best-documented of which was the "gin-craze" that was believed to have taken hold in parts of England between 1700 and 1750. ("Gin" was a generic term for a wide range of distilled spirits, and it was not specifically the juniper-flavored spirit that was at issue here, but all grain-based alcohol.)

It is difficult to separate reality from rhetoric when looking at this phenomenon.[44] It was probably not nearly as serious as it was portrayed in the most alarming accounts of contemporaries and some later historians. The 1925 description by the historian Dorothy George that "it would be hardly possible to exaggerate the cumulatively disastrous effects of the orgy of spirit-drinking between 1720 and 1751" seems itself to be an exaggeration.[45] And contemporary accounts of widespread ruin and death as a result of gin-drinking are surely examples of moral panic based on a fragile interpretation of verifiable events. Be that as it may, it is clear that the production and con-sumption of spirits did increase dramatically in some parts of England (espe-cially in London) during the first half of the eighteenth century, and that this must have had implications for the health and well-being of many individuals and for the social order more generally. It is difficult, however, to assess the scale of the phenomenon and its consequences and to understand why they provoked a moral panic.

The popularity of gin in England was kick-started by a shortage of brandy, which by the late seventeenth century was being imported from France in substantial volumes: 2 million gallons a year by the 1680s. These imports were interrupted when William of Orange, a Protestant Dutch prince, be-came king of England in 1688, causing a rupture in England's relations with the aggressively Catholic king of France, Louis XIV. Not only were imports of French brandy drastically reduced for a number of years (what did arrive was subjected to punitive duties), but the accession of William popularized gin, a beverage with Dutch origins. At first, gin was imported from the Netherlands, but before long, English distillers were producing it, or adulterated versions of it, in large quantities.

Between 1690 and the 1720s, the English parliament encouraged the pro-duction of spirits, not because it was necessarily considered a good thing in its own right, but to reduce demand for wine and brandy from the Catholic French. Gin became, effectively, a patriotic drink, even if it did not displace beer as England's national beverage. Parliament allowed virtually anyone to distill spirits commercially as long as they paid the required duties of 2 pence a gallon—a low rate that went unchanged when, in 1710, the taxes applied to beer were increased by up to 100 percent. Although restrictions on dis-tilling were occasionally imposed before the 1720s, they reflected concern about grain shortages and were intended to ensure that food supplies were not compromised by alcohol production. As it happened, the period from 1715 to 1755 saw a run of good harvests (there were only three poor years), so that cereal for distilling was plentiful and relatively inexpensive.

The deregulation of distilling led to the establishment of an estimated 1,500 stills in and around London by 1736. Most (perhaps three-quarters of them) were small-scale distillers using equipment worth less than £100, and only perhaps one in six owned equipment valued at more than £1,000.[46] The distilling industry thus differed markedly from brewing, which by the early 1700s was becoming dominated by fewer and fewer large-scale companies.

Not only was the production of spirits taxed at a lower rate than brewing, but there were benefits to selling spirits. Retailers of spirits did not have to buy licenses, and because they did not sell food or offer accommodations, they needed more modest premises than alehouse keepers. Another incentive was added in 1720 when anyone who distilled and retailed spirits was exempted from the obligation of billeting troops—a detested burden imposed on innkeepers, stable keepers, and others. Under these favorable commercial conditions, and with a buoyant market, the number of dramshops (as small retailers of spirits were known) flourished. According to contemporary reports, which might or might not be accurate, there were more than 8,500 dramshops in London by 1725, or one dramshop for every eleven houses.[47] In poorer districts like Westminster and St. Giles, they were said to account for one in every four houses. This is a staggering density, and it seems possible that the number of dramshops was exaggerated; it is hard to see how a retailer could stay in business selling to customers from ten houses, on average, let alone three houses.

These figures were collected and made known at the time, and accurate or not, they can only have fueled anxiety about what appeared to be an insatiable appetite for spirits. Taxed production of gin rose from half a million gallons in 1688 to 2.5 million gallons in 1720,[48] and to that must be added an unknown volume of spirits produced illicitly and therefore not recorded in the excise figures. But the duty on spirits was so low that even when it was applied, spirits remained an attractive addition or alternative to ale and beer in the all-important consumer calculation of cost to alcoholic strength. The flavor of the spirits might have added to their attractiveness. Most were made from corn, but they were generally flavored—sometimes with juniper berries (like the original Dutch gin) and sometimes by such additives as coriander, sulfuric acid, and oil of turpentine—and often sweetened with sugar. The sweetness is thought to have contributed to gin's appeal to women in particular, although the arrival of sugar in Europe in the 1600s had generally pushed sensory preferences toward sweetness, and men frequently sweetened their wine with sugar.

Conditions favored the English spirits industry in the early 1700s, and its very success was the problem, for by the 1720s, levels of spirits consumption and their perceived effects on health and social order rang alarm bells among the upper and middle classes. The 2.5 million gallons legally produced in 1720 were enough to provide every Londoner each year with 3 gallons of spirits, the equivalent of fifteen standard modern bottles—enough for every man, woman, and child in the metropolis to have an ounce a day.[49] But as we have noted before, the formula "man, woman, and child" is a misleading abstraction when expressing the per capita consumption of alcohol in Western societies, because children historically drank far less than adults, and women consumed less than men.

Yet "man, woman and child" has a particular resonance in the context of the eighteenth-century English gin-craze because much of the anxiety rested on the belief that gin was being abused not only by men, the traditional consumers to excess, but also—and especially—by women and children. Gin was called "Mother Gin" and "Mother Geneva," names that linked it to women and children. Mothers who guzzled gin were said to feed it to their older children to stop their complaining about being hungry, and indirectly to their infants as they breast-fed. Front and center in the most famous pictorial representation of the gin-craze, William Hogarth's etching *Gin Lane*, is a nursing woman, her breasts exposed. She is sprawled on a flight of steps and so insensibly drunk that she is unaware that her infant has slipped from her arms and is falling headfirst to the street below.

Hogarth, who produced *Gin Lane* in 1751 as the gin-craze drew to a close, must have been inspired by the many written works of the period that vividly described the effects of gin-drinking on women and their families. One writer noted that if "child-bearing Women are habituated to strong inflaming Liquors, the little Embrios must and will have a share" that would cause them to develop "a Love of Strong Liquors before they can call for them, or even see them."[50] He added that many mothers and nurses fed their children gin and that the demand for milk had fallen. Another writer described the children of the gin-drinking mother in these words: "One is bandy-legg'd, another hump-back'd, another goggle-ey'd, another with a Monkey's Face, and all of them wearing some visible Mark of their Mother's Folly."[51]

As monstrous as were the children described here, they were at least the survivors of their mothers' alcoholic habits. Many antispirits writers pointed out that these deadly beverages led to a declining birthrate and rising death rate; Hogarth's representation of the ravages of gin included a number of images of death. The concern expressed here about mortality rates and children's health was not confined to England, for all European states had an interest in fostering robust demographic growth for political, economic, and military purposes. The commentator who so vividly described the children suffering from what would later be called fetal alcohol syndrome described them ironically as "a hopeful Progeny to furnish the succeeding Generation with Patriots and Defenders of their Country, and Supporters of the British Glory, which their Forefathers have acquired both by Sea and Land!"[52]

An array of other arguments was ranged against the consumption of spirits. One was that drinking gin led to a dramatic loss of appetite for nourishing food, although scenarios of an undernourished underclass seem to have been less alarming than the prospect of declining profits for food producers and merchants. Some contemporary accounts told of butchers throwing away meat or feeding it to dogs because no one was buying it. Others reported dairy farmers pouring unsold milk into the sewers. Gin was said to depress the appetite so severely that it reduced the demand for bread, the staple of the eighteenth-century working-class diet. One pamphleteer argued that parliament should step in and raise the price of gin so as to return the poor to "the natural taste of bread, meat and beer."[53] Gin was also socially disruptive in the most banal sense. Not only did it interfere with family stability and the prosperity and health of the population, but it also led to crime and immorality; men and women were said to be driven to theft, prostitution, and murder to support their drinking habits. "Hence follow desperate Attacks, Highway and street robberies, attended sometimes with the most Cruel and unheard of Murthers."[54]

Against the arguments for prohibiting or restricting distilling and the sale of spirits were more modest proposals based on the assumption that the scenarios of social collapse were exaggerated. Some writers in this vein, perhaps with interests in the gin industry, insisted that beer-drinkers were just as unruly as gin-drinkers and that, as far as immorality went, dramshops paled against the excesses to be found in alehouses. They argued that the distilling industry contributed to the prosperity of grain-growers and that others benefited in turn, among them implement-makers, carters, and the seamen who manned the coastal vessels that carried the grain to London. The government also had an interest in the alcohol business: it is estimated that by 1730, a quarter of England's state taxes came from alcohol of all types.

The preoccupation with gin consumption and its social effects continued from the 1720s until the 1750s and resulted in a series of laws that attempted in different ways to deal with the problem. The first act, passed in 1729, attacked the retail end by raising the duty on spirits thirtyfold, from 2 pence to 5 shillings; imposing a licensing fee of £20 a year; and setting a fine of £10 for hawking gin in the streets. But this law, the result of lobbying by London judges and doctors, remained in force only four years before it was repealed because of widespread evasion that the authorities were powerless to stop. The volume of spirits produced legally continued to rise, from 2.5 million gallons in 1720 to 3.8 million in 1730. Once the 1729 law was repealed, the volume shot up, reaching 6.4 million gallons in 1735. Illicit spirits accounted for an unknown quantity on top of these taxed totals.

Soon after the repeal of the 1729 act, another campaign, led by judges and religious organizations, claimed that drunkenness and criminality were increasing and that spirits were to blame. The Grand Jury of the County of Middlesex reported that the poor "are intoxicated and get Drunk and are frequently seen in our Streets in such a condition abhorrent to reasonable creatures . . . [and] are thereby rendered useless to themselves as well as to the Community."[55] Such representations led to the passage of a 1736 law that imposed a licensing fee of £50 a year. At this point the defenders of gin again reacted, and there were threats of riots in the streets of London. As unworkable as the 1929 act, this one was abandoned after three years, and the manufacture, sale, and consumption of spirits were effectively unrestrained. Consumption seems to have peaked in 1743, when 8.2 million gallons were taxed. That was more than a gallon per head for the entire English population, but if we take into account illicit production, variations in consumption by gender and age, and the fact that spirits-drinking was concentrated in London and, to a lesser extent, in a few other ports and industrial centers, adult men must have had access to up to 10 gallons of spirits a year, about a modern bottle per week. Clearly there was enough in circulation for a substantial minority of male adults to drink considerable amounts on a regular basis.

But spirits production declined from the mid-1740s, and when another act was passed in 1751, the so-called craze was already ebbing. The 1751 regulations forbade distillers to sell their own product and imposed a modest licensing fee of £2 on retailers. It is easier to understand why spirits became so attractive in the first place than why they lost their appeal. Perhaps the series of laws, as ineffective as they were, dislocated production and made supplies unreliable. Perhaps drinkers moved back to beer, especially to the new, stronger "porter" style. In the later 1750s, too, the thirty-year series of good cereal harvests came to an end; the 1757, 1759, and 1760 harvests were so poor that distilling was banned entirely in order to protect food supplies. By then, spirits production was already in decline, in any case, and the ban simply intensified an existing trend.

The gin panic brought to the surface some of the relationships of alcohol to power. This was the first attempt in Europe to use the full force of the state to control the consumption of alcohol; sixteenth-century regulations against drinking and sitting, or against toasting and treating, paled against the aims of the English parliament to remove a popular alcoholic drink from the market. Because there were no precedents to this scale of regulation, mistakes were made. The first act, of 1729, which raised the cost of retail licenses, was probably intended to drive many retailers out of business and to force the rest to pass on the cost of the license to their customers, thus depressing demand. Parliament subsequently focused on production rather than retailing. Even so, the government was halfhearted in its application of the laws. Mindful of the tax revenues that a legally operating drinks industry provided, it had no wish to see distilling and gin retailing driven underground.

The battle waged against gin was also a class and gender war. The middle and upper classes portrayed the industry as one largely maintained by and for the indigent, unruly, and dangerous popular classes. Gin shops were described as squalid hangouts for the dregs of society, and dram-sellers were considered shiftless at best, criminal at worst. The links between spirits and morals were carefully drawn in class terms. Better-off citizens were portrayed as able to enjoy their beer, wine, brandy, and cordials (flavored spirits) responsibly, but the lower classes were shown as able neither to afford their coarse liquor without condemning their families to destitution at best or to death at worst, nor to drink it without doing so to excess and driving their families into immorality and crime. The stress on the particular evils of women's drinking echoed a contemporary reassertion of the belief that women were destined by nature to be mothers and that they bore particular responsibilities toward their families. Excessive drinking by women was not only deplorable but unnatural.

But affordable gin must have been attractive to many of London's workers as a pleasant experience in a life that offered few. Many of the working poor were recent migrants from the country, used to drinking festivities reined in by informal social mechanisms that were either absent from or less effective in the urban environment. It is believable that the better-off interpreted any widespread public intoxication as evidence of social disorder and collapse. The critical point might well have been the public character of working-class drinking; laws have historically penalized public drunkenness rather than domestic intoxication. The critics of London's gin-drinking poor were anything but abstemious, but they could drink themselves insensible in private. A contemporary poem drew attention to the double standard:

> Now greedy Great Ones, their inferiors Grind
> And Vice monopolize of ev'ry kind.
> In costly Riot they may waste the Wealth,
> The Poor must rest content with Temp'rate Health.[56]

Although much attention was directed to the dramshops as places of disorder and crime, the bulk of spirits retailers appear to have been drawn from the same social groups as other food and drink retailers, and their premises were no different from those of other small-scale traders.[57] But in some respects the gin trade was different from others, and again there was a link to women.

It seems likely, first, that women were more highly represented as gin-sellers in England, just as women were prominent as distillers throughout Europe. About a quarter of licensed sellers and perhaps a third of unlicensed traders were women, and a disproportionate three-quarters of gin-sellers jailed in 1738–39 because they could not pay the £10 fine were women. Although it is possible that the authorities targeted women traders, these figures suggest that women were more highly represented in the gin trade than among, say, food-sellers (where they made up 10 to 15 percent), and that they were especially common at the poorer levels, probably among street sellers who offered gin from stalls or barrows.[58] This would have reinforced the feminization of the gin panic.

It is possible, too, that women patronized dramshops more frequently than they did alehouses. Women rarely visited alehouses, which were often resolutely masculine in their patronage, but they might well have drunk spirits at a dramshop run by a woman. Gin was often identified as a women's drink, especially when it was sweetened, and the fact that many dram-sellers were women might have made dramshops new places of female sociability, historically a source of anxiety for men. The recurrent association of gin and women in the antispirits campaigns could have reflected hostility to the presence of women in public places as much as to the social implications of lower-class drinking.

Viewed from the underside of society, the attempts to regulate gin—which meant making it more expensive and difficult to obtain—turned gin-drinking into a form of cultural resistance. The poor seem to have had allies in some magistrates and commissioners of excise who turned a blind eye to many infractions of the laws and, in some cases, even refunded fines that had been paid.[59] Distillers mocked the impotence of the laws by producing beverages called "parliament brandy" and "parliament gin." Disturbances greeted each Gin Act, and when the particularly draconian 1736 act was passed, there were mock funerals in London to mark the death of "Madame Geneva." Quite possibly, the attempts to suppress gin increased its appeal, and gin became a field of class conflict.

The gin-craze was a short period in the longer history of distilled spirits and of alcohol more generally, but it vividly illustrated issues that often fermented below the surface. The most notable aspect of it was the attempt to deal rigorously with what some of the upper classes saw as a dangerous misuse of alcohol that threatened to undermine the social order. The scope of the Gin Acts in trying to reduce consumption by forcing poor retailers to close down and by raising the price of gin to consumers was unprecedented.

The acts failed because of popular resistance and lack of enforcement mechanisms, and also because the government both relied on tax revenue from alcohol and was nervous about the public disorder that might erupt if serious attempts were made to cut off access to cheap gin. The Gin Acts were not an attempt to impose prohibition, but they resembled some twentieth-century efforts to reduce alcohol production and consumption.

It was no accident that the attempts at control in the 1700s centered on distilled spirits. Their entry into mainstream markets from the early 1500s had provoked anxiety and a range of ad hoc regulations. Even though they became normalized in most jurisdictions, in the sense that they became subjected to regulations similar to or the same as those for beer and wine, they continued to be subjects of social anxiety. When the antialcohol movements emerged in the 1800s, their prime targets were distilled spirits. This is a reminder that when we speak of the history of alcohol, we constantly need to bear in mind that the various alcoholic beverages often had distinct histories.

European Alcohol in Contact
1500-1700

NON-EUROPEAN WORLDS

Alcoholic beverages did not originate in Europe, but in the thousand years up to 1500, they became entrenched in European popular and elite cultures to an extent that was not only unprecedented but also unparalleled anywhere else in the contemporary world. Even though large numbers of Europeans must (for simple financial reasons) have drunk only water on a daily basis, beer and wine had become so widely consumed in Europe by 1500 that we must consider them staples of the region's diet. When Europeans began systematically to contact, conquer, and colonize regions in the Americas, Africa, and Asia in the sixteenth and seventeenth centuries, alcohol was so integral to their material, social, and cultural lives that living without it was almost as inconceivable as living without bread.

When Europeans sailed the vast distances to the Americas, Africa, and Asia, they took alcohol as part of their subsistence supplies during the voyages that involved weeks and months at sea. Early explorers shared alcohol with the indigenous inhabitants they encountered, just as they used alcohol for hospitality purposes in Europe. Then, as contact with specific regions became more regular and European settlements were established, traders and settlers began to introduce their alcoholic beverages on a more regular basis to the indigenous populations of regions as disparate as Peru, New England, and India. They used alcohol as a medium of exchange to purchase everything from beaver pelts in North America and spices in south Asia to slaves in West Africa and sex everywhere. Eventually, as Europeans established permanent settlements, they planted vineyards, built breweries, and later constructed distilleries, making themselves self-sufficient in alcohol in many parts of the non-European world.

But the Europeans who settled far from their points of origin did not simply replicate the drinking patterns of the places they came from. Alcohol consumption has historically reflected more general social and cultural conditions, and these were often quite different in colonial contexts from those in Europe. Colonial populations were often (especially during early phases of settlement) composed largely of adult men, the heaviest-drinking demographic in Europe. This meant that per capita alcohol consumption in the colonies was higher than in Europe, where it was moderated by the presence of women and children, who drank much less. Indigenous populations that began to consume the European settlers' alcohol created their own patterns of consumption, and the interplay between the two drinking cultures frequently gave rise to problematic relationships.

But before these relationships developed, Europeans had to reach the far-flung destinations they would eventually turn into colonies. The importance of alcohol on long-distance voyages is well known. Crews expected regular, if modest, servings of alcohol, and alcohol lasted better than other beverages at sea. Barrels of beer, wine, and brandy were generally among the supplies of food and drink taken onboard to sustain the crew for weeks and months at a time. When the *Arbella* ferried Puritans from England to Massachusetts in 1630, it carried 10,000 gallons of wine, 42 tons of beer, 14 tons of water, and 12 gallons of brandy. On longer voyages that followed coastlines more closely than a transatlantic crossing, stops might be made to restock food and fresh water. But there were few, if any, opportunities to replenish alcohol supplies. Longer voyages necessitated more alcohol, and it is estimated that the Portuguese expedition to India in 1500 carried more than a quarter of a million liters of wine, and that the 1,200 men involved in the expedition drank about 1.2 liters of wine a day. Wine not only was a vital part of the crew's diet and helped sailors overcome their fears about sailing through unknown waters; it was also useful ballast for the ships, even though its effectiveness was reduced as it was consumed.[1]

Maintaining food in edible condition was often difficult, and keeping water safe and potable was no easier. Stored in wooden barrels, water fouled within weeks and took on unpleasant odors and flavors. In the late 1600s there were projects to construct desalinization plants onboard ships so that seawater could be made potable enough for drinking by crews. But effective and efficient desalinization plants were far off, and one way to preserve water in potable condition in the meantime was to add brandy to the water barrels.

The concentrated alcohol, even when diluted, killed some of the bacteria and slowed, if it did not prevent entirely, the spoilage of a ship's water supplies. Beer and wine were also taken onboard and served (often diluted) to the crew, but they could also spoil over time, especially when ships sailed through hot climates. Distilled spirits alone survived these voyages in good condition.

Very long voyages, such as those from Europe to Asia around Africa, posed particular problems. When, in the seventeenth century, the Dutch established a lucrative trade in spices with the Dutch East Indies (Indonesia), their ships were at sea for more than six months each way. These voyages taxed supplies onboard, and even though ships stopped at stations on the African and Indian coasts to take on food and water, alcohol provisions were stretched thin. The Dutch planted vines in their colony near what is now Cape Town—thus inaugurating the important South African wine industry—for the express purpose of providing wine for their ships at this halfway point. Jan van Riebeeck, a doctor, established the first vineyard in 1658, and the first wine was made the following year. Cape wine was consumed by the local settlers, taken onboard ships for consumption during voyages, and shipped for consumption by Dutch settlers in their Asian colonies—although these settlers complained that the quality was much lower than the European wines they received.[2]

Alcohol was by no means unknown to most of the populations with whom Europeans made contact in the sixteenth and seventeenth centuries. Van Riebeeck might have been the first person to make wine from grapes in sub-Saharan Africa, but peoples in many parts of Africa had long made low-alcohol beverages by fermenting such products as cereals, honey, fruit, sap from palm trees, and milk.[3] They were consumed at myriad ceremonies, such as marriages, and were used to mark social and economic transactions, as well as for ancestor worship. They were also served as a sign of hospitality: when the first Portuguese emissary visited the kingdom of Kongo in 1491, he was given palm wine.[4] Subsequent Portuguese visitors probably reciprocated sporadically with gifts of wine, and European alcohol began to reach southern African populations in a consistent way in the sixteenth and seventeenth centuries, when Portuguese explorers and traders deployed wine as a commercial medium of exchange. At this time, wine was an important Portuguese export product, and it had value to Africans, even though they had their own fermented beverages, because wine had a much higher alcohol content. The local cereal-based beer probably had about 2 percent alcohol; palm wine, 5 percent. But the wine imported from Portugal very likely had an alcohol content of

10 percent or more and was much more potent than the locally produced beverages.

Distilled spirits were much stronger, of course, and in the 1700s, volumes of rum and grain-based spirits began to flow into regions of Africa, and alcohol and firearms became the preferred commodities of exchange. Much of the grain-based alcohol originated in Hamburg, Europe's second-largest port after London. Some rum arrived on the west coast of Africa from New England, while distilleries were built in Liverpool, the English port, to produce gin specifically for export to Africa.[5]

Portuguese wine, much of it transshipped through the Canary Islands, played an important role in the slave trade from Angola to Brazil, starting from the mid-1500s. Violent disputes between indigenous and Portuguese slave parties led the governor of Luanda, the region at the heart of the Portuguese slave trade, to ban the transport of alcohol to the interior slave markets. But by then wine was established as a valued medium of exchange, and in some cases it was the main means of payment for slaves. The importance of wine was thrown into relief when the Dutch seized Luanda for several years in the 1640s. Although they found about 70,000 liters of wine, it was soon consumed or traded away, and the Dutch discovered that the indigenous slave dealers were unwilling to sell slaves without some payment in wine. They were forced to order wine from Spain.[6]

The Dutch were also active in the Caribbean region, where the Carib peoples of the Lesser Antilles (and the nearby regions of South America) produced a fermented drink from the root of the cassava (or manioc) plant.[7] Called variously *oüicou* and *perino*, it was made by Carib women who grated the cassava root, added water, and let it soak until it became a thick, brown, gravylike substance. It was then strained, and the moist flour was formed into cakes and baked. Women chewed the cakes and spat the masticated liquid into a container, where it fermented into a beverage with an alcohol level similar to beer's.[8]

Chewing introduces enzymes from saliva that transform the starches in the cassava root to sugar, which allows fermentation to occur, and this process both fascinated and disgusted Europeans—not least because they knew that the cassava root is extremely toxic, as it produces cyanide on contact with the human digestive system. One account from Barbados in the mid-1600s describes a drink "made of *cassavy* root, which I told you is a strong poison; and this they cause their old wives, who have a small remainder of teeth, to chaw and spit out into water. . . . This juyce in three or four hours will work [ferment] and purge itself of the poisonous quality." Some Europeans reported trying the drink, and a few found it "fine" and "delicate"; at least one noted that the flavor belied the "beastly Preparation" that produced it.[9] Charles Darwin described the practice in Tierra del Fuego as "disgusting."[10] But Europeans had no such qualms about *mobbie* (or *mabi*), an alcoholic drink made by the Carib from sweet potatoes, and it became popular among whites until the eighteenth century.[11]

When the Spanish conquistadores invaded Central and South America, they brought wine with them and were continually reprovisioned, but they soon set about planting vines to make themselves independent of supplies from Spain that must often have arrived in poor condition. But the indigenous peoples they encountered already knew various kinds of alcohol, made from the raw materials readily available to them. In preconquest Mayan society, public ceremonies were accompanied by the drinking of *balche*, a beverage with strong religious associations that was made from fermented honey and tree bark. It was low in alcohol, so considerable quantities had to be consumed before anyone would get drunk on it.[12] But public intoxication did occur, and it was often followed by ritualized violence that is said to have reinforced rather than disturbed the social order.[13]

In many Andean regions, people drank beer (called *chicha*) made from maize (as well as yucca and other fruit) as part of their daily diet and had possibly done so for more than a thousand years when the Spanish arrived. Maize beer was part of the diet of the Inca, who also used it on ritual and ceremonial occasions, such as funerals, when chicha was offered to the dead. It was produced by women in every community within the Inca empire but always under central control, and the state looked after its distribution to people employed on massive public projects such as roads, canals, and buildings. The Spanish were initially hostile to chicha and banned its production, but it was so embedded in the Inca economy as a medium of exchange that they soon abandoned this early prohibition policy.[14]

In Mexico, too, the Spanish encountered peoples who for thousands of years had consumed various fermented beverages. The best known is *pulque*, a milky beverage with an alcohol content of about 5 percent made from the fermented sap of the agave (or maguey) plant (but a different variety of agave than that used for making tequila). A big agave could yield 4 to 7 liters of sap a day and produce up to a thousand liters of pulque before it died. A plantation could thus produce considerable volumes of pulque. Pulque had dietary and health benefits (it is a rich source of vitamin B1) and might have played a role in reducing the incidence of dysentery and other diseases. It would also have been a safer drink when water supplies were polluted and a source of liquid where water supplies were scarce.[15] Even so, pulque must be consumed within a day or two of being made because it degrades quickly and takes on a strong, unpleasant odor. One Spanish account from 1552 suggested that the smell was worse that the stench given off by a dead dog.[16]

Pulque was not part of the daily diet of Mexico's peoples; but it was used in religious celebrations, and there are parallels between the cultural uses of pulque in Mexico and of wine in ancient Middle Eastern and Chinese cultures. The indigenous Mexicans had many wine gods, all known under the generic name Ometochtli (Two Rabbits). A Huaxtec (Aztec) account of the origins of pulque has a woman discover how to tap the agave for its sap, just as Babylonian and other ancient cultures stressed the roles of women in the discovery of wine. A story of the first pulque feast has all present being given only four cups so that no one would get drunk, except a Huaxtec chieftain who had five. Echoing the biblical story of Noah, who stripped naked after becoming intoxicated by wine, the Huaxtec leader is said to have become so drunk from pulque that he took off his clothes, so offending the others present that they decided to punish him.[17]

Although the Spanish were spectacularly successful in establishing wine production throughout Latin America in the sixteenth century, especially in Chile and Peru, viticulture failed in Mexico. Pulque retained its importance as a source of alcohol; indeed, it not only survived but became known as Mexico's national drink in the first half of the twentieth century. But the early colonial Spanish authorities became concerned when production increased and pulque, which was much less expensive than wine, became a regular drink not only of the indigenous peoples but also of poorer Spanish settlers. The authorities thought that simple, white pulque (*pulque blanco*) was not problematic, but that when mixed with herbs, roots, and other additives (*pulque mezclado*), its effects were extreme, bordering on what might be called hallucinogenic. Although the colonial authorities tried to discover what the additives were, they only came up with an unwieldy list that included orange peel, the root of various trees, peppers, meat, and animal excrement.[18] As early as 1529, only ten years after Spanish settlement began, edicts were issued against mixing pulque with other substances, but unadulterated pulque was freely produced, sold, and consumed. By the late 1500s, the church and secular authorities were expressing alarm at increased consumption,[19] and in 1608 the Spanish viceroy gave jurisdiction over pulque to the indigenous leaders. In 1648, a commission of judges was established to regulate the beverage.[20]

Tolerance of pulque was cemented by the 1650 decision to allow the colonial government to tax it and by the realization soon afterward that the revenues thus raised were considerable: according to a report sent to Spain in 1663, the pulque tax could raise as much as 150,000 pesos a year. The prospect of such fiscal benefits led to a new appreciation of the beverage. A report to the royal government drew attention to its "healthy and medicinal" properties and suggested that even when people abused it, the consumer, not the drink itself, was the problem. The report pointed out that if excess consumption were a ground for outlawing pulque, it could just as well be argued that wine should be banned. Still, there was some concern about the effects of pulque on the indigenous peoples, and the viceroy of Mexico was asked to report on whether it caused them "more drunkenness than wine" and led them into "public sins and other insults to the service of God."[21]

Pulque remained an issue between the Spanish government, which wanted the tax revenues that the drink brought in, and the Spanish viceroy in Mexico, who regarded *pulquerías* (the stands where pulque was sold and which could attract large crowds of drinkers) as sites of immorality and criminality. The colonial authorities blamed pulque for fueling the violence that led to the destruction of the royal palace and other government buildings in Mexico City in June 1692, even though the uprising reflected popular frustration with food shortages. The Spanish viceroy immediately banned the consumption of pulque in Mexico City, and ten days later he extended the ban to the entire colony. But two weeks after that, pulque was again legalized, as long as it was pulque blanco, unmixed with roots and herbs. One historian has drawn attention to the parallel between the duality of "good, healthy" pulque (pure pulque) and "bad, dangerous" pulque (mixed pulque), on one hand, and the desire to prevent the mixing of ethnic communities in the Spanish colony, on the other: three weeks after the uprising, the viceroy commissioned a proposal to divide Mexico City into separate Spanish and indigenous zones, the way it had originally been set out. The danger of mixing pulque became, then, a metaphor for the danger of mixing ethnic communities.[22]

But when the Spanish first conquered the Americas, they were far less interested in pulque than in fostering the production of wine. By the early 1500s, when the Spanish extended their empire down the west coast of South America, wine was consumed by all levels of the population of Spain. The expulsion of the Muslims had cleared the way for the recovery of Spanish viticulture and wine production, and consumption had risen. Most Spaniards were accustomed to drinking wine every day, so it is not surprising that when they settled in the Americas, one of their priorities was planting vineyards. In 1519, a royal instruction ordered that vine cuttings and rootstock should be sent on every ship bound for the New World, particularly in regions where water suitable for drinking was scarce.[23] Wine was also needed for religious purposes, and viticulture became closely associated with the Jesuit and other missions throughout Latin America. Even so, only the priest drank wine at communion at that time, so the volume of wine required for religious rituals was very small; the specific needs of the church cannot explain the vast amounts of wine that the Spanish American colonies were soon producing, and it was clearly far more a secular commodity than a religious one.

Although wine could be—and for some time was—shipped from Spain to the New World, doing so was not only expensive but also risky, because the wine was unstable and often arrived on the other side of the Atlantic in poor condition. Even so, Spanish producers saw the colonies as potentially lucrative markets for their wine, and they attempted to restrict wine production there. In 1595, under pressure from Spanish producers, Philip II forbade the planting of more grapevines, except by the Jesuit missions, in the American colonies. But his edict was largely ignored, and by then, in any case, the Spanish settlers and missions had firmly established viticulture throughout the region. The first vines in Latin America were planted in Mexico in the early 1520s, and vineyards were established in Peru by about 1540, in Chile in the 1540s, in Argentina in the 1550s, and in Bolivia and Colombia in the following decade. In short, viticulture was extended throughout much of the continent (and in many specific regions now known for quality wine production) within fifty years of the beginning of Spanish colonization. Compared to this, the millennia-long progress of viticulture from Mesopotamia to Egypt and then to Greece moved at a glacial pace.

The church took a pioneering role in promoting viticulture in many regions, and the skill of Jesuits and Augustinians in identifying suitable vineyard sites was important. But the authorities also encouraged secular participation in wine production. In 1524, Hernán Cortes, the commander of New Spain, ordered settlers in the district that was to become Mexico City to plant vines; any settler who had been granted land and indigenous laborers to work it was required to plant a thousand best-quality vines for every hundred indigenous people he owned. But the attempt to make wine in the area was futile because the climate was unsuitable. Northern Mexico was another matter, and by the end of the 1500s, wine was being produced near the current border with Texas. One winery established there, on land granted by King Philip II in 1597, is still in operation. The first vines in Baja California, close to the Pacific Ocean and now Mexico's main wine-producing region, were planted more than a century later, in the early 1700s.

Maintaining and extending the area in vines remained a preoccupation of the early colonial administrations, and soon Peru became the key wine-producing region in Latin America. Vines were first planted about 1540, and in 1567 an official visiting southern Peru called for the planting of more vines in a vineyard near Lake Titicaca. The aim—to guarantee a local supply of wine so as to free settlers from dependence on imports from Spain—was soon realized. Growing conditions in some Peruvian river valleys were so good that by the 1560s, only twenty years after the first vines were planted, there were 40,000 hectares of vineyards. One of the most important regions, the Moquegua Valley in the south of Peru, also benefited from proximity to silver-mining communities, which became important markets.[24] Peruvian wine and, later, brandy not only served local markets but were important commodities in trade with other regions of Latin America, and they became second in importance only to silver in the development of the Peruvian economy.[25]

The Peruvian wine industry hit a boom cycle in the late 1500s with growing demand for wine, and the number of wineries increased rapidly. Perhaps they increased too rapidly, for in the early seventeenth century a glut of wine depressed prices. Together with some natural disasters (a volcanic eruption in 1600 and an earthquake in 1604), the depression caused the industry to contract, although it expanded again in the eighteenth century when the growing popularity of brandy created renewed demand for grapes. By the late 1700s, a frenzy of planting had led to vineyards replacing other crops in the fertile Moquegua Valley, forcing the inhabitants to buy the beans, corn, wheat, and potatoes they had previously grown. By then the region was producing massive volumes of wine for distillation into brandy for export. In 1786 nearly 7 million liters of wine were produced for this purpose.[26]

The extension of grapevines and the production of massive volumes of wine throughout the Spanish colonies of Latin America in the 1500s were an inspiration and a model for the English when they began to colonize North America early in the following century. Apparently unaware of, or discounting the significance of, the vastly different climatic and other conditions that distinguished South from North America, the English planned to cultivate grapes on the eastern seaboard of North America and thus free England from dependence on France for its wine and brandy supplies. In the first permanent English settlement, Jamestown, in Virginia, there were attempts to grow grapes during the first two years of settlement, from 1607, but despite constant failures, the inhabitants came under regular pressure to make wine. In 1619 each householder was instructed to plant and maintain ten vines a year and to learn viticulture. The results must not have been impressive because three years later each household received, on the king's command, a manual on cultivating vines and making wine. The French author, who had never been to America, recommended using indigenous grapes; he suggested optimistically that those who followed his advice "may presently have wine in Virginia to drink."[27]

Further acts mandating the planting of vines in Virginia followed in 1623 and 1624, but as with Spanish attempts a century earlier to get settlers in Mexico City to grow vines, official policy foundered on climatic and other conditions. Vines imported to Virginia from Europe died from winter cold or from diseases they were not accustomed to. Meanwhile, wine made from indigenous grapes was rejected as having unattractive flavors. A few individuals claimed to have made excellent wine with native grapes, and some barrels of Virginia wine were sent to London in 1622 to demonstrate the colony's potential. But it spoiled en route and probably did more harm than good to the colony's prospects as a wine region. Only when tobacco became a successful crop in Virginia did the English lose interest in trying to make wine there.

Producing wine proved as elusive to other settlers in North America. Dutch colonists planted vineyards near New York in the 1640s, Swedish settlers did the same along the Delaware River, and Germans tried to cultivate vines for wine in Pennsylvania.[28] Later, in the 1680s, William Penn, after whom the state was named, vigorously supported viticulture and expressed the hope that his land would soon be producing "as good wine as any European countries of the same latitude do yield."[29] He planted Spanish and French vines in eastern Pennsylvania, but there are no records of the success of the wine. There are, however, records of Penn's purchases of French, Spanish, and Portuguese wines from an importer, and they probably speak loudly about the success of his own vineyards.

The Virginia settlers eventually turned to brewing beer using indigenous corn, but Dutch migrants in their New Amsterdam colony are generally credited with making the first European-style beer in America as early as 1613. Beer became the staple alcohol for Europeans in North America during the seventeenth century, as production of wine—the drink of the upper classes in northern Europe, where most of the migrants came from—seemed to pose an insurmountable challenge. When a group of English migrants, the Puritans, arrived in Plymouth Bay in 1621 onboard the *Mayflower*, they reported seeing "vines everywhere." These were the indigenous vines that were failing to make acceptable wine in Virginia at that time, but they caught the eyes of the Puritans, who undoubtedly imagined bountiful supplies of wine, and not only for communion.

The Puritans saw rivers and streams everywhere, too, but their English experience made them suspicious of drinking the local water. Having run out of beer, the first Plymouth settlers had to drink water for some time, but they did so reluctantly and only as a last resort. The irony was that the available water was (unlike much water in England) quite safe to drink, as the settlers discovered. William Wood wrote of it in 1635 that "there can be no better water in the world, yet dare I not prefer it before a good Beere, as some have done, but any man will choose it before bad Beere, Wheay, or Buttermilk. Those that drinke it be as healthfull, fresh and lustie, as they that drinke beere."[30] Living in Massachusetts, the Puritans seem to have been more fortunate than their compatriots in Virginia. As early as 1625, the water in Virginia was described as "at a flood verily salt, at a low tide full of slime and filth, which was the destruction of many of our men."[31] Not only were many Virginia wells contaminated by salt, but the warmer climate enabled bacterial growths that produced epidemics in 1657–59 and for much of the 1680s and 1690s.

Although drinking water ran against almost all medical advice in contemporary England, many Puritans clearly did so, perhaps on a regular basis. But for cultural and probably aesthetic and sensory reasons, they preferred alcohol, especially beer. Their ships carried substantial supplies. The *Mayflower* had provisions of beer and brandy; the *Talbot*, which arrived in 1628, offloaded 45 tuns (about 10,000 gallons) of beer, while the *Arbella*, which took Puritans to Boston in 1630, brought thousands of gallons of alcohol in the form of wine, beer, and brandy. Immigrants to Massachusetts, whose number increased dramatically during the 1630s, were advised to bring with them barley, hop roots, and copper kettles—the basic necessities of beer production. In the same decade, rye, barley, and wheat were planted, and many Massachusetts inhabitants became self-sufficient in beer by the mid-1630s.[32]

Most brewing was done by women in their kitchens, as it had been in England a century or two earlier. In 1656, women in the Chesapeake area were denounced for being too lazy to brew: "Beare is indeed in some places constantly drunken, in other some, nothing but Water or Milk and Water or Beverage; and that is where the good wives (if I may call them so) are negligent and idle; for it is not for want of Corn to make Malt with (for the Country affords enough) but because they are sloathful and careless."[33] In this respect, America represented an earlier stage of brewing organization than contemporary Europe, where much domestic brewing by women had been replaced by commercial brewing by men. But a 1637 law requiring a £100 license to brew beer for sale—far too steep for most women to afford—indicated that brewing in the American colonies would take the same direction. Additional regulations controlled the price and alcohol content of beer, but although they were repealed as unworkable within two years, they set the tone of the complex regulation of alcohol that would follow in British North America.

For a time after the 1637 rules were repealed, brewing in Massachusetts was unregulated, and it continued to fall to domestic brewsters (women brewers) who probably made a batch of beer every four or five days. Most was made for consumption within the household where it was brewed, but some was sold or bartered for goods as disparate as fish and millstones. When it was not drunk within the household where it was made, it might also be consumed in public, on festive occasions, at funerals, and at the completion of building projects. Knowing beer's nutritive value, women purchased it to drink during pregnancy and childbirth, and the elderly bought it to drink when they were ill. For the great part, however, brewing at this time was irregular and unorganized; beer was made simply when and where it was needed.

Beer was embraced by Puritans as a healthy beverage. "Puritanism" has become associated generically with an abhorrence of drinking and many expressions of sexuality, but while it is true that seventeenth-century Puritans opposed activities such as gambling, playing games, and dancing, they were not worried about moderate drinking for nutritional purposes; consuming alcoholic beverages on a daily basis was as acceptable as eating bread. The Puritans recognized the particular cultural and religious value of wine among the other alcoholic drinks available; but it did not travel well across the Atlantic, and sporadic attempts to make it from indigenous vines failed. One prominent preacher, Increase Mather, called wine "a good creature of God" but warned that no one should drink "a Cup of Wine more than is good for him."[34] The Puritans, boat-people who fled the Anglican religious settlement in England, were largely followers of John Calvin, who had imposed rigorous drinking laws on Geneva in the mid-1500s. Calvin approved of moderate drinking but drew a line at the point where consuming any form of alcohol became simply a social act for pleasure, when a drinker might easily slip over the line into drunkenness.

Drunkenness alone was sin enough, but it was compounded when it resulted in blasphemy, immorality, and violence. This was a mainstream attitude common to all Christian denominations, and it informed policies toward alcohol throughout the English colonies in America during the 1600s. But no authorities strove as hard to implement it as the Puritan leaders of Massachusetts. They believed the Catholic and Anglican churches in England had been lax in enforcing God's laws and had allowed alcohol to undermine morality and social order. They were determined to prevent the same thing from happening in Massachusetts, and throughout the seventeenth century, they fought a continuous battle against the excessive consumption of alcohol.

Many of their regulations focused on the providers of alcohol: taverns, inns, and "ordinaries," the American version of the alehouse, typically a room in a private dwelling where neighbors could drink homemade beer served by members of the family. Most ordinaries, which probably provided their owners with no more than a secondary income, were modest and spartan, but a few provided luxuries such as cloths on the tables, cushions on the chairs, and candles. One partial financial account from Essex County, Massachusetts, shows that a Samuel Bennett drank at Thomas Clark's ordinary nineteen times between June 1657 and September 1658 and downed 3 quarts of beer (at 2 pence a quart) on each occasion. Visiting once every three weeks cannot have made him a regular patron, and his spending all of 9 shillings and 6 pence in a fifteen-month period would not have made Thomas Clark rich. Other public drinking establishments in the colonies—inns and taverns— varied in their services. Some served food, some provided accommodations, and depending on the licensing rules in force, they served beer, wine, cider, and spirits.

All were regulated in some way. In the 1630s, laws specified how much owners could charge for meals and beer, how many nights a guest could stay in a tavern, and even the maximum time a patron could spend drinking in a tavern or ordinary: "ye space of halfe an houre."[35] As early as 1637, the General Court of Massachusetts expressed its horror at behavior in drinking establishments: "It hath appeared unto this Court, upon many said complaints, that much drunkenness, wast of the good creatures of God, mispence of precious time, & other disorders have frequently fallen out in the inns, & common victualling houses within this jurisdiction, whereby God is much dishonored, the profession of religion reproached, & the welfare of this commonwealth greatly impaired."[36] The magistrates' solution was to limit the price of all alcohol to a penny a quart, which effectively restricted sales to beer. Constables were urged to investigate and prosecute all suspected alcohol offenses.

For all that laws focused on drinking in taverns, much colonial drinking took place where alcohol (especially beer and cider, but also distilled spirits) was produced: in the home. In 1636 and 1654, Massachusetts law specified that only members of families (not strangers) were permitted to drink homemade alcohol, and they were forbidden to drink to excess. In 1675, Massachusetts established the office of tithingman—one for every ten or twelve families—whose responsibility was to report violations of alcohol laws in the colony's homes.[37] Because these "sober and discreet" men were appointed in open meetings, all the people under their surveillance knew who they were, so it is unlikely that they were very effective—although their very presence might well have been a deterrent to excessive drinking.

Massachusetts laws also regulated beer production. Brewing was forbidden on Sundays, and in 1651 brewers were required to make their beer from barley, not from the less expensive maize. Regulations stipulated the price of beer according to the amount of malt used; the higher the malt content, the higher the price. More stringent measures followed in the 1670s, when beverages with much higher alcohol levels became widely available. In 1672, three-quarters of Boston's ordinaries sold only beer, but by 1679, all sold beer and cider, two-thirds also sold wine, and half sold distilled spirits, in addition. There was also a steady growth in the number of liquor retailers, and they far outnumbered the ordinaries. In response to the widening availability of alcohol, a 1680 Massachusetts law limited the number of drinking places in each town. Boston, with a population of 4,500, was allocated only sixteen (ten inns and six wine taverns), a reduction of about half, plus "eight retaylors for wine & strong licquors out of doores."[38] Other major towns were permitted between two and six establishments, and smaller communities were allowed just one each. One result was the decline of small-scale brewing and the rise of fewer, larger, commercial breweries, each associated with an ordinary.

Massachusetts also set down guidelines for acceptable levels of drinking, just as many modern governments recommend maximum daily servings of alcohol. In 1645, the General Court declared that it was "excessive drinking of wine when above halfe a pinte is allowed at one time to one [person] to drinke," and that a fine of 2 shillings and 6 pence would be levied on anyone "for sitting idle, & continuing drinking above halfe an houre."[39] Later laws provided a fine of 5 shillings for drinking "at unseasonable times" or after 9:00 PM and set down penalties for alcohol-sellers who permitted patrons to drink excessively, for more than half an hour, or too late at night. Needless to say, gambling, playing games, and dancing were forbidden in taverns. The result was a complex of regulations surrounding the production, sale, and consumption of alcohol, all designed to prevent the excessive drinking that Massachusetts leaders thought so harmful to religion, morals, and social order.

The penalties for drunkenness were set out time and time again, which suggests that compliance was far from common, and there were ascending scales of punishments for recidivists. In the 1670s and 1680s, anyone who drank excessively was fined 3 shillings and 4 pence, while anyone found drunk was fined 10 shillings. Second and third offenses were punished by double and treble the fines, and anyone unable to pay was whipped "to the number of ten stripes" and could be put in the stocks for three hours. Anyone convicted of excessive drinking or drunkenness a fourth time was imprisoned until two people provided sureties for the offender's good behavior.[40]

Despite the anxiety about excessive drinking, access to alcohol was clearly a priority in the early settlement of America, so much so that when Georgia was established in 1733, each new settler was offered 44 gallons of beer.[41] At 2 quarts a day per person, that would have lasted one person about three months (if the beer remained drinkable that long), time enough to start brewing to satisfy their own needs. The plan was to encourage beer-drinking in the colony, but the governor's generosity went further and undermined the intention, for he also offered settlers 65 gallons of molasses, the raw material for rum. The settlers quickly fermented and then distilled the molasses, making themselves a much stronger alcohol that lasted much longer than beer in Georgia's climate.

Rum became popular in taverns in European and North American port towns that were frequented by crews on shore leave. Although it never gained much of a market in the main inland population centers of Britain and Europe, rum became a very popular drink throughout North America. Rum and molasses, as well as sugar, became key export commodities from the Caribbean to the North American colonies from the middle of the seventeenth century. Molasses was used for sweetening foods and for rum production at distilleries closer to markets in the American colonies, and sugar producers in the Caribbean were happy to export the raw material to North America, thereby saving themselves the cost and risks of making and shipping rum. By the end of the 1600s, there were numerous rum distilleries in the British colonies, especially in Massachusetts and Rhode Island.

Even after Americans began making whiskey from corn, rum was the preferred "strong drink" and the main alternative to beer until the American War of Independence disrupted the sugar trade with British colonies in the Caribbean. In this sense, the European (especially the British) settlers in North America established drinking patterns different from those they had left on the other side of the Atlantic. Beer was the most widely consumed alcohol in Britain and many of its widely scattered colonies, but distilled spirits—mainly rum—had a much higher profile in North America. The raw materials were readily available, and given the lower volume per unit of alcohol, it was much more easily shipped—a real advantage, when supplies needed to be transported by land to the remote communities that were established deeper and deeper in the interior of North America.

Not only did European settlers in North America diverge from European patterns of alcohol consumption; they introduced alcohol to the continent's indigenous peoples. Despite occasional references to beer made from birch bark, there is general agreement that fermentation was not known, even for limited ceremonial purposes, in native North American cultures before the arrival of Europeans. The exception was several tribes in the southwestern United States who made alcohol for religious purposes by fermenting cactus juice. Elsewhere on the continent, there were beverages containing caffeine and others having a stimulant effect. Although this effect can result from alcohol consumption, the peculiar series of effects of alcohol—including elation and risk-taking—were unknown before European contact. Native Americans had no words to describe alcohol, the kind of drinking it made possible, and the sensory effects it produced, and new words were introduced to their languages to denote them.[42]

Early European explorers gave Native Americans wine and brandy (as well as food, firearms, and other goods) for many reasons, sometimes as greetings and offerings, sometimes as trading commodities, and sometimes for other purposes. Europeans are said to have plied Native Americans with alcohol until they agreed to transactions they would not have made if they were sober.[43] In the early 1600s, English explorer Henry Hudson provided alcohol to the people he encountered "to find out if they had any treacherie in them"—presumably meaning that under the influence of alcohol they would reveal any plans to attack Hudson's party. The voyage's chronicler noted that when one of them became intoxicated, "it was strange to them, for they could not tell how to take it," reinforcing the belief that alcohol had been unknown to this population.[44]

Transactions involving alcohol between Europeans and Native Americans seem to have become increasingly common in the first half of the seventeenth century. As European settlement extended down the eastern seaboard of North America and inland, and as supplies of locally produced beer and rum became more plentiful, the indigenous populations had ready access to alcohol. It was supplied by explorers and merchants at remote trading posts to such an extent that, by the 1630s, exchange rates between alcohol and beaver skins had been formalized. In Maine, 4 pounds of skins could be exchanged for 7 gallons of brandy and spice, while 2 pounds of skins netted the hunters 6 gallons of mead.[45] Indigenous peoples also had access to alcohol in the heart of European settlements. Some bought alcohol directly from producers, such as women who made beer in their homes; some were given alcohol as payment for work they did for Europeans, while others occasionally drank alcohol alongside Europeans in town taverns.[46]

These increasingly common transactions aroused anxiety among the colonial authorities, and from the middle of the seventeenth century, one colony after another enacted laws forbidding the sale of alcohol to Native Americans. The Dutch in New Netherlands did so in 1643, and Connecticut followed suit in 1687.[47] There was a general belief that Native Americans could not hold their alcohol, that they frequently drank to a point of severe intoxication and often drank only to get drunk, and that their drunkenness created problems of social order. In 1684, a woman was charged with having provided alcohol to "an Indian Squaw." She pleaded in her defense that her husband was at sea, she was supporting small children, and "the Indian tempting me with Sixpence for my pains, I was willing to get a penny to relieve my Self and children, and so fell into this offence."[48]

It is clear that whatever the advantages Europeans got from these transactions, the native peoples themselves regarded the alcohol they received as a valuable commodity. It was not part of their daily diet, as Indians drank the potable water that was readily available in colonial America and drank other beverages for ceremonial purposes. Throughout the Southwest, Native Americans ritually consumed "black drink," a tea made from leaves of the yaupon holly tree, which contained caffeine and theobromine.[49] The rituals involved vomiting, either artificially induced or brought on by the volume of the beverage consumed while the drinker was fasting. After alcohol was introduced to Native American societies, it was not only consumed for the pleasure it gave but also integrated into hospitality ceremonies, marriages, ceremonial dances, and mourning rituals.[50] In short, Native Americans employed alcohol for as many and as varied purposes as Europeans did.

We should note that if alcohol was part of the daily diet of early European colonists, it was no longer because it was a safer beverage than the polluted water that was available, because North America offered plenty of potable water, at least in the colonial period. Rather, Europeans drank alcohol for cultural reasons: it was embedded in their daily diet and in the relationships of exchange and sociability they carried over from Europe, and alcohol gave them pleasure. In functional terms, then, both Europeans and Indians consumed alcohol for largely the same purposes: it gave individuals pleasure, marked cultural exchanges of many kinds, and could be a force for sociability, both within and between social and ethnic groups. It has also been suggested that Native Americans in the Northeast used alcohol for its ability to engender a dreamlike, spiritual state that had religious meanings, but this is a contested notion.[51] The major difference between the consumption patterns of the two populations was that alcohol was not integral to the daily diet of Native Americans, as it was among Europeans.

Despite the varied contexts of alcohol consumption by Native Americans, many of the contemporary European accounts of their drinking patterns focused on episodes of severe intoxication and of disorder and violence that were attributed to alcohol. There is some evidence that among the Iroquois, at least, offenses committed when the perpetrator was drunk were not punished, as intoxication was viewed as exculpatory. One historian writes that Iroquois men drank not for pleasure but to get drunk, such that they would only start drinking if there was enough alcohol to ensure intoxication. Once they were intoxicated, they often destroyed property and assaulted and killed one another. Clearly, these acts were considered problematic, at the very least, because Iroquois chiefs requested traders and the political authorities to stop selling alcohol to their people. At the same time, "Iroquois society was willing to excuse even the most horrendous behavior provided the perpetrator was intoxicated."[52]

Intoxication and drunken violence were themes repeated over and over in descriptions of Native American drinking behavior in the early period of European contact. Paul Le Jeune, a Jesuit missionary in the St. Lawrence Valley in the 1630s, commented, "The savages have always been gluttons, but since the coming of the Europeans they have become such drunkards that . . . they cannot abstain from drinking, taking pride in getting drunk, and making others drunk."[53] In New France (Québec), the indigenous people were said to become "swinishly intoxicated" on brandy, get into fights with one another, and murder colonists. By the 1660s, the bishop of Québec ordered the excommunication of any traders who supplied alcohol to the local native peoples.[54] One of the problems that missionaries associated with alcohol was that it made Native Americans more difficult to convert to Christianity. One Jesuit in New France wrote that "the greatest evil done here by drunkenness is, that its consequences Utterly estrange the savages from Christianity."[55]

Such accounts of intoxicated natives gave rise to the image of the "drunken Indian," with its implication that Native Americans had an innate propensity to become intoxicated that distinguished them from Europeans, and that drunkenness was more pervasive in Native American than in settler society. Undoubtedly some Native Americans became drunk, and some became violent when intoxicated. But we have no way of knowing how reliable or accurate the accounts are, even when they purport to be eyewitness descriptions, or how often violence was associated with drinking. Given the anecdotal and episodic character of the evidence, it is no more possible to assess or quantify Native American behavior than to calculate what proportion of Europeans at that time regularly drank heavily to the point of intoxication. It is possible that some or many of the accounts of alcohol-driven mayhem and killing were constructed to conform to the contemporary European imagination, as was the case with many accounts of cannibalism by indigenous peoples elsewhere.[56]

Accepting the premise that Native Americans who drank alcohol generally did so heavily, some scholars have suggested a genetic explanation: that Native Americans process alcohol differently from Europeans. But there is no evidence of such a difference, and the wide variations in drinking patterns among Native Americans argue against it—as do the patterns of heavy drinking and persistent intoxication within the European populations themselves.[57] Some historians have suggested a cultural explanation: that some Native Americans learned heavy drinking behavior from the traders who provided them with the beverages. There is another assumption at work here, of course: that these traders themselves were heavy drinkers and given to drunkenness. Perhaps they generally were. They were adult males who worked in remote locations far from the surveillance and social controls of their communities of origin. In the mid-eighteenth century, Jean Bossu, a French traveler in the Mississippi Valley, wrote that "drunkenness . . . is corrected with difficulty even amongst the French. The Indians imitate them easily in it, and say the white people have taught them to drink the *fiery water* [brandy]."[58]

There is another important point to remember here: European populations developed their cultures of alcohol consumption over thousands of years. At first, alcohol was available in limited quantities, and as it became more commonly consumed, protocols for drinking were established and the consequences of excessive drinking became known, if not always heeded. Some people broke the protocols, and some were punished. The indigenous peoples of North America, in contrast, had no alcohol tradition until Europeans introduced rum and other beverages, and there was no gradual, centuries-long phase-in of alcohol to their communities. Thanks to the fur trade, some of the indigenous populations were awash in alcohol within decades of European contact. In the absence of effective communal restraints, excessive consumption might quickly have become established as their alcohol culture, whether or not European traders and merchants were their models.

We do know that heavy drinking and intoxication were far from uncommon among European colonists. As we have seen, as early as 1637 the General

Court of Massachusetts took steps to curb what it believed was widespread drunkenness. A drunk person was defined as someone who "either lisps or falters in his speech by reason of much drink, or that staggers in his going, or that vomits by reason of excessive drinking, or cannot follow his calling,"[59] or who was "disabled in the use of his understanding, appearing in his speech or gesture."[60] Colonists convicted of drunkenness were sometimes whipped, on the ground that a drunk was no better than a beast and deserved to be beaten as a beast would be.

Despite consequences that could be quite severe, drunkenness seems to have increased in the early colonies as locally produced alcohol added to imported supplies. John Winthrop, a Puritan leader, noted that young people commonly "gave themselves to drinke hott waters [spirits] verye immoderately."[61] As early as 1622, the Virginia Company called on the colony's governor to do something about excessive drinking there, news of which "hath spread itself to all that have but heard the name of Virginia."[62] The court records of all the American colonies are full of charges for drunkenness, despite the efforts of the authorities to reduce its incidence. Although young people and the transient population were often cited as being particularly problematic, it is not clear whether any demographic was overrepresented among the consumers convicted of alcohol offenses. (Innkeepers and other retailers were sometimes charged—for allowing drunkenness or serving alcohol past closing hours, for example—but they are a group apart.)

There remains the fundamental question of whether there was a significant difference in the frequency and scale of intoxication between the indigenous and European communities. The insistence by European commentators on the ubiquity of native intoxication is all too reminiscent of middle-class commentaries on the drinking behavior of the poor and working classes in Europe or the allegations made by any number of groups that other populations drank to excess and disturbed the social order. The colonial authorities in America clearly thought there was a difference between the two drinking cultures because they adopted divergent policies for each community. As we have seen, they attempted to regulate alcohol distribution in colonial towns so as to limit the places colonists might drink—although the aim was clearly to limit the volume that colonists might drink. Policies directed at Native Americans, on the other hand, attempted to prevent their access to any alcohol whatsoever.

The difference might well have rested on the authorities' assumptions about the ability of the respective populations to drink moderately: impossible in the case of Native Americans, but generally possible as far as the colonists were concerned. On the other hand, the divergent policies might have reflected more pragmatic judgments: it was possible to cut off the alcohol supply to Native Americans, for whom alcohol was still a novelty, but it was unthinkable to do the same to Europeans, for whom alcohol was a nutritional and cultural necessity. The authorities who tried to impose prohibitionist policies on Native Americans in the 1600s (and later) were themselves consumers of alcohol and had no thought of depriving themselves or their fellow colonists of a staple commodity. Prohibition was a policy that made sense in universal rather than ethnic terms only three centuries later.

The seventeenth century saw the beginning of a complicated relationship between Native Americans, Europeans, and alcohol. Almost from the very beginning, Europeans attributed pathological drinking behavior to Native Americans and strung episodic accounts into a narrative of the "drunk Indian" who was unable to resist alcohol and who drank to the point of oblivion or violence. It proved to be an enduring stereotype that underpinned government policies toward indigenous peoples in the United States and Canada until the twentieth century. Like most stereotypes, it generalized uncritically. In this case, it treated Native Americans as an undifferentiated group, rather than recognizing that experiences with alcohol varied from region to region and from population to population. As we shall see, many Native Americans were dispossessed of their lands and cultures, forced to abandon their family and social networks, and coerced to adopt European religions. Like the dispossessed in other societies and social classes, some native populations turned to alcohol and other drugs. The introduction of alcohol, then, was one facet of a broad upheaval experienced by Native Americans. This was no less true of indigenous peoples in other parts of the world, but only in North America did such a particular and enduring drinking stereotype emerge.

8

Europe and America
1700–1800

ALCOHOL, ENLIGHTENMENT,
AND REVOLUTIONS

In 1797, Benjamin Rush, physician, vineyard investor, temperance advocate, and signatory to the American Declaration of Independence, published what has become one of the best-known documents in the history of American alcohol: "A Moral and Physical Thermometer: A scale of the progress of Temperance and Intemperance—Liquors with effects in their usual order." This "thermometer" divided beverages into two categories, those that fostered "Temperance" and those that fostered "Intemperance," and it showed the supposed effects of drinking each. Under Temperance, Rush first listed water and gave its effects as "Health and Wealth." Next came milk and water (consumed together) and "small beer," all of which resulted in "Serenity of Mind, Reputation, Long Life, & Happiness." They were followed by cider and perry (pear-based cider), wine, porter and "strong beer," which resulted in "Cheerfulness, Strength and Nourishment, when taken only in small quantities, and at meals."

These positive attributes changed dramatically when Rush turned to the drinks associated with Intemperance. The least harmful, punch, was portrayed as leading to idleness, gambling, sickness, and debt. Most of the other alcohols, such as "Toddy and Egg Rum," "Grog—Brandy and Water," and "Drams of Gin, Brandy, and Rum, in the morning," led to vices such as quarreling, fighting, horse-racing, lying, swearing, perjury, burglary, and murder; to diseases that included tremors of the hands in the morning, puking, inflamed eyes, sore and swelled legs, madness, and despair; and to consequences that encompassed jail, black eyes and rags, hospital, poor house, state prison for life, and the gallows.[1]

The "Moral and Physical Thermometer" was an eye-catching graphic that set out more clearly than ever the distinction between good alcohol and bad alcohol and the positive and negative consequences of each. Although its language might strike us as quaint and some of the effects of drinking spirits seem more than a little far-fetched as generalizations, it reflected a common view that drunkenness was often the first link in a chain of sins and crimes. In the late seventeenth century, Owen Stockton's *A warning to drunkards* had described drunkenness as "the root of all evil, the rot of all good" that "disposeth a man to many other great and crying sins," from blasphemy to murder.[2] This view, that most pathological behavior could be traced back to alcohol, flourished well into the twentieth century and underlay much of the support for temperance and prohibition policies in the nineteenth century.

But Rush introduced some interesting concepts and made an important distinction between Temperance alcohols (cider, wine, and beer) and Intemperance alcohols (distilled spirits). The former were described as good and healthy when consumed in small volumes with meals, but there was no such allowance for the modest enjoyment of whiskey or rum. Instead, Rush implied that while people could enjoy wine, cider, and beer moderately, the same was not true of spirits. The consequences Rush listed as flowing from alcohol—crimes and their punishments—were what others attributed to drunkenness, suggesting that, in Rush's mind, one sip of alcohol inevitably led to more and to eventual inebriation. While "temperance" and "intemperance" refer to human drinking behavior, Rush attached the terms to categories of alcohol (although there was no appreciation at the time that alcohol was common to all these beverages). Rush clearly regarded gin, brandy, rum, and other distilled alcohols as inherently addictive, in the sense that it was not possible to drink them moderately. To put it another way, the explanation of drunkenness (and what would later be called "alcoholism") lay not only with the consumer but also with the nature of the type of alcoholic beverage itself.

Benjamin Rush was born in the mid-1740s and wrote during the late 1790s. He was able to survey the social landscape of much of the eighteenth century, and we can assume that his work on alcohol was informed by his experiences as a physician and public figure. Clearly, he was concerned about the extent and patterns of alcohol consumption in America around the time of the Revolution. But it is difficult to determine what alcohol consumption was like at that time, in America or elsewhere. Except for a few periods (such as the phase of gin-drinking in some English cities, discussed in Chapter 6), there is no good evidence as to whether alcohol consumption rose or fell (or both) during the eighteenth century. A number of themes emerge that sometimes associated alcohol consumption with the social elites, unlike in the following century (discussed in Chapter 9), when the focus was primarily on the working classes.

In the eighteenth century, two types of fortified wine (wine whose alcohol level is raised by the addition of brandy or distilled grape spirit) from Portugal became popular among the English and American upper classes. One was madeira, named for the Portuguese-owned island in the Atlantic Ocean where it was made. Madeira, now generally a sweet wine in the style of some sherries, was virtually invented during the eighteenth century. At the beginning of the 1700s, it was an undistinguished and inexpensive table wine, but within a hundred years it had become an expensive fortified beverage that only the well-to-do could afford.

The initial attraction of Madeira's wine was strategic rather than sensory. The island of Madeira was a popular port of call for ships on several Atlantic routes from Europe to Africa, India, the Caribbean, and North America, and during the 1500s, many would take on casks of the island's wine, mainly as cargo but also for consumption by the crew during the voyage. Until the early 1700s, typical Madeira wine was made from white grapes to which juice from black grapes was added to give the wine varying shades of pink and red. But the wine, exposed to summer heat and rough seas, often spoiled, and by the middle of the eighteenth century, some of Madeira's winemakers began to add distilled grape spirit to the wine (thus fortifying it) as a stabilizer. On one occasion, some barrels of this fortified wine returned to Madeira still full, and the producers discovered that it not only had survived the demanding sea voyage but had been improved by it. From mid-century, some producers began to ship their wine back and forth across the Atlantic and even as far as India before selling it, and wine labeled *vinha da roda* (wine that had made the round trip) commanded a premium price. Eventually, producers built storerooms under the roofs of their wineries, or special hothouses, where madeira could age in the heat. Barrels were rocked back and forth, later by steam-powered machines, to simulate the action of waves.

Madeira came in many styles, each customized to the preferences of a specific market, the way champagne was to be marketed in the following century. Madeira wine exported to Caribbean plantation owners was sometimes sent unfortified but accompanied by red grape must (unfermented juice) and brandy, so that the recipients could color, flavor, and fortify it to their own liking. Customers in South Carolina and Virginia preferred a dry, white, heavily fortified madeira; Philadelphians sought a sweeter, gold-colored madeira with less brandy, and New Yorkers wanted a reddish color with even less brandy and more sweetness.[3]

As madeira gained in popularity, it was sold as a wealthy person's drink, and barrel-aged madeira in particular became one of the eighteenth century's luxury products; from about 1780, producers marketed older wines (more than ten years old) as especially suitable for "intelligent" consumers—"the older the wine, the more distinguished its drinker," as one historian puts it.[4] In line with its luxury status, the price of madeira rose steadily. In the first decade of the eighteenth century, a pipe (a barrel holding about 435 liters) of madeira fetched about £5 on the island for export, but by the 1720s the price had risen to £8, by the 1740s to £22, and by the early 1800s to £43. Taking inflation into account, the price of madeira tripled in 100 years, a period that saw it transformed from the least to the most expensive wine on the Kingston (Jamaica), Boston, and London markets.[5] One sign of its status was widespread counterfeiting, and some markets were flooded with wine that had been fabricated to taste like madeira.

Although it was popular throughout Britain and its empire, madeira's greatest success was in North America and the Caribbean, where it was the alcohol of choice among wealthy colonists. An account of the liquid elements of one Barbados sugar plantation owner's breakfast at the end of the eighteenth century ran, "a dish of tea, another of coffee, a bumper of claret, another large one of hock negus; then Madeira, sangaree."[6] Its prestige was great enough that madeira was used to toast the work of the First Continental Congress in 1775 and to launch the *Constitution*, one of the first frigates of the U.S. Navy, in 1797.

Port, the other fortified wine to gain a following in the eighteenth century, also came from Portugal, but from the mainland. It was first made in the 1600s when spirits were added to red wines from the Douro Valley to stabilize them for shipping. The alcohol was added not to the finished wine, however, but during the fermentation process, thus raising the alcohol level to a point that killed the yeasts and stopped the fermentation before it was complete. The remaining unfermented sugar gave sweetness to the wine, while the added alcohol contributed alcoholic strength, thus producing the character of most modern port: a sweet red wine with an alcohol level higher than the range common in unfortified wines.

There was no standard alcohol content during the eighteenth century, and the volume of spirits added to the wine rose over time. In the early 1700s, producers added 10 to 15 liters of brandy to each 435-liter barrel of wine (about 3 percent), but the volume rose to 10 percent and then 17 percent toward the end of the century. By 1820 it had stabilized at 22 percent.[7] Modern port producers, such as Taylor Fladgate, add about 115 liters of alcohol to each 435-liter barrel of wine (26 percent of its volume), suggesting that for most of the eighteenth century, port contained less alcohol than it does today (usually 20 percent).

The 1703 Methuen Treaty between England and Portugal allowed the importation of port at low levels of duty to compensate for the decline of imports of French wine and brandy while France and England were at war. The flow of port into England grew rapidly, and by 1728 some 116,000 hectoliters of the wine—the equivalent of more than 15 million standard bottles—entered the country. The demand created a problem of supply because port came only from one part of the Douro Valley and could therefore be produced only in limited volumes. As in Madeira, enterprising producers in the Douro Valley began to fabricate port by using wines from other regions. They then "improved" the wines to bring them up to the flavors and quality expected on the English market, by blending inferior with superior wines and by adding sugar and more alcohol for sweetness, crushed elderberries to give color, and spices such as cinnamon, pepper, and ginger to enhance the flavor.

These concoctions were soon discovered by English importers and consumers and were denounced as dangerous to health. Demand fell off quickly, and imports declined from the 116,000 hectoliters of 1728 to 87,000 hectoliters in 1744 and to 54,000 hectoliters by 1756. The bottom fell out of the price of port on the London market: a barrel that had fetched £16 in the late 1730s could be bought for just over £2 in 1756. Faced with disaster, the Portuguese government introduced one of the world's first comprehensive wine laws to regulate the production of port. It specified the area of the Douro Valley where port could be produced, making it one of the world's first officially delimited wine regions, and regulated the winemaking process. The addition of substances to add color and flavor was prohibited, and to prevent temptation, the government ordered all elderberry bushes in the Douro region to be ripped out.[8]

Although it was impossible to ensure that there were no fraudulent practices, these decisive actions restored confidence to the English market, and imports and prices rebounded. By the 1770s, 160,000 to 180,000 hectoliters of port entered England each year, and in 1799, imports reached 440,000 hectoliters, the equivalent of almost 60 million bottles. The population of

England was about 9 million, so there was enough port that year for 6 bottles for every man, woman, and child.

But children did not drink port, and even though it was culturally identified as a man's drink (thus eliminating women from its consuming market), most men could not afford it. Those who could clearly consumed more than 6 bottles a year, and many might well have gone through 6 bottles a week, for the century is known for "3-bottle men"—men who could down 3 bottles of port in one session. What is now decried as "binge-drinking" was admired in British eighteenth-century upper-class male circles, and the ability to drink vast volumes of port was among the attributes of contemporary masculinity. Some who overachieved—"6-bottle men"—included the playwright Richard Sheridan and a prime minister, William Pitt the Younger. John Porter, a classical scholar at Oxford University, is said to have been able to drink 13 bottles of port at a sitting—the sitting presumably being part of the achievement.[9]

Port underpinned a culture of heavy drinking that seems to have become widespread among upper-class British men in the later eighteenth century— although it is possible that heavy drinking was not so much a new phenomenon as a continuity that was more openly discussed in the eighteenth century as drinking became associated with elite masculinity. The drinking careers of the Scottish writer James Boswell are well known, and it is possible that Boswell's "indulgence in port" and other beverages so disabled him that he was almost unable to complete his famous *Life of Samuel Johnson*.[10] So closely were elite males linked to heavy drinking that the term "drunk as a lord" seems to have become entirely literal in its force. In 1770 the *Gentleman's Magazine* listed 99 ways to call a man drunk, including the genteel "sipping the spirit of Adonis" and the cruder "stripping me naked."

Yet port was not the only beverage that gentlemen drank, nor did they all necessarily drink to get drunk. Cyril Jackson, dean of Christ Church, Oxford, thanked his wine merchant in 1799 for sending some French brandy: "For myself I confess to you that it is something so very much beyond anything I have ever tasted before, that I keep it sacredly to be used only in case of illness."[11] Dean Jackson might indeed have believed that excellent flavor made for a more therapeutic beverage, but it is interesting that he felt the need to assure his wine merchant that he did not intend to guzzle alcohol the way that so many of his contemporaries appear to have.

Dean Jackson might well have been enjoying one of the higher-quality brandies that were produced in the 1700s. In the early part of the century, brandy was made in many parts of France, but the Charente region, near the Atlantic coast north of Bordeaux, began to take off. Fewer than 7,000 barrels of brandy were shipped from Charente annually in the early 1700s, but the number rose to 27,000 barrels by 1727, 50,000 by 1780, and 87,000 by 1791—a twelvefold increase during the century. Like madeira, brandy rose from rags to riches. Although it was initially an affordable beverage for seamen, soldiers, and the poor and was originally distilled from the worst surplus wines, brandy soon appealed to the upper classes, and a hierarchy of brandies emerged. By the 1720s, brandy from the Cognac district of Charente was selling for about 25 percent more than brandies from other regions.[12] As with madeira and port, so with brandy: success led to counterfeiting, and in 1791 Charente's producers formed an association to regulate their industry and to guarantee the provenance and quality of their brandy, especially the higher-end brandies destined for better-off consumers.

The other alcohol industry that took off in the 1700s was whiskey distilling, in Scotland. It was practiced as a cottage industry in the Highlands but was virtually unknown in Lowland areas before the 1780s. During that decade, however, a number of large distilleries were constructed. One, at Kilbagie, cost the huge sum of £40,000 to construct and equip, employed 300 workers, and raised 7,000 cattle and 2,000 pigs on the spent grains left over after distilling.[13] Exports of Scottish whiskey to England rose at a staggering rate, from a mere 2,000 gallons in 1777 to more than 400,000 gallons by the mid-1780s. Like port, whiskey was often associated with excessive drinking.[14]

In this period, too, elite males began to flaunt their wine cellars. Voltaire, who hosted sumptuous dinners on his estate at Ferney, bought large volumes of beaujolais (his favorite), burgundy (which he used to top up his barrels of beaujolais), and Spanish wine from Malaga. The cellar of the Duke of Tavanes was mainly stocked with hundreds of bottles of wines from Beaune and Médoc, but he also had wines from Cyprus and Hungary. The first president of the Parlement (royal law court) of Dijon seems to have been loyal to his locality: most of his fine wines were burgundies from estates such as Chambertin, Vougeot, and Montrachet.

Quite possibly the wine they drank improved in quality as the century progressed, just as their brandy might have, because in many parts of France there was growing interest in improving the quality of wines. The Academies of Bordeaux and of Dijon (representing Burgundy) sponsored several competitions for treatises dealing with winemaking techniques. Wine producers began to pay more attention to the grape varieties they used, to the ripeness of the grapes, and to the fermentation and aging processes. By the middle of the century, the wines of some of the great Bordeaux estates (not yet known as châteaux), such as Haut-Brion, Lafite, Latour, and Margaux, were already well known, and wines from prestigious Burgundy estates, such as Romanée and Montrachet, attracted the highest prices—always a good guide to reputation, if not to quality.

New techniques, many of which are well known to modern winemakers, were introduced. One was the addition of sugar to the must (grape juice) before fermentation, in order to increase the potential alcohol content of the finished wine. The process is now called "chaptalization," after Jean-Antoine-Claude Chaptal (a chemist and, later, minister in one of Napoleon's governments), who advocated the process in a work published in 1801. But adding sugar to must was practiced well before that date. The article on wine in the *Encyclopedia* (1765) recommended using sugar, and a succession of French scientists recommended adding sugar, honey, or sugar-syrup as a means of starting the fermentation process as quickly as possible. As an experiment, one chemist, Pierre-Joseph Macquer, added sugar to the sour juice of under-ripe grapes from the 1776 harvest and declared that it tasted as good as any other wine from that vintage: there was nothing syrupy about it and no sensory evidence that the juice had been artificially sweetened.[15]

The vast amount of research on wine, all directed toward improving quality, involved scientists from a number of fields, and it was summarized in a book, *The Art of Making Wine according to the Method of Chaptal*, which Napoleon's government distributed to grape-growers throughout France in 1803. (It was part of an attempt to stimulate France's economy and exports following the setbacks of the Revolutionary period.) The book drew not only on scientific research but also on the experience of grape-growers, as Chaptal had sent questionnaires to leading producers. It summarized what was known about soil (pointing out the benefits of the light, porous soils found in the best areas of Bordeaux), climate, and winemaking techniques. If these approaches and practices were being widely adopted in France during the 1700s, the overall quality of the top-tier wines ought to have improved steadily.

Needless to say, quality did not extend to the wine consumed by the poorer members of French society, many of whom must, in any case, have had no choice but to drink whatever potable water was available. Voltaire might have enjoyed his beaujolais and burgundies, but he cultivated his own vineyard and gave his servants homemade wine, which he described as "my own bad wine, which is by no means unwholesome."[16] Little wonder that (as Voltaire complained) his servants stole his good wine from time to time. The wine consumed by the poor, who made up a third or more of France's population, must have been thin, flavorless, and acidic. In 1794, the Paris authorities took samples of wine from sixty-eight restaurants and bars and declared that only eight could reasonably be described as wine. While it is true that the Revolutionary period brought particular challenges and hardships, it is likely that much of the wine that circulated before the Revolution was equally suspect. Wine has historically included many styles and levels of quality (however quality is judged), but it is possible that improvements in winemaking in the eighteenth century led to a wider gap than ever before between the best and the worst of wines.

The cultural meaning of wine and other alcoholic beverages might have varied among social classes and between genders during the eighteenth century, but alcohol retained its widespread attraction. Whether they sipped and enjoyed it for its sensory pleasures or gulped it down as an anesthetic against poor conditions of life and work (these are only two stereotypes of drinking behavior and motivation), eighteenth-century men, in particular, drank deeply, and drunkenness seems to have been a pervasive condition. As we have seen, heavy drinking in homosocial contexts such as clubs and being able to hold one's drink were marks of upper-class masculinity. The point was distilled in Dr. Johnson's famous comment, "Claret is the liquor for boys; port for men; but he who aspires to be a hero . . . drinks brandy."[17] Although there is no mention here of how much brandy was heroic, it was unlikely to have been a nip. This sort of attitude worried many commentators, such as Benjamin Rush, who regarded intemperate consumption as the beginning of a chain of actions that included sins such as Sabbath-breaking and blasphemy and crimes that ranged from theft to murder.

But during the eighteenth century, in England at least, upper-class commentators began to draw a distinction between drunkenness by the wealthy and by the poor. This class-specific distinction marked a shift away from the undifferentiated condemnation of drunkenness as sinful and as a first step on a life of immorality and crime. By the mid-eighteenth century, elite drunkenness was more likely to be seen as a private vice that had no social consequences (and which society and the law might therefore overlook), while heavy drinking by the working poor (the very poor and the indigent could not afford to drink alcohol, let alone drink enough to get drunk) was associated with crime and social disorder.[18]

This perspective emerged from a vigorous debate, coinciding with the so-called gin-craze in the first half of the 1700s, about the legal consequences of drunkenness. There was some recognition of, if little sympathy for, the conditions that might drive people to drink. The Dutch philosopher Bernard Mandeville referred to the poverty-stricken wretch who "drowns his most pinching cares, and with his reason all anxious reflexion on brats that cry for food, hard winters' frosts, and horrid empty home." Like most other commentators of the period, Mandeville explicitly focused on the poorer strata of society. Henry Fielding, the writer whose work as a magistrate gave him a privileged and particular view of crime in London, blamed drink for increasing criminality by "the very dregs of people."[19]

Drunkenness among the well-off, which many commentators readily acknowledged was widespread, was perceived as having different consequences. If the poor were socially disruptive when they drank too much, and therefore invited and deserved intervention by the authorities, the intoxicated well-off were guilty of moral weakness that, no matter how deplorable, was beyond the legitimate reach of the law. The direct issue here was not whether a crime had been committed—a murder was essentially a murder, whether committed by a drunk lord or a drunk laborer—but the meaning attached to drunkenness. Heavy drinking by the wealthy might be morally objectionable, but it was a private problem. Heavy drinking by the poor was a social threat that could be identified: drunk men neglected their work and their family responsibilities, while women (who were seen as especially vulnerable to drunkenness) neglected their families and their children. It is clear that this discourse had emerged by the gin-craze of the early to mid-1700s, with its emphasis on women and children (see Chapter 6).

The question of crime was also important, and jurists debated the meaning of criminal responsibility when a crime was committed by an intoxicated person. What came into play was the tension between accepting, on one hand, that drunkenness could deprive a person of reason and thus lead him or her to behave out of character and, on the other, believing that even a drunk person should be held accountable for his or her actions. There was no formal provision in English law for pleading drunkenness as an extenuating condition when one committed a crime, but some defendants tried to excuse their behavior that way. Legal authorities generally agreed that the courts should reject such pleas: Matthew Hale argued that a defendant "shall have no privilege by his voluntarily contracted madness," while William Blackstone, the eighteenth century's greatest jurist, called it a "weak excuse." For his part, John Locke argued that only insanity could be an exception to the rule of responsibility because a judge or jury could not verify a drunk person's state of mind at the time he or she committed a crime.[20]

In practice, few defendants tried to claim drunkenness as a mitigating condition. Between 1680 and 1750, less than 2 percent of defendants at London's central criminal court (the Old Bailey) did so, and in only a few cases did the drunkenness defense seem to have played a part in either acquittal or conviction on a lesser charge.[21] But as the century progressed, some defendants were more likely to allege that drink had effected a change in their normal character such that they had committed the offense without any malicious intent. The murder of a friend in a tavern fight was a prime example of this sort of plea. Other defendants conflated drunkenness and insanity, as did one Elizabeth Lawler who, charged with stealing a carcass of lamb, "pleaded that she was disordered in her head and crazy, and did not know what she did."[22]

Defendants in some divorce cases in France during the 1790s also argued that their responsibility was diminished when they were drunk. One told a court that "he admits having ill-treated his wife, that he has no complaints about her behavior, but that the abuse, harsh words and threats he directed at her ... often occurred when he was drunk."[23] Women plaintiffs complained that men often returned home drunk and assaulted them, and many women associated the worst episodes of ill treatment with religious festivals, such as Easter and Pentecost, when men were able to drink all day. On the other hand, one woman in Rouen complained to a divorce court that "her husband gets drunk every day and profits from his drunkenness to abuse her." Where married women were alleged to have been drunk, their husbands associated it not with violence but with sexual immorality. One woman was said to have "drunk and become intoxicated to such an extent that she gave herself up to the greatest immorality possible."

If the family was a common location for the effects of drunkenness to be played out, a specific and highly stratified site for alcohol consumption was the military. There, drunkenness could lead not only to immorality, violence, and crime but also to military-specific problems of insubordination, indiscipline, and reduced efficiency. Little wonder that there was particular concern about the extent of heavy drinking in the British army, where ordinary soldiers had ready access to as much alcohol as they wanted and could afford, whether from the merchants who provisioned armies, from taverns, or even from their officers. Additional alcohol—usually rum—was served before battles, after victories, and on special occasions, such as royal births or anniversaries.[24] The official provision of alcohol appears to have risen during the 1700s, and by the time the British army fought in the American War of Independence, rum rations were no longer reserved for special occasions and generally amounted to a gill (about 5 ounces) a day, or about a gallon each month. But there appear to have been no hard-and-fast rules, and one officer seems to have provided his men with half a pint of rum a day.[25] Because it was so inexpensive in North America, rum was the liquor of choice there, but other beverages were popular elsewhere: in Britain, whiskey and gin, along with beer and ale (depending on cost), and in India, arrack, which was distilled from various fruits and grains or from the fermented sap of coconut flowers, and which was much less expensive than beer.

But the British army's alcohol rations paled against those provided to sailors while at sea. The standard daily allotment was a pint of wine or half a pint of brandy or rum (served with water) or, on shorter voyages, a gallon of beer. Although these amounts were more than those doled out to soldiers, sailors at sea did not have the opportunity to purchase additional supplies (although they did smuggle extra alcohol onboard), and they were under the continuous surveillance of the ship's officers. Soldiers, on the other hand, were seldom under strict surveillance. Although they might be involved in campaigns for extended periods, most of the time they were stationed at forts or garrisons, where they seldom lived in barracks. Billeted in barns, private houses, and taverns, and far from the watchful eyes of their officers, they could drink as they wished.

The extent of heavy drinking and drunkenness in the eighteenth-century British army is a matter for speculation. Unrestricted supplies were generally available, and the main limitation on access was cost. Ordinary soldiers received very little cash, but they obtained alcohol by theft, bartering their (and sometimes their colleagues') other provisions and possessions. In the West Indies, soldiers traded their rations of older rum for greater volumes of new, stronger rum.[26] Some might have curtailed their drinking out of a sense of responsibility, and soldiers who could read might have been influenced by a tract, *The Soldier's Monitor*, that was widely distributed to soldiers during the eighteenth century. Written by Josiah Woodward, an Anglican social reformer, it directed the usual warnings about alcohol toward soldiers. Intemperance, Woodward wrote, "perfectly bereaves the brave Soldier of all that is great and noble in his Character. A very Child exceeds him in Strength, and an Idiot is his Equal in Discretion."[27]

There are plenty of reports that British soldiers drank deeply and often. A surgeon's mate wrote in 1744 that soldiers in the Flanders campaign were "reeling about continually drunk with gin brandy etc that they got at Bruges." There was some discussion about the relative drunkenness of English and Irish troops. Lord Castlereagh thought the English abused whiskey more, but an army surgeon pointed out that Irish soldiers were far more likely than the English to suffer from ulcerated legs as a result of heavy drinking.[28]

The consequences of heavy drinking by soldiers spanned issues of health, morality, crime, and military efficiency. Military doctors warned of the physical dangers of alcohol abuse and even warned that drinking new rum (as distinct from the older rum that comprised military rations) could be fatal—a possibility, because much new rum was contaminated with lead. One officer reported in 1762 from Martinique: "Upon my arrival here I found the troops very Sickly, many dead, & the Sick list increasingly dayly, chiefly owing to the bad rum they got on shore."[29] Of equal concern was the breakdown of discipline under the impact of alcohol. General Wolfe noted in 1758 that "too much rum necessarily affects the discipline of an army. We have glaring evidence of its ill consequences every moment. Sergeants drunk upon duty, two sentries upon their posts and the rest grovelling in the dirt."[30]

Alcohol seems, then, to have posed challenges to all military forces in the eighteenth century. In the early years of the Fortress of Louisbourg, on Canada's Cape Breton Island, soldiers garrisoned there had access to unlimited supplies of wine and brandy. But widespread illness, problems with military discipline, and a 1717 report from the governor that "the inn-keepers are completely ruining the colony" made the authorities rethink their alcohol policies.[31] Until the end of the colony, in the 1750s, there were continual attempts to distance soldiers from alcohol. Some regulations forbade the sale of alcohol to soldiers on workdays; others limited the number of drinking places in the colony, while others were directed at the troops themselves, such as one that prohibited soldiers and sailors from trading their clothes for drink.

Although no general policies were adopted to curb drunkenness by soldiers, various local solutions were adopted by individual commanders. Some tried to restrict the availability of spirits entirely, while others merely forbade drinking while on sentry duty. Yet other officers adopted more draconian policies and attempted to prevent soldiers' having access to any spirits other than the rations issued by the army, although this effectively involved confining the troops to barracks. In 1759 the commander of British forces in Quebec canceled all licenses to sell liquor to the troops and ordered any soldier found drunk to receive twenty lashes a day until he revealed where he had obtained the liquor. In addition, his rum ration was stopped for six weeks. Drunkenness alone, even when not aggravated by insubordination or other misbehavior, was a punishable offense in the British army. The penalties were generally extra duty or drill, but more serious consequences followed on breaches of discipline and other offenses committed while inebriated. Incidences of this kind appear to have been more common among troops stationed in the Americas because of the ready availability of inexpensive rum.

These policies were directed almost exclusively toward distilled spirits, mainly rum, gin, and brandy. Little attention was given to beer and ale, and even less to wine, even though all led to intoxication if consumed in sufficient volumes. John Bell, a medical officer who was generally opposed to the military providing liquor rations and even questioned the medical orthodoxy that wine had specific therapeutic qualities, was relatively positive about wine and beer as everyday drinks. Wine, he thought, should be given to troops on a regular basis because of its general health-promoting properties, while beer was "an invigorating, antiseptic, salutary beverage . . . highly nutritive." As for liquor, Bell allowed that it might be given to cold or fatigued soldiers but not to others.[32]

Soldiers must have hydrated themselves with beer (they could not do it with spirits alone) or with water, and it is noteworthy that all references to drunkenness in the British army assume that it resulted from liquor consumption, not from heavy beer-drinking. It is quite possible, though, that eighteenth-century soldiers drank more water than historians have generally thought. Hector McLean, a medical officer in the West Indies, recommended that hard-worked troops should be allowed to drink only water or lemonade, although he advised that officers should drink wine moderately for their general health.[33] In 1780 the commander of the Royal Artillery in Charleston received a petition from some of the troops complaining that they had been deprived of their rum ration. They wrote that rum is "an Article we humbly conceive to be essentially necessary to the health of Labouring Men in this sultry Climate. . . . Neither can it be thought that [we] can work hard from 6 o'Clock in the Morning to 6 in the Evening on simple Water, which is peculiarly bad in this Town."[34] There is a report of an eminent physician who cured several people of habitual drunkenness by progressively diluting their liquor until they were drinking pure water.[35]

In his "Moral and Physical Thermometer," Benjamin Rush recommended drinking water decades before governments began to construct systems for providing their citizens with regular supplies of potable water. But elsewhere Rush cautioned against drinking cold water in hot conditions or drinking too much water. He noted that "few summers elapse in Philadelphia in which there are not instances of many persons being affected by drinking cold water. In some seasons four or five persons have died suddenly from this cause, in one day." These deaths usually occurred among "the labouring part of the community," who drank from the public pumps "and who are too impatient or too ignorant, to use the necessary precautions for preventing its morbid or deadly effects upon them."[36] The impact of very cold water on a warm body, Rush wrote, resulted in such symptoms as dimness of sight, staggering and collapsing, difficulty breathing, a rattle in the throat, and cold extremities.

Death could follow in four or five minutes. In less serious cases, people who drink very cold water while warm would suffer chest and stomach spasms.

But in Rush's view, the problem was not water in itself but the relative temperatures of the water and the consumer's body and the volume of water consumed. He pointed out that the same problems could occur when punch or beer were drunk under the same conditions. The "precautions" that Rush referred to were to mitigate the shock of cold water. If drinking from a cup or bowl, drinkers should hold their hands around it for a while to warm the water. If drinking directly from the stream or a pump, they should splash the cold water on their hands and faces to accustom their body to its temperature before drinking any.[37] Yet nowhere, unlike many of his contemporaries, did Rush actually advise against drinking water.

Although water was an effective way of hydrating, alcohol was culturally embedded, and it would have been as difficult to deprive soldiers of it as it would civilians. In 1791 an army surgeon stationed in Jamaica noted that if rum were withheld for a single day, "discontent immediately begins to shew itself among the men. If with-held for any length of time, complaints sometimes rise to a state of mutiny, and desertions become notorious."[38] In fact, apart from sporadic attempts by some officers, there was little interest in depriving soldiers of liquor. A culture of drinking was as embedded in the officer corps as among their men, and alcohol was believed to have medical properties and to be advantageous in hot and cold weather and when soldiers faced trying conditions.

Soldiers who failed to perform their tasks or were insubordinate because of drinking were dealt with, but drinking itself—even heavy drinking—was widely tolerated because there were few alternatives. From this perspective, the army did not quite parallel civilian society. By the middle of the eighteenth century, the upper classes had determined that the simple act of drinking liquor by the working poor was morally problematic. In the military hierarchy, the officers tended to accept drinking by their men and to take action only when drinking led to behavior that undermined military discipline and efficiency.

The two great revolutions of the eighteenth century had quite distinct impacts on alcohol, but in both the American and French cases, taxation was a mediating influence. One of the major challenges facing the newly founded United States was financing the debt it had incurred from the War of Independence. Like many politicians before and since, Alexander Hamilton, the first secretary of the treasury, looked to taxes on alcohol as a rich and permanent revenue stream. Even though we cannot quantify consumption with any reliability, all accounts suggest that Americans were heavy drinkers in that period. One often-cited source suggests that in 1790–1800, Americans of drinking age consumed more than 6 gallons of pure alcohol from all sources (spirits, wine, and beer) per capita. The same source suggests a level of consumption about a third of that 100 years later (2.2 gallons in the 1890s),[39] and somewhat less than half 100 years after that (2.5 gallons in 2003–5).[40] If such calculations are correct, it is hardly surprising that Hamilton cast a covetous fiscal eye on his compatriots' drinking habits. Taxing alcohol must have seemed less likely to provoke a reaction than the English government's attempts to tax tea, and Hamilton and others were probably influenced by their sympathy for temperance ideas.

At the same time, Hamilton might have noted the problems the English government had faced when, financially exhausted by the American War of Independence, it had tried to increase alcohol revenues. Receipts were notoriously undermined by widespread smuggling and other forms of tax avoidance, and Prime Minister William Pitt attempted to impose new taxes on the steady stream of whiskey entering England from Scotland. Various systems of taxing whiskey were tried, including simple licensing and levies on the volume of fermented "wash" a distillery prepared for distilling. But the various methods set Lowland distillers against their Highland counterparts and both against London distillers, who wanted to keep Scottish whiskey out of England. It also raised issues of England's constitutional relationship with Scotland.[41]

In March 1791, Congress passed a law enabling the federal government to collect taxes on distilled spirits. Spirits produced in the United States from imported ingredients (such as rum made from molasses imported from the Caribbean) were taxed at a lower rate than imported spirits (such as French brandy), and spirits produced in the United States from local ingredients were taxed at an even lower rate. Distinctions were made between large- and small-scale distillers. Several states already had such taxes on spirits (some at the retail level rather than on production), although they are thought to have been inconsistently applied. Much of the whiskey (by far the main form of distilled alcohol) was produced in small volumes by corn farmers in remote frontier regions. Far from centers of population, these farmers turned grain into alcohol for more efficient and cheaper overland transportation, sold much of their whiskey locally, and used it as a means of exchange to purchase goods for their own use. The 1791 tax was imposed not only on whiskey made for these commercial purposes but even on what farmers produced for their own consumption. Moreover, rather than being levied on receipts from the sale of whiskey, the tax could be imposed in advance; rural producers had to pay an annual fee based on the capacity of their stills, or 9 cents a gallon of whiskey distilled. It meant that producers, many of whom were farmers of modest means, paid taxes on everything they produced, even if some was lost (by leakage or spillage) while being shipped, reducing their revenue at the point of sale.[42]

The government saw the tax as necessary and fair. It was far lower than similar taxes imposed in other countries, and the fact that the tax on all-American spirits was much less than that imposed on imports gave local distillers a competitive advantage. But farmers viewed distilling as a way to get by rather than as a commercial operation, and they considered the new tax grossly unfair. It targeted farmers who were just trying to survive, and it threatened to drain the frontier regions of hard currency, which was already in short supply. Avoiding the tax entailed further hardships, as anyone charged with evasion would be tried in Philadelphia, far from their homes. Overall, the spirits tax, imposed on westerners by easterners, smacked of earlier taxes imposed on colonists by the English.[43]

At first, protests against the tax took the form of letters to newspapers and petitions, but in the autumn of 1791 (despite a concession by the government that reduced the tax from 9 to 7 cents a gallon), opposition escalated into what has become known as the Whiskey Rebellion. Refusal to pay the tax spread, and the initial reaction was to threaten, beat, and even tar and feather the agents who came to farmers' properties to collect the tax. From 1792, actions against tax collectors intensified, especially in western Pennsylvania but also in other states. In 1794, when the government sent a U.S. marshal and forces led by a general to charge several distillers, a battle between federal soldiers and local militiamen led to deaths on both sides. The tax resisters were given an opportunity to abandon their cause and declare their loyalty to the U.S. government and its laws, and when they refused, President George Washington raised a militia force of 13,000. Accompanied by Hamilton and by Washington himself, the soldiers marched into the region where resistance to the whiskey tax was strongest, and in the face of armed force, the insurgents dispersed. Several dozen were seized, and although two were convicted of treason and sentenced to death, Washington pardoned them.

The Whiskey Rebellion not only highlighted conflicts between regions and classes in the early United States but showed the importance of distilling at the time. The same source that shows Americans of drinking age consuming more than 6 gallons of pure alcohol a year around 1800 suggests that half the alcohol came from distilled spirits. Beer came second, while wine trailed a poor third. For example, of 6.6 gallons of pure alcohol in 1800, 3.3 gallons came from spirits, 3.2 from beer, and 0.1 from wine.[44] Alexander Hamilton justified the 1791 whiskey tax in part as a deterrent to drinking; because producers could pass the tax on to consumers, a higher price might lower consumption. Hamilton noted that the use of spirits seemed "to depend more on relative habits of sobriety or intemperance than on any other cause."[45]

It could be said that Hamilton's whiskey tax embodied a tension: the expectation of sufficient revenues to help the U.S. Treasury rested on the very drinking he deplored. In the end, although the tax led to higher prices for all kind of spirits, domestic and imported, demand continued to grow. Whiskey tax revenues from Pennsylvania, the state at the heart of the rebellion, more than doubled between 1794–95 ($66,401) and 1797–98 ($123,491).[46] Although some of the increase might have been due to more efficient collection, it is likely that demand and consumption expanded.

In France, wine rather than spirits attracted the attention of reformers. The French Revolution of 1789 made a significant impact on wine and set the stage for the development of the modern French wine industry, not least by fostering consumption by removing many of the taxes imposed on it under the old regime. The grievance lists drawn up before the Revolution in 1789 show widespread detestation of taxes of all kinds, including those on consumer goods such as wine. One community in the Menetou region of the Loire Valley complained that the tax on wine "is perhaps the most harmful to all people and the least profitable to the king," while another noted that it was even impossible for a charitable person to send a bottle of wine to the home of some "unfortunate" without some zealous official trying to tax it. The taxes were said to lead to all manner of criminal behavior: "How many clandestine wine-shops there are in the country! Often they are the refuge of that sort of person who, having lost their minds through drinking so much wine, are reduced to a level below animals . . . from which follow assaults, violence, loss of health, changes in character, and scorn for decent people."[47]

One of the most burdensome taxes was the duty imposed as wine entered cities. In Paris, whose half-million inhabitants were by far France's largest urban consumer market, wine was subjected to duties at the city gates and at posts on the River Seine. Although they were initially fairly light, the duties on wine rose until by 1789 they effectively tripled the initial cost of the wine. Moreover, because taxes were levied by the barrel, regardless of quality and value of the wine, consumers of less-expensive, poor-quality wine ended up subsidizing the drinking preferences on their better-off fellow citizens. One result of the higher urban prices was a regular migration of Parisians, especially on Sundays and other holidays, to taverns and bars outside the city walls, where they could enjoy duty-free alcohol. One of the most popular taverns, Le Tambour Royal, was said to have sold about 1.3 million liters of wine a year.

The people of Paris employed a variety of subterfuges to lessen the impact of the taxes in the city itself. Merchants brought high-alcohol wine through the gates, then diluted it so as to lessen the impact of duties. More wine—probably great volumes, but we can never know for certain—was smuggled into the city by hiding barrels under other goods on the carts as they passed through the gates. Smaller volumes of brandy could be concealed under the voluminous skirts of women smugglers. Then there were the tunnels and channels—lined with wood, iron, leather, or lead—that were drilled through the city walls. In 1784, the authorities decided to extend the perimeter of the city walls in order to encompass the growing population outside the existing ones. The project was unpopular—not least because it would push the cheaper taverns outside the walls even farther from the center of the city—and officials found and closed eighty wine tunnels drilled through the new walls by 1788.

Opposition to duties on wine and other goods grew in France during the late 1780s as prices rose steadily, employment fell, and the mass of the population came under increasing pressure. As political, economic, and social crises mounted toward the end of the decade, violence broke out in Paris, and on the night of July 12–13, 1789, most of the customs barriers at the city gates were destroyed or burned by angry crowds. It was not wanton and random violence but the precise targeting of institutions that threatened the living standards of common citizens, the livelihoods of vine-growers, and even merchants. Although the beginning of the French Revolution is conventionally marked by the storming of the Bastille, on July 14, the destruction of the customs barriers has as good a claim. The Bastille, a royal prison, was as hugely symbolic as its great bulk, but the sacking of the customs barriers represented the struggle of ordinary Parisians to destroy institutions that were driving them deeper and deeper into poverty.

Yet the early years of the Revolution were disappointing for wine-drinkers in Paris and elsewhere. The city needed the tax revenues from wine and completed the new walls in 1790, and national taxes were retained until a new tax code was developed. But in 1791, the Revolutionary government abolished all indirect taxes, including those on wine, and as soon as the policy went into effect at midnight on May 1, a convoy of hundreds of carts entered Paris carrying 2 million liters of wine. Patriotic Parisians partied all night with wine that sold at 3 sous a pint. Huge volumes of brandy were sold off the same way, and similar scenes played out throughout France. Even though prices rose during the 1790s, largely because of poor harvests, and although indirect taxes were reintroduced by the impoverished government in 1798, wine remained less expensive during the Revolution than it had been before.[48]

It is likely that the consumption of wine rose during the Revolution, not only because the price was lower, but also because there was an increase in the land under vines and in wine production. The statistics are uncertain, but one estimate has an increase from 27.2 million hectoliters before the Revolution to an average of 36.8 million in the period 1805–12, an increase of a third in about twenty years. It had to be the result of increased vineyards, higher yields, or both, and it represented much more rapid growth than the population, meaning that per capita consumption of wine must have risen. At this time, wine exports were minimal, as France was at war with its export markets for most of the period.

Taken as a whole, the eighteenth century saw the emergence of clearly defined, class-based drinking cultures and a much starker differentiation between elite and popular drinking. Not only did the better-off, whether in North America, Britain, or Europe, drink beverages like port, madeira, and brands of wine that carried social cachet, but they more explicitly and frequently distinguished their drinking cultures from those of the common people. In stressing not the volumes concerned but what was drunk and how it was drunk, the elites echoed the alcohol ideologies of the Greeks and Romans centuries before, as they condemned beer-drinking peoples as "barbarians." Meanwhile people in the lower echelons of society defended what they perceived as their rights to alcohol at a fair price. In this sense, we might see the burning of the customs barriers around Paris in July 1789 and the Whiskey Rebellion in the United States five years later as sharing the same source of inspiration.

9

Alcohol and the City

1800–1900

CLASS AND SOCIAL ORDER

Although there was no general pattern in alcohol consumption throughout Western society during the nineteenth century—it rose in some countries and fell in others, and there were regional and demographic variations in all—a common thread in alcohol discourse throughout Europe and North America was the association of alcohol abuse with the growing industrial working class. Alcohol became the focal point of many anxieties, whether they concerned social and economic changes or shifts in values and behavior. It was held responsible for sickening or killing its consumers, for ruining families, and for causing behavior as varied as prostitution, suicide, insanity, and criminality. Historically, as we have seen, alcohol has been blamed for many social ills, but the tendency went further in the 1800s (see Chapter 10) as many critics abandoned the temperance solution—the notion that moderate drinking was the answer—and embraced the idea of total abstinence, whether voluntary or coerced. One of the innovations underpinning this shift in policy was the provision of safe drinking water to many urban populations. This technological and material development, driven by concerns for public health and ideas about personal and social hygiene and morality, provided one of the bases for the radical antialcohol movements of the nineteenth century.

Until the nineteenth century, when a statistical revolution put masses of more reliable data into the hands of Western states and from there into the hands of historians, our sense of alcohol production and consumption remains just that: a sense. But from the middle of the 1800s, and in some places a little earlier, we have fairly reliable figures of production and taxation, and we can infer broad levels of consumption. They show that there was no pattern common to Europe and North America as a whole. In the most general terms, and without considering regional variations, the consumption of alcohol in England rose steadily during the 1800s; in the United States it declined from the 1840s, while in Germany it rose from the 1850s and declined twenty years later. Beer and brandy were the most popular alcohols in Germany; many French consumers turned from wine to spirits from the 1870s, while the English balanced beer and spirits. But uniting all these variations was a common discourse among published commentators: whether or not alcohol consumption was rising—and even if it were falling—urban working people (the stress was on working men rather than on women) were drinking far too much, and something had to be done about it.

This belief reflected middle- and upper-class anxiety about the speed and scale of social and economic changes in the 1800s. Population rose rapidly in most countries, and the number of large cities multiplied dramatically as economies began to industrialize. The cities teemed with tens of thousands of workers whose public and often alcohol-fueled sociability unnerved the better-off classes, who could afford to drink themselves into subdued rowdiness or simple insensibility in the privacy of their homes, clubs, and other gathering places. Although there are no reliable statistics on differences in drinking behavior between country and town, it is likely that city dwellers, most of whom were workers, consumed alcohol at higher rates. Taverns and bars were certainly more common in cities, and men gathered in these places after work and on weekends. While this might conjure up an image of boisterous sociability, alcohol must also have provided a liquid haven from the hard-working lives of these men. Women, who lived equally hard (if not harder) lives, were generally barred from these drinking places, and they consumed their alcohol in what passed for privacy in their homes. It is notable that although pre-1830 antialcohol campaigners routinely discussed excessive drinking by women, the rise of notions of domesticity seems to have led to women's drinking becoming culturally invisible. From the 1830s, temperance campaigners focused resolutely on drinking by male workers.[1] One commentator noted that the English aristocracy "have very much improved in their drinking habits" and that the alcohol problem was concentrated in the "vicious classes," the lower classes.[2]

A general belief that the working classes were afflicted by alcohol abuse is reflected by the concern among Australian employers that the migrants they attracted were "respectable" and "of good character." One advertisement

seeking migrants for South Australia specified, "We want no idlers here—
no drunkards. But steady, sober men, who are not ashamed to live 'by the
sweat of their brow,' will be welcomed." The application form that would-be
migrants had to fill out had to be signed by two "respectable householders"
who could vouch for the applicant's character, but the form specified, "This
is not to be signed by Publicans or Dealers in Beer or Spirits." To get migrants
off on the right footing, some of the ships used to bring migrants from England to Australia (a grueling four-month voyage) carried no alcohol and were
known as "temperance ships." Others provided alcohol for sale to passengers,
whether they were traveling first class, second-class intermediate, or third-
class steerage. A banker, traveling first class on an 1835 voyage, described his
fellow passengers as "the most inveterate drunkards, fit only for a penal settlement."[3] It is not clear which category of passenger he was referring to, but
the rhetoric (and the suggestion of criminality) echoes contemporary upper-
class attitudes toward working-class drinking.

Much of the increase in alcohol consumption can be attributed to distilled
spirits. It became common in the nineteenth century to make a distinction
between "natural" beverages, such as wine and beer, and their "industrial"
counterparts, such as distilled spirits. The distinction, which is difficult to
justify, helped temperance campaigners in France and elsewhere defend wine
while they condemned spirits (as Benjamin Rush had done at the end of the
1700s). For them, it was obvious that wine was a natural product. It was made
in the country, and grape-growing was a form of agriculture; all the winemaker did was press the grapes and let nature take its course. (There was a
debate in nineteenth-century Germany over adding sugar to grape juice to
raise the potential alcohol level. Opponents of the practice began to refer to
their unsugared wine as "natural.")[4] Spirits, on the other hand, were produced
at urban distilleries that looked like factories. Smoke poured from their chim-
neys, and horse-drawn carts delivered the raw material (grain) and carried the
finished product out. Even though spirits long pre-dated the Industrial Revolution, they became thought of as the mass-produced alcohol of industrial-
ism, and it seemed appropriate that many industrial workers rallied to them.

Although French workers consumed most of their alcohol as wine, an increasing percentage was represented by spirits. On a per capita basis, Parisians drank about 2.9 liters of pure alcohol from spirits in the early 1800s, but
the figure rose to 5.1 liters in the 1840s and 7.3 liters at the end of the century.[5]
The English working classes certainly adopted spirits (generically called "gin")
in the early nineteenth century. If England had a "national drink," it was beer,
but the output of breweries scarcely changed during the first three decades

of the 1800s, even though the population rose by almost a third in the same period. On the other hand, the consumption of spirits almost doubled, from between 3.7 and 4.7 million gallons a year in the first half of the 1820s to more than 7.4 million gallons each year from 1826 to 1830.[6] Governments by this time were starting to collect and pay attention to statistics, and they noted this trend in alcohol consumption with alarm. In 1830 the British parliament passed a Beer Act designed partly to steer workers back to the more nutritious national beverage, partly to appease workers at a time of economic hardship, and partly to weaken the near-monopoly (85 percent of production) that the twelve biggest breweries had over beer in England.[7] Under the Beer Act, any householder who paid a small fee of 2 guineas (a little more than 2 pounds) could brew beer and sell it on their own premises. The only restriction was that they had to close at 10:00 PM, unlike public houses, which could stay open at any hour, except during church services.

Within six months, 24,000 of these beer-houses had opened all over England and Wales, and many thousands more opened in the following year, so there was a bar in almost every neighborhood. It is likely that alcohol had never been so readily available. The Beer Act also repealed the taxes on strong beers and cider, which immediately reduced the price of beer by about a fifth. Under these circumstances, consumption could have been expected to rise, although it is difficult to calculate production, with so much of it deregulated and untaxed. But there was no doubt in the minds of solid middle- and upper-class citizens that drinking had increased, and within hours of the Beer Act coming into effect, there were complaints about beer-generated debauchery, idleness, and criminality on the part of the workers. The Reverend Sydney Smith reported, "Everybody is drunk. Those who are not singing are sprawling. The sovereign people are in a beastly state."[8] Others were soon describing the ravages the Beer Act had wrought on families and portrayed the beer-shops as havens for prostitutes, criminals, and radicals. There are echoes here of the allegations against gin and the dramshops a century earlier.

By the end of the 1830s, more than 40,000 beer-houses were licensed under the act in England and Wales, almost as many as the 56,000 public houses then in operation. That might have been anticipated, given the small cost required to open a beer-house. But if one of the intentions had been to turn gin-drinking workers into beer-consumers, it had only partial success. Faced with competition from the beer-houses, which offered quite basic furnishings and only beer, many of the public houses renovated their drinking spaces and began to offer spirits as well as beer. With comfortable furnishings and sometimes musicians for entertainment, they became known as "gin-palaces" and were said to have stimulated yet another wave of gin-drinking.

Attention was focused squarely on the working classes, as a parliamentary committee made clear: "The vice of intoxication has been for some years past on the decline in the higher and middle ranks of society; but has increased within the same period among the labouring classes."[9] As a result, the Beer Act was revised in 1834 to raise the license fee by 50 percent, to give police the right to search beer-shops, to require owners to have a certificate of "good character," and to divide beer-shops into two classes: those that sold beer to be consumed on the premises and those selling beer to be consumed elsewhere. The former were to display a sign that read, ambiguously, "To be drunk on the premises." In 1869 the licensing of beer-houses came under the control of local magistrates, and their number declined steadily.

The beer-houses became the center of a broader debate on the state of the working classes in nineteenth-century England. Polemicists such as Friedrich Engels, Karl Marx's collaborator, blamed the government and employers for creating such conditions of life and work that workers could be excused for finding relief in sexual and alcoholic excess. Even so, whether the contributors to the debate were hostile or sympathetic to workers, all assumed that there was a high level of consumption and frequent intoxication on their part. The statistics certainly show that sales of alcohol well outpaced population growth: from 1824 to 1874, England's population grew by 88 percent, but beer sales rose by 92 percent, spirits distilled in Britain by 237 percent, foreign spirits by 152 percent, and wine by 250 percent.

While the working classes represented the great majority of the British population and must have contributed to the increased consumption of spirits and wine, these figures do not and cannot tell us whether the increase was greater among workers than among middle- and upper-class drinkers. Wine and spirits, as well as tea, had become the common beverages of the better-off by the middle of the 1800s. One French doctor reported that heavy drinking took place at all levels of French society but that patterns and circumstances varied by class. Workers, generally living on poor diets, tended to drink heavily on a regular basis but also drank "enormous" volumes of brandy in periodic binges. Heavy drinkers in the upper class, on the other hand, were better-nourished and tended to avoid binge-drinking. The working-class pattern, he found, was more likely to manifest as diseases of the liver,[10] and it is possible that the overrepresentation of workers in some disease categories reinforced the prevailing belief that workers generally drank more than their social superiors. An influential 1872 work declared that excessive drinking was concentrated among beggars, vagabonds, criminals, and workers.[11]

In France, another factor came into play in drinking patterns: a tiny, yellow aphid called phylloxera that devastated the country's vineyards from the 1860s and caused a dramatic reduction in French wine production for several decades. Phylloxera aphids are indigenous to North America, where native grapevines are resistant to them. But when they arrived in France in the 1850s and 1860s on the roots of American vines brought over for experimental purposes, they soon migrated to European vines that had no resistance to them. Distressed and dying vines were first identified in southern France in the early 1860s, and by the 1890s phylloxera had devastated vineyards throughout France's major wine regions, including Bordeaux, Burgundy, and the Rhône Valley. From France the disease spread throughout the rest of Europe's vineyards; it reached Spain in 1873 and Italy in the 1880s and then spread (on imported vines) as far afield as California, Peru, and Australia. Unable to eradicate it, French scientists eventually developed a way of dealing with phylloxera—by grafting European vines onto the resistant American rootstock. But by then Europe's wine industry had suffered a serious, if temporary, setback.

French wine production suffered more than that of other European countries, which quickly adopted the grafting solution that French scientists had taken years to discover. Throughout France, the land planted in vines decreased by about a third, with some regions losing as much as four-fifths of their vines. French wine production fell by half between the 1860s and 1880s, and production did not fully recover until the early 1900s. The result was a shortage of wine for two decades, despite success in expanding wine production in France's North African colony Algeria and the widespread adulteration and diluting of wine. Wine made from imported raisins and then blended with red wine from the south of France made up about a tenth of the wine on the French market in 1890.

Phylloxera was a mixed blessing for the French wine industry. It did short-term damage but also led to more rational relocation and replanting of vineyards. Meanwhile, the need to rebuild France's wine market and to reassure domestic and foreign consumers that they were getting real wine, rather than some phylloxera-era concoction, led to the adoption of an early form of *Appellation d'Origine Contrôlée*, which was designed to guarantee the provenance and quality of wine.[12] But over the short term, consumers of French wine turned to other beverages—other alcoholic beverages, that is, for there is no evidence that many seized the opportunity to became water-drinkers.

In Britain, the shortage of French wine stimulated the production of whiskey in Scotland. In the United States, the California wine industry was taking off just as vines in France started to die, and the completion of the continental railway enabled wine-drinkers in the cities of the eastern United States to replace French wine with Californian.

In France itself, alcohol consumption had climbed steadily during the century. In the 1840s, each adult consumed an average of 19 liters of alcohol from all sources (wine, beer, and distilled spirits), and that rose to 25 liters in the 1870s and 35 liters in 1900. It stabilized at that level for the next fifty years, making the 1800s a period of significant growth. Even so, these global figures conceal important variations, not the least important of which was gender: men drank far more alcohol than women. There were also significant regional variations, with higher-than-average consumption in areas where alcohol was produced: the beer and spirits-producing northeast and the wine-producing regions of the south and southwest.[13]

Wine was an important component in the alcohol intake of the French, but it was more important in the south, where the bulk of it was produced and where it represented most of the alcohol consumed. In the northern half of France, beer and spirits played a more significant role. The volume of wine on the market varied, sometimes dramatically from year to year, depending on the harvest. Average wine production between 1805 and 1840 was about 37 million hectoliters, and that rose to 48 million in 1852–62 and 52 million in the 1870s, before falling under the impact of phylloxera. In the 1880s, only 30 million hectoliters of wine were produced each year, just 60 percent of the volume of the previous decade, and in the 1890s, output was 36 million hectoliters. From that point, production began to return to pre-phylloxera levels.[14]

Faced with a shortage of wine, many French wine-drinkers turned also to beer and distilled spirits, and the production of spirits (made from grain, beets, and molasses) doubled between 1870 and 1890. One of these spirits was absinthe, the first alcoholic beverage to be banned outright in many countries. Absinthe is made by macerating the leaves and top part of the wormwood plant, along with ingredients such as anise and fennel, in distilled alcohol, and then distilling it again. In its most popular form, it is a bright green liquid that turns to a cloudy yellow when water is added—commonly by being poured through a cube of sugar sitting on a special slotted spoon.

Absinthe was first introduced to France in the 1840s, in the backpacks of soldiers returning from the war of conquest in Algeria, where it had been used as a cure for dysentery, fever, and malaria. It became popular in the bistros and bars of Paris in the 1860s and 1870s, when five o'clock in the afternoon, the time after work when people drank absinthe, became known as *l'heure verte*, or "the green hour." It was quickly associated with the cultural elite, with Vincent Van Gogh, Edouard Manet, Paul Verlaine, Guy de Maupassant, and Edgar Degas being high-profile consumers. Absinthe was celebrated in many French paintings of the later 1800s, especially in the cabaret paintings of Henri Toulouse-Lautrec.

What gave absinthe such fame (or notoriety) was the belief that it was not only an intoxicant—and a potent one, because the alcohol level was often well above 40 percent—but also a hallucinogen. The active ingredient is thujone, a derivative of wormwood, and the effects of drinking absinthe were described as more akin to a drug like cocaine than to other alcoholic beverages. It was credited with being an aid to cultural inspiration, a quality that seemed to explain its popularity among artists, novelists, and poets, although the hallucinogenic qualities have undoubtedly been overstated. For one thing, the alcohol level of absinthe was generally so high, and the level of thujone generally so low, that most consumers would pass out from the alcohol before feeling the effects of the thujone.

Critics of absinthe portrayed its drinkers as nothing more than drug-takers, and they pointed to its addictive and other harmful qualities. In an 1890 novel called *Wormwood*, the main character, an absinthe-drinker, sums up his life this way: "I am a thing more abject than the lowest beggar that crawls through Paris whining for a sou!—I am a slinking, shuffling beast, half monkey, half man, whose aspect is so vile, whose body is so shaken with delirium, whose eyes are so murderous. . . . At night I live;—at night I creep out with the other obscene things of Paris, and by my very presence, add fresh pollution to the moral poisons in the air."[15] Absinthe addicts were said to have a characteristic hoarse and guttural voice, glazed eyes, and cold, clammy hands.

Just as the production of wine, one of the mainstays of France's bars, cafés, and bistros, started to decline because of the phylloxera epidemic, alcohol consumption in France was given a boost. Through the 1850s and 1860s, the policy of Emperor Napoleon III had been to reduce the number of bars, because they were often places where people gathered to debate political issues. Between 1851 and 1855 alone, the number of bars and bistros selling alcohol in France fell from 350,000 to under 300,000, but it rose to more than 360,000 by the end of the 1860s as regional administrators failed to enforce the law. But in the 1880s, just as wine supplies were falling, the liberal government of the Third Republic made opening a bar even easier, and by the early 1890s the number of drinking establishments swelled to 450,000—one for every sixty-seven inhabitants in France. Competition led some owners to offer more than the basic level of service common in the great majority of bars. They installed counters made of zinc, offered a wider range of drinks, and even hired women to serve the drinks.

With wine in short supply, absinthe production rose, and soon it became the drink of choice among workers in Paris and other major cities in France. The increase in absinthe consumption was nothing short of staggering; it rose from 700,000 liters in 1874 to 36 million liters by 1910, a few years before the French government banned production. This volume was small compared even to the reduced wine production of the time, but because absinthe was so much more alcoholic than wine and was considered a much more dangerous drink, the increase in production and consumption was deplored by social critics, the medical profession, and the clergy. There were reports that per capita consumption of pure alcohol in France tripled between 1850 and 1890 and that it was largely accounted for by the increased consumption of brandy, absinthe, and gin.[16]

Before long, the campaign to ban absinthe was ratcheted up to levels never before applied to any kind of alcohol, even gin in England in the early 1700s. A few medical voices insisted that absinthe might be used to combat depression and "nervous irritability," but the weight of opinion was clearly that absinthe was a danger to the moral and physical health of the drinker and a menace to society. At temperance meetings, guinea pigs and rabbits were fed pure absinthe, after which they had convulsions and died. In 1901, lightning struck one of the Pernod company's absinthe plants and a vat exploded. Burning alcohol flowed out, and the fires burned for days, vividly demonstrating the elevated alcohol content of the beverage.

But what really galvanized the campaign to prohibit absinthe was an event in Switzerland four years later. Jean Lanfray, a peasant born in France and known to be a heavy drinker, murdered his pregnant wife and two daughters, apparently because his wife had failed to wax his boots. Although Lanfray regularly drank six bottles of wine a day, attention was focused on his additional penchant for absinthe. When Lanfray was tried, his lawyer argued that he had shot his wife and children while in an "absinthe-induced delirium." His massive intake of alcohol via wine was considered irrelevant, as wine was considered benign. Sentenced to life imprisonment, Lanfray committed suicide, but by then his case had developed political dimensions. Local pressure led the Swiss government to hold a referendum on absinthe in 1907, and although few people participated, 23,000 voted in favor of banning absinthe and 16,000 voted against. The prohibition on its sale in Switzerland encouraged antiabsinthe campaigners elsewhere.[17]

The outbreak of the First World War, in 1914, provided the political conditions for the banning of absinthe. The first years of the war witnessed a wide range of restrictions on alcohol of all sorts. In order to reduce drunkenness among workers so as to maintain wartime productivity, the alcohol level of beer was ordered to be lowered. At the same time, alcohol production was reduced to save grain for bread, rather than beer and spirits. Wartime conditions also enabled governments to enact policies they hesitated to implement in peacetime, and one of the early wartime acts of the French government, in March 1915, was to ban the production of absinthe, still a popular working-class beverage.

The working-class associations of high alcohol consumption in the 1800s were by no means confined to Europe, as we have seen. In the United States, the period from 1790 to 1830 is thought to have seen far more alcohol consumed on a per capita basis than any other time in American history: each American over the age of fifteen years is estimated to have consumed at least 6.5 gallons of pure alcohol at this time, a volume that was more than halved (to between 2 and 3 gallons) between 1850 and the early 1900s.[18] If these estimates of trends are generally accurate, two shifts need to be explained: the high level of alcohol consumption to 1830 and its sudden decline and stability for the next eight decades.

The high intake of alcohol from 1790 to 1830 is generally attributed to the widespread drinking of American whiskey. Rum had been the beverage of choice through much of the seventeenth and eighteenth centuries, but during the American War of Independence, the British cut off supplies of rum and molasses from their colonies in the Caribbean. Americans turned to whiskey made from locally produced corn and rye, and soon whiskey was regarded as a patriotic drink, much as gin had been in England after the accession of William IV in 1688. As if to demonstrate whiskey's status, George Washington, the republic's first president, had five corn whiskey stills operating on his estate at Mount Vernon. Corn whiskey was especially attractive because settlement in the American Midwest had produced such a glut of the grain that whiskey could be sold for 5 cents for a fifth of a gallon, equal to a modern standard bottle of spirits.

Although Americans also drank cider and beer (and a little wine), whiskey became the beverage of choice in the early republic, and whiskey-drinking attracted the attention of moral and social reformers. They blamed whiskey for crime, poverty, and family violence, and employers pointed out that workers arrived at work drunk and ruined expensive equipment. In 1829 Secretary of War John H. Eaton, lamenting the incidence of heavy drinking in the army, declared, "The practice of indulging in the use of spirituous liquors is so general in this country that there is not, it is believed, one man in four among the laboring classes who does not drink, daily, more than one gill [about 4 ounces]; and it is from these classes that our army is recruited."[19]

Recruits to the army might well have been solid drinkers before they joined, but the army did little to change their behavior. Following the British practice of providing soldiers and sailors with a daily ration of alcohol, Congress authorized a military beer ration at the beginning of the Revolutionary War. In 1782 it was replaced by a gill of whiskey, with George Washington arguing, like the good distillery owner he was, that "the benefits arising from moderate use of strong Liquor have been experienced in all Armies, and are not to be disputed."[20] Each soldier's annual allotment amounted to 13.6 gallons (about 4.5 gallons of pure alcohol), so that the military ration amounted to about two-thirds of the estimated 6.5 gallons of pure alcohol that Americans are thought to have consumed annually at this time. This did not include additional whiskey rations provided to soldiers on fatigue duty or in bad weather, or any additional alcohol that soldiers were able to obtain from civilian merchants. Later attempts to substitute beer and wine for the whiskey ration failed in the face of opposition from soldiers, and it remained in place until 1832.

But during the 1820s, various measures were taken to reduce intoxication in the army. They ranged from persuasion (temperance campaigners encouraged soldiers to take a pledge of abstinence), courts-martial, and even flogging. In some army forts, the whiskey ration was issued in two servings, half at breakfast and half at dinner, rather than all before breakfast, and soldiers were limited to buying a single gill each day from the merchants who followed the armies. Even so, there were continual reports of widespread drunkenness in the army, and alcohol was blamed for desertion, insubordination, disease, and death among soldiers. From a welter of proposals, a new policy emerged in 1832. The whiskey ration was replaced by coffee and tea, except for men on fatigue duty or in hospital (who continued to receive alcohol), and the sale of spirits to soldiers by civilians was prohibited. Reports on the effects of the new policy varied. Some said that discipline had improved, while others claimed that merchants were illicitly supplying soldiers with ever more liquor so that drunkenness was more widespread than before. Either way, the 1832 policy created the first officially dry army in the Western world.

Other military forces, such as the British, Russian, French, and German, continued to provide their soldiers with regular rations of alcohol, but their policies were not without their critics. There was a vigorous debate about the effects of alcohol on military efficiency (discussed in Chapter 12) as well as its implications for the health and physical fitness of soldiers and sailors. Some navies doled out daily rations of alcohol that were sometimes higher than those served to land-based troops because sailors had fewer opportunities to obtain additional alcohol. In the Royal Navy, the alcohol of choice was rum diluted by water, a mixture known as "grog." From the mid-eighteenth century, the ration had been half a pint of rum mixed with a quart of water (one part rum to four parts water), which was doled out in two servings each day. This ration carried over to the American navy, although it was modified in 1794 to provide for either half a pint of whiskey or a quart of beer. The beer option was soon dropped (perhaps because of the volume needed onboard ship), and by 1805 the navy was going through 45,000 gallons of spirits a year. These volumes of alcohol might not, in themselves, have been problematic, but critics argued that they produced in sailors a craving for more and led to sailors' smuggling alcohol onto their ships.[21]

Reports from various stations showed that relatively small percentages of sailors in the Royal Navy suffered from delirium tremens (a form of delirium, or "the shakes," which is often associated with withdrawal from alcohol). There were 2,033 reported cases in the Royal Navy (of an aggregate strength of nearly three-quarters of a million) between 1858 and 1872, and of those, 112 died. The highest mortality rates came from naval stations in the West Indies, Bermuda, Canada, and South America, but even those translated into very low rates compared with the number of serving sailors. Moreover, mortality rates fell during 1858–88.[22] One historian concluded, "It seems that in spite of their reputations as 'drunken sailors,' the seamen of that time displayed a low incidence of delirium tremens."[23]

Policies reducing the alcohol available to American soldiers and sailors were born of their time, because restrictive policies were emerging in civilian society, too. The temperance movement got under way in the 1820s (this is discussed in more detail in Chapter 10) and seems to have had early successes. Some of the groups that were prominent in the temperance movement led by example: it is said that by 1840, 80 percent of the Protestant clergy and half the doctors in New York state had stopped drinking alcohol. If that were true (it is the sort of claim that cannot be verified), it was the leading edge of dramatic changes in alcohol consumption. By 1850, according to some reports, half the population living in small towns and the country had given up alcohol. And if that were true, it was not only a stunning turn of events, given that alcohol had been integral to American social life since the early 1600s, but it had no parallel anywhere else. What we do know is that the first state prohibition policy was enacted in Maine in 1851, and that is an indication of the strength of antialcohol ideas in the first half of the 1800s.

The apparently sudden and widespread embrace of abstinence raises the question of what Americans were drinking to hydrate themselves once they gave up alcohol. It is important to recognize that the United States had a drinking culture different from that of almost anywhere else, in that the dominant alcoholic beverages were distilled spirits: rum in the colonial period, whiskey in the early republic. Distilled spirits, even when diluted with water, do not have the same hydrating purpose or effects as beer or cider and even wine. Although spirits are mostly water, their high alcohol content means that drinking enough for hydration would quickly lead to intoxication. If the whiskey were sufficiently diluted with water, of course, it would (depending on the ratio of whiskey to water) have purified the water to some extent and been a more effectively hydrating beverage, although not very satisfying as an alcoholic beverage.

It is possible that rural America had sufficient supplies of clean drinking water to hydrate its population safely. Even though the claim that half the rural and small-town population of the United States had quickly abandoned alcohol seems unlikely to be true, the availability of safe, potable water would lead us to expect that they could have given up alcohol more readily than their city counterparts, who had no such alternative. Water in the cities was far more problematic, and urban workers (and others) must have been more reluctant to abstain from alcohol. There was, in addition, growing consumption of nonalcoholic beverages, such as coffee and tea, which provided safe hydration.

The effect of the antialcohol movements on nineteenth-century American drinking patterns is discussed in Chapter 10, but it is worth noting that at that time America experienced waves of immigration that might have been expected to push alcohol consumption up. Many Germans began to arrive in the 1820s, and they brought their beer-drinking culture with them. Three decades later, a wave of beer- and whiskey-drinking Irish immigrants arrived, fleeing the famine in their homeland. Yet although alcohol consumption rates in contemporary Germany and Ireland were undoubtedly higher than in the United States, and the immigrants might well have consumed more than the resident population, their numbers were nowhere near big enough to affect the overall level of American alcohol consumption. The effect of these two groups on America's drinking culture was felt in other ways. From the 1850s, German immigrants began to open the breweries that became some of the biggest in the United States, Coors, Miller, Anheuser-Busch, Pabst, and

Schlitz among them. For their part, Irish immigrants contributed to American culture Irish-themed saloons and St. Patrick's Day, an alcohol-centered festivity for Irish and non-Irish alike.

As the examples of Britain, France, and the United States show, alcohol was widely consumed in the nineteenth century, but critics focused mainly on urban drinking and on the working class. It was true even more broadly. In Germany, industrialization took off in the 1850s and 1860s, and by the mid-1870s, one in six workers was employed in industry. As real wages improved in the early period of industrial growth, alcohol consumption rose: between 1855 and 1873, consumption of Schnapps (which referred to any distilled spirits) increased by 50 percent and sales of beer nearly doubled, increases that far outstripped population growth. Per capita consumption reached its peak in the early 1870s, when each adult consumed an average 10.2 liters of pure alcohol, equally represented by beer and spirits. But at that point the German economy entered an industrial depression, and brandy was largely priced out of workers' budgets. Although beer sales rose steadily through the early 1900s, spirits declined steeply, lowering the per capita volume of pure alcohol consumed.[24]

Alcohol regularly punctuated the workday in mid-century Germany. Employers provided alcohol to their workers until they realized that it had a harmful effect on labor discipline and productivity. Even though per capita consumption was not high in relative terms, the steady intake of alcohol, combined with the novelty of urban industrial life, stirred anxiety in middle-class observers. It was not that workers were perceived as drunken and debauched—the sort of allegations made in England—but that their drinking made them "lazy, unreliable, disruptive and dissatisfied," as one temperance leader put it.[25] By 1885, two-thirds of factories in one survey had banned the use of spirits on their premises, but half of them reported problems of resistance by workers who smuggled alcohol in.[26]

The nineteenth-century social lens was firmly focused on the new urban working class, the unprecedented, growing, and often threatening social class of the industrial economy everywhere. Alcohol was consumed in small towns, villages, and isolated farms, too, but it was far less visible. Drinking establishments in small communities and the country were thought of as places where agricultural workers socialized. Small-town and rural social pressure and convention might well have ensured that they remained reasonably orderly. The cities, on the other hand, produced a profusion of drinking places, and whether they were French cabarets, British beer-houses, German beer-cellars, or American saloons, they were portrayed as places of immorality and criminality. Urban society did not regulate itself the way country society did, and nor was there, in the 1800s, a police force big enough to reassure the middle and upper classes. By the nineteenth century, any notion of people of vastly different social class rubbing elbows at the bar (if it was ever generally true) disappeared as the upper and middle classes retreated to their homes and private clubs in the face of growing crowds of unruly workers. If alcohol in itself were considered problematic, alcohol in the hands of urban workers was regarded as an imminent threat to the social and moral order.

And the number of large industrial cities grew. In Europe in 1800 there were twenty-two cities with more than 100,000 inhabitants. By 1900, there were seventy-nine, and they were only the largest of many more large concentrations of population. Cities meant not only more people crammed together but also problems of social order and health. The upper and middle classes deplored the behavior of what they thought of as the "dangerous classes"—the workers and the poor—whose living arrangements, relationships, hygiene, and social comportment left so much to be desired. As one French commentator put it, "Savages alone take to drink with the fervor displayed by the most degraded part of the poor classes, like the Negro on the African coast, who sells his children and himself for a bottle of spirits. . . . To the savage, intoxication is supreme felicity; to the destitute of the great cities it is an invincible passion, an indulgence which they cannot do without."[27]

What was the cure for the many ills of the city? Water. Safe, clean drinking water.

Water is necessary for human life, but in the cities of the nineteenth century, it was often polluted, especially by their inhabitants who disposed of human and industrial waste in ways that made rivers and other bodies of water unsuitable for drinking. The pollution of water supplies began long before the nineteenth century, but it reached a critical point then. Historian Peter Mathias describes the early 1800s as "an age when drinking water was the most dangerous habit of all."[28] In the mid-1800s, water from the River Thames taken onboard Royal Navy ships in London for consumption by sailors on long voyages was described this way: "It purifies itself, say the apologists; and so to a certain extent it does: but the process of purification is far from rapid, during which it exhibits various forms of putridity, and a variety of colours, as the runnings from gas-works or sewers may predominate in each particular cask."[29]

London was far from unique in having water problems. An 1830s report on Boston, Massachusetts, noted that a quarter of the wells that provided the city's water were bad, and the rest left much to be desired. "There are many persons upon whom the well water of Boston acts very unpleasantly, making them sick at the stomach. . . . In most persons it produces constipation of the bowels and many other . . . symptoms of diseased functions. It is much desired that good water should be supplied to the city so as to reach every dwelling and supply every person."[30] That was a need in many places. Inhabitants of the poorer districts of Leeds, in northern England, had no water within a quarter of a mile of their dwellings, and very few even had vessels in which they could fetch water.[31] The drinking water of Brussels, in Belgium, was described in the 1830s and 1840s as having a "disgusting flavour," a "foul odor," an "extremely disagreeable smell of rotten wood," and a "nauseating taste." An 1844 study of Paris concluded that barely 10 percent of the water drawn from the public fountains was drinkable.[32]

From the mid-1800s, central and urban governments began to address the water problem by constructing systems that piped clean water to cities. They were driven by several considerations. First, there were waves of epidemics of waterborne diseases such as cholera and typhoid fever between the 1830s and 1850s. An outbreak of cholera in the Soho district of London in 1854 killed more than 500 people in ten days.[33] Second, the ruling classes believed that the urban masses needed the means to keep themselves and their environments clean and hygienic, and that meant providing water suitable for washing as well as sewage systems to carry waste away. Third, the simple existence of water was sometimes construed as having the power to improve morality. Urban planners in Boston and elsewhere included fountains in their designs on the ground that the sight and sound of water had the power to tame urban passions and bring order and decency to the disorder and degradation of the city. Fourth, safe drinking water would be an alternative to the alcohol that was increasingly blamed for social and moral disorder. Water, then, would cleanse the city and the bodies of its teeming inhabitants of many of their physical and moral maladies. And as the Reverend John Garwood of the London City Mission observed in 1859, water would fix the drinking problem: "A very large amount of drunkenness is occasioned by the great difficulty of obtaining pure water to drink in many of the poor parts of London."[34]

By the time Garwood made that observation, dozens of municipalities in England, Scotland, and Wales had begun to create systems for piping filtered water to cities, sometimes to public fountains, sometimes to individual dwellings. These major public works, which involved establishing reservoirs of water together with piping systems, took decades to complete, but gradually during the 1800s many urban populations were supplied with water that was suitable for drinking, food preparation, and washing. From the 1840s through the end of the century, some 180 British towns and cities established clean water supplies, and by 1911, 96 percent of dwellings in London were connected to a water supply. This was a much higher percentage than in Paris, where most water was piped to public outlets rather than to individual dwellings.[35] In the Netherlands, piped water was introduced to Amsterdam first, in 1854, before being extended to Rotterdam and The Hague in the 1860s and to Leiden, Utrecht, and Arnhem in the 1870s and 1880s. By the end of the century, about 40 percent of the Dutch population had access to piped drinking water.[36]

The technologies developed in Europe were soon applied around the world. An English engineer oversaw the waterworks that was completed in Yokohama in 1887, and in the following years he consulted on water supplies for other Japanese cities, including Tokyo, Osaka, and Kobe. Other Europeans were actively involved in projects to supply drinking water in Asian cities that included Mumbai, Hong Kong, Colombo, Karachi, and Singapore.[37] They were undertaken in the spirit of colonial interest. Henry Conybeare, an English engineer heavily involved in water reform, wrote that fresh water would reduce illness caused by bad water: "For every death . . . there are . . . at least fourteen cases of illness . . . during which the patient is not only unproductive himself, but is a burden on the productive labour of others."[38]

In the United States, providing fresh water had moved ahead more rapidly. New York had tried various methods, but by the 1830s the volume and quality of the city's water was reaching a critical stage. An 1830 report by the Lyceum of Natural History, New York's leading scientific body, concluded that the city was simply unable to provide an "adequate supply of good or wholesome water" from its own rivers and wells. The underlying geological structure of New York was not suitable for wells, and even though urine that seeped into wells from cisterns softened the hard well water, the Lyceum's scientists noted that "the fastidious may revolt from the use of water thus sweetened to our palate."[39] The quality of the water might have been argument enough in favor of a new water supply system, but temperance campaigners argued for it as an alternative to alcohol. Ironically, they found themselves on the same side as the city's brewers, who argued that New Yorkers were turning to beer made in Philadelphia because of the unpleasant taint local water gave to the local beers. The alcohol industry was not an insignificant lobby. In 1835, when New York contained 30,000 houses, there were 2,646 taverns (1 tavern for 12 houses), 63 distilleries, and 12 breweries within the city limits.

But as elsewhere, it was partly an outbreak of disease—in this case, cholera, which killed thousands in 1832—that spurred New York's administrators into action. Three years later, a disastrous fire that could not be doused because of inadequate water supplies reinforced the sense of urgency. Even so, not until 1842 was an aqueduct, which brought water from a river thirty miles from Manhattan, completed. The water was judged "a wholesome temperance beverage," and the celebrations and procession held to mark the arrival of fresh, clean water had a clear antialcohol tone: "The temperance societies . . . won high marks for their display of a water hydrant chasing a rum cask and a banner with an inverted decanter reading 'Right Side Up.'"[40]

In Boston the first municipal water system was completed in 1848 after years of debate among reformers and ordinary citizens.[41] Providing water as an alternative to alcohol was only one of the issues in play; clean, fresh, potable, and free water was seen as a resource that citizens had a right to, and it was portrayed as beneficial to health, morality, and social order. There was little doubt that Boston's water supply was overtaxed and of poor quality. An 1834 survey showed that consumers considered that 30 of the city's nearly 3,000 wells delivered undrinkable water. Water from many of the rest tasted bad, and some was so discolored that it stained clothing washed in it.

The wish to reduce alcohol consumption was only one part of the campaign to provide Bostonians with good drinking water, but it was a prominent argument. Some held that people added alcohol to poor quality water to make it drinkable; one artisan said "he used to mix spirit with water, when it was so bad I could not drink it without." There was also the evidence of a citizen of Philadelphia, which already had a waterworks: "I was in the daily habit of using intoxicating drinks, and scarce ever drank water without mixing them with it. Since the introduction of that [fresh] water, I have almost abandoned the use of such drinks . . . *I do not want them.*" Little wonder that supporters of temperance fell in behind the water movement. They praised water as the pure beverage that was part of nature and compared it to human-made, fabricated, alcoholic beverages. As part of nature, water was God-given, as one writer pointed out graphically: "Not in the simmering still, over smoky fires, choked with poisonous gases and surrounded with the stench of sickening odors and rank corruptions, doth our Father in heaven prepare the precious essence of life—the pure cold water."[42]

Many more examples could be given to illustrate this trend. Throughout Europe and North America (and elsewhere) during the nineteenth century, more and more urban populations had reliable access to the clean, fresh drinking water that moral reformers hoped would replace alcohol. Americans began to use far more water for a wide variety of purposes (including washing and drinking) than Europeans. By the beginning of the twentieth century, people in Europe's largest cities (including London, Paris, and Berlin) went through 86 liters of water per capita each day. In the major cities of the United States, the figure was 341 liters, four times the volume on a per capita basis.[43] The situation in smaller towns and rural areas is less clear, and it is likely that many continued to rely on the water of variable quality that came from local springs and rivers and from artesian wells.

In some places, such as Boston, the antialcohol and pro-water lobbies joined forces to argue explicitly not only that improved water supplies were desirable in themselves but that they would also benefit society by hastening the arrival of an alcohol-free society. Even so, the temperance argument for water reform was not without its opponents. One pamphleteer condemned the "impudence" of Boston's water campaigners in hitching their wagon to the temperance cause and "prating about pure and soft water, while every syllable they utter is accompanied by the compound stench of brandy and tobacco." He doubted whether water would ever be an adequate substitute for brandy: "How little influence has the quality of water, upon the brandy-drinker's habits! He may assign it as an excuse, and when the city shall have removed this excuse, at the cost of millions, he will readily find another."[44]

He was probably right that few alcohol-drinkers were likely to be swayed, or quickly swayed, toward abstinence simply because clean drinking water was—literally—on tap. Later in the century, in 1870, the *British Medical Journal* lamented that "the social movement in favour of water-drinking has been steadily pushed on for nearly forty years," but that no matter where you looked—hospitals, prisons, or the "poorer streets of any British town on Saturday night"—there was clear evidence that "prominent amongst the causes of human misery, in all its legion forms, is DRINK."[45]

Yet the provision of drinking water in major cities had important consequences for the history of alcohol. In many parts of the world, especially in the industrial cities where alcohol abuse was believed to be especially serious, it could no longer be argued that alcohol was necessary for hydration. As such, alcohol could be viewed as an almost exclusively recreational drink, a discretionary beverage that could be given up without any harmful consequences. Indeed, the centuries-old argument for the superiority of alcohol over water could be and was turned on its head: beginning in the nineteenth century, water would be portrayed as the safe choice, and alcohol could be condemned as harmful. But whereas water had been seen as dangerous to the health of individuals, alcohol could be represented as harmful to society and morality as well. The provision of supplies of safe drinking water was thus one of the conditions that made possible a real shift in attitudes toward alcohol and provided a basis for the rise of temperance ideologies in the 1800s.

10

The Enemies of Alcohol

1830–1914

TEMPERANCE AND PROHIBITION

For thousands of years, concerns had been expressed about the harmful effects of alcohol on human health and social order, but they were mere murmurs when compared with the furor of the attack on alcohol that rose during the nineteenth century. Temperance societies appeared in the 1830s, and fifty years later, mass organizations were dedicated to limiting the availability and reducing the consumption of alcoholic beverages or to eliminating them altogether. Powerful temperance and prohibitionist movements, many with religious affiliations, attracted widespread support in many parts of the world, notably in the United States, Canada, the United Kingdom, and Scandinavia. Working in national and subnational arenas and cooperating internationally, they publicized their messages in newspapers, pamphlets, and books and broadcast them in speeches and lectures. Many took to the streets to put pressure on governments to bring the alcohol business under control or to put it out of business altogether. To that time, it was the largest civilian mobilization of people and resources ever assembled to achieve a single policy goal, and it resulted in a wave of prohibition and near-prohibition policies in many countries during and soon after the First World War.

Historians have paid a lot of attention to these antialcohol organizations and their leaderships and, more generally, to the politics of alcohol in the nineteenth century.[1] But far less attention has been given to the social, cultural, and material conditions that enabled the antialcohol movement to have such an impact on political culture and alcohol policies. These conditions included the broad changes that accompanied urbanization and industrialization in the 1800s, as well as more specific phenomena, such as the rise of Christian reform movements and gendered politics. At the material level, the availability and widening consumption of nonalcoholic beverages—especially potable water but also tea and coffee—had a critical impact on the cultural meaning of alcohol and made its consumption vulnerable to the attacks mounted by the organized antialcohol movements.

Although these organizations that emerged in the 1800s shared a general hostility toward alcohol, their broader strategies and immediate goals were often quite diverse. There were, first, important differences among those who called simply for moderation in drinking, those who called for voluntary abstinence by consumers, and those who wanted the total prohibition, by law, of alcohol production, distribution, and consumption. Some placed greatest weight on the health dangers of alcohol; others stressed the social disruption they believed it led to, while yet others drew attention to the dangers of alcohol for the growth and well-being of national populations, a powerful consideration in this period of intensified nationalism in Europe. Organizations with religious affiliations justified their positions by appeal to scripture, while others drew on secular and utilitarian arguments. Finally, women's antialcohol organizations tended to focus on the dangers that drinking men posed to women, children, sexual morality, and the stability of the family.

Overall, the medium-term achievements of the antialcohol movement were impressive, but like the movements themselves, they varied from place to place. The best-known success was national prohibition in the United States, although prohibition policies of varying degrees were also to be found in countries as diverse as Russia, Mexico, Canada, Belgium, and Finland (see Chapter 13). In yet other countries, such as England and Scotland, such rigorous policies were rejected in favor of tighter regulations regarding the sale of alcohol. Many of these policies, we should note, were introduced only after the outbreak of the First World War (see Chapter 12), when the demands of a war economy made it politically feasible for governments to enact policies they had hesitated to impose during peacetime. That said, there is no denying the achievements of the antialcohol movements before the outbreak of the global war.

The strategies the various organizations adopted varied according to the laws, policy-making institutions, and drinking cultures they faced. In the United States, pressure was first put on state governments, and there was a particular focus on saloons as the primary sites of problematic drinking. In France and Germany, temperance campaigners pressed national authorities to ban distilled spirits. But there were some common features. Everywhere there was a wide range of organizations, with one or two dominant. There were divisions between those who campaigned for moderate drinking and those who insisted on total abstention, and between those who wanted voluntary abstinence and those who favored coercive policies of prohibition. Protestant churches generally embraced the antialcohol cause more enthusiastically than the Catholic Church, and women were prominent participants in most movements, sometimes as leaders, sometimes as members.

All these characteristics were to be found in the broad-based antialcohol campaign that arose in the United States from the early 1800s. Drawing on middle-class anxiety about the effects of alcohol on social stability, a number of state-based temperance societies were formed soon after the turn of the century. Rather than embrace voluntary total abstinence or prohibition, many had limited ambitions, like the Massachusetts Society for the Suppression of Intemperance (founded in 1813), which campaigned mainly against the consumption of spirits, the source of most of the alcohol consumed by Americans at that time. But by the 1830s, some organizations were beginning to insist that their members abstain entirely from alcohol (that is, adopt teetotalism), while others started to press for prohibition, which would have imposed abstinence on everyone by cutting off all sources of alcohol. Pressure from these organizations contributed to the adoption of stringent alcohol regulations in a number of states. In 1838, Massachusetts banned the sale of spirits in volumes of less than 15 gallons (effectively ending the retail sale of spirits for personal consumption by the mass of the population), and in the 1840s, other states began to restrict the sale of spirits. In 1847, in response to legal challenges to these restrictions, the U.S. Supreme Court ruled that state governments had the power to refuse licenses to sell spirits.

Legislators in Maine took the fight against alcohol much further. As early as 1837, a committee of the state legislature decided that the most effective way to control drinking was to ban the sale of alcoholic beverages entirely, and after some transitional legislation, Maine became, in 1851, the first state to prohibit the production and sale of alcoholic beverages within its borders. State officials were empowered (if three citizens lodged a complaint against any individual) to search private premises for alcohol intended for sale, and a mandatory prison term was imposed for a third conviction of breaking the prohibition law.[2] However, the Maine law did not prohibit the consumption of alcohol or its importation into the state for personal consumption. This meant that as long as alcohol was available in the contiguous states, many citizens of Maine had reasonable access to alcohol. By 1855, however, all the New England states had adopted prohibition laws, as had New York and a number of other states and territories. This initial tide of state-based prohibition laws crested during the 1850s and then ebbed. Maine's legislators repealed the 1851 law in 1856, reenacted it in 1858 after a referendum, and finally entrenched prohibition in the state's constitution in 1884. But many other states that had enacted prohibition-style laws in the 1850s repealed them by the late 1860s.

In the 1870s, following the Civil War, a second wave of antialcohol sentiment began to build. One of the most important organizations was the Woman's Christian Temperance Union (WCTU), founded in 1874 by women from sixteen states.[3] Membership was limited to women, who were expected to abstain entirely from alcohol, and the organization's initial mandate was to fight the evils of saloons and to lobby for a congressional inquiry into the alcohol trade. The WCTU justified women's participation in political life on the ground that women had a special interest in defending family and home from the ravages of alcohol, and later (in 1881) it invoked the same argument when it added women's suffrage to its agenda. Yet although the WCTU attracted wide support—it had about 150,000 members in the United States by 1890— and gave many women their first experience of political participation, it failed to make the impact on national politics that might have been expected.

The WCTU was dominated by Protestant women. Jewish women tended to distance themselves from it, partly because they objected to the Christian agendas (or the name of the WCTU), but more because they drank wine at Sabbath dinners and social gatherings and did not see alcohol as a problem in the Jewish community.[4] Catholics largely stayed away because, although the WCTU made it clear that there was no "creed test" for membership, many temperance supporters opposed immigration, notably immigration by Catholics and especially from Ireland. Frances Willard, the most prominent leader of the WCTU, called on Congress in 1892 to prohibit "the influx into our land of more of the scum of the Old World, until we have educated those who are here."[5] Some Catholic Irish Americans, inspired by the temperance work of Theobald Mathew ("Father Mathew") in Ireland, took up the cause independently. The major Catholic society, the Catholic Total Abstinence Union, was founded in 1872 (before the WCTU), and it and its affiliates counted 90,000 members by the early 1900s. Temperance was far more popular among Irish than German Catholics, the latter seeing it as a threat to cultural activities such as Sunday beer-gardens. Irish Catholics, however, viewed temperance as a means of assimilating into American society and ridding themselves of the stereotypes that cast them as unclean, rowdy, brawling drinkers. Some of the supporters, like Bishop John Ireland of St. Paul, Minnesota, an immigrant himself, probably did not help the Irish cause by suggesting in 1882 that his compatriots were inherently prone to drunkenness: "Alcohol does them more harm, because their warm nature yields more readily to its flames."[6] It was a strange conflation of the humoral theory of the body and prevailing ideas about the "natural" tendency of some populations, such as Native Americans, toward intoxication.

In time, Catholic organizations turned their attention to saloons, male-only bars that were seen as the worst manifestations of drinking in America; in 1890, one priest referred to them as "an illicit, a morally bad business."[7] But three years later, a Congregationalist minister, H. H. Russell, founded the Anti-Saloon League of America (ASLA), a much more important organization that initially aimed only to close saloons, not to prevent drinking at home, but which soon broadened its mandate to encompass a full-fledged prohibitionist program. Where the WCTU's leadership had created divisions within its membership by allying with political parties that supported prohibition, the ASLA was resolutely nonpartisan and soon worked single-mindedly for prohibition. For the ASLA, the saloon—the working-class public house that had gained a reputation for being a rowdy, disreputable place where coarse men gathered to get drunk, blaspheme, gamble, and enjoy a thousand other vices—was a symbol of all that was wrong with the consumption of alcohol.[8]

The ASLA came into its own in the early 1900s, when it was the leading edge of the often disparate prohibition movement in the United States. It worked with other groups, funded prohibitionist activities at the state level, and became wealthy enough (thanks in part to financial support from millionaire prohibitionist John D. Rockefeller) to build a printing plant where it published its own books and pamphlets. Some were published in foreign languages so that the prohibitionist message would reach the immigrants who flowed into the United States from eastern and southern Europe at the turn of the century.

The influence of the ASLA on personal drinking behavior cannot be measured, but its impact on policy-makers can. Almost all American states adopted restrictive alcohol policies in the twenty years preceding the First World War, and many went so far as to enact strict prohibition. This patchwork of states that were either "dry" or "wet" ("damp" might be more descriptive of states that merely regulated alcohol rigorously) led to one of the ASLA's greatest achievements: the 1913 Webb-Kenyon Act, which prohibited the movement of alcohol from a wet state to a dry one. Having achieved that, and with the wind in the sails of prohibition at the state level, the ASLA redoubled its efforts to secure nationwide prohibition by means of an amendment to the Constitution. By 1916 a prohibition-friendly Congress started the process by which the Eighteenth Amendment, enacting national prohibition, would be passed. Although the ASLA was only one of many antialcohol organizations, it was by far the most important in size and influence, and its contribution to having prohibition enacted in the United States is undeniable.

The English antialcohol movements are a study in both similarities and contrasts to their counterparts in the United States. The temperance movement—inspired by organizations in Scotland—first got under way in 1830 in northern industrial cities such as Manchester and Bradford before working its way south. By 1831 there were thirty societies, all with the relatively modest aim of stemming the excessive consumption of distilled spirits. Far from thinking that alcohol was evil and its consumption wrong, many of the first generation of English alcohol reformers drank wine and beer, and even drinkers of distilled spirits could be admitted as members of their societies.[9] At this point they could not be called enemies of alcohol, as their policies demanded no more than supporters of moderate consumption had sought for centuries. This approach to what became known as "the drink question" achieved limited results. Although moderation succeeded in putting alcohol on the broader social reform agenda, the vast social gap between the middle-class reformers and those they believed to be most in need of reform—working-class men—militated against much practical success. Moreover, by tolerating wine and beer while targeting gin and other distilled spirits, these middle-class men could easily be portrayed as demonizing the common drink of workers while treating their own preferred alcoholic beverages as benign.

In a fairly short time, the moderate approach that aimed for temperate drinking was challenged by demands for more radical reforms, including complete abstinence from alcohol. Members of the original temperance societies who were abstainers formed their own societies, and soon the English antialcohol movement was split. The division was not only one of approach: reformists tended to be middle class, religious, and from London and the southern counties, while proponents of total abstinence were more often from the industrial north of the country, without religious affiliation, and reformed drinkers themselves with working-class roots.[10] Drawing on their social affinity, the teetotalers worked to help heavy drinkers shake the habit, whereas the middle-class reformers had taken the view that existing drunkards were beyond help and that the main task was to prevent anyone from starting to drink heavily.

Working-class, self-help teetotalism became a feature of the antialcohol movement in England by the mid-nineteenth century, and abstinence was portrayed as a way to improve the lives of working men and their families.

Some organizations were resolutely secular, such as the East London Chartist Temperance Association, which prohibited any discussion of religion for fear that it would be divisive and distract attention from the main issue.[11] Members helped one another find work, and they were encouraged to trade among themselves as much as possible. At another level, refraining from alcohol was portrayed as a precondition for workers to obtain the vote and other political rights. Some socialists also argued for teetotalism for political reasons, seeing alcohol as one of the means by which employers kept their workers docile and uninterested in union and political activism.

But teetotalers of all kinds fought an uphill struggle. Drinking was solidly entrenched in English working-class culture, and the public house was the primary place for working men (and women, though less often) to socialize. All manner of events, from births and weddings to funerals, were marked by social drinking, and public houses were the principal or only public meeting places in many communities. (Many antialcohol organizations had difficulty finding locations for their meetings, and the wealthier among them built their own Temperance Halls.)[12] Alcohol was also a medium of exchange, and drinks were offered as payment for small services; women who acted as attendants at funerals were customarily given a serving of rum. Above all, drinking in the company of friends, neighbors, and workmates was enjoyable, and alcohol was not only a social lubricant but also a social adhesive.

There was, of course, another side to drinking: alcohol could be equally effective in dissolving social bonds when provocative words were uttered and arguments and fights broke out in public houses and when drinking led to domestic violence in private homes. Alcohol runs like a steady stream in the records of the growing number of divorces in the nineteenth century. Often the records show a drunk husband beating his wife, but apologists for domestic violence sometimes explained male violence as provoked by women's drinking: "In the vast majority of these cases, the suffering angel . . . is found to be rather an angel of the fallen class, who has made her husband's home an earthly hell, who spends his earnings in drink."[13] In the later nineteenth century, divorce laws in many Western countries (and states in the United States) added persistent drunkenness to the grounds that justified dissolving a marriage. Maine added "gross and confirmed habits of intoxication" in 1883; Virginia added "habitual drunkenness" in 1891, while in Scotland (in 1903), habitual drunkenness was made equivalent to cruelty for the purpose of getting a judicial separation.[14]

But the overwhelming working-class male perception of alcohol was positive, and many English workers were hostile toward teetotalers, seeing them not only as dull and unsociable tea-drinkers but even as implicitly subversive of working-class culture. There were suspicions that teetotalers were in the pay of employers who wanted their workers to stop spending money on drinks so that they could reduce their wages. In fact, some employers fired employees who signed the abstinence pledge, because their presence among workers who continued to drink was disruptive and threatened the harmony of the workplace.

While dynamics such as these operated within the English working class, middle-class reformers began to mobilize against alcohol on a grand scale. One spur to action was the 1851 prohibition law passed in Maine, which was a different and much more rigorous model than any of the English organizations had envisaged. Teetotalers relied on moral persuasion, leaving it to drinkers to see the light and stop drinking voluntarily, but Maine's legislators provided a model that, if adopted, gave drinkers no choice but to stop. It appealed to those who were convinced that alcohol was such a harmful commodity that the state ought to take it out of circulation, and it altered the terms of reference of some English antialcohol movements by shifting the object of their attention. Many advocates of abstention had become frustrated by their failure to convince consumers of alcohol to change their ways, and they began to lobby politicians and governments at all levels to enact policies that would severely limit or end the availability of alcohol. In this sense, the antialcohol activists became an explicitly political movement as much as one for social reform.

But although prohibition became a popular policy in the United States, the notion of a coercive, state-enforced prohibition on alcohol found little support in Britain. It was opposed by most alcohol reform organizations, and it was at odds with the prevailing middle-class ideology of liberalism, which envisaged the state as guaranteeing rather than erasing personal freedoms. John Stuart Mill, the leading liberal theorist, declared that prohibition policies were "monstrous" and an "illegitimate interference with the rightful liberty of the individual." Drinking was a personal choice, he wrote, and even drunkenness "is not a fit subject for legislative interference."[15] Such sentiments seemed to be shared by most British legislators, even those critical of alcohol. Long-serving prime minister William Gladstone, for example, declared, "We have suffered more in our time from intemperance than from any war, pestilence, and famine combined," and he encouraged the drinking of tea instead.[16]

But many British legislators were uneasy about even partial restrictions such as limitations on Sunday drinking. In 1854 a law was passed to prevent drinking places in England from opening on Sundays between 2:30 and 6:00 PM and after 10:00 PM, but it (together with a law prohibiting Sunday trading) generated massive protests. A crowd of working-class Londoners, estimated by Karl Marx (who was there) at 200,000, demonstrated in Hyde Park on a Sunday in June 1855. (Marx, who mistakenly thought this might be the beginning of the workers' revolution, noted that some of the gentry, in the park for their weekly outing, seemed to be somewhat under the weather from their lunchtime wine.) The law was amended to require pubs to close from 3:00 to 5:00 PM and after 11:00 PM, which allowed ninety minutes' more drinking time on Sunday afternoons than the original form.[17]

This compromise represented only a partial victory for supporters of Sunday closing in England, and their counterparts elsewhere in Britain were even more successful. Pubs were ordered closed throughout the day on Sundays in Scotland in 1854, in Ireland (except for the main cities) in 1878, and in Wales in 1881. But despite their general failure to have much impact on policy or (as far as we can tell) consumption patterns, England's antialcohol organizations experienced a new lease on life in the 1860s and 1870s. New organizations were formed, and more important, many of the major Protestant churches rallied to the cause. The Church of England Temperance Society, formed in 1863, became the largest organization of its kind by the end of the century, when it had 7,000 branches and between 150,000 and 200,000 subscribing members.[18]

With other organizations, it pressured the government to enact restrictive policies on alcohol, particularly as it affected children, who until then had been able to obtain alcohol as easily as adults. A series of laws in the last decades of the nineteenth century moved toward establishing a minimum legal drinking age, a common feature of modern alcohol policies. In 1872, children under the age of sixteen were prohibited from purchasing spirits at a public house for consumption on the premises, and in 1886 children under thirteen were prohibited from buying ale for consumption in a public house. But in both cases children could purchase alcohol for consumption elsewhere. Working-class parents often sent their children to buy drinks for them, but there was growing fear that this provided a loophole that allowed children to drink at will. One observer of taverns in Edinburgh noted that "children, sent with jugs for liquor, seemed to enjoy sipping it after emerging from the public house."[19] In response to such concerns, a 1901 Child Messenger Act forbade the sale of beer or spirits to a child under age fourteen unless the alcohol was in a sealed bottle.

Legal reforms like these were part of a contemporary trend to protect children, and the antialcohol movements dedicated much of their energy to educating children about the dangers of alcohol before drink got them in its clutches. In Hull (Yorkshire), temperance workers organized an essay competition among elementary school students on the theme "Physical Deterioration and Alcoholism." The essays produced insights such as the following: "To-day, many people are in jail for committing suicide, while under the influence of drink"; "Seafaring men who are in the habit of drinking are liable to collide with other vessels"; and "Before so much alcohol was taken, the British were sturdy, strong, square-shouldered men. But what do you see at the present day? Thin, puny, round-shouldered men."[20]

Reformers saw children affected by alcohol in several ways. First, many unplanned births were said to result from women drinking and allowing men to take advantage of them—a process described pithily by one author as combining "brutality, female degradation, and reckless prodigality."[21] Second, drinking habits were passed from generation to generation, although one author noted that "happily, drunkenness is a direct cause of sterility."[22] Third, children (and their mothers) often suffered neglect and pauperization, as men squandered on alcohol the money that was needed for shelter and food. Protecting the family was central to antialcohol discourses everywhere, from Europe to North America and beyond.[23]

Alcohol was said to have ruined what should have been many joyous family occasions. One series of illustrations portrayed the way alcohol spoiled Christmas, a festival coming into its own in the later 1800s. The "Drunkard's Christmas" showed a bar scene with men drinking, sleeping, and being sick. One was clearly a father, and his children cowered under the bar counter. An accompanying verse read,

> Behold the effects of intemperance here,
> No comfort at this happy time of the year;
> For the little children no pudding, no play,
> And no home but the pot-house on dear Christmas-day.

In contrast was the "Teetotaller's Christmas," a scene of a happy family with lots of food, the children also on the floor, but here gazing greedily at plates laden with pies.

> By industry and temperance the board is well-spread
> With a nice furnished home o'er the family's head;
> Here is plenty and peace, such as all men may win,
> With a blessing from God, by refraining from gin.[24]

Antialcohol movements elsewhere adopted different strategies. In France the temperance movement did not get under way, in any serious sense, until after the French defeat by the Prussians in 1870—a defeat attributed to, among other things, a weakening of the population (and young men of military age in particular) by the consumption of distilled spirits. Until that point, leading French political and other commentators insisted that, unlike the United States and Great Britain, France did not have a drinking problem because its people drank wine, a healthy beverage. In 1853 the Académie Française confidently asserted that "France has many drunkards but, happily, no alcoholics."[25] Drunkenness in itself was not perceived as a problem, as apologists argued that there was a particular kind of French drunk, not boorish and violent like drunks of other nationalities, but one that was witty, vivacious, and intelligent.

This set the tone for the temperance movement in France, which focused on spirits but supported the drinking of wine and beer. They and other fruit-based alcoholic beverages had, after all, been consumed in France for centuries without the country encountering problems. The disastrous defeat in the Franco-Prussian War had to be attributable to distilled spirits made from grain and sugar beets that were becoming increasingly popular as working-class drinks. By the 1890s, absinthe had displaced beer and brandy to become, after wine, the most popular drink in Paris.[26]

A temperance campaign, led by the Société française de tempérance from the early 1870s, called for the French to abstain from "industrial" alcohols such as brandy, absinthe, and other grain-based spirits and to drink instead unadulterated wine. The message could hardly have been timed worse. Just as it got under way, France's vineyards were being struck by phylloxera, and wine production began to plummet (See Chapter 9). To meet consumer demand, producers throughout France began to tamper with their wine, sometimes blending it with wines from Spain or Algeria and sometimes making wine from raisins instead of fresh grapes. But there were still shortages, and many wine-drinkers turned to distilled spirits. The temperance attack on spirits was further weakened when French scientists began to argue that alcohol was alcohol, whether it was consumed as wine, beer, or spirits, and that above certain volumes it was as dangerous.

This argument undermined the privileged position of wine and made nonsense of the notion that consuming unlimited amounts of wine was alright but that drinking any spirits at all was harmful. But there were still some scientists, as late as the 1890s, willing to differentiate among alcohols. A prominent Belgian physician declared that there were eight different kinds of alcohol, of which only one was innocuous: "Pure beer and pure wine consist of this good alcohol; but all spirits, unless properly rectified, contain the most deadly poisons."[27]

As French temperance organizations faltered, they were replaced in 1895 by a new body, the French Anti-Alcohol League (Union française antialcoolique, or UFA), which adopted a program calling for total abstinence, including from wine. It faced a formidable task, for at the turn of the century France had one of the highest rates of alcohol consumption in the world. At 15.9 liters of pure alcohol per capita, it was almost twice the rate in Great Britain (8.2 liters) and three times the rate in the United States and Russia (5.8 liters and 5.2 liters, respectively). The UFA hoped to become a mass organization and appealed in particular to women, whom it portrayed as the most common victims of alcoholic and heavy-drinking men. But it faced stiff opposition, not only from the alcohol industry but also from many physicians who persisted in promoting the health benefits of wine. One advertisement, endorsed by several professors of medicine, claimed that a liter of wine had the nutritional value of 900 centiliters of milk, 370 grams of bread, 585 grams of good (deboned) meat, and 5 eggs. It carried the statement by Jacques Bertillon, an eminent French demographer, that "alcoholism is held in check by the consumption of wine."[28]

Even the government, concerned for the economic impact if France's alcohol industries (especially the wine industry) were to shut down, weighed in against any attempt to reduce wine consumption. Wine was France's fourth-biggest export, 1.5 million people were grape-growers, and almost 10 percent of the total population was involved in some aspect of the wine industry.[29] Many more people were employed in the brewing and distilling industries. The finance minister stated that France was "not rich enough to fight alcohol," and the National Assembly passed a resolution in 1900 declaring wine to be the national beverage of France.[30]

The defense of wine echoed widely throughout France. One writer denounced abstinence in ringing nationalistic terms: "Young men or sad old men may advocate water as the only healthy drink and hurl anathemas at those who enjoy the pleasures of a glass of old wine or fine cognac. No! In our beautiful France, a country of wine, joy, openness and happy temperament, let us not talk about abstinence. Your water, your Lenten drinks, your Ceylon tea, fig or acorn coffee, your lemonade and camomile, be hanged. You are not only bad hygienists, but bad Frenchmen." Another sneered that La Croix Bleue, a temperance organization active in France but based in Switzerland, was represented by "Geneva clergymen with high collars and skin yellowed from not drinking wine."[31] La Croix Bleue merged with the Société française de tempérance in 1903 to promote a common message that stressed moderate consumption of beer, wine, and cider. This platform was more successful than calls for abstention, and the organization was supported by the French government, which allowed it to set up education programs in the army and in schools. It campaigned hard against spirits, however, especially against absinthe, and was influential in having it banned in 1915, soon after the First World War began.

In Germany, temperance movements were more active in the predominantly Protestant north than in the Catholic south, and as in France, they focused on distilled spirits rather than on beer or wine. In the mid-nineteenth century, the consumption of spirits increased at the expense of beer, particularly in the north and northeast but also, though to a lesser extent, in the south. Temperance campaigners argued that the ready availability of cheap Schnapps (spirits made from grain or potatoes) led to criminality, godlessness, and immorality. By 1846 there were more than 1,200 local temperance organizations, often led by Protestant pastors, and most were in the rural areas of northern and eastern Germany and in Prussia's Polish districts. Tens of thousands of men are said to have taken the temperance pledge.[32] They had little impact, and temperance did not enter political debate until the 1880s, when Germany entered a phase of rapid industrialization. In 1883 the German Association for the Prevention of Alcohol Abuse was formed, and it argued for the drinking of beer rather than Schnapps and the banning of Schnapps (a *Schnappsboykott*) from factories. As in France, the temperance message was undermined by the scientific discovery that all alcoholic beverages were harmful if consumed in sufficient quantities, and organizations favoring total abstinence came to the fore. Some seventy of them merged into a powerful association that pressed the government to adopt policies such as local option (giving municipalities, which were more vulnerable to lobbying, the power to restrict the sale of alcohol within their jurisdictions) and the compulsory sterilization of alcoholics.

By the time the abstinence movement got under way in Germany in the 1880s, alcohol consumption had begun to fall; it peaked in the early 1870s, when Germans consumed 10.2 liters of pure alcohol in almost equal volumes of Schnapps and beer. From that time, the consumption of beer rose while the consumption of the higher-alcohol Schnapps fell steadily. Even so, the place of all alcoholic beverages in the German diet seems to have declined by the turn of the century. Between 1896 and 1910 there were transformative changes in the German diet. It became more diversified, and products like fruit, sugar, and rice became much more widely consumed. On a per capita basis, tropical fruit consumption rose 92 percent, consumption of fruit rose 67 percent, and consumption of sugar rose 52 percent. Rice, fish, and eggs also made big gains. In contrast, more traditional foods, such as potatoes (down 25 percent), were less represented on German tables, as were Schnapps (down 24 percent) and even beer, which declined by 8 percent.[33] The decline in Germans' potato consumption occurred just as potato yields were rising, and increasing proportions of the harvest were converted into spirits when high-volume, steam-powered distilleries came online. At the same time, consumer drinking preferences in Europe shifted from potato- to grain-based spirits, leaving producers to look for new markets. They found them in the African colonies where, from the late 1800s, German spirits were the source of most of the cheap alcohol used by Europeans as a trading commodity.[34]

The temperance message also found its way into Japan, not coincidentally about the same time that European alcohol began to make an impact on Japanese drinking patterns. The commercial production of beer in Japan—based on German practices and styles—began in the 1870s, and by the 1890s it had won a substantial part of the domestic market: imports of foreign beer fell from more than 611 kiloliters in 1890 to 100 kiloliters in 1900. At the same time, imports of wines and spirits rose and remained robust.[35] The first beer-hall opened in Tokyo in 1899, and soon beer was being served in beer-gardens, restaurants, and teahouses. But for the most part, consumption was confined to the better-off, and there were few complaints about excessive drinking. All one Western resident of Tokyo could complain about was that although "the Japanese had not required much instruction in the art of beer-drinking . . . he does not, however, quite understand yet how to handle his beer, and frequently allows it to get too hot in summer and too cold in winter."[36]

Western temperance activities began in Japan about the same time as beer production, and the first branch of the WCTU opened there in 1886. Westerners played prominent roles in the WCTU and other Japanese temperance organizations as they campaigned against not only alcohol but also prostitution. WCTU books aimed at young readers, such as *Health for Little Folks*, were translated into Japanese, but although they were used in mission schools, they made little headway in public and private schools.[37] Overall, the temperance movement had little discernible impact on patterns of drinking and on government alcohol policies in Japan. Temperance was not necessarily an ideology alien to Japan; but the WCTU was resolutely Christian in its approach, and the authorities were not impressed by activities such as the WCTU's sending copies of the Bible to soldiers fighting in Japan's early twentieth-century wars with China and Russia.

The WCTU's frustration in Japan contrasted with the successes of the antialcohol movements in Western countries, where the drink issue began to appear on the policy agendas of local, regional, and national governments. Yet it is important to appreciate the broader social and cultural conditions that gave traction to the drive for changes in alcohol policy. Through the nineteenth century, anxiety grew about the moral state and cultural directions of Western societies. As we have seen (Chapter 9), industrialization created a mass working class and drew huge populations of poor workers to lives of hardship in the crowded new cities. There, middle-class observers began to express concern about the ever-larger working class, which they perceived as a threat to moral and social stability. Everything in the cultures of the urban working class and the poor seemed to run against the expressed ideals of the burgeoning middle class, which stressed restraint and self-discipline, religious piety, moderation in all things, sobriety, and the values of family life. Workers were boisterous in their leisure activities, whether playing football in the city streets or drinking inside and outside taverns. Men and women were as likely to cohabit as to marry, and urban illegitimacy rates rose during the nineteenth century. Workers were less likely than members of the middle class to attend church.

All of these tendencies looked threatening to the social and moral order, and whereas a more religious age might simply have looked to the devil as the cause, nineteenth-century observers focused on alcohol—although for many religious commentators this might be a fine distinction, as they argued that alcohol was simply the devil's weapon of choice. Alcohol led drinkers to lose control of their minds and bodies, and they made irrational decisions that led them to embrace poverty, indolence, crime, immorality, and impiety. Stop the consumption of alcohol, the argument went, and you would solve most of the problems that bedeviled workers and the poor and that threatened social stability. As Richard Cobden, the English reformer, put it, "The temperance cause lies at the foundation of all social and political reform."[38]

One of the responses to the perceived degeneration of Western populations was the eugenics movement, which professed to take a scientific approach to issues of heredity. There were several schools of thought within the movement, but their common principle was that people with inherited physical, emotional, or intellectual disabilities should, for the good of the general population, refrain from reproducing. As with the antialcohol movement, some eugenicists believed that the decision not to reproduce ought to be voluntary, while some adopted a coercive approach and advocated compulsory sterilization.

Among the hereditary disabilities—including epilepsy, blindness, and what was called "feeble-mindedness"—identified by many eugenicists were patterns of persistent or heavy alcohol consumption, usually referred to generically at the time as "alcoholism." Insofar as undesirable alcohol behavior was transmitted from generation to generation, heavy drinkers could be shown to be threats to the health of any population, or to "the race," as white Europeans were often called.

Eugenics became closely connected to nationalism and militarism, both of which intensified in Europe during the late 1800s. The antialcohol campaign fed into both by means of eugenics theories insofar as alcohol was seen as a threat to military efficiency and national strength. The campaign against drink often adopted military metaphors. The United Brothers of Temperance in the United States referred to their members as "effective soldiers" in the "battle" against alcohol and pointed out that "no country can with safety rely on raw recruits alone." In the United States, many temperance rallies took place on Independence Day, and the republican mood already in the air was heightened by references to "the war . . . against the hosts of King Alcohol."[39] Americans had defeated one king to win their independence, and they would overcome the next to attain their freedom from drink.

In this period of international tensions and increasing military preparation, considerable attention was paid to the effects of alcohol on the fitness of men for military service, and there was a vigorous debate on the provision of alcohol to European armed forces. Even Turkish soldiers, seldom held up by the British as models of military efficiency, were praised for their abstinence from alcohol, although their officers were said to be "not so free of this pernicious habit."[40] Numerous surveys of military efficiency purported to show the advantages of alcohol-free troops. Statistics from one British regiment in India during the 1860s showed that as policy shifted from allowing alcohol freely to restricting its availability and finally banning it altogether, the annual number of cases of drunkenness fell from thirty-four to seven and courts-martial declined from six to zero.[41] On the impressionistic side, one British naval officer reported to a parliamentary committee that "during the [Crimean] war, almost every accident that I ever witnessed on board ship was owing to drunkenness. Drink was more dangerous than gunpowder."[42]

Spirits, notably rum and brandy, had been provided to soldiers and sailors not to hydrate them (the amounts were too small for that, even when the spirits were diluted with water) but because spirits were considered beneficial to health. If there was a shift in this position on the part of the military authorities, it reflected a general decline in the belief that alcohol had therapeutic properties. For thousands of years, physicians had recommended moderate intakes of alcohol—first wine and beer and, later, spirits—as beneficial to health, and they had prescribed specific forms and quantities for specific ailments. Many early advocates of temperance were medical men who yet believed in the therapeutic value of fermented drinks. The famous temperance barometer devised by Dr. Benjamin Rush allowed that beer and wine, consumed in moderation and with food, were healthy, and Rush himself invested in a vineyard property.

The use of alcohol as therapy by doctors seems to have declined somewhat by the early twentieth century. In London hospitals, for example, spending on alcohol declined by between 50 and 90 percent between 1884 and 1904.[43] The Salisbury Infirmary spent a total of £302 on wine, beer, and spirits in 1865, £142 in 1885, and a mere £18 in 1905.[44] These trends might well have reflected advances made in drug therapy in the late 1800s, such as the development of aspirin. Proprietary medicines of this kind could be tested scientifically and shown to be effective. All that could be reasonably claimed of wine and other forms of alcohol was that they generally promoted physical and intellectual well-being or, more specifically, that they were helpful to the digestion. One investigation at Yale University, reported in 1896, showed that small volumes of alcohol (the researchers tried whiskey, brandy, rum, and gin) accelerated digestion and impeded it "only when taken immoderately and in intoxicating quantities."[45] But when doctors wrote of the benefits of a particular wine for a specific ailment or of brandy for some malady, they had difficulty explaining in prevailing scientific terms just how alcohol achieved the results they claimed for it.

The continuing sense that alcohol was generally a good tonic was expressed in a 1903 book on alcohol and mountaineering written by a Swiss doctor. When 1,200 members of alpine clubs responded to a survey on their alcohol consumption, 78 percent replied that they consumed alcohol regularly, and 72 percent claimed that they carried alcohol while climbing, in case of need. Swiss alpine guides believed that white wine was refreshing, red wine was a restorative when a climber began to tire, brandy gave courage, and hot red wine fixed almost all minor illnesses. After making many qualifications about the value of alcohol and suggesting alternatives (such as water, tea, lemonade, fruits, and coffee), the author concluded that alcohol might be useful as a restorative, but only when it was taken in moderation and when it was really necessary.[46]

Many doctors, and not only those in Europe, continued to believe that alcoholic beverages definitely had a place in medical treatment. At the turn of the century, the WCTU was involved in a debate with medical researchers over its claims for the health benefits of total abstinence.[47] A 1921 survey of 53,900 randomly selected physicians in the United States showed that 51 percent were in favor of prescribing whiskey for certain ailments, 26 percent thought that beer was therapeutic, and a small percentage argued for wine. Then there were the various "medicinal" wines infused with various substances. One was Triner's American Elixir of Bitter Wine, which was sold in the United States at the turn of the century. It was primarily a laxative made of "red wine and medicinal herbs" to deal with the constipation "that is a common occurrence in our families." Not only were the herbs a "scientific combination" whose efficacy was undeniable, but the red wine "strengthens the intestines and regulates their work. It also increases the appetite, stimulates and strengthens the body."[48]

The debate about the health-giving properties of alcohol was complicated by the belief that much of it, especially distilled spirits, was adulterated to the point of being an even greater risk to health than the antialcohol movements argued that it was in its pure state. Anxiety about the adulteration of food and drink has a long a history, but developments in analytical chemistry in the 1800s allowed for greater precision in determining the presence of harmful additives. It was often alleged that strychnine instead of hops was commonly added to ale in order to provide bitterness, an allegation denied by English brewers.[49] Even so, most beers analyzed in one English sample in the mid-1800s were found to be unacceptably adulterated in some way.[50] As for wines and spirits, there seemed to be no end of substances that could be employed to impart color, body, or flavor. An American report warned that adulteration was common everywhere and claimed that if all imported alcoholic beverages were pure, the "quantity would be a mere item compared to the amount now drunk in this country." According to the author, New York City annually sold three times as much "pure, imported brandy" and four times as much "pure imported wine" as all producing countries exported. Some 12 million bottles of "champagne" were sold each year in the United States alone, more than the total champagne exports of 10 million bottles.[51]

One form of adulteration was the widespread practice of adding plaster (gypsum or calcium sulfate) to wine. Plaster improved acidity and therefore acted as a preservative, and it also gave wine a brighter and clearer color. It was particularly common in the mass-produced wines of southern France, Italy, and Spain, which were frequently shipped long distances to their markets and benefited from the preservative qualities of plaster. But plaster found its way into many "quality" wines in the 1880s, as Bordeaux producers blended these plastered wines with their own to make up for losses due to phylloxera. (At the end of the 1880s, twice as much Bordeaux wine was in circulation as was produced in the region.)

Plastering was widely debated in the second half of the 1800s, with various committees and scientists unable to agree on its harmfulness despite reports of illnesses following the consumption of plastered wines. In 1857, people who drank plastered wine in Aveyron, in southern France, were reported to have experienced "unquenchable thirst and an insupportable dryness of the throat" as well as lesions.[52] French legislators decided that 2 grams of plaster per liter of wine posed no threat to health, but there were complaints that winemakers simply tossed handfuls of plaster into the fermentation vats without bothering to weigh it. From 1880 to 1891, the most intense period of the phylloxera crisis, even the regulation dictating a maximum of 2 grams was suspended because of the shortage of wine.

Some forms of adulteration, such as the addition of water, were clearly harmless and might actually have made alcoholic drinks more healthy by reducing their alcohol content. Similarly, using grapes grown in one region to make wine labeled by a different region—Bordeaux merchants often included grapes from Spain and the Rhône Valley in their wines, especially when their own production was reduced by phylloxera—was not a danger to health. But such practices caused more and more concern as authorities groped their way toward an appellation system that would tie wines to demarcated regions and give consumers more certainty as to the provenance of what they were buying.

But even practices that were not harmful to health—like diluting wine and blending foreign and regionally labeled wines—were increasingly considered inappropriate alterations to drinks. They were often treated the same way as the addition of sugar (chaptalization) to raise the alcohol level in wine, the addition of coloring agents, and the use of plaster. The authorities appeared to be as concerned about what are now called consumer rights as they were about consumer health. Consumers who purchased alcohol, it was argued, were entitled to certain expectations, including the expectation that wine did not contain added water or plaster. When one member of the French Chamber of Deputies declared, in a debate on adulteration, that such alcohols were "poisons" that "filled up the insane asylums," the minister of agriculture responded, "We are discussing a law on fraud, not a law on public health. . . . At the same time, I would be pleased if certain provisions of the bill could fight against fraud and also protect public health."[53]

Antialcohol campaigners were not worried about the consumer fraud implied by adulteration. But they exploited it to show that drinkers not only took risks by drinking alcoholic beverages when they were pure but incurred even greater risks by consuming drinks that were likely contaminated by deadly substances. Some doctors insisted that, adulterated or not, "alcohol has a direct tendency to cause death."[54] This was not a novel claim, but by the late nineteenth century, allegations such as these were often backed by statistics—often spurious statistics, but statistics, nonetheless. During the 1800s, governments and institutions had begun to compile social statistics systematically for a wide range of purposes, and no group exploited them more eagerly than campaigners against drink. Mortality statistics were an obvious target, for there was no more cogent argument against alcohol than that it killed. Not only causes of death were at play here, but also the exposure of certain occupations to alcohol. In the early 1900s, for example, English innkeepers and inn workers had mortality rates higher than those of lead workers and two to three times greater than the rates for coal miners.[55]

As they were presented, the figures seemed to bear out claims that alcohol was ravaging peoples and societies, although the statistics varied from source to source. One blamed alcohol for four-fifths of all crime, two-thirds of all poverty, half of all suicides, two-thirds of all madness, and nine-tenths of all shipwrecks, as well as "idleness, Sabbath-breaking, lying, swearing, uncleanness, accidents, etc."[56] Another author gave different estimates: alcohol caused three-quarters of crime, nine-tenths of poverty, a third of suicides, a third of insanity, a third of shipwrecks, and also half of all disease and three-quarters of all "juvenile depravity."[57] Clearly we are in the realm of impressionism rather than any serious statistical analysis, but readers might well have taken such assertions at face value (and even the lower of the two sets of figures would be alarming).

From time to time, more reliable statistics emerged. In contrast to claims that alcohol was responsible for a third to two-thirds of insanity, statistics collected by individual asylums showed a less frequent relationship. The Royal Asylum in Edinburgh reported that in the early 1870s, "intemperance" was an assigned cause of insanity in 13 percent of admissions and 20 percent of cases where the cause of insanity was known. Most other asylums in Britain reported that alcohol was related to insanity in less than 10 percent of admissions.[58] These figures were low in comparison with the rates of about 25 percent reported by a large asylum in Paris, but even that is far from the figures of a third or two-thirds that were often bandied about by antialcohol campaigners.[59] The statistical revolution of the nineteenth century might well have given statistics status and credibility in political discourses, and antialcohol writers enthusiastically embraced them.

The medical profession had not turned entirely from alcohol, but alcohol was no longer unquestioned as having therapeutic value and could, instead, generate its own illness: alcoholism. This is a condition that has many definitions, but it generally refers to an addiction to alcohol, usually manifested in persistent and heavy drinking of a pathological kind. The term was first used by a Swedish physician, Magnus Huss, in 1849 to describe a condition where regular and heavy consumption of alcohol led to adverse effects that interfered with an individual's ability to manage his or her personal and work lives. Alcoholism was defined as a "disease of the will," in that it sprang from a deficit of the will and required the patient to apply his or her will in order to cure it. At the end of the nineteenth century, most people diagnosed as alcoholic belonged to social groups believed to have little willpower or self-discipline: the poor of both sexes and middle- and upper-class women.[60] In France, a physician suggested that the will of workers was impaired by the nature and conditions of their work, their housing conditions, their diet, and their income. He suggested that the solution to drinking problems lay in broad social reforms.[61]

Alcoholism was and has remained a concept with uncertain contours and boundaries, for it is not clear that all regular and heavy drinkers can be classified as alcoholics. Among the ongoing discussions about alcoholism are whether it is a disease and whether it is curable or merely treatable.[62] These issues engaged some temperance and prohibition supporters in the nineteenth century, but for the most part, antialcohol writers seized on the word once it had been coined and applied it to almost anyone who drank daily or who seemed to drink above average volumes of alcohol. Surprisingly, overuse of the term and a tendency to stretch its definition did not weaken its force. Many antialcohol organizations that set out to combat alcohol abuse did so by referring to it as alcoholism.

If confidence in the health-giving properties of alcoholic beverages declined during the nineteenth century, the same can be said of the religious significance of wine, as growing antipathy toward alcoholic beverages called into question its use in Christian communion services. The fact that wine had for nearly 2,000 years been central to Christian imagery and ritual posed a major problem to advocates of complete abstinence from alcoholic beverages. Some temperance campaigners could accommodate a periodic sip of sacramental wine, but even they had to contend with the notion that wine, a "soft" alcohol in comparison to spirits, might be a gateway to harder varieties.

Hard-core abstaining Christians, however, were appalled at the suggestion that their God might have blessed any form of alcohol and that Christ's blood was represented by an intoxicating beverage that was intrinsically evil and responsible for widespread misery and immorality. They developed an imaginative theology of enology, the two-wine theory, according to which the biblical references to "wine" involve two distinct beverages. The first, "good wine," was grape juice (often referred to in antialcohol literature as "unfermented wine," an oxymoron); this, they said, was the beverage that Christ created from water at the marriage of Cana and that the disciples consumed at the Last Supper. The second beverage, "bad wine," was real, fermented, alcoholic, intoxicating wine.[63] It was this beverage that Noah consumed to the point of inebriation and that Lot's daughters plied their father with so that they could have intercourse with him. In other words, when "wine" was associated with good things in the Bible, it was grape juice, but when "wine" was associated with immorality, it was wine.

As they felt it would be blasphemous to represent Christ by wine, teetotalers began a campaign to persuade churches to replace communion wine with grape juice. A structural development assisted the teetotalers in this endeavor. Louis Pasteur and other scientists who carried out research on fermentation discovered that heating up grape juice (the process later known as pasteurization) killed off the yeasts needed to turn its sugars into alcohol. This enabled the production of a stable juice that was free from the risk of fermentation. Grape juice was soon in commercial production, and church authorities were urged to buy this "unfermented wine" for use in communion.

The campaign had scattered successes in the United States, where the Methodist Episcopal Church adopted grape juice in 1880. An influential Methodist theologian argued that grape juice was an "emblem of mercy and salvation" and a "symbol of blessing and life," while wine was "pronounced a poison both by Scripture and science."[64] On the other hand, the Church of Jesus Christ of Latter-day Saints (Mormons) used wine in communion from the 1830s and even owned vineyards to make their own wine. Later in the century, congregations bypassed grape juice and opted for water in their communion services, and water became the rule for Mormons in 1912. In England the Anglican Church resisted all attempts to replace wine with juice.[65] The Catholic Church, which was only marginally involved in the nineteenth-century campaigns against alcohol, continued to use wine.

Pasteurized fruit juices were a new addition to the nonalcoholic beverages available in the later nineteenth century. They joined hot beverages, such as coffee, tea, and chocolate, and most important of all, water. As these drinks became more widely consumed, and as fresh, potable water was made available to people in Europe and North America, the cultural meaning of alcohol was permanently changed. The consumption of alcoholic beverages for recreational purposes was, by the nineteenth century, deeply embedded in the cultures of Western societies. But historically they also had a parallel and primary dietary purpose as beverages safer than the existing sources of drinking water. That was still true in many places at the beginning of the 1800s, and it is clear that campaigns to reduce alcohol consumption—and especially to eliminate it entirely—could make no progress until alternative beverages were available.

Coffee and tea, which had been introduced to Europe and North America in the seventeenth century, were widely consumed by the nineteenth century. Both could be considered alternatives to alcohol for the purpose of hydration; even though tea is a diuretic, its overall effective is to hydrate. Because both coffee and tea called for boiled or almost-boiled water, they were safer ways of drinking the water that was used in their preparation. The consumption of both of these hot beverages increased during the nineteenth century and permeated all levels of society in some countries. Tea became especially popular in Great Britain (where per capita consumption more than doubled between 1850 and 1875) and its colonies and in Russia, while coffee was dominant in France, Italy, and North America. For all that, safe water supplies were necessary before an alcohol-free society could realistically be contemplated and advocated. An English physician noted this in 1898: "The first thing a teetotaler requires . . . is pure water."[66] Who would give up the safety of beer or wine to drink water that smelled and tasted bad and was believed to make its consumers sick? It is surely no coincidence, then, that at the very time the antialcohol campaigns hit their stride, serious efforts were made to ensure that Europeans and North Americans had access to regular supplies of potable water. As we have seen, potable water began to be provided to the populations of cities and towns in Europe, North America, and elsewhere from the second third of the nineteenth century, and by the outbreak of the First World War, the bulk of urban inhabitants had access to safe water, piped directly either to their homes or to public fountains.

The two trends were not driven by the same pressures. Opposition to alcohol emerged from an interpretation of deteriorating social conditions and their causes, but the concern about water resulted from the growth of cities and the increasing threat of epidemic disease. Deadly outbreaks of cholera and dysentery in many parts of the Western world in the 1830s and 1850s concentrated the attention of urban authorities everywhere on the need to provide the populations with secure water supplies for drinking and washing. Few alcohol-drinkers were likely to be swayed toward abstinence by the simple provision of good drinking water, but on the other hand, the absence of safe water supplies could be used as an argument in favor of the continued consumption of alcohol. Until safe water was in good and regular supply, the abstinence argument was bound to gather little popular traction. But once it could no longer be argued that alcohol was necessary for health and dietary reasons, alcohol could be viewed as an exclusively recreational drink, a discretionary beverage that could be given up without harm. Indeed, the centuries-old argument that alcohol was a healthier choice than water could be—and was—turned on its head: from the middle of the nineteenth century, water could be portrayed as the safe choice, and alcohol could be condemned as harmful. Water had been merely dangerous to the health of its consumers, but alcohol could be depicted as harmful to society and morality as well.

In short, the nineteenth- and early twentieth-century antialcohol movements must be understood in broad cultural and material contexts. A number of trends undermined positive attitudes toward the medicinal and religious associations of alcohol, class distinctions created anxieties about drinking by the masses, and sensibilities concerning women, children, and the family sharpened concerns about male drunkenness. Nationalism and eugenics added their own dimensions. Meanwhile, the availability of alternative, nonalcoholic beverages was the necessary material underpinning to the transformation of alcohol from a necessary and desirable part of the diet to a discretionary commodity. This shift in the cultural meaning of alcohol was one of the most important events in the history of alcohol for a thousand years, and it reframed attitudes and alcohol policies in the twentieth century.

11

Alcohol and Native Peoples
1800–1930

RACE, ORDER, AND CONTROL

While alcohol was under attack by temperance and prohibition advocates in Europe, Europeans were channeling vast volumes of alcohol into their overseas empires, where, along with textiles, beads, and guns, it was used as a trading commodity. The flow of alcohol swelled during the nineteenth century, especially in Africa after the territory not already claimed by European powers was divided up among them at the 1884 Berlin conference. Alcohol was also implicated as Europeans extended their domination over the whole of North America during the 1800s, as spirits were traded and sold to the native peoples. In both Africa and North America, the European administrators and governments wrestled with the implications of drinking by the indigenous populations, and most applied prohibition policies to them well in advance of such policies being widely imposed on Europeans anywhere. Just as the temperance movement in Europe and elsewhere informed policies enacted in the African colonies and imposed on the native populations of North America, it is possible that the lessons learned were absorbed by European, American, and Canadian governments as they dealt with demands for greater alcohol regulation in their own countries.

Europeans brought their alcoholic beverages, attitudes, and patterns of consumption with them, and in Africa they encountered indigenous peoples with their own alcoholic beverages and modes of consuming them. The interplay was complex and the results were sometimes unexpected, but they were always informed by the relationships of power in colonial societies. Within that framework, each colony presented unique cultural, political, and

216

economic conditions. The degree of contact between European and African populations varied and could be minimal even where railroads were extended into the interior of the continent. Trading networks employed alcohol more in some colonies than in others, and while missionaries urged the indigenous people to drink moderately if they could not abstain entirely, their influence on local alcohol consumption appears to have ranged from a little to a lot. Some colonial administrators were content to see vast quantities of alcohol flow into their colonies because they brought a steady flow of tax revenues into their treasuries; others, motivated by economic or moral concerns, tried to control the access that local populations had to alcohol. Colonialism in Africa was a complex narrative, and alcohol was a constant theme.

Throughout the continent, alcohol became an important medium of exchange—less among the Muslim populations of North Africa than in the south—and it was used, sometimes alone and sometimes in conjunction with other trading commodities, for the purchase of the goods in demand by Europeans: palm oil, rubber, ivory, gold, diamonds, and slaves. A British trade commissioner sent to Nigeria in 1895 reported to the Colonial Office that trade was impossible without spirits because liquor was the most popular currency.[1] Alcohol played an extremely important role in the acquisition of slaves; sometimes it was part of the actual price, and sometimes it was a gift to ensure that local leaders made slaves available for Europeans to purchase. In 1724, for example, French traders purchased fifty slaves for cloth, beads, guns, gunpowder, lead shot, and brandy.[2] Alcohol was also used as payment for territorial concessions. In 1843, the king of Assinie (a small state in Côte d'Ivoire) gave up sovereignty to King Louis-Philippe of France for cloth, gunpowder, guns, tobacco, hats, a mirror, an organ, beads, six 200-liter barrels of brandy, and 4 cases of distilled spirits. In 1894, a British trading company that wanted to extend its riverside frontage by twenty feet agreed to pay 20 cases of gin a year.[3] In Cameroon, chiefs along the coast agreed to a treaty placing themselves "under the protection" of the Germans rather than the British because the German authorities provided them with liquor.[4]

During the nineteenth century, the consumption of European alcohol became far more common throughout native communities. By the middle of the century, the same alarm bells that were being sounded in Europe at what was believed to be the widespread abuse of alcohol among the working classes were also ringing in the colonies. European missionaries reported on the havoc that alcohol played on indigenous cultures, and accounts were published by temperance advocates in Europe to amplify their descriptions of the harm liquor was causing at home. Critics assumed that African villages were full of drunk men and women and that conditions in communities such as Cape Coast, Accra, and Lagos were worse than in the back alleys of London, Manchester, and Glasgow.[5] In England, a crisply named United Committee for the Prevention of the Demoralization of the Native Races by the Liquor Traffic was formed in the 1880s, and similar lobbying groups were formed in the other major colonial powers, France and Germany. Decrying the effects of alcohol on the yet-to-be-civilized native peoples in Africa reinforced the notion that alcohol addiction (often referred to as alcoholism) was more prevalent among populations that lacked willpower and self-discipline.[6]

A number of indigenous leaders petitioned the European nations to halt the flow of alcohol. In the 1880s, Etsu Maliki, emir of Bida, an emirate in central Nigeria, wrote to the bishop of Nigeria, "Rum has ruined my country; it has ruined my people. It has made them become mad." He asked the bishop to beg "the English queen to prevent the bringing of rum into this land . . . to spoil our country."[7] Rather than wait for Queen Victoria to act, the emir outlawed the sale of imported spirits and demanded that the Europeans remove their stocks of gin. The issue was taken up at the 1889–90 Brussels conference convened to deal with the slave trade and the commerce in arms and alcohol. The conference banned the extension of trafficking in alcohol and the local distilling of alcohol in regions where they did not already exist, between latitudes 20 degrees north and 22 degrees south. This ban excluded South Africa, which by then was a major alcohol-producing colony and was regulating its own affairs, and France's mainly Muslim North African colonies (such as Algeria and Tunisia), whose wine was, at the time the conference was held, helping the French deal with the shortages of French wine caused by phylloxera. On the other hand, the conference's decision intended to end the further spread of the alcohol trade throughout most of Africa.

What brought the situation to this point was the rapid diffusion of European alcohol throughout much of Africa during the later 1800s. Before European contact (and afterward in many interior regions little touched by Europeans), various kinds of alcohol were regularly made in many parts of Africa and were consumed in a range of contexts. In some areas, enough alcohol was made for it to be consumed on a daily basis. In other areas, it was consumed primarily at occasions such as festivals and funerals. In eastern Africa, for example, the Haya, who live in the northwest of what is now Tanzania, made beer from bananas, the staple element in their diet, before European contact. Bananas were artificially ripened by hanging them above the hearth or burying them in the ground for several days until their starches were transformed into sugars. They were then mashed, the juice was extracted and mixed with an equal volume of water, then the mixture was allowed to ferment. The result of this process, carried out only by men, was a fairly low-alcohol (4 to 5 percent) beverage that was drunk by men and women at celebrations and rituals of all kinds, including marriage negotiations and offerings to ancestors. Adult men expected to drink banana beer during the day, and while becoming "happy" as a result was approved of, the Haya disapproved of drunkenness. One form of punishment was to force someone to drink to the point of drunkenness and suffer the humiliation it brought upon them.[8]

On the Atlantic side of the continent, in west central Africa, two alcoholic beverages were commonly made before European contact: a milky wine (called *malavu* in Angola) made from the sap of a palm tree and having an alcohol content of about 5 percent, and a beer (*walo*) made from either millet, sorghum, or corn, with an alcohol level less than half that. (It is possible that some of these beverages could reach higher levels of alcohol.) Palm wine seems to have been made in quite small volumes, as each tree gave up at most a liter of sap a day. Moreover, the wine seems to have become very acidic within twenty-four hours of being made. It seems to have served many purposes: as a widely consumed beverage at meals, as a complement to festive and other occasions, and as an offering to social superiors. Palm wine, which required relatively little labor, was made by men, but beer, which demanded a series of brewing processes, was the responsibility of women, as brewing generally was throughout Africa. As we might expect, because cereals grew more widely than palm trees, beer was produced in larger volumes and was even more widely consumed. It appears to have been drunk by the mass of the population, but its consumption is poorly documented because the early European explorers were more interested in the indigenous elites than in the diets of ordinary women and men.[9]

When Europeans began to establish settlements in the coastal regions of Africa, many tried the indigenous beverages, but few appear to have been impressed. Instead, Europeans brought their own supplies of alcohol, and after they settled, they arranged for regular shipments to provide alcohol for their own consumption and as a trading commodity. In Angola, wine, brandy, and *gerebita* (a cheap rum made from the waste of sugar production) were used by the Portuguese not only to acquire slaves—by enticing local leaders to make slaves available for purchase—but also to pay various taxes imposed by indigenous leaders on Europeans who wanted to do business in their territory, and as diplomatic presents to lubricate relationships between the Portuguese and local political leaders. In 1807 and 1810, the governor of Luanda tried to smooth relations with the king of Kasanje, an important source of slaves, by giving him 59 liters of gerebita and 56 liters of brandy for his personal consumption and another 30 liters of gerebita to be shared among his councillors.[10]

Alcohol had also been used to acquire slaves, as well as gold and ivory, from the southern regions of Nigeria in the seventeenth and eighteenth centuries. It had a higher value than other trading commodities such as beads, textiles, guns, and gunpowder, and it retained its status after the end of the slave trade in the first half of the 1800s. European merchants established trading posts on the Nigerian coast to consolidate shipments of rubber, palm oil, gold, elephant tusks, and other commodities for shipping to England, Germany, and other destinations. They negotiated directly with Nigerian agents, and they in turn acted as intermediaries for suppliers who brought their products from the interior to the coast. The intermediaries were paid in gin (a generic name for any grain-based spirits in England) and rum, and they paid their suppliers the same way. The latter then returned to their homes in the interior to drink some of the alcohol and use the rest as a trading commodity in their own communities. In this way, alcohol became effectively a currency throughout the colonies, and between a third and two-fifths of southern Nigeria's exports were exchanged for alcohol by the early twentieth century. Exchange rates were fixed but subject to change as commodity prices fluctuated. In the 1890s, 60 to 75 cases of gin could be exchanged for a 180-gallon barrel of palm oil, an almost equal (at 75 cases of gin) gallon-for-gallon exchange of gin for oil. But as the price of gin increased, less was needed, until by 1925 the barrel of oil cost only 20 cases of gin.[11]

Although this flow of alcohol to the British colonies in southern Nigeria declined with the start of the First World War, it was so important in the 1800s that the tax revenues paid for much of the cost of colonial administration. From the 1860s, alcohol was the single most important import, in terms of value and volume, to these colonies, and the duties on it accounted for half to three-quarters of all the colonies' revenues. Insofar as the taxes were factored into the value of the alcohol for bartering purposes, they were effectively paid by the Nigerian producers and merchants. The colonial administrations could never have collected these revenues in money, as the indigenous population shied away from coins and bills. Alcohol fueled so much of colonial Nigeria's economy that Herbert Tugwell, the Anglican bishop of Western Equatorial Africa and a strong supporter of alcohol control, noted in 1901, "How is the Railway being built? By Gin. How was the Carter-Denton

Bridge built? By Gin. How is the town lighted? By Gin. And now if it be asked, how is the town to be drained, or how are we to secure a good supply of good clean water? The answer is with gin."[12]

Because alcohol was used as currency in southern Nigeria, much of it was never consumed but continually changed hands. Owners were known to open bottles and drink some of the contents before topping them up with water and carefully resealing them. If this happened often enough, eventually one recipient would end up with a bottle of water that had the value of a bottle of alcohol. Even so, and despite the weight of a case of alcohol and the risks of bottles breaking, distilled spirits were an ideal currency because they did not deteriorate like wine and beer or like other trading commodities such as textiles and tobacco. So pervasive was this "gin currency" that currency exchanges were established at some courts, enabling people convicted of offenses to convert their gin to money in order to pay fines in cash. Moreover, a case of spirits was a flexible unit of currency, as it could be traded intact or broken down into its constituent dozen bottles. When the British introduced money into the Nigerian economy, they found that the native population was already prepared to grasp the principle that there were 12 pennies in a shilling.[13]

Even so, the use of money rather than gin was resisted. Gin was so cheap that it was useful as payment for small items, while the coins initially put into circulation were of too large denomination. (The authorities eventually issued a coin worth a tenth of a penny.) Alcohol was a tangible asset with visible exchange value, not like a metal disc or a piece of flimsy paper that was merely reputed to represent some value and could be easily lost or stolen.[14] In a sense, the prevalence of alcohol as currency might have been a deterrent to alcohol consumption. It is one thing to use money to purchase alcohol for drinking and thus to consume money indirectly. It is another thing literally to consume "money" in the form of gin. It is notable that Bishop Tugwell's main criticisms were directed at the role of alcohol in Nigeria's economy, which he characterized as immoral. Unlike his counterparts elsewhere, he was not as preoccupied with drunkenness and the other sorts of immorality that were generally associated with alcohol, possibly because of the role of alcohol as currency in southern Nigeria's economy.

As a general rule, because most colonial administrations relied on revenues from taxing alcohol, they resisted calls to introduce temperance or prohibition policies. Alcohol accounted for 46 percent of all import duties in Côte d'Ivoire in 1911 and 38 percent of total government revenue in the Gold Coast (now Ghana) the following year.[15] Revenues like these represented the difference between colonies that were self-sustaining and colonies that were financially dependent on the colonial power. All colonial powers wanted their colonies to be profitable, not drains on finances, and it is hardly surprising that they resisted any policy that would reduce the steady income stream that duties on alcohol represented.

An exception was the French colony of Côte d'Ivoire, where one governor launched a temperance campaign in the first decades of the twentieth century. Gabriel Angoulvant became governor in 1908 and soon saw alcohol as an impediment to the economic development of his colony. There were minor matters of respect, such as when local chiefs met the governor-general of French West Africa drunk, seated, hats on heads, and pipes in mouths. There was the problem of drunkenness that arose when French employers paid their workers in alcohol, as railroad builders did with their African migrant workers. But the a bigger issue lay in the threat that Angoulvant thought alcohol posed to colonial economic development. He drew on prevailing French temperance arguments that alcohol led to a decline in fertility, to poor-quality offspring, and to various diseases, and he argued that an inebriated African workforce would be unstable and unproductive and that Africans who drank would be unreliable taxpayers.[16] Alcohol, in short, was an obstacle to the economic development of French colonies and the moral improvement of their populations.

Côte d'Ivoire was part of a federation of French colonies, and in 1912 Angoulvant persuaded his fellow governors and the governor-general of the federation to raise the tariffs on alcohol in order to make it more expensive and to reduce consumption. To lessen the dangers of alcohol consumption, the importation of absinthe to these colonies was banned, and in the interest of health, the inexpensive Dutch and German spirits that made up most of the alcohol consumed by the local population were analyzed. They were found generally unfit for human consumption. The governors discussed the possibility of importing more wine, which was, in the eyes of French temperance advocates, a safe beverage. In the meantime, colonial administrators throughout Côte d'Ivoire were charged with explaining the new alcohol policy to the African population. They warned about the addictive properties of alcohol, stressed the need for self-discipline, and advised Ivoiriens to think beyond the short-term pleasures of drinking and consider the long-term implications for their health and fertility and the well-being of their societies. They were also advised not to start producing more palm wine to compensate for the reduced supplies of European spirits, and here we can see colonial moral and economic interests align: taking too much sap from palm trees for wine killed the trees and reduced the supply of palm oil that was so valuable to the French as an industrial lubricant and in the manufacture of soap.[17]

Angoulvant was not the only colonial administrator to see alcohol as a problem. While Angoulvant was working toward reducing the flow of alcohol into Côte d'Ivoire, Theodor Seitz, the governor of the nearby German colony of Cameroon, wanted to prohibit alcohol entirely but was reluctant to do so for fear that it would result in smuggling from adjacent colonies and make alcohol even less controllable. Instead, he limited sales of spirits in many parts of the colony and allowed unrestricted sales to a small area near the coast. The result was a decline in spirits imports but an increase in commodities that contained spirits: cosmetics, patent medicines, and perfumes, including lavender water with an alcohol content of 47 percent. Not only did these products circumvent the alcohol restrictions, but they entered Cameroon free of taxes. Merchants could make good profits from them, and the colonial government lost the revenue from duties. But beer was not affected by the regulations, and imports rose, with the taxes imposed partly offsetting the loss of taxes on spirits. Any regulations imposed on alcohol distribution and sale in the colonies exempted Europeans, as it was understood that they needed or were entitled to drink as much as they wanted. With the exception of missionaries (and not all missionaries), Europeans who lived in the colonies are thought to have been regular and sometimes heavy drinkers.

As the colonial economies developed during the nineteenth century, European employers began to provide local workers with alcohol, sometimes as part of their wages and sometimes to purchase with their wages. This appears to be similar to the practice in early modern Europe (although payment of wages in alcohol had almost died out by the nineteenth century), but there was a key difference. In Europe, alcohol (especially wine and beer) had been part of the daily diet, so that paying workers in alcohol provided them with a necessity. In most of Africa, in contrast, payments in alcohol were generally far above the quantities that local workers would otherwise have consumed. Indigenous alcohols, generally beer and palm wine, were relatively low in alcohol, and the distilled spirits supplied by European employers were much higher, generally about ten times stronger than beer and palm wine. (Spirits were preferred by colonial employers because their high alcohol-to-volume ratio made them less expensive than other beverages to ship.) Europeans used this sort of alcohol not only to provide their workers with energy but also to dull the impact of their working and living conditions and to keep them in a state of subordination. If the European socialists were correct in thinking that alcohol was a weapon used by factory owners to keep their workers docile, it was that much more correct in the race-based economies of the colonies.

Yet there were regions where alcohol appears to have played a smaller role in European colonization. In Ghana, alcohol imports certainly rose at the end of the nineteenth century, by 107 percent from 1879 to 1895, but the rate of increase was half that (206 percent) of other commodities. Liquor represented a declining share of all imports: 19 percent in 1879, 15 percent in 1894, and 7 percent in 1910.[18] Recollections of older Ghanaians suggest that alcohol ranked well behind other commodities (cotton textiles, salt, tobacco, and gunpowder) in purchasing and consumption patterns at the turn of the century. One much-qualified calculation of per capita alcohol consumption puts it at about 1.83 liters in 1895, well below contemporary European rates and almost certainly below the likely rates in other West African colonies.[19] In Akan, the dominant society in Ghana, women and young people (even in their twenties) seldom drank, and children never did, so that consumption was concentrated among older men, who thus had access to a much higher volume of alcohol.

Even so, and insofar as we can rely on accounts of such culturally sensitive behavior, intoxication appears to have been rare. Social controls on drinking seem to have been strong, even if they weakened during the nineteenth century, but many accounts note the rarity of drunkenness. In the 1880s, a temperance-minded and nondrinking Methodist missionary wrote, "I have not the slightest hesitation in saying that instances of drunkenness are comparatively rare in the streets of Cape Coast." He also reported the comment of a district commissioner, also a temperance supporter: "Out of hundreds of cases tried at his court during [his] first 12 months [in the colony], not one was traceable to the use of strong drink." A British district officer wrote in 1897, "Notwithstanding the enormous quantities [of liquor] imported into the Colony, it is very exceptional indeed to see a drunken native. . . . It would be absurd to deny that there is drunkenness among the natives, but habitual drunkenness is practically unknown."[20] Comments like these are extraordinary, given the cultural lens through which most Europeans—especially those who supported temperance or prohibition policies—viewed African society. If there were episodes of heavy drinking (often accompanied by quarreling and brawling), they seem to have been associated with certain festivals.

Alcohol was a less common ingredient in European colonization in the Muslim regions, which were concentrated in the northern half of the continent. But the alcohol trade penetrated even these areas because not all Muslims abstained from alcohol, and because even populations in which Muslims made up the majority contained alcohol-consuming non-Muslim members. Most of the alcohol was smuggled into areas of prohibition from colonies where it was more freely available, but some was carried by train after railroads facilitated the movement of goods and people into interior districts. In Nigeria, temperance organizations tried in 1901 to have alcohol, locally known as "firewater," banned as railway freight. The governor, anxious to see the new railroad make money (spirits accounted for between 8 and 13 percent of freight in the early 1900s), rebuffed them, pointing out that if the alcohol was not carried by rail, it would be taken by river transport, the railroad's main competition.[21] Later, in 1913, a different governor raised the rates charged to carry alcohol on the railroad, but there was continuous evidence of alcohol reaching the areas of prohibition. Many reports told of Muslims of all social classes drinking alcohol, sometimes to the point of intoxication. Access to liquor was said to be a status symbol in Muslim ruling circles, and it was consumed openly at occasions such as weddings. Overall, concludes one historian, liquor was consumed in these areas "without any external inducement."[22]

The First World War reduced imports of European alcohol to many African colonies. The bulk of the alcohol supplied to Africa had taken the form of cheap Dutch and German spirits, and with the outbreak of war, German supplies were cut off. As for distillers in the Netherlands (which was neutral during the war), their shipments declined dramatically because they depended on Germany for bottles. Nor did French wine take the place of these spirits in the French colonies during the war, even though there had been some talk of replacing "harmful" spirits with "healthy" wine. The French government supplied huge volumes of wine to its armies on the western front (1,200 million liters by 1917), and when combined with high civilian consumption, there was little left for export. British colonies felt the same impact, as supplies of German spirits disappeared, and throughout Africa many colonial administrations found ways to raise revenues—generally from taxes imposed directly on Africans—to replace the duties on alcohol.[23]

During and immediately after the war, various ordinances to restrict alcohol were put in place in some colonies, as they were in Europe itself. In 1917, Nigeria was divided into "prohibition" zones, where the indigenous population was forbidden to drink imported alcohol; "licensed" zones, where alcohol could be sold only by licensed retailers; and "restricted" zones, where Africans could sell imported alcohol if they had a license. But in 1919, British colonial governments were instructed to prohibit the importation of any distilled spirits that were destined for sale to the indigenous population.[24]

After the First World War, an international commission was set up to consider revising the terms of the conferences of the 1880s that had divided Africa among the European powers and set controls on the importation of alcohol. The result was a convention, signed in 1919, to control the liquor traffic so as to continue "the struggle against the dangers of alcoholism" in Africa. It banned the importation of "trade spirits" of any kind throughout Africa, except in South Africa and the Muslim countries of North Africa, but left the governments in each colony to decide which distilled spirits should be classified as "trade spirits." In addition, they agreed to impose prohibition in areas where spirits had not been used, although "non-native persons" could bring alcohol into these areas for their personal consumption. Finally, local distillation was prohibited, as was the importation and sale of any distilling equipment. The big loophole, of course, was that each government could decide which distilled beverages were trade spirits. The treaty proved largely unworkable because of this, and in practice it made little difference to the availability of alcohol in the colonies.

In the late nineteenth and early twentieth centuries, the European colonies displayed a range of alcohol policies and patterns of consumption that was as varied as in Europe itself. But the policies were rarely simple echoes of the policies adopted in Europe. There was a continuous expression of concern for the effects of alcohol on indigenous people and their culture, from missionaries on the ground, from temperance organizations at home, and from some colonial administrators. All reflected the sentiments current in Europe, where nearly all governments tightened alcohol policies, even if not to the extent that many antialcohol groups wanted. But they went much further in the colonies. Even though they were deficient in applying restrictions, the European powers negotiated regions where prohibition was mandated, at least to the extent that the indigenous population would be deprived of access to imported spirits. Britain, France, and Germany would never have adopted policies like this domestically, and they did so in the colonies because they could expect little resistance. Areas designated for prohibition were areas where European alcohol had not reached, so that prohibition did not so much involve withdrawing an existing commodity as preventing its arrival. Beyond that, European governments more readily imposed restrictive policies on their colonial subjects, to whom they did not have to answer directly. All these alcohol policies, then, must be understood as emerging from the interplay of many considerations: the reception of temperance arguments, calculations of economic loss and advantage, a paternalistic view of colonial populations, and the perception of power in the colonial context.

South Africa had a distinctive alcohol history through Africa's late colonial and postcolonial periods because it was at times divided into self-governing republics until the Union of South Africa was formed in 1910. Moreover, formal dominance by whites lasted longer there than elsewhere in Africa, ending only in 1994 with the fall of the apartheid system. One of the main uses of alcohol was in the "dop" or "tot" system, by which wages were paid in alcohol. This system stretched back to the early settlement of the Cape region by the Dutch in the seventeenth century and continued to the end of the twentieth century. Although the system was abolished by law in 1960, the ban was not seriously enforced until the postapartheid period. By the 1800s, when Europeans began to extract gold and diamonds commercially from the region, the provision of alcohol to South African workers was a well-entrenched practice. In 1891 the benefits to mine owners of providing alcohol to African workers in the Kimberley diamond mines was described this way: "Familiarity with the glass [of alcohol] has built moderation in the black man, while it is admitted that better work is got out of him when he sees the prospect of a cheering glass at the end of a day's labour. . . . At not a few works, [alcohol] permits are regularly issued for supplies to the native hands, the reasonableness of the request for refreshment being amiably admitted on the grounds that the 'boy' so humoured and so refreshed is the better labourer."[25]

Vast quantities of cheap alcohol were made available to black workers in other South African industries. In the gold mining districts of Transvaal from the 1880s onward, canteens designated for blacks sold distilled spirits. Some were made from local grain in a massive distillery that turned out thousands of gallons of alcohol a day, and some were imported spirits shipped from Germany and the Netherlands via Mozambique. The German spirits were analyzed in 1902 and declared "unfit for internal use," and most of the locally made spirits ended up in concoctions with names like "Kaffir Brandy" ("Kaffir" was a derogatory term applied to blacks in general), "Kaffir Whisky," and "Dutch Gin for Kaffirs." The first of these consisted of equal volumes of proof spirit and water, cayenne pepper tincture, mashed prunes, and small volumes of sulfuric nitric acid. The other drinks included additives such as orange peel, fennel, green tea, creosote, and turpentine. White workers were provided more or less the same beverages (with additives such as oak sawdust to give them a distinctive flavor), but they had to pay more, as would be expected of better-paid workers: "Kaffir Ginger Brandy" sold for 16 shillings and 6 pence a dozen bottles, while the "White" version cost 22 shillings and 6 pence.[26]

Between 1893 and 1896, the one distillery near the gold mines at Witwatersrand sold an average of 318,000 gallons of spirits a year to be made into these beverages, and hundreds of thousands of liters of poor-quality gin, rum, and other forms of alcohol flowed across the border from Mozambique. The market in the mining districts was massive—there were 100,000 black miners in the Transvaal by 1899—and the alcohol served the purposes of the mine owners well. Most of the black miners were migrant workers from Mozambique, and the more they spent on alcohol, the less they saved and the longer they had to stay at the mines before returning home. Not only did whites profit from sales of alcohol, but mine owners enjoyed a more stable workforce because of the lower turnover rates. The quality of the liquor caused some turnover as a result of mortality, because hundreds of workers, black and white, died from drinking the beverages. One report noted that it was "a common thing to find 'boys' lying dead on the veld from exposure and the effects of the vile liquids sold them by unscrupulous dealers." The superintendant of the Johannesburg Cemetery is said to have commented, as he looked at one corpse, "Several of these every week—the cursed stuff burns their insides, and they never recover after a drinking bout."[27]

These were the worst effects of the alcohol provided for workers, although they were not so important for mine owners who had a seemingly endless supply of labor. What worried them more than a few deaths was the extent to which alcohol consumption affected productivity. On average, they estimated, about 15 percent of their workforce was disabled by drink each day, but some put the figure as high as 25 percent. There was clearly a contradiction when alcohol both contributed to a docile and stable labor force in the mines and reduced the efficiency of the mining industry. (The same was true of agriculture; workers might be induced by alcohol to work on a farm, but in the long run, alcohol undermined farming operations.)[28] After first trying to tighten up the liquor supply by cracking down on unlicensed suppliers and effectively becoming the only legal dispensers of alcohol to their workers, the Transvaal mine owners took the radical step of agreeing that the sale of alcohol in the mining districts should be banned altogether. They were successful in having parliament pass legislation to that effect in 1896, thus creating an island of near-prohibition (better-off whites could purchase their alcoholic beverages from farther away) in South Africa.

With the assumption of British control following the South African War of 1899–1902, new alcohol policies were put in place, but total prohibition was continued for blacks, with severe penalties for any contravention. Alcohol was smuggled into the mining camps, as we would expect—prohibition has everywhere generated resistance—but it appears to have been a trickle compared with the volumes that the mine owners had facilitated in the 1880s and 1890s. Those very mine owners reported that, as a result of prohibition, a mere 1 percent of their workforce was disabled each day, a big drop from the 15 percent accepted as the norm only ten years earlier.[29]

As we can see, in one African colony after another, some form of prohibition was eventually imposed on the indigenous population for ideological, cultural, or economic reasons. Similar policies were applied to Africans who were taken to the Americas, most as slaves. As early as 1692, a New Jersey law forbade selling or giving rum or any distilled spirits to African Americans, and by the mid-eighteenth century, most colonies had adopted similar rules, just as they attempted to keep alcohol from Native Americans. Slave owners similarly prevented their slaves from having access to alcohol, partly for fear of disorder should they become intoxicated. The exceptions were holidays, such as Christmas, when drinking privileges were extended. Reports suggest that at this time, when slaves were given up to a week off work, plantation owners would actively encourage the slaves to drink until they were so drunk that they passed out.[30] Clearly, what was threatening to social order was drinking to the point of moderate intoxication, when slaves could coordinate their thoughts and their actions. Being cold sober or dead drunk was not threatening.

The prohibition of alcohol was also among the policies pursued by Europeans as they extended their control over North America's indigenous populations in the nineteenth century. As European settlement moved west, European Americans confronted the issues they had first met in the seventeenth and eighteenth centuries: whether to offer alcohol to the Native Americans they encountered. They took with them the belief that Native Americans could not drink moderately, that they were innately prone to addiction, and that intoxication led them to all manner of rash decisions that often culminated in violence. Despite this alarming scenario, Europeans persisted in supplying Native Americans with alcohol because of short-term benefits. Alcohol was a very profitable retail commodity, especially when prices could be inflated and whiskey and rum watered down. Alcohol was also an important trading medium, and it became a feature of land negotiations, employed so that native negotiators made concessions they would not agree to when sober. Some Native American leaders recognized the strategy, and in 1801 representatives of the Choctaws refused alcohol before, during, and after their meetings with federal commissioners at Fort Adams.

Other Native Americans were aware of the broader effects of alcohol on their communities. In 1802, Chief Little Turtle of the Miami people pleaded with President Thomas Jefferson (referring to him in the then-customary way as "Father" and to his own people as "children") to stop the flow of alcohol to his communities. "Your children are not wanting in industry; but it is this fatal poison which keeps them poor. Father: Your children have not that command over themselves, which you have, therefore, before anything can be done to advantage, this evil must be remedied. Father: When our white brothers came to this land, our forefathers were numerous and happy; but, since their intercourse with white people, and owing to the introduction of this fatal poison, we have become less numerous and happy."[31] Little Turtle might or might not have believed that Native Americans were more prone to addiction than Europeans, and he surely realized that not only alcohol but also European diseases and cultural dispossession had reduced the native population. But nothing could be done about diseases to which Native Americans had no immunity, and it was pointless to resist the diffuse forces that supported European hegemony. But stopping the flow of alcohol, which played a definable role in the cultural degradation of his people, must have seemed to be within the realm of possibility.

By approaching the president, Chief Little Turtle acknowledged a major change that had taken place as a result of the creation of the United States of America a quarter-century earlier. In the colonial period, attempts to restrict the supply of alcohol to Native Americans had largely failed, as there was no central authority with the power to do so. But after independence, Congress had the power to regulate trade with Native Americans, and that implied the right to stop trade. Jefferson responded sympathetically and urged Congress to heed calls from Native Americans for prohibitions on spirits, "in the spirit of benevolence and liberality" and in order to gain their friendship. But instead of imposing a blanket ban on trading or selling spirits to Native Americans, Congress empowered the president to "prevent or restrain the vending or distribution of spirituous liquors among all or any of the said Indian tribes" in federal territory.[32] Between 1805 and 1815, a number of territories (Indiana, Illinois, Michigan, Mississippi, and Louisiana) passed laws prohibiting the sale of spirits to Native Americans, but despite penalties of fines and jail sentences, the alcohol trade prospered. Policy was inconsistent. On one day in 1817, an Indian agent in Michigan informed the governor that he had prohibited all spirits intended for trade with Native Americans, but the next day he gave permission to a trader to exchange up to 6 gallons of whiskey for sturgeon.[33] Weak enforcement was easily overwhelmed by the desire of merchants to sell and Native Americans to buy, notwithstanding the opposition to alcohol on the part of some of their leaders.

In 1815 a federal law prohibited the operation of distilleries in the poorly defined "Indian Country," but this was also ineffective, as transporting distilled spirits efficiently and inexpensively, just as traders were doing in Africa at the same time, was not difficult. Nonetheless, these acts by Congress were the start of a long effort to limit or cut off Native American access to alcohol, especially to whiskey, which was easily and inexpensively produced in the 1800s. Whiskey was not only more intoxicating because of its high alcohol content—even when it was diluted to a third, it was far more potent than beer—but its advantageous alcohol-to-volume ratio made it efficient to transport along waterways and overland. Efforts to prohibit Native American access to alcohol continued until a clear prohibition policy was enacted in 1892. Until then, various attempts to keep alcohol from Native Americans failed for the same reasons that prohibition failed in the United States and elsewhere in the twentieth century: the production and sale of alcohol were profitable, and there was more than enough consumer demand to keep producers and merchants in business.

The commitment of the federal government to eliminating drinking by Native Americans fluctuated, and at times the government employed alcohol as an aid to land and treaty negotiations. Some 662 gallons of whiskey were supplied for the negotiations of the Saginaw Chippewa treaty of 1819, and 932 gallons were used for the Ottawa, Chippewa, and Potawatomi treaty in Chicago two years later.[34] Still, most of the alcohol that flowed into Indian Country was channeled by private merchants. It was transported along waterways, notably the Missouri River, and overland, and traders employed various subterfuges. Fur trading companies insisted, reasonably, that their white employees needed rations of whiskey while working in remote areas and purchasing pelts. They were issued permits to take whiskey, based on the number of employees and the length of time they expected to be away. It was easy enough to exaggerate both and to take plenty of whiskey to sell to Native Americans. The commander of Fort Leavenworth estimated that twice as much whiskey was shipped up the Missouri River in 1831 than was legally permitted, while an Indian agent reported that a mere 1 percent of whiskey transported overland to Indian Country was covered by permits.[35] These were clearly impressionistic assessments, but they show that officials believed there was a substantial flow of illicit alcohol.

Reports of the harmful consequences of drinking for Native Americans began to increase. In 1831 the Upper Missouri agent wrote to William Clark, the noted explorer, former governor of Missouri Territory, and at that time superintendent of Indian affairs, "Liquor flows as freely here as the Missouri.... For

God's sake, for the sake of humanity, exert yourself to have this article stopped in this country." On the same day in 1831, Clark was writing that he considered it his duty to recommend "the total & entire prohibition" of spirits from Indian Country. It was clear, he wrote, that the regulations on selling alcohol to Native Americans had been abused by traders, who had thus shown "such disrespect for the government as to violate its most immanent laws & so little humanity toward the Indians themselves, as to disregard the most sacred provision for their protection." Clark's decision was predicated on the belief that Native Americans had an irresistible attraction to alcohol: "It is well known that not an Indian could be found among a thousand, who would not (after a first drink) sell his horse, his gun, or his last blanket for another drink—or even commit a murder to gratify his passion for spirits."[36]

In 1832 a new federal law was passed making it illegal to take distilled spirits "under any pretense" into Indian Country. Soon after, in 1834, Indian Country was defined to encompass almost the whole of the United States west of the Mississippi River, except for the states of Missouri and Louisiana and Arkansas Territory, and alcohol would be confiscated from any trader who brought it into this region. These laws have been seen as an infringement on the rights and sovereignty of Native Americans, but they indicate the determination of the federal government to deprive them of alcohol.[37] Unlike colonial governments in Africa, the federal government in the United States saw no benefit in continuing the alcohol trade with Native Americans—it did not provide the government with tax revenues—but only harm in its effects on the stability of communities and public health. Supplying Native Americans with alcohol was an obstacle to the proclaimed aim of the government to bring them into the mainstream of American society as productive citizens.

In 1834 there was no thought of creating new states farther west, and there was an expectation that the vast expanse of land called Indian Country would permanently remain alcohol-free. But despite the threat of heavy fines, the alcohol trade continued, as many merchants set up shop just over the border from Indian Country. The law was later amended to specify that sales to Native Americans were prohibited, as European Americans expected to be able to sell alcohol to military personnel, but that cleared the way for alcohol ostensibly destined for consumption by whites to be sold instead to Native Americans. Soldiers at garrisons sold some of their supplies, and emigrants traveling west took enough whiskey with them to cover their personal consumption, with surplus to sell to Native Americans for a tidy profit.

Native American leaders and revivalist prophets, who tied abstinence to cultural and spiritual rebirth, fought to halt the trade. Native American temperance organizations were formed, starting with the Cherokee Temperance Society in 1829, while some Native American women joined the WCTU.[38] But the flow of alcohol was virtually unchecked. Indian Country itself shrank under the continued expansion of European settlement, and even the definition of "Indian" was called into question. By the 1860s, writes one historian, "it was virtually impossible to determine who an Indian was or, for that matter, where Indian Country was for purposes of enforcing the Indian alcohol statutes."[39] Eventually the term "Indian Country" became too unstable to be useful, and it was dropped from statutes. By then, a growing number of states were passing laws that either prohibited or severely restricted the sale of alcohol within their borders. Temperance and prohibition organizations were gaining the popular and political support at state and federal levels that eventually culminated in national prohibition. If alcohol was portrayed as harmful to European Americans, it could be shown to have had devastating effects on Native Americans.

When Alaska was purchased from Russia in 1867, more indigenous populations fell under the jurisdiction of the American government. By this time they had been exposed to alcohol for several decades, despite treaties of 1824 and 1828 in which the Russian, British, and American governments agreed that distilled spirits and firearms should not be sold to the indigenous populations in the regions of the northwest coast that each power controlled. The system broke down as traders from each country competed to purchase skins from the native hunters. In 1835 the Hudson's Bay Company would exchange a gallon of spirits and a blanket, or 3 gallons of spirits, for a large beaver skin.[40] In 1842, concern about the effects of imported spirits on indigenous communities led both the Hudson's Bay Company and its Russian counterpart, the Russian-American Company, to agree to a ban on supplying them with spirits. In that year, the director of the Hudson's Bay Company and the governor of Alaska were present at an alcohol-fueled clash between two native communities when the chief of one killed a member of the other. But this ban, too, was frequently ignored by European traders, and by 1860 the Hudson's Bay Company had resumed using alcohol as a trading commodity. The official Russian policy of imposing prohibition on the indigenous populations was occasionally enforced; a steward of the Russian-American Company had his salary reduced from 1,000 to 600 rubles in 1862 when he was found selling spirits to two Aleuts.[41] But Russian control over Alaska was partial at best, and any restrictions their authorities might make were ignored or easily circumvented by independent or organized traders, whether they were Russian, British, or American.

When the governance of Alaska was transferred to the United States in 1867, the captain of the revenue cutter sent to establish control declared that, in the absence of any instructions, he would consider the territory as Indian Country and destroy any alcohol brought into it by any vessel, no matter what its nationality. This policy was confirmed by Congress the following year.[42] As in the rest of the United States, alcohol flowed liberally into Native and white communities despite what appear to have been rigorous attempts to suppress illicit alcohol production. Federal agents searched Aleut houses for distilling equipment, imposed fines and mandatory work for drinking, put people in irons for being drunk in public, and even banned the sale of sugar, a necessary ingredient for alcohol production where ripe produce was in short supply.[43]

In 1892, Congress passed a definitive and comprehensive law enacting prohibition on all Native Americans under U.S. jurisdiction. This legislation encompassed not only spirits, which had historically been viewed as the main problem alcoholic beverage, but also wine and beer. It was a recognition that many Native Americans no longer lived in isolated locations far from centers of European American population. Shipping alcohol over long distances was no longer necessary, so Native Americans now had access to the more bulky beverages, beer and wine. By the late 1800s, except where state prohibition laws prevented it, beer was being brewed widely in communities across the United States, and significant wine industries were located in Indiana, Ohio, and California. As of 1892, it was forbidden to "sell, give away, dispose of, exchange, or barter" any of these alcoholic beverages or any beverage "which produces intoxication" to any Indian. In 1920 this legislation effectively became redundant, as national prohibition applied the same rules to all Americans; but unlike prohibition for other Americans, Native American prohibition was not repealed in 1933, and it persisted until 1953.

Native peoples in Canada experienced a narrative similar to that of Native Americans, although with differences in chronology. They, too, were believed to be innately prone to abusing alcohol, but until the early nineteenth century, they were amply provided with it by traders who exchanged rum for furs. In the late 1700s, there were attempts to prevent the sale of rum to Aboriginals, partly to guarantee their effectiveness in aiding the British against attacks from Americans. As the military threats ended following the War of 1812, Aboriginals were transferred from military to civilian authority, first British and then Canadian, and were designated to undergo a "civilizing" process. This meant they were dispatched to reserves (designated Aboriginal territories) where they would learn agriculture and convert to Christianity.[44]

Between 1777 and 1860, there had been a number of ordinances restricting or prohibiting the sale of alcohol to native peoples. Some were responses to petitions from Aboriginal leaders, while others reflected Europeans' concern for heavy drinking in Aboriginal communities. As in the United States, Native Canadians were widely portrayed by whites as generally lazy and immoral and given to intoxication and alcohol-fueled violence, qualities invoked to justify the seizure of their lands.[45]

With the creation of Canada as a federal state in 1867, authority over Aboriginals passed to the federal government, and in 1876 the Indian Act imposed complete prohibition on anyone who had legal "Indian status" and anyone who followed "the Indian mode of life." Any Aboriginal who was found in possession of alcohol or selling alcohol could be imprisoned for up to six months. The only way an Aboriginal could legally drink was to be enfranchised, which meant surrendering Indian status and becoming a Canadian citizen. As in the United States, to become a citizen a native person had to demonstrate good character, which meant abstaining from alcohol.[46] The essential terms of the 1876 Indian Act remained in force until 1985, when band councils were given the authority to permit or prohibit alcohol and other intoxicants on reserves.

There were vast differences in the material and cultural conditions among the indigenous inhabitants of the African colonies and the native peoples of North America, but there were significant similarities in the policies adopted by authorities in the nineteenth and early twentieth centuries. All were influenced by the temperance and prohibition sentiments current in Europe and North America, but the European authorities were far more ready to impose prohibition on indigenous peoples than on their own populations at home. The American case is more complicated and less clear-cut as a race-specific policy applied to indigenous peoples, because in the 1800s, before the blanket ban on alcohol applied to Native Americans in 1892, many white populations had been subjected to coercive prohibition. By that date, a dozen states had imposed prohibition on all their inhabitants, and many more would do so before national prohibition came into force in 1920.

Beyond Africa and North America, European alcohol was a factor in cultural contacts in Asia and the Pacific region. Taxes drove colonial policies in parts of Asia as well as Africa. In Indochina, for example, the French began in the 1890s to tax rice alcohol, the alcoholic beverage most widely consumed by the Vietnamese population. The tax was initially resisted and difficult to enforce because much of the alcohol was produced clandestinely. But in 1902 a French company developed a method of purifying rice alcohol that not only was less expensive than the small-scale domestic production common among the Vietnamese but was easily distinguishable from it. The government gave the company a monopoly on production, expecting increased revenues.[47] Instead, the attempt to impose a European style of rice alcohol ignited vigorous objections that were often expressed in sensory terms. In 1907, Vietnamese members of the colony's governing council complained that the French were "forcing the natives to drink an alcohol that is not to their taste, that lacks the aroma of the alcohol made by Asian methods."[48]

Whether the French alcohol really represented a sensory affront to the Vietnamese or whether the Vietnamese wanted to avoid appearing that they did not want to pay for the taxed beverage, the Vietnamese won important concessions. The price of the beverage was lowered, as was the rate of tax on it, and the distilling company was ordered to improve the purity of its product (it had used water of dubious quality to dilute it to 40 percent alcohol) and to bring it more in line with the aromas and flavors of the traditional beverage.[49] It was a rare example of a colonial power treating its subjects as consumers. A historian able to shelve skepticism might think that the French authorities, with their cultural attachment to wine, were able to empathize with their Vietnamese subjects.

Japan is a case apart, as it was not colonized by Europeans. For centuries, from the mid-1600s, the only outsiders to have regular contact with Japan were the Dutch, who had access to Nagasaki. The Dutch brought beer for themselves, and gradually it infiltrated small segments of Japanese society. But the main alcoholic beverages consumed by the Japanese remained, by far, sake and plum wine. The policy of national seclusion ended when, in 1854, the Japanese government agreed to open diplomatic relations with the United States. Commodore Matthew Perry, who signed the agreement for the Americans, brought gifts that demonstrated American modernity: a small-scale working steam locomotive, a telegraph, and three casks of beer. Japanese descriptions of the beer were mixed, ranging from "magic water" to "bitter horse-piss wine."[50] As Japan opened for trade, alcoholic beverages of all sorts began to be imported, and within two decades a domestic brewing industry began production. But attempts by American temperance organizations to dampen the Japanese demand for alcohol were fundamentally unsuccessful (see Chapter 10).

As Europeans dealt with alcohol in many parts of Asia, their preoccupation in China was with opium, which had many of the characteristics attributed to alcohol: it was addictive, it had stimulant and intoxicating effects that bring on euphoria, and it was believed to have medicinal and therapeutic properties. Ironically, however, opium was said to be an effective cure for drunkenness. In the commentaries of missionaries in China, the word "alcohol" could easily be substituted for "opium," as in this 1856 report: "The ravages of opium we meet with here on every hand, and the deterioration of the morals of the people . . . I cannot but ascribe, in great part, to the use of this ensnaring and destructive drug." At least one Western commentator, a botanist, objected to those who criticized opium: "I would recommend the well-intentioned persons who have of late been raising such an outcry on the subject of opium, to reform their own [rum-sodden] countrymen."[51]

In the Pacific region, some alcoholic beverages were known before European contact, but Europeans introduced their own varieties, as they did elsewhere. For much of the nineteenth century, however, supplies of European alcohol to the distant and relatively remote colonies were anything but consistent, a fact that was lamented by many of the heavy-drinking missionaries. In the early 1800s, missionaries on Tahiti lived on fish, breadfruit, and water and received alcohol only from the ships that occasionally visited the islands.[52] Despite the limited supplies, alcohol made its way into the native communities, and there was growing concern among the missionaries for the consequences. Already in the early 1800s, Tahitians were said to have developed a taste for gin ("the waters of Britain"), and King Pomare II—plied with alcohol by visiting captains as a way of lubricating their arrangements to resupply their ships—was said to have became not only a habitual drinker but a habitual drunk.

Tahitians began to distill their own spirits by the 1820s, and there are reports of common intoxication as much among the European missionaries as among the indigenous population. In 1833 the Tahitian Temperance Society was formed (its founder was a missionary with a reputation for hard drinking), and the following year the Tahitian Assembly forbade the importation and use of distilled spirits on the islands. A native found guilty of having "in his possession, even one glass of ardent spirits" would be fined ten hogs; a foreigner would be fined $10 and be banished from Tahiti.[53] One result was that fewer ships visited the island, as they were no longer able to resupply with alcohol. Notably scarce were the "temperance ships" from America, which carried no alcohol for the crew. But their crews were notorious for drinking onshore, leading one missionary to observe, "The word 'temperance' applies only to the ships, and not to their crews."[54]

Europeans also dealt with alcohol in other parts of the Pacific region. Missionaries to Fiji found the population consuming *kava*, a beverage made from the root of the kava plant (variously known as *yagona* and *ava*), which promotes mild euphoria and relaxation. In 1862 the Reverend Joseph Waterhouse denounced kava in the same breath as spirits: "In addition to ardent spirits the yagona or kava root, is the curse of Fiji. For 12 years I have preached moderation, but in vain. With the Fijian of the present day it is all or none,—stupefaction or sense."[55] Europeans took part in kava ceremonies, and some noted that they were dignified and orderly occasions, like this report from 1845: "The cava [*sic*] has been considered sacred; and almost everything to be settled in these islands is done at a cava meeting, at which great order is observed."[56]

Such an account contrasts with the situation in Micronesia (thousands of small islands between Hawai'i and the Philippines), where many Europeans of marginal status had settled by the mid-1800s. One ship's captain described them as "runaway convicts, expirees or deserters from whalers" who lived "in a manner easily to be imagined from men of this class, without either law, or education to control them, with an unlimited quantity of ardent spirits which they obtain from distilling the toddy that exudes from the coco-nut tree."[57] When trading ships began systematically to visit the islands, much commerce was done using alcohol (and other commodities, such as firearms and tobacco) as the medium of exchange. Cheap gin was the usual beverage, and it was used to purchase copra and other products from the native populations. On the Tuamotu islands, pearl divers were paid in whiskey or rum, and there are reports of land trading hands for alcohol and firearms.

Such transactions, and the use of alcohol and tobacco generally, were opposed by Christian missionaries as they spread through Micronesia from the 1850s onward. They were appalled by the levels of crime, violence, and sexual promiscuity, and because they attributed such behavior to alcohol, they blamed the Europeans who had introduced alcohol to the islands.[58] Alcohol became a pivotal issue in the competition between the early European settlers and the missionaries for influence over the indigenous elites. Foreseeing a threat to their position, the resident Europeans had warned local leaders that the missionaries would try to take over the government, and in a few cases the missionaries were forbidden by chiefs to come ashore. Most were welcomed, however, and over time they converted many of the indigenous people to both Christianity and abstinence. In Kiti, in the Caroline Islands, a sort of prohibition was enacted by 1876 when missionaries persuaded Christian chiefs to appoint policemen to enforce the policy of abstinence.[59] In Micronesia, abstinence from alcohol became a defining characteristic of a Christian, a quality that distinguished Christians from non-Christians. (In a rare case, as on the island of Truk, where there was no alcohol, Christians were defined by their abstinence from tobacco.)

There is no defining pattern to be discerned as Europeans confronted alcohol in their far-flung colonies. In each case, the policies they applied ranged from laissez-faire to prohibition, and in most cases policies went through a number of phases, each representing a different level of coercion and rigor. There is no doubt that colonial alcohol policies were fashioned from competing interests, notable among which was the revenues that colonial powers could obtain from taxing alcohol in their colonies. At the same time, they had to deal with the demands of temperance organizations at home, often informed by their missionaries on the ground, and many policies (such as those forged in the international conventions dealing with alcohol in Africa) were compromises that attempted to balance restricting alcohol supplies while securing existing fiscal advantages.

12

The First World War
1914–1920

THE BATTLES AGAINST ALCOHOL

The First World War (1914–18) was a turning point in European and global history. It destroyed great empires, radically redrew Europe's political boundaries, altered the global balance of power, forced governments to mobilize state power, and ushered in new social policies. The war was also a watershed in the history of alcohol. Under the pressure of extended military conflict, growing concerns about alcohol crystallized, and many governments introduced regulations that were unprecedented in their rigor and extent. Although many of these policies were adopted as emergency wartime measures, they were largely maintained and even intensified long after the conflict ended, and the period between the world wars saw temperance and prohibition policies extended throughout the Western world. The best-known case is the United States, which introduced national prohibition in 1920, but it was only one country that tried to stamp out the supposed evils of alcohol during and immediately following the First World War.

The anxieties about the effects of alcohol consumption on health and social order that had been building during the nineteenth century sharpened with the outbreak of war in the summer of 1914. If alcohol had a negative effect on health, then it had the potential to be particularly serious in the case of soldiers. They were expected to be fit and robust models of manhood, rather than the weak, hollow-chested, and mentally deficient specimens that temperance literature generally portrayed drinkers as being. If alcohol undermined moral order and the stability of civilian society—which became crucially important as the "home front" during the war—it threatened havoc and defeat in military society, where men had to be in peak physical and emotional form, unquestioningly patriotic, and ready to obey orders, no matter what the consequences.

Alcohol also became a sharper issue from 1914 onward because wartime conditions gave extraordinary opportunities for the antialcohol campaigners to press their case more effectively. Temperance and prohibitionist rhetoric had long employed military metaphors: theirs was a war against drink that involved recruiting forces in the campaign against the enemy alcohol. This rhetoric meshed easily with the nationalist language of war that was normalized before and during the hostilities that began in 1914. Temperance and political leaders armed themselves with one language to fight two simultaneous wars—one against the foreign enemy beyond their borders and the other against the alcohol enemy within them. The most explicit statement of this sort was the 1915 declaration of British prime minister David Lloyd George: "We are fighting Germany, Austria, and Drink, and as far as I can see, the greatest of these deadly foes is Drink."[1] It was an astonishing statement, given that the British forces had already suffered hundreds of thousands of dead and wounded at the hands of the German armies. An earlier prime minister, William Gladstone, had claimed that alcohol had been more disastrous than all the wars, plagues, and famines, but at least he had not said that while Britain was in the grip of a deadly epidemic.

The war focused on two distinct drinking populations—soldiers and civilians—and the varied responses to each displayed the ambiguities that were evident in much of the antialcohol rhetoric of the day. As far as drinking by the military was concerned, opponents of alcohol had to contend with the centuries-old practice of providing daily rations of alcohol to soldiers and sailors. Fermented beverages were often the safest drinks in battle zones, where water supplies were often contaminated by human waste and dead bodies (humans and animals) and could be a source of epidemic diseases such as cholera and typhoid fever. At sea, beer was often served, and many navies included a daily ration of rum or other distilled spirit.

Temperance movements had focused on alcohol use in the military and had drawn attention to what they considered the particular iniquity of the state, through the army, appearing to encourage alcohol consumption by young men. Some temperance advocates argued that many young soldiers had no experience of alcohol until they joined up. Others, including serving and retired officers, challenged the conventional assumptions that alcohol was beneficial to health and argued that alcohol consumption was positively correlated with problems of discipline. Some raised the question of the impact of drinking on military efficiency in the narrow sense. Former British naval officers declared that most accidents aboard warships were the result of alcohol (one asserted unequivocally that alcohol was more dangerous than gunpowder), and army officers insisted that alcohol impaired the aiming accuracy of both riflemen and the artillery.

Before the First World War, the military authorities of a number of states carried out independent studies on the effects of alcohol on various military activities. A German survey of soldiers who fired some 36,000 rounds over sixteen consecutive days showed that their marksmanship was not affected by the normal ration of alcohol.[2] French military authorities seem to have been more realistic about the chances of keeping alcohol out of the hands of soldiers: instead of comparing the success of soldiers who drank with that of those who did not, they compared the marksmanship of wine-drinking and beer-drinking soldiers. They concluded that both beverages impaired accuracy, but wine less so. During the war itself, other estimates of the effects of alcohol on military efficiency were bandied about. According to one account, even half the rum ration of a British soldier produced a 40 to 50 percent reduction in accuracy of rifle shooting, while the naval rum ration led to a loss of 30 percent in gunnery accuracy.[3]

Yet despite the familiar moral strictures and the more pointed warnings of the practical effects of alcohol consumption on military effectiveness, most European armies continued to supply their soldiers in the field with spirits or wine. By the end of November 1915, after sixteen months of war, the British had sent a quarter of a million gallons of rum to their forces in France.[4] It was used mainly as a ration, each man receiving a modest twice-weekly serving that was increased for soldiers in the trenches and increased again when the weather was very bad. The justification was set out in a 1914 regulation: "On very exceptional occasions, as when the troops have been drenched or chilled through exposure on manoeuvres or training, a free ration . . . of rum . . . [may be issued] when certified by the Senior Medical Officer to be absolutely necessary for safeguarding the health of the troops." Antialcohol activists, who had long abandoned the notion that alcohol offered any health benefits, condemned the rum ration, which, they said, should be replaced by truly nutritious foods like hot milk and soup.[5]

Rum was also provided as a stimulant, and an extra ration was doled out to troops before they were sent "over the top," swarming from their trenches across no-man's-land toward the enemy lines. One soldier recalled, "Though the rum was potent, the amount given to each man was strictly limited and the effect was little more than that of a whiskey after some nasty shock. With most of the men keyed up for the coming assault, the alcohol tended to sharpen their senses rather than to deaden them."[6]

Still, there were concerns about mixing alcohol and military service. Legislation gave military authorities powers to regulate the hours alcohol could be sold in localities close to defended harbors, to seize alcohol on any premises used for military purposes, and to take action against any sailor who was drunk when he joined his ship.[7] Reformers in Britain were appalled at the thought of the moral effects that an extended period on the Continent with alcohol would wreak on the millions of young Britons who were in military service. Their anxiety reflected a tendency of the British upper class to think of Europeans (and the French in particular) as morally loose and lacking self-discipline. Never mind that soldiers were engaged in an atrocious military conflict, enduring shocking living conditions, and suffering the most appalling casualties; antialcohol campaigners, including the prime minister, seemed more concerned about the effects of a daily ration of rum than of incoming shells.

But British temperance campaigners who criticized the alcohol ration knew they walked a narrow line. They wanted to stress the harm that intoxicating drink did to military morale, discipline, and efficiency, but they did not want to appear unpatriotic by suggesting that their fighting forces were undisciplined, unmotivated, and ineffective. One way out of the difficulty was to draw an implicit contrast between the British troops and those forces that were believed to be fighting without any alcohol rations.

A number of British commentators pointed to Russia, Britain's ally against Germany, because the Russian government had ordered the country's 26,000 vodka shops closed during the mobilization of millions of men in August 1914. This was a significant break with tradition, because bouts of vodka-drinking had been the common way that communities sent their young men off on military service. This time, the huge Russian armies were massed in an orderly and efficient way, a sharp contrast with the drunken sprees that had passed for mobilization on earlier occasions. As a result (and also to preserve grain supplies for food) the next month the tsar's government ordered liquor shops closed for the duration of the hostilities. For its part, the Russian army command banned the consumption of all forms of alcohol by troops on active service, and this, too, broke with tradition. Until then, Russian soldiers had been given vodka on nine holidays during the year and on special occasions determined by commanders. During war, rations of vodka had traditionally been distributed to soldiers three times a week (with more doled out as a reward for good performance), while Russian sailors had a ration of vodka every day while they were at sea.[8]

Western temperance organizations described the results of Russia's dry wartime policies as both amazing and predictable. British prime minister Lloyd George said productivity had increased by 30 to 50 percent on the Russian home front, "just as if she had added millions of labourers to the labour force."[9] As for the battle front, Russian soldiers were said to exhibit as much enthusiasm for battle when they were cold sober as other soldiers did when fortified by drink; but the Russians were more disciplined and fought as well or better, and those who were wounded recovered more rapidly. "There was never a more clear-headed or more sober army in the field," one author exclaimed, "than that which is now facing the hordes of the Teutons at this present moment." He continued that, because Russia was "one of the most democratic of countries" (an assertion that would have astounded most Russians), "once the peasant had been deprived of vodka it was unseemly that the wealthier classes should be able to enjoy champagne," and that as a result, all alcohol consumption in Russia had been suspended for the duration of the war.[10]

Such accounts of a dry Russian army contrast vividly with descriptions of heavy drinking on the eastern front during the war. Alcohol was no less prominent on the Russian home front. Illicit distilleries sprang up to serve a ready market, and peasants and workers produced vast volumes of *samogon* (homemade alcohol). In Tushino, near Moscow, illicit vodka was so plentiful and inexpensive by 1916 that peasants no longer bothered to make their own, and reports throughout the war suggest that alcohol was widely and readily available, despite government regulations.[11] Temperance supporters in the West ignored the failure of wartime prohibition in Russia and instead stressed the apparent resolve of the government so as to highlight what they portrayed as the British government's weak-kneed policy of doling out alcohol to the troops.

Nor did the Russian upper classes let the war interfere with the appetite that had made them one of the largest markets for champagne during the nineteenth century. Imports continued, although the war could interrupt supplies: one ship carrying vintage champagne (Heidsieck 1907) for the imperial court in St. Petersburg was sunk by a German submarine in the Gulf of Finland in 1916. (The bottles were recovered in 1998, and the wine was found to be in excellent condition.) If anything choked off the supply of champagne to the Russian elites, it was not any sense of wartime duty or wish to set an example for peasants and workers, but the Bolshevik Revolution of 1917.

The real loser from Russia's wartime prohibition was not consumers (although most probably drank poorer-quality alcohol than before) but the government. Before the war, taxes on liquor sales accounted for more than a quarter of the Russian state's revenues, but illicit producers, of course, evaded taxation.[12] The loss of this major contribution to the state budget undermined Russia's ability to sustain its war effort and contributed to the unrest that led to revolutions in 1917.

The French took a much less restrictive view of the military alcohol ration and made provisions for it from the beginning of the war. It was not rum they issued to their soldiers, however, but wine, the beverage that even the French temperance movement accepted as healthy. The 1914 grape harvest, brought in largely by children, women, and older men during the first months of the war because the younger men had been called up on military service, was an especially good one, up 50 percent from the previous year. The winemakers of Languedoc, the southern region that produced vast volumes of inexpensive wine for working-class consumption, presented 20 million liters to the army for distribution in military hospitals. As patriotic as this gift was, it was also profitable, for it prompted the French military authorities to purchase much more Languedoc wine to provide soldiers with generous rations throughout the war.

In 1914 the French military wine ration was set at a quarter of a liter a day, but in 1916, as the war dragged on and conditions at the front deteriorated, it was increased to half a liter. In 1918 officers were permitted to add a further quarter-liter and soldiers had the option of purchasing another quarter-liter at subsidized prices. By the end of the war, then, French soldiers had legitimate access to as much as a liter of wine a day, and no doubt there was a brisk trade in illicit supplies of wine and other alcoholic beverages. Reflecting current views of the effects of different forms of alcohol, the authorities fought a constant battle to keep spirits out of the hands of French soldiers, and the generous ration of wine was intended to reduce the demand for stronger alcoholic drinks. In 1916 the Academy of Medicine in Paris issued a statement to soldiers that addressed a number of myths, such as that alcohol gives strength and warmth. It warned against distilled spirits but allowed that a man might drink a liter of wine a day, as long as it was with meals.[13]

During 1917 the French army went through 1,200 million liters of wine, and it was estimated that it would have consumed 1,600 million liters in 1918 if the war had continued to the end of that year. Thousands of railroad tankers were requisitioned to supply French troops with wine. Supplying military rations helped sustain the French wine industry through the war; the men in military service were in the prime drinking demographic, and the loss of this market for years on end would have been disastrous for wine producers. Government requisitions of wine for soldiers were a boon to southern producers of cheap wine, although the prices paid were well below the peacetime market rates for the producers of the more expensive wines in regions like Bordeaux and Burgundy.

French soldiers consumed red wine, which was thought to be more masculine and more likely than white wine to put fire into men's blood. Other nationalities seem not to have had the same qualms. Australian soldiers are said to have drunk cheap (and almost certainly awful-tasting) white wine, and they pronounced *vin blanc* "van blonk," a phrase that was soon corrupted to "plonk" and applied to any cheap, poor-quality wine. But the French drank red, and one of them, writing to the London *Times* in 1917 in response to criticism of French drinking habits, noted, "The fine health of the French troops in Gallipoli and in France is considered to have been largely due to their consumption of red wine—our light Burgundies and Bordeaux."[14] This overlooked the fact that most of the wine provided to soldiers came from southern France, not from prestigious regions like Burgundy and Bordeaux. Even so, wine was given some credit for the final victory when, at the end of hostilities, a French military newspaper proclaimed, "No doubt our brilliant generals and heroic soldiers were the immortal architects of victory. But would they have been without the ordinary wine [*pinard*] that kept them going to the end, that endowed them with spirit, courage, tenacity, and scorn for danger, and made them repeat with unbreakable conviction, 'We will prevail!'?"[15]

It is pointless to wonder whether the French and their allies prevailed because of alcohol or despite it. If a modest wine or rum ration helped make conditions more bearable, there were occasions when drinking interfered with the military effort. Ernest Hemingway wrote of one experience in the war: "Everybody was drunk. The whole battery was drunk, going along the road in the dark. We were going to the Champagne. The lieutenant kept riding his horse out into the fields and saying, 'I'm drunk, I tell you *mon vieux*. Oh, I am so soused.'"[16]

In the end, alcohol on the battlefronts proved to be a less contentious issue than regulating its supply and consumption on the home fronts, and European governments enacted restrictions on alcohol during the war with urgency and decisiveness they had not shown before it. Most of the restrictions were aimed at the production and sale of beer and distilled spirits. Some reflected wartime conditions, such as the need to protect grain supplies for bread by limiting beer production or to reduce drunkenness so as to maximize industrial productivity. In other cases, specific policies were adopted not because wartime conditions made them urgent but because the war provided the opportunity to impose regulations that would have been unacceptable in peacetime.

Among the war-related policies were the British alcohol regulations issued in 1914 under the Defence of the Realm Act that ushered in a wide range of emergency measures, including restrictions on the production and sale of alcohol. Then, in mid-1915, the government set up the Central Control Board, the first bureaucratic body designed specifically to develop and oversee alcohol policy. Legislation and cabinet orders, buttressed by local regulations issued by municipalities and military authorities, created a web of restrictions designed to keep alcohol from interfering with the war effort. They reflected the concern expressed by the prime minister: "A considerable percentage of workers failed to turn up on a Monday morning, and when they appeared on Tuesday they were much the worse for their week-end debauch. . . . One bank holiday a great number of men failed to turn up for the whole week. No wonder output was unsatisfactory."[17]

Early measures included raising the price of all forms of alcohol and lowering the strength of beer. The latter was designed partly to reduce the breweries' consumption of grain and partly to reduce the frequency of drunkenness among workers in the all-important war-related industries. Although no limits were initially placed on the production of beer in England, output fell during 1915, and in July 1916 it was reduced by government order to about three-quarters of prewar production. Further restrictions were added the next year amid a vigorous debate within the cabinet over two issues: whether to nationalize or to simply regulate the brewing industry during the war and whether to ban production entirely or to merely limit production of the diluted product.[18]

Other measures designed to achieve maximum economic wartime efficiency in Britain included restrictions on the hours that bars could open. They were limited to serving drinks at lunchtime and in the evening, thus encouraging the consumption of alcohol with food and discouraging drinking during regular working hours. Confronted by evidence that drinking was still interfering with munitions production—the *British Medical Journal* wrote that "the critical supply of munitions and armament of war is imperiled by whisky drinking in Glasgow"—the government imposed further limits in 1915.[19] Bars were permitted to sell alcohol for only five and a half hours a day (noon to 2:30 PM and 6:00 to 9:00 PM), rather than the sixteen to nineteen and a half hours (hours varied by district) permitted up to that point. Other regulations included restrictions on the hours that spirits could be sold for consumption off the premises (two and a half hours a day during the week and none at all on weekends), and bans on selling alcohol on credit, serving bonus measures, and treating. Additional restrictions were imposed in militarily sensitive areas near dockyards and munitions factories. Such measures limited opportunities for drinking, but workers were also urged to exercise self-restraint. The royal family was persuaded to set an example by abstaining from alcohol for the duration of the war.

These policies were not without their critics. An editorial in the influential *British Medical Journal* argued that the failure in the supply of munitions was due not to alcohol, which it argued was inherently no worse to health than tea, coffee, sugar, and lack of exercise. Rather, the productivity problems should be attributed to the strain of overtime and poor work conditions that delivered bad air, noise, high pressure on workers, and monotonous tasks. The editors explicitly linked drinking to the environment: "The excessive spirit drinking occurs in those parts of the country where the atmosphere is begrimed with smoke and the natural beauty of the world most hidden by the dirt of man's handiwork—in London, Lancashire, Glasgow, Tyneside." It recounted the story of a little girl who, seeing a picture of the sun rising behind a mountain, exclaimed, "Oh, it's as beautiful as a public-house!" In order to improve wartime productivity, the editorial suggested the government improve working conditions and limit alcohol to drinks with a maximum of 4 percent alcohol. Whiskey would be served already diluted, at a ratio of one ounce of whiskey to half a pint of water.[20]

There was an irony inherent in the various alcohol policies adopted by governments such as Britain's during the war. They were put in place while a sizeable proportion of the country's prime drinking population—adult males—was absent. By 1917 some 4 million British men of drinking age were on military service abroad, and the ratio of females to males over eighteen years of age in Britain was 61:39, a big shift in favor of women, compared with the 52:48 ratio of 1914.[21] This meant that rigorous alcohol policies of the kind long advocated by temperance campaigners were applied to a population that was now skewed toward the two broad demographic groups that historically consumed relatively little alcohol: women and children.

The shift in gender ratios in wartime civilian society underlay a broader cultural movement that in some respects blurred existing boundaries between women and men. Hundreds of thousands of women were employed in war-related industries where they enjoyed relatively good wages, and they took advantage of the new context of drinking (restricted hours and lower alcohol levels in drink) to patronize pubs in unprecedented numbers. This was a radical break with existing behavior that had seen "respectable" women—especially single women who did not want to be mistaken for prostitutes—avoid pubs. From 1916 on, however, middle-class and better-off working-class women appear to have patronized public bars in considerable numbers, a phenomenon described by one historian as "the first major shift in popular drinking habits in more than a century."[22]

This change in the balance of men and women in British pubs was, if anything, encouraged by the regulatory body set up by the government to control all aspects of drinking. It overruled regulations imposed by the military authorities in some naval and garrison towns that would have banned all women from bars—regulations imposed to deal with perceived heavy drinking by the wives of enlisted men. The official spirit of gender equality was not entirely a matter of principle. The women's suffrage movement had suspended its agitation for the women's vote for the duration the war, but its leaders had threatened to renew their activities if the government fostered inequality in any sphere to the disadvantage of women.

Even adjusted for the demographic shift that Britain experienced during the war, per capita consumption of all forms of alcohol declined. After rising 2 percent in 1915, consumption by people eighteen and older declined by 6 percent in 1916 and 39 percent in 1917. But there were differences between the consumption rates of spirits and beer (very little wine was consumed in Britain). Consumption of spirits rose 18 percent in 1915, fell slightly (by 1 percent) in 1916, and then more sharply by 30 percent in 1917. Beer consumption declined every year: by 6, 7, and 44 percent, respectively.[23] It is possible that the declining availability and quality of beer persuaded some drinkers—perhaps heavier drinkers—to switch to spirits, even though they were more expensive. The fact that income and living standards in Britain remained buoyant during the war (far more so than elsewhere in Europe) would explain how some people were able to afford spirits.

The decline in overall alcohol consumption was reflected in a drop in the number of arrests for public drunkenness. They fell by a quarter in 1915 (compared to 1914) and slid by another two-thirds in 1916 and 1917. By the end of the war the annual number of such arrests in England and Wales was 33,000, less than a sixth of the 212,000 in 1914, largely because so many men in the twenty-to-forty age group, which so generously contributed to the drinking population, were on active service.[24]

Despite the increasingly important share of the market represented by spirits during the war, beer remained the staple alcoholic beverage of the British working class, and the government was reluctant to go too far too quickly in restricting its availability. In 1917 the American government, which was within two years of legislating prohibition throughout the United States, tried to persuade its European allies to ban brewing entirely as part of more rigorous rationing programs. The British declined, citing "the difficulties and dangers of imposing upon the working classes any sweeping measures of prohibition especially at a moment when drastic compulsory rations are coming into force."[25] Even if beer were no longer an essential element of the British diet, enjoying a couple of pints at the local pub was deeply embedded in male working-class culture. Cutting off supplies might have led to the sort of disturbances that food shortages provoked in Germany and elsewhere in the last two years of the war.

If the British wartime administration acted cautiously to restrict alcohol to its population, the French acted with even greater care. Alcohol possessed a particular economic and cultural significance in France, where a considerable proportion of French workers were employed in viticulture and where exports of wine and brandy made important contributions to the balance of trade. These considerations alone made legislators nervous about attacking alcohol, and there was the additional fact that spirits and wine were culturally important throughout French society.

There was widespread official concern about levels of drinking in France before the war—per capita consumption of alcohol from wine and spirits amounted to 23 liters, compared with 10 liters in England and 7 liters in Germany—but governments had resisted pressure to impose serious restrictions. The law required bars to display official posters warning of the penalties for being drunk in public, measures that temperance supporters considered derisory in the face of what they believed to be widespread alcohol abuse and alcoholism. There was particular concern about the level of absinthe consumption, but even here successive prewar governments had dragged their feet, partly for fear of the reaction from consumers and producers.

The advent of war made all the difference. Within two weeks of the beginning of hostilities, the minister of the interior issued a regulation banning the sale not only of absinthe but also of similar beverages, such as the anise-flavored alcohols (made without wormwood) known by their brand names, Pernod and Pastis. Despite arguments that the government would lose tax revenue and would have to pay massive compensation to producers and farmers, and ignoring claims that the real danger to health was from cheap, adulterated versions, the Chamber of Deputies voted in March 1915 to prohibit their production and sale.

Absinthe was an easy target. It had been singled out as a particularly dangerous beverage not only by antialcohol campaigners but also by groups (such as the army) that were anything but hostile to alcohol itself. The ban on absinthe during the war is, in many respects, less surprising than the failure of governments to prohibit it before the war. But having acted resolutely on absinthe, the French wartime administration adopted very limited restrictions on other alcoholic beverages. Legislators took little issue with soldiers having a generous daily ration of wine, and attempts to regulate the availability of alcohol to civilians were modest. They included restrictions on the opening hours of existing bars and cafés and a decision not to issue any additional licenses to sell alcohol during the war.

Policies such as these were mild responses to the vivid scenarios of national disaster painted by some French temperance campaigners during the war. They criticized the army for introducing young men to alcohol, and some carried reports of heavy drinking by soldiers before they went into combat. A leading public health periodical carried an article claiming that alcohol made "the good soldier . . . undisciplined, lazy, perverted," and it went on to ask, "How will he behave when he returns from the Front? What will be the consequences of this invasion of drinkers?"[26]

Like their English counterparts, some French commentators portrayed drink as an enemy as dangerous as Germany and represented the wars against both as inseparable. But the French antialcohol lobby gave particular prominence to the negative effects of heavy drinking and alcoholism on fertility. This was a response to the chronic French concern about population decline—a fear that had intensified after the Prussian defeat of France in 1871 and became especially acute during the First World War, when France faced the far more populous German Empire. Seen as obstructing population growth, alcohol could be portrayed as weakening France from within and making it vulnerable to defeat by Germany.

If France's wartime administration did not respond to these anxieties about alcohol, some military and regional civilian authorities did. One French general banned the consumption of all spirits in the region under his control, a regulation that encompassed not only French soldiers but their British and Belgian counterparts and soldiers' families. In some localities, civilian authorities forbade the employment of minor females (except for owners' children) in taverns, required bars to have windows so that drinkers could be seen from the street outside (presumably to prevent clandestine drinking), and banned advertisements for absinthe (which was no longer legally available).[27] But such measures were only local in their reach, and even then, they tended to target spirits and largely left untouched the broader alcohol-positive culture of the French.

For the most part, the difficulties faced by French civilians in terms of getting alcohol were caused not by obstacles thrown up by the government but by wartime price inflation. Even in the Charente region, on the Atlantic coast, where vast volumes of cheap wine were produced for distilling into brandy, the price of wine rose from 20 francs in 1914 to 60 francs the next year and then to 110 francs by 1918. The price of few other commodities increased as much. Compared with the more than fivefold rise in the price of wine, bread doubled in price, meat rose threefold, and milk and cheese went up fourfold.[28]

On the other side of the conflict, the German administration also implemented measures to restrict alcohol, but they too were generally modest. In order to maximize efficiency and save grain for food, beer production was ordered cut by a quarter, and per capita consumption of all forms of alcohol fell by two-thirds between 1914 and 1917.[29] Overall, however, the decline in consumption was due less to government regulations than to problems of production, as the grain needed for beer and spirits became increasingly scarce.

Wartime regulations extended well outside Europe, for the world war earned its name by drawing in countries from all parts of the globe, particularly colonies of the European belligerents. Restrictions on alcohol production and sales were imposed in countries as far-flung as Canada, South Africa, and New Zealand. In Canada, the federal government enacted a system of almost total prohibition in April 1918, just seven months before the end of hostilities. It expired at the end of 1919, but wartime restrictions, applied by all the provinces but one, continued into the 1920s and beyond. These had been encouraged by temperance organizations that tried to leverage the war as a means of getting restrictions placed on alcohol. For example, in 1916 the Montreal Anti-Alcoholic League denounced beer as an "unsanitary and mischievous beverage" and cited as evidence "the brutality of the German nation," which was well-known for its beer consumption. The brewing industry replied, in full-page newspaper advertisements, that "beer is a Veritable Food Product." Ignoring the German reference and striking a slightly anti-American note, the Quebec brewers quoted the president of the British Medical Association: "Bread, cheese and beer for a meal is infinitely more scientific than the American meal of bread, tea, and jam."[30]

Quebec lagged behind the other Canadian provinces in regulating alcohol during the war, for by 1917 all the others had introduced prohibition policies in some form. Ontario passed a temperance act in 1916 that banned the sale of alcohol with the exception (designed to protect local grape-growers) of wine made from grapes grown in the province. In compliance with the law, the wine could be sold only from the winery and in quantities of at least 5 gallons—presumably to reduce purchase by the poor, who could not afford to buy wine in bulk volumes. Other exemptions were allowed: clergymen could obtain sacramental wine; physicians could prescribe spirits, beer, and other forms of alcohol for medicinal reasons; dentists could administer alcohol "as a stimulant or restorative"; and veterinarians were permitted to keep up to a quart of liquor as long as it was not used for human consumption.

In New Zealand, in contrast, the nascent wine industry almost became a fatality of the war, not because of objections to wine itself but because most of the pioneer winemakers were immigrants from Dalmatia, a region on the Adriatic coast that in 1914 was part of the enemy Austrian Empire. There is no evidence that the Dalmatians were supporters of the Austrian war effort— indeed, they were as likely to be supporters of Dalmatian independence from Austria—but the New Zealand government treated them as enemy aliens and confiscated their vineyards.

Far more rigorous alcohol regulations were also adopted by the Bolshevik authorities after the Russian Revolution of 1917. They continued the prohibition policy enacted by the tsar in 1914, but they also nationalized the alcohol industry and declared any existing stocks of alcohol to be state property. To some extent they were motivated by an ideological objection to alcohol, which Karl Marx had criticized as a means by which capitalists ensured the docility of workers. Marx is better-known for having written that "religion is the opiate of the people," but he might just as well have added alcohol to religion, because levels of consumption seem to have been very high at the time of the revolution, despite the formal prohibition imposed during the war. In more practical terms, the new Bolshevik authorities were concerned at the socially disruptive effects of alcohol. Drink was implicated in a number of the Petrograd riots in 1917, with Lenin writing that the bourgeoisie was "bribing the scum of society and the déclassé elements, getting them drunk for pogroms." The next year there were reports of units of Red Guards looting state alcohol warehouses, even though Red Guards were required to "struggle with drunkenness so as not to allow liberty and revolution to drown in wine."[31] Beyond this there was a determination to keep grain supplies for baking and cooking, rather than for producing alcohol.

Concerns such as these confirmed the need for prohibition, but the government was faced with widespread illicit production, which it alleged was carried out by wealthier peasants (kulaks) to lure poor peasants to the anti-Bolshevik side. A series of regulations dealt with alcohol production and consumption in what was to become the new Soviet state. In December 1919 the government codified its liquor policy and made home-brewing and -distilling a crime punishable by a minimum five-year jail sentence and confiscation of property. An unusual clause—because most prohibition laws have historically not criminalized consumers—made it an offense, punishable by a minimum of a year in jail, to drink illicitly produced alcohol.[32] This was the beginning of a series of policies that ran up against (mostly male) drinking cultures that proved almost impossible to change. By the mid-1920s another consideration became pressing: the state's need for the taxes that alcohol generated. Conflicting pressures led successive Soviet governments to adopt varying policies on alcohol, which proved to be a persistent problem throughout the life of the Soviet Union.

One more country needs to be mentioned as a belligerent in the First World War: the United States, which declared war in 1917, little more than a year before hostilities ended. The American army was officially dry, having abandoned the alcohol ration many decades earlier. But when General Pershing, the commander of the American Expeditionary Force, issued orders against drinking, he exempted light wines and beer. In his memoirs he observed that there was "comparatively little drinking in our armies, and what there was decreased noticeably after the prohibition of strong drink."[33]

In other respects the U.S. government pursued more comprehensive antialcohol policies during the war. When negotiating the supply of grain, American officials tried to persuade Britain and its partners to ban brewing entirely so as to conserve cereal stocks for bread. Several of the American agencies that accompanied U.S. forces to France lent their support to temperance campaigns there. The YMCA set up establishments where young men and women could meet in a wholesome, alcohol-free environment, while the Rockefeller Foundation published brochures for French children that contrasted two ways of life: one with alcohol, which included violence and poverty, and the other without alcohol, which led to happiness and plenty.[34]

The antialcohol policies fostered by the United States government and by American organizations in Europe reflected the widespread adoption of prohibition policies in the United States by the time it entered the war. Although they varied in their terms and rigor, some forty-five states had enacted prohibition statutes by 1916. There was, therefore, an important difference between European states and the United States. The First World War represented a turning point in European alcohol policies, because the more rigorous regulations enacted during the war were, to a large extent, maintained for decades after. But the war was largely irrelevant to the course of alcohol policies in the United States. By the time the war broke out, prohibition looked like an unstoppable force, and there is no sense that American participation in the European conflict for twenty months slowed or accelerated the process that culminated in prohibition.

Prohibitions
1910–1935

NOBLE EXPERIMENTS,
IGNOBLE FAILURES

The word "prohibition" is often shorthand for prohibition in the United States, the national policy in force from 1920 to 1933 that banned the production and sale of beverage alcohol throughout the country. This period, together with the antialcohol movements that led to it, has dominated American histories of alcohol. But although American prohibition is important to the alcohol and broader cultural history of the United States, it is also important in the wider, global context. While American prohibition was arguably the most stringent policy of its kind enacted on a comprehensive national basis since Islam banned the making and drinking of alcohol by Muslims (and by others in Muslim-ruled territories), it was far from the only policy of its kind at the time it was introduced.

Many countries enacted prohibition laws during and soon after the First World War. They included Russia, which went dry at the outbreak of war in 1914, and its successor Soviet state, which continued the imperial prohibition policies into the 1920s. Some Scandinavian countries passed prohibition legislation, as did some Mexican states and most Canadian provinces. The British government imposed prohibition policies on the indigenous populations of some of its African colonies in 1919. These examples generally fell within the same period, but there were even earlier, race-based examples: the U.S. government imposed prohibition on Native American populations during the 1800s, and the government of the Republic of Transvaal and its successor white South African governments did so on native African populations from 1896 to the 1960s.

Prohibition policies have seldom been total and absolute, and there is always a question of how strictly we should define prohibition. Some prohibition policies made exceptions for lower-alcohol beverages such as light beer and wine while banning higher-alcohol spirits; some banned production and sale but not consumption, while others included consumption; some allowed consumption for religious or medical purposes. Even under Islamic law, according to some interpretations, there is some allowance for alcohol as a medical remedy when no alternative is available.[1] In Britain's African colonies, indigenous peoples were permitted to make and consume their traditional grain-based beer and palm wine, which were generally considered harmless, but not to drink the stronger European alcoholic beverages. All these examples are qualified versions of prohibition, but all represented serious attempts to deprive specific populations of alcohol or, at the very least, to severely restrict their access to it.

Russia first introduced nationwide prohibition when Tsar Nicolas II decreed at the outbreak of the First World War that alcohol would not be produced or sold for the duration of the hostilities. This policy was based on the same considerations that motivated other wartime governments to restrict alcohol: the fear that alcohol would disrupt military discipline on the battlefronts and impair industrial efficiency on the home front. But although other participants in the war eventually adopted measures such as reducing the alcohol content of beer and limiting the hours during which alcohol could be sold, as the British government did, Russia opted for outright prohibition. The tsarist government was able to do so not only for the practical reason that the state's monopoly on vodka production made it easy to control, but also because it was an autocratic regime that believed it would not have to face a political backlash such as democratic governments feared. In Britain, for example, Lloyd George's administration was reluctant to take alcohol restrictions too far because a pint (or more) of beer at the pub was a staple of men who were not only workers but also voters.

As we have seen (Chapter 12), the Russian ban on alcohol production was widely ignored during the First World War. Clandestinely and not-so-clandestinely produced vodka quickly replaced legal alcohol, and consumption not only continued among civilians (including the imperial family) but was widespread among Russian troops. And even though the autocratic tsarist government believed itself immune from any backlash against its wartime policies, including prohibition, mounting dissatisfaction reinforced the opposition to the tsar and paved the way for revolutions in 1917.

Ironically, the adoption of prohibition had brought the tsarist government to the same position (although for different reasons) that some of its socialist opponents had been advocating for decades. While the government's policy was based on considerations of wartime efficiency, many unions and socialist organizations had long argued that drinking was against the interests of the working class. The alcohol question was to have been taken up by the meeting of the Second International, in August 1914, and the dominant concern was the effect that alcohol abuse had on workers, not only on their health as individuals but on their ability to organize politically.[2] Russian socialists had made a distinction between two ideal types of worker: backward workers who lacked intellectual and cultural character, and progressive workers who were politically engaged in the struggle against capitalism. One critical aspect of these categories hinged on alcohol: backward workers were heavy drinkers as well as womanizers, bawdy, and generally coarse, in contrast to progressive workers, who were sober, neatly dressed, and sexually restrained.[3]

In this sense, the continuation of prohibition after the Russian Revolution of October 1917 was consistent with the antialcohol position adopted by many workers' organizations before it. One of the first measures taken by the new Bolshevik government (in November 1917) was to close all existing distilleries and wineries and prohibit the production and sale of all alcoholic beverages. A commissar "for the struggle against alcoholism and gambling" was established, and in the Red Army, alcoholism was included among offenses that were punishable by death. A year later, all existing stocks of alcohol were declared to be the property of the state. It was estimated that millions of rubles of alcohol were stored in 700 warehouses in St. Petersburg and that the tsar's residence had a cellar that held alcohol valued at $5 million.[4]

The aim of these policies was to produce a nondrinking population, but the authorities soon had to confront the reality that most workers drank and that alcohol was embedded in their culture; drinking was a social act, and among workers, refusal to have a drink was interpreted as a gesture of unfriendliness, if not outright hostility. In early Soviet factories, managers demanded a bottle of vodka as the price of hiring new workers, and older workers required the same for training them in their jobs.[5] Rather than take the pragmatic course of encouraging temperance and reserving moral condemnation for excessive drinking and drunkenness, the Soviet authorities insisted on strict abstinence. (Contrary to many accounts, Vladimir Lenin, the first Soviet leader, drank wine, beer, and vodka, although by the time of the Revolution, he might well have portrayed himself as an abstainer for political purposes.)[6]

In addition to pointing out the negative health and social consequences of drinking, Soviet commentators added a political dimension: drunkenness was equated with counterrevolution, and heavy drinkers were portrayed as traitors. A Soviet newspaper declared in 1929 that any worker who drank alcohol committed a "crime . . . against himself, his family, production and the state."[7] This position, which effectively obliterated the notion of private life, gave the state a vested interest in the bodies of workers and a claim to regulate their diets.

The reality on the factory floor was very different from the official prescription. During the Soviet period of prohibition, as before, there were countless incidents of workers arriving for their shifts intoxicated, and many workers brought before courts and tribunals vigorously defended their customary right to drink. Workers consumed the illicit alcohol that was plentiful on the black market and treated the new revolutionary holidays as they had treated holidays under the tsar: as occasions for festive and sometimes heavy drinking. When they did not make their own alcohol (a third of rural households were said to be making vodka in the 1920s), they were able to draw on widespread production in tens of thousands of illicit breweries and distilleries. In 1918 one village in Voronezh province (in southwest Russia) distilled grain equivalent to the amount that would have fed a town of 9,000 to 12,000 people for a year. In the spring of 1918, twice as much grain was distilled into vodka in Siberia as was shipped across the Urals as food.[8]

This massive diversion of grain supplies alarmed the authorities as much as the fact of illicit distilling, and they blamed the kulaks, a wealthy peasant class that later became a target of Stalin's repressive policies. Yet despite serious penalties for making illicit alcohol (set in 1918 at a minimum of five years' imprisonment, with hard labor), many citizens evidently considered the risk worth taking; in 1922 alone, there were more than half a million prosecutions for liquor crimes in the Russian republic, and that was after strict prohibition rules had been eased somewhat.

Faced with resistance by consumers, the inability to halt illicit production, threats to the grain supply, and the loss of tax revenue from alcohol, the Soviet government changed course and gradually abandoned prohibition. In August 1921, after seven years of total prohibition (four of them in the Soviet period), the government permitted the production and sale of wine, and in early 1922 it authorized beer sales. In January 1923 the production of low-alcohol (20 percent) vodka was permitted, and in October 1925 regular-strength (40 percent) vodka was allowed. All alcohol production was in the hands of a state monopoly. Despite making alcohol again available to the population and wanting to maximize the tax revenues that alcohol produced, the Soviet government continued its antialcohol campaigns, but alcohol consumption persisted at high levels. In Leningrad there were 2,000 arrests for drunkenness in 1923, but by 1927 there were 113,000—one arrest for every four adults in the city.[9] (Many were probably repeat offenders.) It is unlikely that such an increase can be explained simply by changes in policing and enforcement, and it must indicate an increase in heavy drinking.

The strict prohibition policies adopted by the tsarist and Soviet governments lasted for seven years (1914–21), half as long as prohibition in the United States. Often referred to as the "Noble Experiment," American prohibition was not enacted simply out of a desire to stop Americans from drinking. The framers of the Eighteenth Amendment, which banned the production, sale, transportation, and importation of alcohol for beverage purposes, were motivated by a desire to improve their society. They believed that the citizens of an alcohol-free America would be healthier, more moral, and more law-abiding. Life expectancy would rise as alcohol-related mortality fell, offenses against the person and property would decline as alcohol-related crime rates plummeted, and there would be less poverty and better health as people redirected their spending on alcohol to food and housing. Marriages would be more stable as alcohol-driven divorce rates fell. If alcohol was the foundation of almost all of America's social ills, prohibition was the cure. That was what made it noble.

National prohibition was the culmination of decades of lobbying by politicians, church groups, and ordinary citizens, and it came long after individual states began to enact their own prohibition laws. By 1919, twenty-seven states were dry and twenty-one remained wet, with the greatest support for prohibition in the South and West and the greatest resistance in the Northeast. State prohibition policies were buttressed by federal legislation: the 1913 Webb-Kenyon Act prohibited the transportation of alcohol into states with prohibition policies. The federal government took further action in 1917 when the United States entered the First World War. Distilleries were closed down in the interests of wartime efficiency and grain conservation; then grain shipments to breweries were limited, and the alcohol level of beer was set at a maximum 2.75 percent. At the end of the same year, Congress passed the Eighteenth Amendment and sent it to the states for ratification. But Congress was so keen to stop the flow of drink that it passed the Wartime Prohibition Act on November 21, 1918, ten days after the end of the war. This act banned the sale of intoxicating beverages effective July 1, 1919. Before that date, the Eighteenth Amendment received the overwhelming support of forty-six of the forty-eight states, and national prohibition was set to take effect on January 1, 1920.

When national prohibition came into force on that date, it was far more inclusive than many people had expected. The specific terms of prohibition and its enforcement were set down in the Volstead Act, which instead of focusing on distilled spirits and exempting wine and beer, as many people had expected and hoped, prohibited any alcoholic beverage that had more than half of 1 percent of alcohol by volume. Protests by brewers, who had hoped to be able to continue producing the low-alcohol beer mandated during the war, were unsuccessful, and they were among the casualties as prohibition virtually wiped out America's beverage alcohol industry.

The number of breweries producing regular-strength beer fell from about 1,300 in 1916 to 0 ten years later; the number of distilleries declined by 85 percent (the survivors made industrial alcohol and alcohol for medicinal purpose); wineries declined from 318 in 1914 to 27 in 1925 (the survivors made wine for religious purposes and grew table grapes); and only 4 percent of liquor wholesalers and 10 percent of retailers remained in some kind of business.[10] The economic costs to governments and individuals were enormous, not only in terms of lost tax revenues but because the near-closure of the alcohol industry threw thousands of employees out of work. It also affected workers in other sectors of the economy associated with alcohol, such as glass manufacturing, transportation, and hospitality (saloons and bars), although some new employment was generated when the saloons (many strategically located on street corners in cities) were replaced by retail stores.

The few exceptions to total prohibition were predictable and few and were based on the principle that the ban applied only to alcohol used for *beverage* purposes. This meant that alcohol could be made for industrial use and that alcoholic beverages (fermented and distilled) could be made in small quantities for nonbeverage purposes. Doctors could prescribe wine and spirits, for example, and priests, ministers, and rabbis could obtain and serve wine in religious rituals. Apart from these exceptions, which were expected to represent minuscule volumes of alcohol, breweries, wineries, and distilleries would go out of business, and bars, saloons, and taverns would close.

Finally, Americans were permitted to keep alcohol in their homes for consumption by family members and bona fide guests, a provision intended to allow for existing alcohol stocks to be used up. Many of those who could had probably stocked up on alcohol. One Virginia newspaper publisher ordered 16 gallons of whiskey in advance of a state vote on prohibition, noting, "I believe in looking ahead. I don't know what the pro-hibs will do in September, but I do not mean for them to catch me high and dry in any event."[11] As they consumed the last dregs of their bottles, which could not legally be replaced, Americans were expected to abjure their alcohol-drinking habits and turn en masse to healthy beverages like milk, water, fruit juices, coffee, and tea, none of which was linked to mortality, crime, immorality, and social disorder.

The popular image of prohibition, reinforced by movies and television series like *The Untouchables*, is a far cry from this ideal. It is an image of speakeasies (clandestine bars where men and women continued to drink), illicit stills producing moonshine, rum-running and other forms of alcohol smuggling, shootouts between enforcement officials and prohibition breakers, and the rise of organized crime led by gangsters such as Al Capone. These sensational images distort the complex picture of prohibition in the United States, but they do highlight an important theme: just as soldiers, workers, peasants, and the middle and upper classes resisted prohibition in Russia and the Soviet Union, so did millions of Americans, whether they were men or women, whether they lived in town or country, whether they were workers, farmers, and professionals or in business.

Resistance took many forms. Some emanated from individual states, even though the great majority had ratified the Eighteenth Amendment. While states that had enacted prohibition regimes before 1920 were happy to see it adopted federally—for one thing, it promised to put an end to the importing of alcohol from other states—some state legislatures soon rebelled against being drawn into the federal liquor regime. Several tried to override the Volstead Act; the legislatures of Massachusetts, New York, and New Jersey passed laws in 1920 to permit the sale of wine and light beer in their respective states. But in each case, the Supreme Court struck the state legislation down and upheld prohibition throughout the whole country.

Some states passively resisted prohibition and thus undermined joint state-federal enforcement of prohibition. Maryland never passed enforcement regulations, and starting with New York in 1923, a number of states that did repealed their legislation. By 1927, twenty-seven of the forty-eight states made no budgetary provision at all for enforcing prohibition. But although such acts—or failures to act—weakened the impact of prohibition, they could not restore the right of citizens to obtain legal alcohol.

More resistance came from wineries and clandestine distilleries. A number of wineries began to sell dehydrated grapes and concentrated grape juice, both of which could be turned into regular grape juice and then fermented into wine by the addition of yeast. Wine made under these conditions might not have been commercially viable, let alone of high quality; but it was wine of sorts, and it contained alcohol. Much more alcohol was produced by small-time moonshiners (illicit distillers) and by the smaller number of large-scale clandestine distilleries. Whiskey was the main alcohol sold on the black market because its far higher alcohol level by volume made it much more efficient to store and transport. To this extent, the period saw a dramatic shift away from beer and also from wine, which had historically run a distant third in alcohol popularity in the United States.

Beyond the alcohol illicitly produced in the United States, volumes were smuggled in from outside the country. Some came from Canada, where provinces began to enact prohibition policies from 1915. But when the Canadian government regulated the production of alcohol in the nation and its movement among the provinces, it permitted distilleries, breweries, and wineries to continue making alcoholic beverages for export, and much of this production went clandestinely to the United States. Some was shipped across Lake Ontario to the north shore of New York, while on the east coast, rum was shipped to New England from Nova Scotia. The 1920s saw a depression in the fishing industry, and smuggling was a welcome source of income. It was reported in 1925 that half the Lunenberg (Nova Scotia) fishing fleet of 100 vessels were engaged in the rum trade, with many leased to American syndicates for $2,500 a month.[12] Yet more alcohol reached the United States from Europe. Ships laden with wine and spirits lay outside American territorial waters, beyond the reach of prohibition enforcement officers and the U.S. Coast Guard, and the alcohol was ferried to shore at night by flotillas of small boats.

Further supplies of alcohol moved across the American border from Mexico. Many Mexican states had introduced prohibition after the 1910 Revolution, but there was little popular or even official support for it. By the 1920s, just as prohibition was applied in the United States, most Mexican prohibition policies were being abandoned, and production of alcohol was again in full swing. Some Mexican alcohol crossed the border in the bellies of Americans who had traveled to Mexico to drink in the saloons that multiplied to cater to a new phenomenon, alcohol tourism, but most was simply smuggled across the border. The bulk of it was beer, and the Mexican brewing industry, no longer facing competition from American beers, flourished during American prohibition. In addition, a number of Americans set up distilleries in the Mexican border states with the aim of smuggling liquor to the United States. A whiskey distillery jointly owned by Mexicans and Americans opened in Piedras Negras, Coahuila, in 1920, and another with owners from Colorado started production in Ciudad Juárez six years later.[13]

The continuous supply of alcohol that flowed into the United States during prohibition—a precursor to the later flow of narcotics—speaks not only to strong demand but also to ineffective federal enforcement. The enforcement of prohibition fell to the Treasury Department, and its agents were given the power to seize, close, or sell any property (including houses and vehicles) that was used to make, sell, or transport illegal alcohol. First offenses against the law could be punished by fines of $1,000 and imprisonment for up to six months, while repeat offenses carried penalties of up to $10,000 in fines and five years in jail.

The Volstead Act provided for overall enforcement to be shared between the federal and state governments, and there was an implicit understanding that state police and courts would carry most of the burden. In fact, many states were reluctant participants, and as we have seen, most had canceled enforcement funding entirely by 1927. The result was that the burden fell on federal enforcement offices, and they were underfunded. Although their annual budgets rose from $3 million to $15 million during the 1920s, enforcement was thin, and there were never more than 3,000 agents in the field at any time. Another problem was the high turnover of enforcement staff, which meant that there were few experienced agents. Nearly 18,000 men were appointed to positions between 1920 and 1930, many of them to replace agents who had been dismissed. One in twelve agents was fired, most for drunkenness or for taking bribes, although there seems to have been an improvement in training and professionalism toward the end of the 1920s.

Although enforcement was uneven and seemed, to many observers, arbitrary and capricious, it was possibly most effective in states that had enacted prohibition policies before the federal law came into effect. When Kansas enacted state prohibition in 1881, many Kansans (living on "an island entirely surrounded by liquid territory," as one commentator described it)[14] brought liquor in from other nearby states, but once national prohibition was in place, illicit alcohol production sprang up throughout Kansas. Much of it, according to prohibition officials, contained toxic ingredients such as ether, chloroform, and fusil oil. The officials claimed to have reduced the flow of alcohol in Kansas to a trickle, but they were likely to exaggerate their success, since they had an interest in appearing to be effective and efficient.

The detection and prosecution of moonshine (illicit liquor) production often depended on the diligence of the agents, and it was often inconsistent, at best. In many cases, agents were effective at identifying and prosecuting small-scale producers, resulting in an impressive number of arrests, but they did not have the resources (or failed to use them) to do the investigative work necessary to track down the major sources of illegal alcohol. Informers were also important. In some cases they were antidrink citizens who alerted the authorities to the existence of illicit stills, but other, less civic-minded informers were motivated by different considerations. Some moonshiners blew the whistle on their competitors so as to increase their own market share, some clients informed on producers who refused to give them credit, and one woman in Florida turned in her husband because his heavy drinking was affecting their family's well-being.

The sheer number of prosecutions overwhelmed some court systems. In the Southern District of Florida in 1921, the federal courts handled 551 criminal prosecutions, 463 of which were violations of the federal liquor law. By 1928 there were 1,319 prosecutions, 85 percent of which concerned liquor. Florida's long coastline made it an obvious destination for alcohol smuggling, a factor that contributed to the high proportion of liquor prosecutions on the courts' dockets. In order to clear a backlog of nearly 3,000 cases, a third judge was added to the Southern District in 1928.[15]

Although most prohibition prosecutions across the United States involved small producers, many people were concerned with the involvement of organized crime in liquor production and distribution. The relationship of criminal syndicates to prohibition is debated by historians. Organized crime did not come into being with prohibition, and it did not disappear when prohibition was repealed. The relationship could be no more complicated than that organized criminals have historically exploited goods and services that are illegal but in demand, including not only alcohol during prohibition but also prostitution, gambling, firearms, and narcotic drugs. Still, the activities and exploits of criminal syndicates received substantial media coverage during the 1920s. One of the most sensational events was the St. Valentine's Day Massacre in Chicago in February 1929, when seven men associated with one of the city's gangs were shot, apparently by men working for gang boss Al Capone. It is thought that, as part of a conflict over territory, the victims' syndicate had been hijacking Capone's liquor shipments. The killings outraged citizens and drew attention to the role of organized crime in the supply of liquor, especially to speakeasies. In addition to provoking anger at the criminal syndicates, the massacre also fueled demands for the repeal of prohibition—or at least a liberalization of policies to allow low-alcohol beverages—on the ground that the law, as it stood, was causing a crime wave.

Consumers also felt the force of the law as prohibition focused attention on public intoxication. In Philadelphia, arrests for intoxication, intoxication and disorderly conduct, and habitual drunkenness rose dramatically during the 1920s. From a total of 23,740 in 1919 they increased to 44,746 in 1922 (including intoxicated drivers, a category added in 1921) and then to more than 58,000 in 1925.[16] In other words, there were more than 1,000 arrests a week for public intoxication in Philadelphia (with a population of about 1.3 million) in the mid-1920s. Of course, we should bear in mind that these statistics need not reflect an increase in drunkenness; more rigorous enforcement might explain some of the increase in arrests. But it is also likely that more alcohol was consumed at home during prohibition than before and that this shift in patterns of consumption and sociability ought to have depressed the incidence of public drunkenness.

One of the unintended consequences of prohibition was what might be called the normalization of public drinking. During the nineteenth century, the antialcohol movement had been fairly successful in portraying drinking as pathological behavior. From being a shared social activity on festive and other occasions, as it had been for centuries, public drinking was gradually confined to the saloon and to men. The saloon was then demonized as a space where men, fueled by alcohol, swore, gambled, neglected their families, and generally behaved coarsely, lewdly, and criminally. Prohibition closed the saloons but inadvertently gave rise to new sites of alcohol-centered sociability, the speakeasies. Despite the constant threat of being raided and having their alcohol stocks confiscated, they flourished in many cities, and the police in New York City, which was one of the leading centers of opposition to prohibition, estimated that there were 32,000 speakeasies in operation by 1931.

Speakeasies ranged from gloomy basement bars that encouraged solitary male drinking to bright clubs that served cocktails and where bands and singers entertained clients.[17] Ironically, speakeasies attracted middle- and upper-class clients, including women who would never have stepped into a saloon for fear of compromising their reputations. Women had been the invisible drinkers of nineteenth-century America: physically invisible because, effectively excluded from saloons, they drank in the privacy of their homes; culturally invisible because the rhetoric of the antialcohol movement gave the impression that men were the drunkards and that women did not drink. The club style of speakeasy was far more welcoming to women, who could drink there without being regarded as immoral—despite the fact that they were supporting criminal activity by doing so. The fact that some women frequented speakeasies, rather than continuing to drink alcohol (illicit alcohol) at home, speaks to the unintended emergence of a new drinking culture during prohibition.

In the small communities and rural areas of the United States, illicit alcohol consumption had little of the romance of the speakeasies, which with their middle-class clientele and music were forerunners of the clubs and cabarets of the 1930s and 1940s. The experience of prohibition in the countryside was a network of small-time producers making whiskey in 5-gallon milk cans, 50-gallon steel drums, or any other vessel that did the job, in their houses, in barns, or in shacks hidden in forests and swamps. Most producers were poor—or at least most of the producers who were prosecuted were poor. A sample of convicted moonshiners in Florida showed that three-quarters of them had an average net worth of only $74.50; many were women, and some were African Americans who turned to making moonshine when prohibition made it an activity that promised a regular income. Their customers paid prices like 50 cents a pint or $3 a gallon for a beverage whose flavor and quality can only be imagined and that might well have been dangerous to consume.

But while the Volstead Act, which set out the practicalities of prohibition, made producing and selling alcohol for beverage purposes a crime, it specified that "liquor" could be prescribed for medicinal purposes, to "afford relief . . . from some known ailment." It was limited to 1 pint in a ten-day period (about an ounce and a half a day), and a prescription could be filled only once. To write a prescription for liquor, a doctor needed to obtain a permit from a federal official. Many doctors opposed these provisions, not because they were against prohibition (the medical profession was divided on the issue), but because the law effectively gave the government the power to interfere in the way doctors practiced medicine.

A further issue arose because the law referred only to "liquor" and not to beer, and many doctors as well as laypeople believed that beer had therapeutic qualities. One of the prominent physicians who led the campaign against government regulation of prescriptions, John Patrick Davin, executive secretary of the New York Medical Association, argued that beer had been shown to cure diseases as diverse as anemia and anthrax poisoning.[18] In the months following prohibition, physicians deluged the authorities with applications to prescribe beer, and the attorney general agreed that, because the intention was not to regulate doctors, each physician should be free to set the amount of beer each patient needed for therapeutic purposes. A government survey showed that "many physicians said that they had patients who should have from one to three bottles of beer a day to help them recuperate" and that beer was especially useful for "certain ailments of women."[19]

These doctors were not quacks; it is clear that well into the twentieth century, mainstream doctors in America regarded alcohol as therapeutic. A

1921 survey of 53,900 randomly selected physicians showed that 51 percent were in favor of prescribing whiskey, and 26 percent thought that beer was "a necessary therapeutic agent." A smaller percentage of physicians argued for wine; even though it had a long therapeutic tradition in Europe, wine was not consumed nearly as widely in the United States as whiskey and beer. Still, one Texas doctor told of the successful use of champagne in treating some of the symptoms of scarlet fever. Such arguments in favor of medicinal alcohol were not necessarily part of a broader antiprohibition stance. Many doctors shared the argument of one respondent to the survey, that "whiskey as a medicine is fine, as a beverage it is absolutely unnecessary." Others condemned the Volstead Act as creating "state medicine," while some told of cases where patients deprived of alcohol had suffered needlessly and even died.[20]

In April 1921 Andrew Volstead, who had crafted the initial legislation, tried to pass an amended law to ban the prescribing of beer for medical purposes and to restrict the therapeutic use of spirits even more. The loophole allowing for therapeutic beer threatened to undo prohibition. There were estimates that doctors would be able to prescribe three bottles a day per patient and arguments that, in those circumstances, the government might just as well legalize brewing. Despite concern that upsetting the medical profession would have political consequences, as doctors could wield influence in their communities, Congress passed legislation in November 1921 closing the loophole that allowed beer to be prescribed. One result was that the American Medical Association, which in 1917 had supported prohibition and taken a stand against therapeutic alcohol, reversed itself. Physicians took their fight to prescribe alcohol as far as the Supreme Court, but in a split decision in 1926, the justices sided with the government.

Pharmacists were no happier than physicians with their role in prohibition. Alcohol was the single most important ingredient in many prescription drugs, and because they had licenses to possess alcohol, the country's 50,000 pharmacists were given responsibility for dispensing alcohol, in the form of whiskey, when it had been prescribed by a doctor. To do this, they needed to apply for a license that cost $25, and although many were reluctant to do so, most did for fear of losing collateral business. Not only did pharmacists resent becoming, in their own eyes, liquor retailers, but the number of pharmacies increased rapidly as entrepreneurs realized the profits to be made by dispensing liquor. To deal with this trend, the government passed regulations limiting revenue from liquor prescriptions to a maximum of 10 percent of any pharmacy's sales.[21]

The scope and enforcement of prohibition were still evolving when it was repealed in 1933. The Democratic candidate for president in the 1932 election, Franklin D. Roosevelt, ran on a repeal platform that reflected a shift in public sentiment during the 1920s. In addition to declining support for prohibition in Washington, D.C., there was growing pressure from the states, some of it driven by the economic and financial realities of the Great Depression, which struck the United States in 1929. As industrial and agricultural production declined and unemployment rose, federal, state, and municipal budgets shrank, and politicians grew nostalgic for the revenues that alcoholic beverages had brought in before prohibition. Federal tax revenues on distilled spirits were less than $13 million in 1929, a far cry from the $365 million collected in 1919. Revenue from beer and wine was virtually nil in 1929, compared with $117 million ten years earlier.[22] The revival of alcohol production would not only enrich governments but also bring back to life an industry that, directly and indirectly, employed millions of Americans.

There was also the experience of prohibition that, among other things, had represented a massive intrusion by the state into what many Americans regarded as their private lives. Prohibition supporters pointed to tangible benefits such as declines in the incidence of some diseases and illnesses, fewer traffic accidents, and falling homicide rates, but prohibition had also entangled millions of Americans in the criminal law. The number of small-time moonshiners seems to have risen during the depression, as the unemployed turned to making and selling illegal alcohol as way to make a living. One man who went to Florida from Georgia in 1932 in search of work started "selling whiskey to negroes for fifty cents per pint" when no jobs were available.[23]

The arrival of the depression must, in itself, have undermined support for prohibition. A drink-free America was supposed to be a place of peace, happiness, and prosperity, but as the 1930s opened, the nation seemed populated by the miserable and the poor. Prohibition cannot be blamed for the depression, of course, but it must have been caught up in the mood of despair. In the most banal sense, prohibition deprived ordinary, moderate-drinking Americans of the bottle of beer or shot of whiskey that might have provided a little pleasure in an otherwise bleak landscape.

New movements emerged, such as the Women's Organization for National Prohibition Reform (WONPR), formed in 1929, which showed that women were far from unanimous in their support for prohibition. Within two years of being founded, it had more than 300,000 members, and when prohibition was repealed in 1933, it claimed a membership of 1.3 million. Turning the prohibitionist argument on its head, the WONPR argued that prohibition had been harmful to the family, women, children, and the home by halting a trend toward moderate drinking, stimulating alcohol abuse, and encouraging crime, political corruption, and disrespect for the law. Most members of the WONPR were middle- and upper-class women, not the sort of people to trifle with important social and moral issues. Their work contributed a dimension of respectability to the repeal movement, which had been portrayed by die-hard prohibitionists as made up of unreconstructed males who wanted nothing more than a return to the bad old days of uncontrolled drinking in saloons.

Opposition to and disillusionment with prohibition, together with a desire for more general change, contributed to the election of President Roosevelt in 1932. One of his first acts on taking office in January 1933 was to amend the Volstead Act to allow the production and sale of alcoholic beverages with an alcohol level up to 3.2 percent. Breweries began to open, and soon Americans were enjoying "near-beer." Alcohol-related prosecutions fell dramatically. Later that year, Congress passed the Twenty-First Amendment to the Constitution, which repealed the Eighteenth, and national prohibition came to an end. Responsibility for alcohol policies reverted to the states, with federal oversight (which included the interstate transportation of alcohol) vested in the Bureau of Alcohol, Tobacco, and Firearms.

It is difficult to determine whether prohibition in the United States was a success or a failure, not least because it is not clear how success and failure should be defined. A simple criterion would be a decline in drinking, but it is impossible to establish consumption rates with any confidence. The great bulk of the alcohol consumed during prohibition was illicit, and by definition it largely escaped official regulation and records. The exception was the alcohol seized by the authorities, but we have no way of knowing what proportion that represented of all illicit alcohol on the market. One study of the effects of prohibition used surrogate trends to calculate shifts in alcohol consumption: deaths due to cirrhosis of the liver and alcoholism, admissions to hospital for alcoholic psychosis, and arrests for drunkenness. The authors concluded that immediately after prohibition was enacted, alcohol consumption fell to 20-40 percent of pre-prohibition levels, but that it soon began to rise and by the late 1920s had reached about 70 percent of the pre-prohibition rate.[24] There is a logic to this trend, in that it took some time to develop clandestine production facilities and foreign sources of alcohol and to organize distribution channels and retail outlets.

Even though we cannot know rates of alcohol consumption during prohibition with any certainty, all the evidence points to levels that were lower than before prohibition but still considerable. The explanations for lower consumption rates seem quite straightforward. Alcohol was no longer publicly available but had to be purchased clandestinely; consumers had to know a person to buy it from or a place where it could be consumed. Purchasing alcohol, whether it was backyard moonshine or whiskey in a speakeasy, meant participating in a criminal act, even though purchasing and consuming alcohol were not themselves criminal. And the price of alcohol was generally much higher—some was said to be 500 percent higher—than in pre-prohibition times, as producers and sellers covered their costs, factored in their risks, and set their prices to a sellers' market. Under these culturally and financially restrictive conditions, it is not so surprising that Americans continued to drink, but that a relatively high level of consumption seems to have prevailed.

Beyond shifts in consumption levels, which persisted after prohibition was repealed, there were changes in America's drinking cultures. Many clandestine bars catered to men and provided the basic facilities that pre-prohibition saloons had. But the higher-end speakeasies had ushered in a new form of public drinking, if illegal and clandestine drinking can be called public. "Respectable" women and men mingled in these places, and although these speakeasies existed primarily as places where alcohol was available, it was served with food and entertainment. We can see the emergence of alcohol's integration into nongendered public sociability, a new phenomenon in the United States. The overall image of prohibition, then, is complex and defies easy generalization. How it was experienced by Americans depended on where they lived, their financial circumstances, and their gender, race, and age. In the end, though, more Americans found it wanting and effectively voted for its repeal.

The progress of prohibition at the state and federal levels in the United States had parallels beyond the country's borders. In Mexico the Revolution of 1910 had ushered in periods of prohibition in various states, often not because of popular pressure, as in America, but because it was favored by the new political leadership, as in the Soviet Union. The new political elites in Mexico were concerned about the levels of drinking, which they believed lay behind much of the nation's poverty and backwardness, and they saw prohibition as an integral part of social renewal. One vigorous proponent of alcohol control was Salvador Alvarado, governor of Yucatán, a state with a thriving rum industry. During 1915, Alvarado passed a series of increasingly rigorous regulations known as La Ley Seca, the Dry Law. He started with a law forbidding the sale of alcohol to women and minors, then he banned women from working or drinking in cantinas and later prohibited the sale of alcohol in restaurants. Cantinas, now the only source of alcohol, had to relocate if they were near schools. In the face of continued drinking at an unacceptable level, the governor banned the sale of alcohol during siestas, after 10:00 PM, on Sundays, and on national holidays—all favored occasions for drinking. When what seemed to him to be heavy drinking persisted, he banned the production and sale of all beverages with an alcohol level higher than 5 percent.[25]

This level of alcohol was generous compared with the half of 1 percent benchmark adopted in the United States five years later, but Yucatán's citizens yearned for even stronger drinks. In a scenario all too familiar when prohibition has been imposed, a clandestine liquor industry sprang up to service a thirsty and receptive market. But at the same time, many women rallied to a popular antialcohol movement that drew strength partly from the belief that rum-drinking was responsible for widespread social problems (including male sexual infidelity), and partly because landowners used rum to create a system of forced labor: poor peasants were allowed to run up debts at the cantina, and employers would then assume the debts on condition that the peasants live on the landowner's property and work off the debt.

The link between economic exploitation and alcohol reinforced a preference for prohibition among Mexico's socialists, and at the First Socialist Workers' Congress in 1918, women delegates pushed prohibition to the top of the agenda. But prohibition remained a policy enacted only sporadically in Mexico, and it depended on specific conditions and the leadership in specific regions. When Yucatán's new socialist governor visited a village in 1918, he was besieged by women demanding he close all the cantinas "because in these places their husbands lost all their wages, leaving them and their children without clothes or food." The governor closed the cantinas, and as a reprisal, the men of the village expelled the village priest, thus depriving their more pious wives of communion. By 1922, seven other villages in the state had banned alcohol (and priests).[26]

Even so, the socialists did not enforce prohibition in Yucatán rigorously. Although ideologically committed, the party's male leaders were reluctant, in practice, to challenge long-standing practices of sociable drinking. They also found that offering alcohol was an effective way to persuade men to align themselves with the Socialist Party. Candidates held meetings in cantinas, and once in office, many Socialist officials profited from the illegal trade in alcohol. In 1923 there was a military coup, and one of the first acts of the rebel administration was to remove restrictions on alcohol. When the Socialists returned to power the next year, they effectively abandoned controls on consuming alcohol but created a regime that embedded alcohol within a system of corruption that profited many political leaders. Prohibition in Yucatán had initially brought the state, a popular movement, and women into an alliance, but it effectively broke down after ten years.

Elsewhere in Mexico after the 1910 Revolution, the state of Durango banned alcohol production and consumption, and all pulquerías in Mexico City were closed. In Chihuahua and Sinaloa, breaking prohibition laws was punishable by death. Even so, the general assessment is that prohibition was loosely enforced and little observed in Mexico. Governments needed the income from taxes on alcohol, and prohibition laws produced widespread corruption and a flourishing black market.[27]

Mexican liquor laws were important to U.S. officials, as we have seen, and Mexico eventually became a source of illicit alcohol when prohibition policies were imposed on Americans. Even before that time, however, the availability of alcohol in Mexico aroused anxiety among antidrink campaigners in the United States. In 1915, members of the WCTU branch in Imperial Valley, California, realized that their community's water supply originated near the Mexican town of Mexicali, close to the U.S. border. Fearful that the water might be polluted by Mexicali's many bars, they lobbied to have prohibition extended not only to California but also to the Mexican town. As far-fetched as it sounds that water with any perceptible alcohol would flow from the faucets in Imperial Valley, the U.S. secretary of state took the idea seriously enough to initiate discussions with the Mexican government.[28]

Alcohol policies in Canada were of interest to American authorities, too, for similar reasons. The long and (at that time) lightly monitored border between Canada and the United States provided ample opportunities for alcohol to be smuggled into the United States, and the best prevention was prohibition in Canada. Any illicit alcohol produced there under a prohibition regime would then be sold locally, since producers would rather not take the greater risks of moving their goods across an international border, as porous as it was. A problem was that alcohol was regulated primarily by provincial governments, and there was no certainty that all would adopt prohibition. From the late 1800s, all had allowed municipalities to vote on alcohol sales, and by the First World War, many districts had gone dry. Pro-prohibition organizations pressed for more comprehensive restrictions, and during the war, as so many governments did, Canada's provinces capitulated to the pressure, even though few enacted absolute prohibition.

In 1915, Saskatchewan closed all drinking establishments and restricted sales of alcohol to government-owned stores in wet municipalities. The next year, following a referendum, even these stores were closed. Also in 1916, voters in Alberta, Manitoba, and British Columbia opted for prohibition, and the governments of Ontario, Nova Scotia, and New Brunswick agreed to enact prohibition without referenda. Newfoundland, which was still a British colony, voted for prohibition the same year, and the federal government extended the policy to the Yukon Territory in 1918 after an indecisive referendum. The outsider was Quebec, whose government and population were unenthusiastic about prohibition. Early in 1918 the government scheduled a ban on retail sales of alcohol for May 1919 and permitted business as usual in the interim. But a month before this total ban on sales was to start, the government backtracked and applied it only to spirits; wine, light beer, and cider could be sold.[29] In Ontario, too, prohibition was selective; under pressure from the grape and wine producers, the government allowed the sale of wine, but only from wineries and in minimum volumes of 5 gallons. This effectively eliminated the poor from the legal alcohol market.

This patchwork of provincial prohibition policies in Canada was sewn together by federal regulations that controlled aspects of alcohol policy that were not within provincial jurisdiction. In 1918 the importation of alcohol into Canada was forbidden, as were production and interprovincial trade in alcohol. All were to last until a year after the end of the war, which eventually meant November 1919. For about eighteen months, Canadians in all provinces except Ontario and Quebec lived without legal access to beverages with an alcohol level above 1.5 or 2 percent, depending on the province. Stronger alcoholic beverages could be produced for export, however, and much of it was shipped clandestinely to the United States, even though cargo manifests showed other destinations.

With the war over and Canada's federal regulations lapsing, provinces had to decide whether to continue, modify, or abandon their wartime alcohol policies. Referenda in Ontario and New Brunswick confirmed existing policies, but British Columbia and Quebec voted to liberalize alcohol sales. In a flurry of legislating between 1919 and 1923, the federal and provincial governments put restrictions on the movement of alcohol and sharply increased the taxes on it. In national terms, Canada never enacted prohibition as comprehensively as the United States did, but the antialcohol forces were convinced that the country was part of a global movement. In 1925 the president of Canada's WCTU declared, "The world is going dry."[30]

Even by 1925 the claim was hollow, as several provinces had abandoned prohibition and allowed the sale of alcohol in province-owned stores. Quebec had done so in 1919; British Columbia, Manitoba, Alberta, and Yukon followed by 1925; and Ontario followed in 1927. By 1930 the only Canadian province not to have abandoned prohibition was Prince Edward Island, which held out until 1948. Having permitted retail sales of alcohol, the provinces then moved rapidly to allow public drinking in bars, taverns, and other licensed establishments; nearly all did so in the 1920s.

Across the Atlantic, few European nations attempted prohibition. It was never a likely proposition in Britain, France, Italy, Germany, or Spain, where alcohol consumption was part of daily life for most adult men. But prohibition did take tenuous hold in Scandinavia, which had strong traditions of social reform. Finland adopted the most stringent regulations when, in 1919, the government banned all beverages with an alcohol level over 2 percent. The policy lasted until 1932, when it was abolished in the face of widespread resistance. Alcohol consumption is reported to have risen during prohibition, as Finns consumed locally made alcohol as well as vast volumes smuggled into the country across its coastal borders.

In Norway, citizens voted in local referenda on prohibition, and by 1916, only nine towns permitted the sale of alcohol. That year, faced with wartime shortage of foods, the government banned spirits and, in the following year, beer (including light beer). In 1919 there was a referendum on prohibition, and 62 percent of Norwegians voted to prohibit the sale of spirits and fortified wine but to allow access to table wine and beer. However, producers of fortified wine (especially Spain and Portugal) insisted that Norway buy their product if they were to import Norwegian fish and seafood. That, together with what is thought to have been significant prescribing of spirits by doctors and veterinarians, led to a change of course. The prohibition on fortified wine was lifted in 1923, and four years later, spirits sales were permitted in the towns that had allowed them in 1916.[31]

In Sweden, alcohol legislation built on widespread support for control. By the early 1900s, 10 percent of all Swedes were members of temperance societies, women's organizations had embraced temperance and abstinence as means of improving family life, and leading sections of the labor movement argued that alcohol was used by the bourgeoisie to control workers. Their efforts at the local level led to a number of communities taking over management of alcohol sales so as to remove the profit motive that was believed to lead retailers to encourage alcohol sales. This system of "disinterested management" guaranteed modest returns (about 5 percent) to shareholders, with the remainder of the profits disbursed to the community. This arrangement, called the "Gothenburg system," after the city that was one of the first communities to adopt it, became mandatory throughout Sweden in 1905.[32]

While this system might have reduced alcohol consumption, popular opinion in Sweden favored outright prohibition. Prohibitionists were successful in persuading the government to impose prohibition for the duration of a general strike in 1909, on the ground that alcohol would only exacerbate the labor strife. But after the five-week period of prohibition ended, temperance organizations held an unofficial referendum on making prohibition permanent. As one historian says, "The results were staggering": 55 percent of Swedish adults voted in the referendum, and 99 percent of them voted in favor of prohibition.[33] It was much more difficult to get such a policy through Sweden's parliament, however. The lower house agreed to laws that would allow local authorities to impose prohibition in their jurisdictions and to institute a system of passbooks to regulate individual drinking where alcohol was permitted. But the upper house rejected the local option for fear of the consequences for employment and the economy.

In 1913, Gothenburg established a system of passbooks to control individual purchases of alcohol and limited each person to 5 liters of alcoholic beverages every three months; the success of this system undermined the options of national and local prohibition. When, in 1917, parliament passed its long-awaited alcohol legislation, it opted for the passbook system, partly because it feared that local prohibition would have a severe impact on state revenues from taxes. When a state referendum on prohibition was held in 1922, the result was far different from the unofficial sounding of 1909: only 49 percent of Swedes voted in favor of prohibition, far short of the two-thirds needed.[34]

"Local option," the power of municipalities or regions to impose prohibition or restrictive rules on alcohol production and distribution, was often a compromise when a national government was unable or unwilling to apply such policies to its entire population. It was the solution in India, where the legislature set up a local option system in 1921. Temperance found much support in parts of India, where it drew on the Hindu rule that intoxicating substances should be avoided. Alcohol was also part of the early twentieth-century Indian nationalist critique of imperialism, and prohibition was embraced by nationalists such as Mahatma Gandhi. In 1937 he deplored the use of alcohol revenues to fund education: "The cruelest irony . . . lies in the fact that we are left with nothing but the liquor revenue to fall back upon to give our children education. . . . The solution to the problem should not involve a compromise of the ideal of prohibition, cost whatever else it might."[35]

Prohibition was introduced in the state of Madras in 1937. The law not only banned the production and sale of alcohol but also encompassed anyone who "consumes or buys liquor or any intoxicating drug." The penalties ran as high as six months in jail and a fine of 1,000 rupees. Moreover, the definition of an alcoholic beverage was more comprehensive than most: "toddy, spirits of wine, methylated spirits, wine, beer and all liquid consisting of or containing alcohol."[36] Prohibition was extended to other parts of India, and when the colony gained its independence in 1947, the principle of prohibition was included in its constitution.

Belgium, a much smaller and less populous country, introduced national prohibition—applied only to distilled alcoholic beverages—for a short time in 1918. This was named the "Vandervelde law," after a parliamentarian of the Belgian Workers' Party who had campaigned for prohibition. But this limited form of prohibition (which permitted the sale of wine and beer) was modified the following year in favor of a more permanent system that lasted for most of the twentieth century. It allowed the sale of spirits from retailers in minimum volumes of 2 liters, so as to prevent access to it by the poor. But it retained a ban on the sale of strong drinks (beverages with more than 22 percent alcohol) in bars and cafés.[37]

Other countries flirted with the idea of prohibition, but the closest any came to imposing it was New Zealand, where referenda on liquor policy were held with every general election through most of the twentieth century. In 1911, 56 percent of the votes were cast for prohibition, but the threshold had been set at 60 percent. In 1919 the prohibition vote was a mere 3,000 short of the number needed, and the country was saved from prohibition thanks largely to the antiprohibition votes of soldiers who had returned from the war. Thereafter, support for prohibition declined steadily, falling to 30 percent in referenda in the mid-1930s, and much lower later in the century.[38]

Mexico, the United States, Canada, Finland, Iceland, Norway, India, and Russia/the Soviet Union all experimented seriously with prohibition, all within the period from 1914 to 1933. Other countries put in place a range of restrictions on the production, distribution, and consumption of alcohol. After decades of antialcohol campaigning, prohibition's moment came and went remarkably quickly. But the national case studies were linked by a transnational antialcohol movement, and one historian describes the wave of prohibition as a "perfect storm" where the world war "provided a common reagent for the dramatic translation of internationally shared temperance ideas into concrete policies through the broad national institutional channels of policymaking."[39]

The experiments with and experiences of prohibition had lasting consequences for alcohol policies and cultures of drinking in a number of countries. Even though prohibition was rejected as a failed policy, alcohol remained tightly regulated throughout the Western world. In some countries and regions (notably Canada and Scandinavia), prohibition was replaced by state alcohol monopolies where before prohibition there had been a free market in alcohol. Perhaps even more important, the lessons of the prohibition era took on a more general application, convincing many people of the futility of attempting to ban any commodity (such as drugs) or service (such as prostitution) for which there is significant consumer demand.

14

After Prohibitions
1930–1945

NORMALIZING ALCOHOL

The first two decades of the twentieth century saw more systematic restrictions placed on alcohol production and consumption than the preceding two millennia. They included the noble and not-so-noble experiments with prohibition in Russia/the Soviet Union and the United States and the quasi-prohibition regimes in Canada, Scandinavia, and parts of Mexico. There was also the complex web of regulations enacted during the First World War in many countries to deal with particular challenges but maintained long after—regulations on production, drinking ages, and the serving hours of taverns and bars. In the following decades, from the mid-1920s to the 1960s, legislators in many countries wrestled with the tensions inherent in returning to more liberal alcohol regimes while simultaneously trying to restrain consumption in the interests of public health and order. Production and consumption sometimes reflected these policies, but they were also affected by economic cycles of depression and prosperity, the class- or race-based policies adopted by authoritarian states, and the Second World War.

In December 1933, President Franklin D. Roosevelt announced that the Twenty-First Amendment to the Constitution, ending prohibition in the United States, had been ratified by the thirty-six states needed to carry it into force. But, not wanting to appear too jubilant that alcohol would flow freely again, Roosevelt drove a careful middle line, praising the amendment for restoring individual freedom but cautioning against the adoption of irresponsible alcohol policies. The amendment specified that the importation of alcohol in violation of state or territorial law was prohibited, effectively giving individual states control over alcohol policy within their borders. But Roosevelt advised them against restoring what the antialcohol lobby campaigners considered the worst aspects of former policies. "I ask especially," he said, "that no state shall, by law or otherwise, authorize the return of the saloon, either in its old form or in some modern guise." In a further gesture to prohibition supporters, Roosevelt called for citizens to be educated to drink responsibly, to prevent the return of "the repugnant conditions" that had preceded prohibition.[1] It was a careful statement that recognized the validity of prohibitionists' concerns while rejecting their solution.

Although alcohol policy was now squarely in the hands of the states, the federal government retained jurisdiction over matters such as interstate commerce in alcohol and the issuing of winery and brewery licenses. It established the Federal Alcohol Control Administration (FACA) to manage these and other issues, but that body (and its successors) largely adopted a hands-off position. The experience with prohibition had no doubt left the federal government with little appetite for driving alcohol policy. The first director of the FACA clearly hoped that public interest in alcohol issues would simply disappear. Much of the drinking during prohibition reflected the attraction of the illicit, he said, and once alcohol was freely available again, consumption would almost certainly decline. But officials must secretly have hoped that it would not decline too much or too quickly; the government badly needed tax revenues from alcohol to finance the public works projects that Roosevelt's administration designed to help the country out of the economic depression. American citizens came through: taxes of $2.60 a gallon on distilled liquor and $5 a barrel on beer accounted for 13 percent of all federal tax revenues by 1936.

The Twenty-First Amendment eventually produced the same patchwork of regulations as had existed before prohibition came into force. Some states were dry and others were wet, but each adopted its own licensing and consumption regulations. Many states that had adopted prohibition policies before 1920, however, chose to permit alcohol after prohibition was repealed. Clearly, the experience of thirteen dry years had soured many state legislatures on the wisdom of trying to choke off alcohol supplies entirely. Most of the dry states were in the Southeast; Mississippi, the last state to remain dry, went wet as late as 1966. While the legislators of some states did not hesitate to make alcohol available again, in other states the repeal of prohibition sparked renewed conflict as temperance organizations campaigned to halt any renewed flow of alcohol in their states.

Florida, which had been more exposed to liquor smuggling than most other states and whose courts had been swamped by alcohol-related cases, is an example. As it became increasingly evident that prohibition was coming to an end, the respective supporters of prohibition and repeal organized to put pressure on Florida's legislators.[2] Polls showed that the state's citizens were split on the issue. Yet within a month of Congress's raising the definition of alcoholic beverage from half a percent to 3.5 percent alcohol in April 1933, the state legislature legalized the production, distribution, sale, and advertising of "near beer," light wine, and similar beverages. Arguments that restoring the alcohol industry, even in this limited form, would provide employment for thousands and much-needed revenues for the state treasury overwhelmed much of the residual prohibitionist strength. The state's newspapers, which expected to (and did) benefit from alcohol advertising, supported the measure. When the Twenty-First Amendment was referred to the states for ratification later in 1933, the delegates to Florida's convention voted unanimously in favor, making Florida the thirty-third of the thirty-six states needed for ratification.

Once prohibition was gone, the federal courts in Florida began to dismiss outstanding charges related to smuggling and bootlegging. In one case where charges were dismissed, the defendants sued in 1935 for the return of some 75 gallons of liquor that had been confiscated in 1933. The liquor was returned to them on the condition that they pay the taxes due on it. But one federal judge warned that once alcohol was legally available, the courts would deal with unlicensed alcohol producers even more severely than they had under prohibition. One man charged with making moonshine in 1934 was told that "there is no prohibition law anymore and it is . . . unfair for a man to operate a liquor still and not pay the tax. . . . [This] business must be stopped." Yet it was not until November 1934, almost a year after the Twenty-First Amendment took effect, that Florida repealed its own statewide prohibition law. By a two-to-one margin, Floridians voted to restore alcohol control to individual counties. This policy was adopted by many states, ensuring there would be as many regulatory variations within states as among them.

In light of many decades of propaganda that portrayed drinking as immoral and inappropriate for decent people, the emergence of a positive view of alcohol into mainstream middle-class American culture seemed almost effortless. Advertisements for beer, wine, and spirits soon filled the pages of newspapers, and by 1935 a fifth of the display advertising in the *New York Times* was for beer and wine. Neon signs in cities and billboards along highways kept alcohol in public view. The production code for movies introduced in 1930 was revised in 1934 (it remained in force until the 1960s) and might have been expected to deal with the portrayal of alcohol on the screen. But its stress was resolutely on sexuality and the representation of gender. Its administrators intervened in the making of the movie *Casablanca* (1942) to delete any suggestion that the two main characters, Rick and Ilsa, had had a sexual relationship, yet there was no objection to the fact that the movie was not only set in a bar (referred to in the movie as a "gin-joint") that had many of the trappings of a saloon but was replete with scenes of alcohol and drinking and references to gambling and other saloonlike activities.

The new urban drinking cultures that had developed in the privacy of homes and speakeasies in much of urban America during prohibition came to the surface after repeal. Cocktails, made popular as a way of concealing the poor quality of much prohibition-era liquor, maintained their popularity afterward—particularly among women, for whom undiluted spirits were widely thought to be unsuitably strong. (Drinking spirits straight or on the rocks was associated with masculinity.) The speakeasy in its sophisticated form (as rare as those might have been) went public as the cocktail lounge and supper club. These new drinking places had none of the cultural baggage of the saloon, with its coarse and masculine associations, but were places where women and men could socialize without any hint of scandal. Drinking at home became more public, too, in the sense that there was no longer any need to pretend that it was not done. Women's magazines carried articles on serving cocktails and wine at dinner parties and gave advice on the etiquette surrounding alcoholic beverages.

Of course it is possible to overstate the cultural shift that the end of prohibition made evident, as the United States encompassed many drinking cultures that were based on class, gender, race, religion, and region. A significant portion of the American population abstained from alcohol altogether; many people regarded it as a threat to morality and social order or abstained in accordance with religious principles (as with Mormons). A lot of alcohol advertising was targeted at men and associated drinking with male activities such as hunting and horseback riding. Nor was all drinking—or much of it—necessarily sophisticated. Neighborhood taverns, bars, and lounges (the word "saloon" was carefully avoided) became the places where working-class men met and socialized, but they were less often the rowdy places said to have been so common before 1920. Nuanced they must be, but the varied drinking cultures of the 1930s seem to have been quite different from their pre-prohibition forerunners.

The image of sophisticated drinking in the 1930s was largely confined to the urban middle and upper classes of the United States, but it was largely absent even from those circles north of the border, in postprohibition Canada.

Each province replaced the temperance or prohibition laws enacted during the First World War with a liquor retailing system that gave provincial governments a monopoly over the sale of alcohol and the power to regulate alcohol production and the licensing of bars and other drinking places. In Canada's largest province, the Liquor Control Board of Ontario (LCBO), established in 1927, created a system of permit books to regulate access to alcohol; this system remained in force, with various changes, until the early 1960s. Any resident of Ontario over the age of twenty-one who wanted to purchase alcohol had to apply for a permit book (which resembled a passport) in which LCBO store clerks would record all their purchases.[3] Store managers could peruse these passbooks from time to time and were empowered to interview customers if they thought something was amiss—that a customer was buying too much alcohol or seemed to be spending more than he or she should, given his or her occupation and income (occupations were shown in passbooks). Managers could warn suspect clients or restrict the passbooks so that individuals could purchase alcohol from only one LCBO store (to give staff more effective surveillance). Anyone the LCBO decided was abusing alcohol was placed on an "interdiction list," meaning that they were not permitted to purchase alcohol for a year, after which their case would be reviewed. The names of people on the interdiction list (400 to 500 a year during the 1930s) were circulated to the police and all LCBO stores.

If some Ontario citizens could have their alcohol privileges cut off because of their perceived alcohol-related behavior, others were deprived simply on the basis of their status. Only men and women "of good character" could obtain a permit book, and this ruled out anyone known or reputed to be an alcoholic or heavy drinker. Native people were disqualified by other legislation from drinking alcohol. A married women not in the workforce, and therefore without an independent income, could obtain a passbook only when she provided information on her husband's occupation. Tourists and transient residents, on the other hand, could apply for a temporary passbook for the duration of their stay in Ontario.

In Europe, only a handful of countries had to deal with the perceived challenges posed by easing of restrictive alcohol policies. Sweden, Norway, and Finland all established state-owned liquor stores that survive to the present day. In the United Kingdom, France, and Italy, moderately restrictive policies had been adopted during the First World War, and many of them, such as limited opening hours for bars in England and the abolition of absinthe production in France, were maintained throughout the interwar period and beyond. Consumption patterns fluctuated with economic cycles, such as the

Great Depression, when massive unemployment reduced spending power dramatically.

In England, the government set up a royal commission in 1929 to study the licensing laws and the social and economic impacts of alcohol consumption. This was not a reaction to a perceived social emergency, however, as per capita consumption of alcohol in 1929 was considerably lower than it had been thirty years earlier: since 1899, spirits consumption had declined from a gallon to a quarter of that, while beer consumption was half what it had been. By these measures, temperance had gained a major foothold in popular drinking patterns in England.

The commission's report, published in 1932, gave little cause for alarm. It recommended maintaining the opening hours of public houses that had been imposed during the First World War, despite arguments from London's commissioner of police and others that allowing pubs to remain open all afternoon (instead of closing between lunch and dinner) was unlikely to produce social problems. As for the drinking habits of the English, the commissioners noted that "the general decrease in the consumption of intoxicants has been accompanied by a marked decrease in insobriety." They singled out young people as drinking more responsibly. While noting that factors such as higher taxation, lower alcohol levels in drinks, the demands of mechanization in industry, and depression-era unemployment had contributed to lower alcohol consumption, the commission declared, "Drunkenness has gone out of fashion."[4] But if they were optimistic, the commissioners were not naive; if there was a broad cultural shift away from alcohol abuse, there was still extensive intoxication, and they recommended measures that included reducing the number of licensed drinking places, improving the character of pubs, and providing more education on alcohol.

In some respects, these recommendations were already being implemented. From the early 1920s, English brewers began to reshape drinking cultures by building bigger, more comfortable pubs, often in a Tudor or Georgian style.[5] Many featured dining rooms with high-quality food prepared by chefs poached from major London hotels, and tearooms that served non-alcoholic beverages during the long afternoon hours when alcohol was not available. A key innovation in many renovated pubs was a lounge. Carpeted, comfortably furnished with upholstered furniture, and with walls hung with prints and paintings, the lounge was created in the image of the rather stuffy middle-class living room. It re-created the safety of drinking at home and reassured women of the respectability of public drinking. The feminization of this space was neatly encapsulated by the instructions of Whitbread, one of England's largest breweries: "A clean sweep should be made of fixed furniture, wall papers, heavy hangings, and such 'works of art' as famous racehorses, prize-fights, almanac portraits of departed statesmen and other mural eyesores."[6]

Many of the improved pubs were located on the major highways and bypasses that were constructed to accommodate the growing number of automobiles. Automobile ownership in Britain rose from 580,000 in 1925 to more than 2 million on the eve of the Second World War, and the more mobile owners made up a significant clientele that was able to break from the tradition of drinking at a local pub. The automobile gave rise to a new category of drinking place, the roadhouse. Designed to appeal to the affluent, motorized class, roadhouses were more luxurious than pubs, even the improved kind, and they offered a bigger range of leisure amenities. Many featured a swimming pool, a high-end restaurant, and a dance floor with popular bands where formal dress was encouraged. Alcohol was served throughout, but roadhouses featured cocktails in addition to beer, wine, and spirits. Far from the risqué clubs of contemporary Berlin but not so different from many American cocktail bars, roadhouses caught the imagination as slightly dangerous places for illicit dalliances accompanied by drink and dancing. They were a far cry from the relatively drab petit bourgeois drinking culture of the pub lounge.

The association of improved pubs and roadhouses almost inevitably raised the question of drinking and driving, as neither offered accommodations where an overenthusiastic drinker might sleep off the effects before getting back behind the wheel. The 1929 royal commission devoted a scant fifteen lines to the subject, and then only to make the modest recommendation that drivers of buses, trucks, and other commercial vehicles should abstain from alcohol while they were on duty. This suggests that, in England at least, driving while intoxicated was not considered a significant problem. Laws against driving while intoxicated were passed only after the First World War, and because no standard measure of intoxication was available until the 1930s, evidence was based on the commonsense assessment of the police: slurred speech and the inability to walk in a straight line and perform acts like touching one's nose with a forefinger were accepted as signs of impairment.

One of the other main recommendations of the 1929 royal commission, alcohol education, was becoming a feature of alcohol policy in a number of countries in this period. It reflected continued anxiety that populations would slide back into the heavier drinking of earlier decades, and it recognized that early education might restrain coming generations from alcohol abuse. The first official English school syllabus on alcohol, which dated from

1909, adopted a somewhat heavy-handed approach infused with temperance moralizing. When it was revised in 1922, the syllabus placed alcohol in broader contexts, and alcohol abuse was related to the abuse of food; drinking responsibly was portrayed as part of the more general exercise of self-discipline that was necessary for a healthy life. The first official textbook, *Alcohol: Its Action on the Human Organism*, published in 1918, became widely used in English schools and colleges in the interwar period. But it was a dry, technical book that was largely confined to the physiological implications of alcohol consumption. It stressed that alcohol was not a food and had little nutritional value, but that its effects on the nervous system could be mitigated by drinking it diluted or by eating food while drinking.[7]

More straightforward, less nuanced advice could be found in the many books on alcohol written in this period for a young readership. One American example, published in the 1930s, also placed the abuse of alcohol on the same plane as that of food: "Some boys, and girls, too, weaken and disease their bodies by cultivating and developing an unnatural appetite for vinegar, salt, cloves, coffee, spice and other substances. . . . Such habits, if not early abandoned, lead to secret and social vice, prepare the person who does them for intemperance, and pave the way for permanent injury, or even for total wreck and ruin." Having established cloves as a gateway drug, it went on: "What is true of eating is also true of drinking. Drink only that which confers good health. Pure water, at the temperature it flows from the spring, is the best form of drink for both young and old. . . . Never take intoxicating liquors in any form. Look about you and see the ruin caused by rum in the lives of others."[8]

The general thrust of such books, as of most government interwar policies—urging citizens to limit alcohol consumption if they could not abstain completely—was thrown into relief in 1931 when the French government launched one of the more unusual episodes in the history of alcohol: a campaign to persuade French consumers to drink more wine.[9] French wine producers had had several big harvests but experienced difficulty selling wine abroad, thanks to the prohibition policy still in force in the United States and the economic depression and high unemployment elsewhere. The producers of high-end wine in Bordeaux, Burgundy, and Champagne were also affected by the disappearance of much of their aristocratic German, Austrian, and Russian markets in the aftermath of the First World War and the Russian Revolution and by the financial impact of the war on the English middle and upper classes. French wine exports fell from over 2 million hectoliters in 1924 to only 700,000 in 1932, and the result was a big surplus that would only get bigger if there were more big harvests. As the surplus grew, prices fell, as did the earnings of producers—including millions of small-scale grape-growers—and anyone involved in transporting and selling wine.

The crisis was so broad-based that the government could not ignore it. Between 1931 and 1935 it enacted the time-honored response to wine surpluses and attempted to limit production, which had increased during the 1920s. Taxes were placed on high yields, new plantings were prohibited for a ten-year period, and compulsory distillation of wine to make fuel was ordered. This last provision was enacted over protests that it would be a "profanity" to allow "the pearls of a Château d'Yquem or the rubies of a Chambertin . . . [to] end up in the fuel-tank of a motor-car."[10] But in addition to cutting supply, the French government decided to try to persuade citizens to drink their way out of the problems posed by the growing wine surplus. It was an optimistic goal. At 206 liters a year per adult in 1931, consumption of wine in France was the highest in the world. It seemed unlikely that it could be increased significantly enough to have much impact on the wine accumulating in vats and barrels all over France.

Any attempt to increase consumption of any alcoholic beverage ran counter to almost all contemporary trends. True, the United States was on the verge of abandoning prohibition, but no one there or elsewhere was calling for increased drinking—except for the chairman of England's Brewers' Society, Sir Edgar Sanders, who launched a campaign to increase beer consumption. This aim was no more than we would expect of such a lobby group, but it was phrased in an unusually explicit way. Sanders's intention was to "get the beer-drinking habit into thousands, almost millions, of young men who do not know at present the taste of beer."[11] The brewing industry launched a campaign to stress the healthy qualities of beer, echoing an advertising campaign by Guinness in the 1920s that highlighted the nutritional properties of the black brew.

In France, wine, not beer, was the healthy beverage. The French had a long-standing tradition of distinguishing between wine (a natural and healthy beverage) and "alcohol," meaning distilled spirits (which were believed to cause health and social problems). Running against the contemporary trend elsewhere, the French medical profession persisted in portraying wine as a healthy beverage, and the purported health benefits of wine were central to the campaign to increase wine consumption. Eminent doctors formed an association called Médecins amis du vin (the Physician Friends of Wine) to support the government's wine-consumption campaign by writing letters and articles for newspapers. Advertisements stressed the health benefits of wine;

one claimed that the average life expectancy of a wine-drinker was sixty-five years, against fifty-nine years for a water-drinker, and that 87 percent of centenarians were wine-drinkers.[12]

Allied to this theme was the message that wine, which had been declared France's national beverage, was rooted in the French soil (occasionally irrigated with the blood of the country's martyrs), so that consuming wine was not only a healthy pleasure but a patriotic obligation. And if drinking wine were patriotic, drinking more wine could only be more so. Wine, indeed, was linked to the sheer existence of France, as one doctor argued in a brilliant non sequitur: "For over a thousand years, wine has been the national drink of the French and although they have been surrounded by enemies against whom they have fought more wars than any other people, the French have not only survived but they are among the two or three most important nations in the world."[13]

The drink-more-wine campaign used various means—posters, billboards at railway stations, newspaper advertisements, local festivals, and conferences—to convey its message, and it eagerly embraced the new mass media. Four hundred flashing neon signs were erected in Paris with pithy messages such as "Make wine your preference" and "A meal without wine is like a day without sunshine." References to wine were encouraged in French movies, an early form of product placement. Between 1934 and 1937, the new state radio broadcast a series of talks on the history of France as traced through wine. Listeners learned that Louis XVI was an unsuccessful king not because his mismanagement of the state's finances led to the French Revolution but because he diluted his wine with water, which prevented him from thinking deeply enough. As for the great ideas of the Enlightenment, they came forth under the influence of wine.

No sector of the population that was perceived as able to drink more wine was spared the attention of the campaign. Young men would learn wine-drinking while they did military service. Over the objections of some teachers' groups—and, of course, temperance associations—the campaign even reached into France's schools. When children took dictation, they would copy out Louis Pasteur's dicta on the health benefits of wine, and when they took geography lessons, they would learn the location of France's wine regions. Mathematics classes included equations such as "One liter of wine at ten degrees [alcohol-level] corresponds as a food-stuff to 900 grams of milk, 370 grams of bread, 585 grams of meat, and five eggs." It was even suggested that wine should be provided to children during lunch and at breaks. The French Olympic Committee got onboard and asked that French athletes at the 1932

Olympic Games in Los Angeles "be given the same consideration as French sailors in American ports. That is to say, that they be accorded a free daily consumption of a liter of wine." The team had French chefs, but "without wine, the food will not be the same."[14]

Outside metropolitan France, the colonies were identified as underperforming in wine consumption. The pro-wine campaigners had not only the expatriate colonists in their sights but the indigenous populations, particularly in France's sprawling possessions in North Africa. Many, of course, were nondrinking Muslims, and it was thought that they could help the national cause by eating more French grapes and drinking unfermented grape juice. A conference to pursue this goal was held in 1936 in Tunis, where speakers addressed topics such as making and conserving grape juice. But the main force of the campaign was in France itself and on those who already drank wine. Restaurants were encouraged to include some wine in the price of food and to price wine fairly. More retail outlets were proposed—including wine trucks on public squares—and many of the restrictions on bars were relaxed.

Even without its sometimes outrageous proposals—such as giving wine to schoolchildren and paying cyclists in the annual Tour de France to be seen drinking wine while they were racing—the campaign to increase wine consumption is astonishing because it ran directly counter to so many trends in the interwar period. As President Roosevelt was warning about a return to the bad old days after the repeal of prohibition, and as Canada's provinces were carefully monitoring and limiting their citizens' alcohol consumption, the French government was urging its citizen to drink, drink, and drink more wine. Yet for all its work and cost, the campaign foundered on the economic realities of the depression, which struck France in 1931, a little later than many other countries. During the 1920s, adult per capita wine consumption averaged 224 liters a year; in the 1930s, despite the wide-ranging campaign, it averaged 203 liters. It was not a dramatic decline, but it was still a decline and not the increase that the government wanted.

If France's wine crisis did not lead to higher consumption, it did contribute to a transformation of French wine. A plan was put in place to pull up vineyards, and a 1934 law forbade the use of hybrid grape varieties for making commercial wine; they could be used for wine for family consumption, even though one of the justifications offered for the law was that wine made from hybrids could lead to insanity. Even more important were measures to guarantee the provenance of wine, because falling prices had led some merchants to label wine from regions that commanded low prices as coming from more prestigious regions that produced higher-priced wines; one merchant sold wine from Spain's La Mancha region as coming from Chablis, in northern Burgundy. A law of 1935 established a method of guaranteeing provenance, the Appellation d'Origine Contrôlée system that is still central to French law and has been a model for wine laws in many other countries. Various forms of the law had been enacted in France as early as 1905 in response to widespread wine fraud during the phylloxera crisis, but the 1935 law extended and codified the appellation system and cleared the way for hundreds of appellations to be created. In each appellation, regulations covered issues such as the varieties of grapes that could be used, the ratios in blends of varieties, minimum alcohol levels, and maximum yields of wine per hectare of vines.

If the democratic nations of Europe and North America adopted a variety of responses to the perceived challenges of drinking, alcohol was of no less concern to the many authoritarian regimes that emerged in Europe in the interwar period. In Germany, for example, there was a perceptible shift in policy as the liberal Weimar Republic, which came into being after the First World War, gave way to the Nazi regime in 1933. The Weimar government, dominated by center-left parties throughout the 1920s, inherited Germany's wartime restrictions on alcohol production but quickly removed them so as to normalize living conditions. Alcohol became freely available, but paradoxically, consumption seems to have declined to historically low levels, perhaps to as little as 3 or 4 liters of pure alcohol per person each year. The reasons for this must have included the weak purchasing power of most Germans as they faced, first, postwar poverty and then the calamitous effects of runaway inflation in 1923, followed by the economic depression and its high unemployment and much-reduced purchasing power from 1929 onward. German beer production had consistently totaled about 70 million hectoliters a year in the two decades before 1914, but from 1919 to 1933 it averaged only 41 million, a decline of 40 percent.[15]

In contrast to the liberal alcohol policies of the Weimar Republic, the Nazi regime adopted a generally antialcohol position, largely based on the same eugenics theories that underlay its radical race policies. Eugenicists had frequently highlighted the dangers of alcohol for individual and social health, and what they broadly termed "alcoholism"—which often meant nothing more than the regular consumption of above-average volumes of alcohol—was considered as clear a sign of degeneracy as insanity, criminality, immorality, and epilepsy. Rather than see addiction as a response to environmental and social conditions, many German alcohol theorists had embraced the eugenics principle that addictions (of any kind) took root only in people congenitally predisposed to them; alcoholism, rather than being an illness in itself, was considered to be, in most cases, a symptom of a more fundamental pathology. This led to the important conclusion that there was no way to prevent or cure most alcoholism using medical or therapeutic methods.

Commonplace drinking—the regular consumption of alcohol in moderate amounts for relaxation and on social occasions, perhaps with an occasional binge during festivities such as weddings—was treated as a different matter altogether. The Nazis recognized that enjoying beer and Schnapps (wine was a distant third) was integral to German culture and sociability. The earliest Nazi political action, the "beer-hall putsch" of 1923, emanated from a place of drinking, and we can assume that some beer was consumed before Hitler led his followers out to the street. (Hitler himself seldom drank, and if he represented himself as an abstainer from alcohol—and from meat and sex—it was to cultivate an image of a man fully in control of his bodily passions and totally dedicated to the well-being of his country and people.)

Yet if the Nazis were critical of drinking in general because of its occasional personal and social effects (including absenteeism from work, illness, domestic violence, crime, and traffic accidents), they were pragmatic enough to know that trying to ban alcohol would cause more conflict and resistance than it was worth. The Nazis came to power the very year that prohibition was repealed in the United States, so they had a privileged position from which to observe the results of that policy. Nor did the Nazi leadership pay much attention to some radical claims from within their ranks, such as that alcohol was a substance employed by Jews to weaken the German people.

Instead, the Nazis initially embraced a moderate antialcohol position and adopted policies that were familiar throughout much of contemporary Europe. In terms of regulations, they included limiting access to alcohol, educating citizens on its dangers, restricting advertising, police supervision of drinking places, and cracking down on drinking and driving. The alcohol industry was required to produce nonalcoholic beverages, such as fruit juice, and alcohol-free restaurants were established for nondrinkers.

On the coercive side, anyone convicted of disturbing the peace while intoxicated could be forbidden to enter a bar or tavern and could be exposed to public shame by being included in lists of "irresponsible drinkers" that were published in the daily newspapers. More serious offenders could be declared legally incapacitated and interned in a sanatorium, work camp, or concentration camp (which at this time was essentially a labor camp). Anyone who committed a crime while intoxicated felt the full force of the law, including confinement in prison, a workhouse, or a place of "secure custody," which frequently meant a concentration camp. Drinking and driving attracted special attention (the Nazis had an automobile fetish), and by 1938 the German police were among the first to adopt a blood-alcohol test developed only six years earlier by Swedish scientist Eric Widmark.[16]

These policies were designed to deal with the problems that arose when ordinary, healthy Germans, as defined by the Nazis, abused alcohol. Alcoholism was a different matter altogether, and it demanded more rigorous responses. The basic policy was embedded in the Law for the Prevention of Descendants affected by Hereditary Disorders, which was promulgated in 1933 soon after the Nazis came to power. It put alcoholism on the same basis as insanity, schizophrenia, bodily deformity, blindness, and other conditions regarded as hereditary, and it was designed not to provide treatment for alcoholics (which the Nazis thought generally futile) but to minimize the incidence of alcoholism in the future. This would be achieved by sterilizing anyone diagnosed as alcoholic. A commentary on the 1933 law noted, "Through the sterilization of inebriates, the number of mentally inferior individuals for coming generations is reduced and with that the number of inebriates from the hereditary pool."[17]

Petitions to sterilize alcoholics were generally brought by medical officers or the administrators of institutions dealing with alcohol problems and were decided by a panel consisting of a judge and two doctors. No evidence of hereditary alcoholism was required, and arguments for sterilization were generally based on heavy drinking, together with behavior such as criminality, neglect of obligations to family or state, and impaired work habits. It is estimated that 90 percent of petitions were granted and that between 15,000 and 30,000 individuals diagnosed as alcoholics were sterilized under this law.

People diagnosed as nonhereditary alcoholics were not sterilized but were prohibited from marrying. The Marriage Health Law of 1935 forbade marriage by anyone suffering from a "mental disturbance" and singled out alcoholism as making "a beneficial coexistence in the community impossible for both the married couple as well as the children." Alcoholics, the law stated, "endanger the orderly raising of children and the economic situation of the family."[18] In 1938 a new German divorce law made alcoholism a ground for dissolving a marriage.

Yet for all that the Nazis campaigned against alcohol, they only moderately regulated production and consumption, and alcohol consumption in Germany rose steadily after they came to power. The consumption of spirits doubled between 1933 and 1939, and beer production reversed its 1920s decline, possibly reflecting improved economic conditions and higher employment, as the Nazi regime embarked on massive public works and armaments programs.[19] In addition, the government actually assisted some branches of the alcohol industry, such as wineries (wine production fell during the 1930s) and taverns; it appreciated that they provided employment and that the state also needed the revenues from all forms of alcohol.

The Communist Party of the Soviet Union also tackled problems of alcohol in this period, but it had its own chronology and motivations. Having gradually moved away from the prohibition policies that were inherited from the tsarist government and maintained during the first years of the Soviet period, Stalin's government adopted policies that permitted easy access to the alcohol produced by state-owned enterprises. Through the 1920s, however, the authorities struggled against the production of samogon, illicitly produced vodka. Reports throughout the decade claimed that vast amounts of grain were diverted to make this alcohol. In 1922 the Commissariat for Justice noted that "the production of [samogon] . . . has become a large-scale enterprise in several areas of the Republic; it damages national health, causes senseless waste and spoilage of grain and other foodstuffs."[20] The government suspected that many of the producers were political opponents who would rather do anything with their surplus grain than turn it over to the state. They often identified samogon producers as kulaks, the wealthier peasant class that Stalin later targeted for persecution and exile during the campaign to collectivize agriculture.

Alcohol was placed firmly in the Soviet political context. Illicit alcohol was not only illegal, but it deprived the people of grain and promoted antisocial behavior. In 1922, *Pravda*, the state-controlled newspaper, embarked on a campaign against samogon in unambiguously political terms: "The struggle against [samogon] is the workers' cause. . . . The bootlegger is a parasite of the working class. Merciless war against him!" Hundreds of thousands of illicit producers were arrested and tried—191,000 in the Russian republic alone in 1923—but the great majority of those who ended up in court (as in the United States while prohibition was in force) turned out to be small-time operators. In the first half of March 1923, the police made 13,748 arrests throughout the Soviet Union and confiscated 25,114 gallons of samogon, less than 2 gallons per apprehended producer.[21] In 1926 the authorities capitulated to reality, decriminalizing the production of samogon for personal consumption and focusing on large-scale, commercial producers.

The Soviet campaign against bootleg alcohol was distinctive because it took place not within a context of official prohibition but while legal alcohol was freely available. Full-strength alcohol was permitted from the end of 1923, so the existence and consumption of alcohol were not the problems in themselves. Rather, the state was losing the revenues from the taxes that made up most of the price of legally produced alcohol. Recognizing that the Soviet Union needed money to develop an industrial economy, and rejecting the option of borrowing from foreign lenders at high interest rates, Stalin posed the options starkly in 1925: "We have to make a choice between debt slavery and vodka."[22] Even so, the resumption of a state monopoly on vodka was supposed to be a temporary measure to tide the government over. As soon as other sources of income were in place, the production of vodka would be reduced and then eliminated altogether.

Soviet alcohol policies thus embodied a contradiction between end (abstinence) and means (the free flow of alcohol). Thus it is not surprising that they fluctuated wildly as they sometimes favored reducing supply so as to lessen the effects of drinking on health and social order and sometimes favored increasing supply so as to maximize state revenues. For example, the 1929 conference of the Communist Party responded to fears about the extent of alcohol abuse by approving a program for the "de-alcoholization of the economy." But a few months later, the Central Committee of the party annulled the resolution, and in the following year, Stalin ordered "the maximum increase" in the production of vodka.[23]

Underlying first the abandonment of prohibition and then the return to full-strength alcohol production was a shift in Soviet thinking about alcohol consumption. The Communists had come to power arguing that alcohol use by workers was a symptom of the otherwise intolerable conditions imposed on them by capitalists and that capitalists encouraged drinking so as to make workers more docile; even if binge-drinking led to absenteeism, workers well-supplied with alcohol were less disposed to revolutionary activism. But faced with the same widespread resistance to prohibition that the tsar's government had experienced, and needing the revenue from taxes, the Soviet government gradually reintroduced alcohol. In ideological terms, it seems to have assumed that alcohol use would wither away as workers adjusted to their improved working and living conditions in Soviet society. In the meantime, however, workers could no longer justify alcohol abuse by appealing to their oppression by capitalists, and they had to take responsibility for their alcohol-affected behavior. This justified harsher penalties for drunkenness and for crimes committed while the perpetrators were intoxicated.

The production of samogon, which continued to be far more popular than official vodka through the 1920s, seems to have declined dramatically in the 1930s, possibly because the collectivization of farms allowed for far less individual enterprise and provided more social surveillance. In contrast, the state-sponsored production of vodka rose steadily through the 1930s, from 36.5 million decaliters in 1932 to 94.5 million in 1939. By 1940, on the eve of the German invasion, there were said to be more retail outlets selling alcohol in the Soviet Union than shops selling meat, fruit, and vegetables put together.[24]

High levels of alcohol consumption were to dog the Soviet Union for decades and even contribute to its economic decline and collapse in the 1980s. But "alcoholism"—as any form of regular, heavy drinking was often generically referred to—became a more prominent target for therapy everywhere once the impossibility of ending alcohol consumption entirely became clear. One of the most important alcohol-reform organizations to emerge in the interwar period was Alcoholics Anonymous, an organization that was distinctive because it abandoned the moralistic approach to alcoholism that dominated temperance and prohibitionist discourses. With its primary purpose being to enable alcoholics to "stay sober and to help other alcoholics to achieve sobriety," Alcoholics Anonymous was founded in the United States in 1935, but it really took off in the early 1940s. By 1945 there were 12,986 members in 556 local groups throughout the United States, and five years later there were 96,000 members and more than 3,500 groups.

The organization calculated that, in its early years, it was successful for about three-quarters of the people who committed themselves to the Alcoholics Anonymous method. That method involved ceasing to drink alcohol entirely, in the belief that a single drink would most likely put the alcoholic on a slippery slope to chronic and heavy drinking again. It was based on the premise that alcoholics were always alcoholics, but that there were alcoholics who drank and those who did not. At the regular meetings that members were expected to attend, there were speakers and discussions, and new members were expected to tell the story of their alcoholism. Each member was paired with another who could be contacted for advice and support when he or she felt the need to drink. Although Alcoholics Anonymous stressed the importance of each member's spiritual and character development, it steered clear of identification with any specific religion.

Alcoholics Anonymous was not, strictly speaking, against alcohol, and it emerged at a time when the antialcohol movements that had been so influential before the First World War were declining in both numbers and influence. Although the Second World War provided another caesura in the history of alcohol, it was by no means the stark break represented by the First World War. At that time, the antialcohol movements had had their moment when the intersection of war and the momentum of temperance and prohibition produced a slew of policies banning or restricting access to alcohol. But the abandonment or dilution of many of these policies by the mid-1930s not only indicated a shift of popular and political attitudes; it also tainted the antialcohol organizations with an aura of failure. Membership in the WCTU in the United States declined from more than 2 million in 1920 to less than half a million twenty years later. It was only one example of the ebbing of support for antialcohol organizations.

In some countries, the Second World War had far less impact than the First World War on alcohol production and consumption. In Great Britain, the price of alcohol rose because of enormous increases in taxation; the duty on a barrel of beer rose from 48 shillings in 1939 to 138 shillings in 1943. Because higher-alcohol beer was taxed more, brewers lowered the alcohol to keep their product as affordable as possible. If anything, consumption of beer rose during the Second World War, but the Second was different from the First in that the mass draining of young men—the key beer-drinking demographic—from the population did not occur until the Allied invasions of continental Europe began in 1943. Even then, England welcomed a constantly revolving population of alcohol-drinking soldiers from other countries throughout the hostilities, including Americans from 1942 onward.

Women began to drink in pubs more frequently during the war, as had occurred between 1914 and 1918. But most of the women who drank in pubs during the war were younger than those who had done so in the 1930s. Many worked in what had been male occupations, their financial independence freed them from parental control, and meeting men in pubs became more acceptable.[25] A survey of pubs in the early 1940s suggested that about a fifth of patrons were women, with more drinking there on weekends than during the week. The author noted that because women occupied only parlors and lounges, "it is often possible to find rooms in which quite half the drinkers are women."[26] (He also noted that women made up a disproportionately small percentage of pub drinkers arrested for drunkenness.)

This is not to say that the conditions of war from 1939 to 1945 did not have an impact of alcohol production and consumption. Whole economies and patterns of everyday life were disrupted throughout the vast expanses of Europe that were occupied by Germany from 1939 to 1945. The German, Italian, British, Soviet, and many other economies were geared up to produce war matériel, not consumer goods. It was impossible for alcohol production and consumption not to have been affected by these conditions or to have been neglected as governments adopted policies to maximize their war efforts.

With the coming of war in 1939 and the greater discipline needed in the German armed forces and among civilians engaged in industry and agriculture, the Nazi government's tolerance of alcohol shrank. In 1939, the year Germany invaded Poland, the Bureau against the Dangers of Alcohol and Tobacco was established, and it fostered a new network of regulations to control alcohol in Germany. The production and sale of alcohol were subject to new limits, and taxes on alcohol were raised. During the war, strict rules covered alcohol consumption by anyone serving in the armed forces, although alcohol and drugs were widely supplied to German soldiers and police to enable them to carry out some of the barbarous policies ordered by the government. Men who served in the Reserve Police battalions in Poland that were responsible for shooting tens of thousands of Jewish men, women, and children at close quarters were given special rations of alcohol during and afterward to help them cope with the horrors of their actions.[27]

On the German home front, any antisocial behavior that could be attributed to drinking—absenteeism, reduced or impaired productivity, being unruly in an air-raid shelter, or being involved in a traffic accident during a blackout—was now regarded as even more harmful to the state than in peacetime. "No dangerous alcoholic, no person who has fallen under the influence of alcohol may . . . remain unknown to the state and party," declared the regime.[28] A wide range of people in positions of authority, including doctors, union officials, and factory nurses, were required to report anyone suspected to be "alcohol-diseased" or "dangerous alcoholics" to the police. Punishments included detention in a concentration camp.

In many parts of Europe occupied by German forces, particularly in eastern Europe and Russia, preexisting patterns of production, exchange, and consumption were shattered. The needs of the local populations were ignored, at best, and we should assume that little survived of prewar alcohol-related diets and sociability. In northern and western Europe, the disruption to non-Jewish populations was less dramatic. German forces occupied important centers of alcohol production such as Alsace (which was annexed to Germany), Bordeaux, Burgundy, and Cognac.

In Vichy France, the collaborationist state dependent on Germany but not occupied by German forces, attitudes toward alcohol were different. Vichy, its capital, is a city closely associated with healing waters and potable mineral water (as the final scene of the movie *Casablanca* reminds us) and might seem unpromising for alcohol. On the other hand, the Vichy regime was headed by Marshal Philippe Pétain, the hero of the First World War who had praised the contribution of French wine to victory in 1918: "For the soldiers, wine was the stimulant of moral strength as well as physical strength. In its own way, it helped us to our victory."[29]

In 1940, however, Pétain established a right-wing authoritarian regime that had a complicated relationship with alcohol in general and wine in particular. On one hand, Pétain valued wine as an emanation of the French soil and saw viticulture as representing all that was good in the French character: hard work and devotion to land and tradition. In recognition of Pétain's appreciation of wine, the authorities in Beaune, Burgundy's famous wine town, presented him with his own vineyard (Clos du Maréchal Pétain) in the prestigious and expensive Hospices de Beaune estate.[30] Yet for all that the marshal embraced the idea of wine, he had problems with people drinking it. Wine was included in Vichy's rationing program (there had been no rationing in the First World War), because even though supplies of wine were buoyant, the Vichy government required vast volumes to be diverted for distilling and the conversion of grape juice to grape sugar to compensate for shortages. Grape seeds were pressed to obtain oil.[31]

The Vichy government's interference with the wine industry, which was significant even for France—there were more than fifty edicts, laws, and ministerial decrees on wine in the regime's brief, four-year life—alienated growers, producers, and consumers. Among other things, new rules reduced the volume of wine that producers could retain tax-free for their family's consumption. Nor did the regime's crackdown on drinking go over well. Pétain regarded alcoholism as a symptom of French decadence, and reversing the pro-wine sentiments he expressed after the First World War, he blamed wine for the French defeat in 1940. In that and the following year, his Vichy administration put new limits on cafés and other drinking places.

Although there were many reasons why French people might not have supported the Vichy government, the sheer scale of its intervention in the availability of wine—a dramatic shift from the campaign to drink more wine a few years earlier—must have contributed to its unpopularity. In contrast, wine retained a strong association with the mostly left-leaning Third Republic that preceded Vichy, and the wartime Resistance frequently made the point that the Vichy government had stolen the people's wine.

In the United States, the coming of war encouraged prohibitionists to press their case, as they had done successfully in the First World War. After the United States declared war on Japan and Germany in 1941, the president of Colgate University declared, "Alcohol and war do not mix any better than alcohol and gasoline. . . . A sober nation with the morale born of clear thinking, determination and courage can eventually defeat Hitler and the Japs, but a drunken nation will travel through the Slough of Despond to inevitable danger of defeat."[32] Despite attempts to legislate prohibition for men serving in the armed forces, military leaders successfully argued that they would resent being deprived of alcohol and would contrive to obtain supplies anyway. In the end, breweries were permitted to produce beer—"as a beverage of moderation and as an aid to national morale," as one industry leader piously put it—for consumption domestically and overseas.[33] Although distilleries were directed to produce industrial alcohol in 1942, they were permitted to make beverage alcohol for short periods in both 1944 and 1945. Beer consumption in the United States increased by 50 percent between 1940 and 1945, probably as a result of the reduced supply of liquor.

By this time, Americans were generally free to purchase and drink alcohol with few restrictions, as the United States had emerged from national prohibition with relatively liberal alcohol policies. They varied from state to state, as we have seen, but many fewer states opted for prohibition after 1933 than had done so before prohibition was implemented on a national basis. In the sense that national policies following prohibition were more liberal than those that preceded it, the United States was an exception: in Norway, Sweden, the Soviet Union, Finland, and Canada's provinces, the state took over direct control of alcohol retailing after the repeal of prohibition so as to regulate alcohol consumption. Even countries that had not had prohibition policies were more restrictive when it came to alcohol during most of the twentieth century than they had been before. In Great Britain and New Zealand, for example, some alcohol-related restrictions imposed during the First World War (such as public-house opening hours) were retained until the end of the 1900s. In these various ways, the postprohibition world was long influenced by the experience of prohibition and its associated temperance ideas.

15

Alcohol in the Modern World

TRENDS IN REGULATION
AND CONSUMPTION

In the postwar world, alcohol consumption and policies have reflected broad social, cultural, and economic shifts as well as specific national and local conditions. They include the baby-boom generation and the decline of fertility rates, which transformed the age structures of almost all Western populations. Demographic movements, including the migration of millions of non-Europeans with distinctive drinking or nondrinking patterns, have had an impact on many European societies. And while official attitudes toward alcohol consumption have generally shifted in more liberal directions since the 1960s, there have also been countervailing tendencies related to specific issues such as drinking and driving and what is called binge-drinking. Finally, some societies faced significant alcohol-related challenges and responded with tighter controls. The governments of the Soviet Union and its successor state, Russia, continued the century-long saga of trying to reduce alcohol consumption among their people and lessen its social and economic effects.

In the immediate postwar period, from 1945 to about 1960, alcohol remained or became a standard feature of daily life in most Western societies. Cocktails, which had been features of the prohibition era, continued to be more popular in the United States than anywhere else, and middle-class men (and fewer women) enjoyed the "cocktail hour" at the end of the workday. The most popular cocktails—martinis, manhattans, and old-fashioneds—became associated with business and suburban sociability. The distinction between the bar, lounge, or country club—the prime locations for middle-class public drinking—and the home was blurred. Advertisements increasingly implied that whiskey and other spirits were part of domestic hospitality.[1] Although we must assume that many Americans drank at home as a matter of course throughout the nineteenth and twentieth centuries, we must also remember that, since the mid-1800s, the dominant discourses in the United States had portrayed drinking alcohol as behavior bordering on the pathological. Two of the unintended consequences of prohibition might have been to normalize public drinking and drinking by women, but consuming alcohol in the privacy of the home, shielded from public surveillance, presented different kinds of dangers.

Reflecting the persistent belief that women were the repositories and guardians of public and family morality, churches and temperance groups placed the onus on women to ensure that drinking in their homes was moderate. As mothers, they were to steer their children away from temptations to experiment with alcohol; as wives, they were to understand how stressful jobs might lead their husbands to drink heavily; and as hostesses, they were to ensure that any alcohol served in their homes was consumed moderately. Clearly success in these challenges was not universal: surveys in the 1950s showed that high proportions of young people below the minimum drinking age consumed alcohol, many with their parents' consent. A survey of college students in 1953 found that 79 to 92 percent of males and 40 to 89 percent of females drank alcohol with some frequency, which increased with family income. A study the next year in Nassau County, Long Island, found that 68 percent of fourteen-year-olds had parental permission to drink alcohol at home, and 29 percent were permitted to drink alcohol away from home on occasion.[2] Although it is difficult to measure and describe, in the 1950s drinking seems to have been culturally accepted in the United States for the first time in a century and a half. There were, of course, constant warnings about heavy drinking and alcoholism, but one of the worst effects of these behaviors—domestic violence against women—was scarcely mentioned until the 1970s.

The United States and France were often contrasted in their attitudes toward alcohol: on one hand, Americans were thought of as mistrustful of alcohol, willing to support prohibition (even if they eventually recanted), and cautious in their policies; on the other hand, the French were relaxed, full of joie de vivre, and heavy but happy drinkers who had integrated alcohol seamlessly into their work and private lives. After German occupation and the fascist Vichy regime, we might have expected the postwar French governments to liberate their citizens from the tight regulations imposed on alcohol production and consumption adopted during the war by Marshal Pétain. Instead, the transitional regime of General Charles de Gaulle confirmed the Vichy policies, limited the number of bars (which had fallen from more than

455,000 in 1940 to 314,000 in 1946), and gave financial support to France's main antialcohol organization.[3] But with the return of parliamentary government and popular elections, French administrations began to liberalize policies. In 1951 the fundamental Vichy regulations of 1941 were repealed, and alcohol advertising (even of spirits-based beverages such as pastis) was again permitted. Wine producers were allowed to expand their vineyards, and production of all kinds of alcohol was encouraged by the state. Wine was again praised as France's national beverage, and even the entry of Coca-Cola to the French market was delayed several years for fear that it would compete with wine.[4]

While such measures can be understood as integral to rebuilding France's economy and exports after the war (it was generally assumed everywhere that French wine was the best), the government also acknowledged the costs of heavy drinking. While it encouraged alcohol consumption, the government in 1954 passed a law that provided for the compulsory treatment of alcoholics who were a danger to themselves or to society. In the face of determined attempts by sections of France's medical profession to show that wine was a healthy beverage, a broader approach was adopted by a new government, including restrictions on alcohol production and consumption and education programs.[5] (The prime minister, Pierre Mendès France, provocatively brought a glass of milk to the rostrum of the National Assembly.) Throughout the 1950s, French alcohol policy was informed more than ever by antialcohol principles, and although the number of bars and cafés serving alcohol continued its steady decline, per capita consumption of pure alcohol in France did not change appreciably. In 1951 it was 26.7 liters; it peaked at 28.8 liters in 1955, and in 1961 it was 27.7 liters. It did not drop below 26 liters until 1971, when it stood at 24.8 liters.[6]

In the United Kingdom, beer production in the 1940s peaked in 1945, then declined steadily through much of the 1950s before rebounding in the 1960s. Only in the 1970s did output exceed the level reached in 1945, and that, of course, served a considerably larger population. At the same time, there was a clear perception of increased public drunkenness in Britain during the 1950s and early 1960s. Between 1955 and 1957, convictions for being drunk in public rose by 27 percent, and between 1960 and 1962 they rose by 23 percent. In each case they subsequently declined, but only slightly. Much of the increase was attributed to record numbers of teenagers in the population, thanks to the postwar baby boom.[7]

Throughout Western societies in the 1960s, alcohol policies, like policies regarding sexual behavior and social life in general, began to be liberalized.

In that and the following decades, the minimum legal drinking age was lowered in a number of countries, and many of the residual negative connotations of alcohol fell away. The behavioral backdrop to concerns about patterns of drinking was a general stabilization in total alcohol consumption throughout much of the world since the 1970s and 1980s. In some countries, there are countervailing trends that cancel each other out, such as an increase in wine consumption and a decrease in beer and spirits, resulting in little or no overall change in the volume of pure alcohol consumed from all sources. That said, there are vast differences on a national and regional basis; sometimes these reflect policies that ban alcohol consumption entirely (as in many Muslim countries), and sometimes they indicate policies that hardly limit access to alcohol at all. In very general terms, the regions with the lowest alcohol consumption (under 7.5 liters of pure alcohol a year) by adults are Africa, the Middle East, and South and East Asia. Low-average consuming regions (7.5 to 9.9 liters) are North America, Brazil, and South Africa. High-average consumers (10 to 12.5 liters) are Argentina, Nigeria, Australia, Spain, Italy, and Sweden, while the countries with the highest levels of alcohol consumption (over 12.5 liters of pure alcohol per adult each year) are Russia, Portugal, France, and almost all central and eastern European countries.[8]

Such statistics give us a general idea of the global distribution of aggregated alcohol consumption patterns, but they conceal important variations within countries by region, class, gender, and generation. For example, in Italy, alcohol consumption declined steadily from 20 liters a head in the 1960s to less than half that in 2006, but consumption is higher among older men than among younger consumers. Unless younger consumers increase their alcohol consumption as they age, overall consumption in Italy can be expected to continue to decline. In Italy, as almost everywhere else, women consumed considerably less alcohol than men. A quarter of Italian women report they have not consumed alcohol in the preceding twelve months, compared to a tenth of men.[9] A similar effect is found in the United Kingdom, where in 2010, men between the ages of forty-five and sixty-four were the most regular and highest consumers of alcohol, compared with men in other age groups. The same was true of women.[10]

In the United States, alcohol consumption was not only lower than Italy's throughout the whole period but rose from 8 liters of pure alcohol in 1961 to 10 liters in 1981 before falling to 9 liters in 2006. American rates of abstention from alcohol were much higher than the Italian: two-fifths of American women and more than a quarter of men reported having consumed no alcohol in the preceding year.[11] In broad terms, then, about a third of American adults do not drink alcohol, compared to less than a fifth of Italians.

Some of the explanations for national, regional, and demographic differences seem obvious. Many Muslim countries report no alcohol consumption simply because alcohol is prohibited, and any consumption must be clandestine. The relatively high level of abstention from alcohol in the United States is partly the result of the presence of several alcohol-averse religious denominations, such as the Church of Jesus Christ of Latter-day Saints (Mormons), which has 6 million adherents. It is possible that the presence of low-consuming ethnic groups in the United States also contributes to the rate of alcohol abstention. But it is clear that broad categories such as "Asian" and "Hispanic" populations, both frequently associated with low alcohol consumption, comprise many different populations with varying traditions, histories, and cultures of drinking. Moreover, drinking patterns sometimes change as minority populations become more assimilated into the dominant culture. In France, the increased immigration by Muslims from North Africa since the 1960s—there are between 5 and 6 million Muslims, about a third of them devout, in the country of 66 million inhabitants—has contributed to the steady decline in France's per capita alcohol consumption. Total alcohol consumption from all sources in France fell from 25 liters per capita in 1961 to 14 liters in 2006, almost entirely the result of a decline in wine consumption. One of the implications has been the disappearance of tens of thousands of cafés and bars and major shifts in patterns of alcohol-centered sociability.[12]

As alcohol consumption stabilized in many countries, fell in others, and rose in only a few, many governments relaxed their alcohol policies. This easing of restrictions was not necessarily acknowledgment that societies could afford to be less vigilant about alcohol because it was no longer being consumed in ever-greater volumes, but it was probably part of the general tendency toward less regulation of the personal lives of citizens. Since the 1960s, laws relating to sexual behavior and orientation have been relaxed, censorship has lightened, and laws that discriminated on the basis of ethnicity and gender have been repealed.

Regarding alcohol, one of the changes was a reduction in the role of the state in its sale. In a number of countries and their subjurisdictions (states and provinces), the sale of alcohol had been carried out by government-owned retailing outlets, generally known as liquor monopolies. From the 1960s onward, many of these systems were dismantled or modified, often after much public debate. One universal result of the transfer of retailing was a significant increase in the number of places where alcohol could be purchased, and there is some evidence that easier availability of alcohol promotes higher levels of consumption. Overall, however, there is no hard-and-fast rule that the privatization of liquor retailing leads to a higher level of consumption; this has occurred in some places, while in other places, consumption has either not changed or has declined following privatization. In the United States, a series of states surrendered the sale of alcohol to private retailers. In Canada, Alberta gave up its role in retailing alcohol—the first and only province to do so—in 1994, while some other provinces maintained their provincial alcohol system but also began to permit privately owned liquor stores to operate.

Another area of liberalization since the 1960s has been a widespread reduction in the legal drinking age, which until that point had been 21 years almost everywhere that drinking was permitted and a minimum age legally prescribed. (In Muslim countries, where alcohol consumption is prohibited, a minimum legal drinking age would be redundant.) In the United States, almost all states set 21 years as the minimum legal drinking age following the repeal of prohibition. However, after a 1971 amendment to the U.S. Constitution that lowered the voting age to 18 years, many states reduced the drinking age to the same level. By 1975, twenty-nine states (more than half) had done so, although a few lowered the drinking age to only 19 or 20 years. This prompted a reaction from advocacy groups, largely on the ground that automobile accidents increased when the drinking age was lowered. Between 1976 and 1983, nineteen states raised the minimum legal drinking age back to 21 years. Setting the minimum drinking age falls to the jurisdiction of individual states, but fears that young people who were underage in their own state could drive to another state where they could buy alcohol legally led the federal government to step in. In 1984, it passed the Uniform Drinking Age Act, which deprived states of 10 percent of their federal highway funding if they did not conform to the 21-year-old rule. All the holdouts fell into line.

Individual American states have followed different trajectories in terms of the minimum drinking age. In Virginia, for example, the age for buying or drinking any alcohol was set at 21 years in 1934, after prohibition was repealed, but in 1974 it was lowered to 18 years for the purchase of beer. In 1981 the drinking age with respect to beer was maintained at 18 years if the beer was consumed where it was bought (such as in a bar) but raised to 19 years if the beer was purchased for consumption elsewhere. In 1983 the minimum age was raised to 19 years for all beer purchases. In 1985, following the federal Uniform Drinking Age Act, the minimum age was raised to 21 years, but anyone who had been able to purchase beer and was under the age of 21 years was permitted to continue to purchase beer legally—to avoid a situation in which a 19- or 20-year-old person might have been able to buy beer but then was forbidden to do so until reaching the age of 21 years. In 1987 the legal drinking age for all alcoholic beverages in Virginia reverted to 21 years, as it had been more than 50 years earlier.[13]

There are not only global variations in the minimum drinking age but also significant national differences in the way an alcoholic beverage is defined. Although a small number of countries do not define alcoholic beverages at all, the great majority do, and they do so in terms of the percentage of alcohol by volume in the drink. Most countries classify a beverage as alcoholic if it contains at least 4.5 percent alcohol, although many opt for a lower threshold. In Germany and France, for example, it is 1.2 percent alcohol by volume; in the United States, Canada, and the United Kingdom, it is 0.5 percent; Italy, which defines a beverage as alcoholic if it has as little as 0.1 percent alcohol by volume, is much more restrictive. Other countries, in contrast, allow a higher threshold. They include Hungary and Eritrea (5 percent), Belarus (6 percent), Dominican Republic (9 percent), and Nicaragua (12 percent).[14] In these cases, relatively low-alcohol beverages, such as beers, are not considered alcoholic for the purposes of sale, consumption, and regulation. Needless to say, variations like these lead to difficulties when we compare alcohol consumption rates transnationally.

Debates about and changes in the minimum drinking age focus on a very small tranche of the population. Dropping the minimum age from 21 to 19 years is essentially a statement that people aged 19 and 20 years are considered old enough to consume alcohol responsibly. It is often argued that if people are considered responsible enough to drive or vote or perform military service, they ought to be old enough to buy and drink alcohol. But although the general tendency (apart from the United States) has been to lower the minimum drinking age, there have been widespread public and policy debates about the relationship between young people and alcohol. It might be argued that this is a new phenomenon in the history of alcohol. Two issues in particular have been associated primarily with younger consumers: drinking and driving, and binge-drinking, which is often defined as the consumption of four or five standard alcoholic drinks in a single drinking session.

Automobile ownership increased rapidly everywhere after the Second World War, and by the 1970s the number of deaths and injuries on the road was causing serious concern. In England and Wales, for example, driving offenses involving alcohol (such as being unfit to drive and driving while under undue influence of alcohol) rose from 3,257 in 1953 to 9,276 in 1963 and to 65,248 in 1973.[15] The increase can be partly explained by an increase in the number of vehicles on the road and perhaps by more rigorous enforcement, but it was also the result of a more precise definition of alcoholic impairment. A 1962 law allowed the police to use blood-alcohol tests in court, and any result of 150mg of alcohol per 100ml of blood was considered evidence of impairment. (The threshold was reduced to 80mg of alcohol in 1967.) But blood tests were permitted only when there had been an accident, and the police had to continue to use other, impressionistic evidence (putting a finger to the nose or being able to walk in a straight line) in other cases. Even though more certain measures of impairment might have captured more drivers who were unfit to be behind the wheel, it seemed evident to many people that there was an epidemic of drinking and driving. This was the very sentiment that caused the federal government in the United States to coerce states to adopt 21 years as the uniform minimum drinking age in 1984.

One of the important advocacy groups to reflect and intensify concern about drinking and driving was (and is) Mothers Against Drunk Driving (MADD). Founded in California in 1980 by a woman whose daughter had been killed by an intoxicated driver, MADD was not only a major force behind the adoption of the uniform minimum drinking age in the United States but was influential in having almost all states toughen their laws regarding drinking and driving. Many American states were perceived as being too lenient with intoxicated drivers (the driver who killed the daughter of MADD's founder was sentenced to two years in jail), and some began to mandate jail sentences for first offenders. In 2000, under pressure from MADD and other organizations, the federal government stepped into alcohol policy again, this time to require states to legislate a maximum 0.08 percent blood-alcohol content for drivers. At that point, the common maximum blood-alcohol was 0.15 percent, a level at which few adults have the ability to drive an automobile competently. The new maximum was half that, and the federal government again used the threat of withdrawing highway funding to persuade states to adopt the new level: the longer states took to comply, the more of their federal highway funding they would lose.

MADD was part of a more general campaign launched in the 1980s and 1990s to stop young people, in particular, from driving after they had been drinking. Its emphasis has been on education, and it stresses personal responsibility for driving while impaired. MADD has achieved a positive reputation in the United States and Canada, where it has partnered with schools and the police in various projects. Since 2000, however, it has attracted criticism for shifting its focus from drinking and driving to drinking per se, and it has become a vocal advocate for action against underage drinking without any reference to driving.

Drinking and driving, and high rates of highway mortality led other countries to take action at this time. Most countries set the blood-alcohol concentration limit at between 0.05 and 0.08 percent, but a number (including Norway, Sweden, Russia, and Brazil) have established a zero-tolerance regime, in which very small traces of alcohol in the blood can lead to prosecution. In Brazil, the Lei Seca (Dry Law) of 2008 allows for drivers to be arrested and charged if they have a blood-alcohol concentration of 0.02 percent. Penalties include imprisonment for up to three years, a hefty fine, and suspension of the driver's license for one year. The law also forbids the sale of alcoholic drinks anywhere along the rural stretches of federal roads and highways.[16]

Concern about the frequency of driving while intoxicated led even France, which had been one of the more lenient countries regarding alcohol, to adopt more restrictive legislation in the 1990s. The Evin Law (named for the minister of health) dealt with both tobacco and alcohol, and it was passed when alcohol consumption in France was steadily falling. The law struck directly at alcohol advertising by prohibiting it on television and in cinemas, imposing rigid control over messages and images, and requiring all advertisements to include a message to the effect that alcohol abuse is dangerous to health. Alcohol advertising could not be directed at young people, and alcoholic beverage producers could not sponsor sports events. Advertising was still permitted on billboards and at events such as wine fairs, and in 2009 the law was amended to permit alcohol advertisements on French-based websites as long as they were not directed at young people.

The second major alcohol issue associated with young people, binge-drinking or heavy episodic drinking, refers to drinking significant volumes of alcohol in a short period with the primary purpose of getting drunk. Concern for binge-drinking (the term is rejected by some alcohol policy-makers) has some of the characteristics of a moral panic, an inflated assessment of some form of behavior, such as the gin-craze of early eighteenth-century England might well have been. At that time, middle- and upper-class men deplored— and undoubtedly exaggerated—the extent of public drinking by women, workers, and the poor, even though they themselves might have regularly drunk themselves into oblivion in the privacy of their homes and clubs.

Similarly, the modern focus on young people drinking at a binge level (commonly defined in the United States as five standard drinks for males and four for females in one session) usually ignores the reality that many older people regularly consume that much alcohol at an evening meal; it can almost be achieved by consuming half a bottle of wine containing 14.5 percent alcohol with dinner. In the United Kingdom, a more expansive threshold of eight standard drinks for men and six for women is widely used, while some organizations suggest that binge-drinking is involved any time an individual's blood-alcohol concentration reaches 0.08 percent, the common threshold for legally driving a vehicle. This last definition more effectively takes into account the period over which alcohol is consumed, the state of the drinker, and whether the alcohol was consumed with or without food. Some definitions refer to consuming a specified number of drinks in a single session without distinguishing between sessions that last one or two hours and those that last all night.

However it is defined, binge-drinking was presented as a problem affecting young people in several countries in the early 2000s, and there was particular attention to students, many of whom are below the legal minimum drinking age, and young people in their early twenties. An international survey of student health in 2004 found a high proportion of students aged thirteen to fifteen years in many countries had consumed alcohol at least once in the preceding thirty days. They ranged from under 10 percent of males and females in places such as Senegal and Myanmar to rates above 50 percent in Seychelles, Uruguay, Argentina, and several Caribbean countries.[17] In Europe the rates varied from 75 percent in the Czech Republic to 17 percent in Iceland. As far as binge-drinking is concerned, in a 1995 survey, 29 percent of European students aged fifteen to seventeen years reported consuming five or more alcoholic drinks during one session in the preceding thirty days. The same survey reported a rise to 41 percent in 2007 and a slight decline to 38 percent in 2011. In only one country, Sweden, did females outperform males as binge-drinkers.[18]

Responses to what has been presented as an epidemic of binge-drinking have varied. In Canada and the United States, university authorities have attempted to curb alcohol consumption, particularly at times of the academic year—such as the first week—when consumption was historically high. In the United Kingdom, the government in 2011 lowered the tax on beer having an alcohol content of 2.8 percent or lower and raised the tax on beer that had 7.5

percent alcohol or higher. The aim was to deter the use of the higher-alcohol beers that were thought to be leading to problem drinking and encourage the consumption of lower-alcohol beers, without penalizing the great majority of beer-drinkers who opted for medium-strength beer. In France, the Evin Law also addressed drinking by young people by prohibiting the advertising of alcohol in media directed toward them.

Other reforms to alcohol policies in the postwar period varied according to national or regional conditions. In New Zealand, regulations enacted during the First World War had required bars to close at 6:00 PM, Monday to Friday, and remain closed on Saturdays and Sundays. The initial purpose was to prevent absenteeism from wartime work following a night's drinking, and in the following half-century the policy was maintained for other reasons—institutional inertia, for one, and because it encouraged men to return to their homes and families rather than spend the evening drinking with their friends. On the less positive side, such early closings gave rise to what was known locally as "the six o'clock swill," as drinkers—almost all male—consumed as much beer as they could in the hour or less between the end of the workday and 6:00 PM. In effect, the policy promoted adult binge-drinking on a mass scale.

By the 1960s, however, the policy seemed outmoded and untenable. The beginning of a restaurant culture in New Zealand meant that diners could drink alcohol with meals until late at night, and private clubs were permitted serve alcohol beyond 6:00 PM. The increasing number of foreign tourists found the 6:00 PM bar closing time irritating and inconvenient. In a 1967 referendum, two-thirds of voters supported extending drinking hours to 10:00 PM, the first of a series of extensions of drinking hours.

More serious alcohol issues arose in the Soviet Union in the last decades of the twentieth century. High per capita alcohol consumption began to play havoc with public health and the economy, and by the 1980s it was a major contributor to the collapse of the Soviet economic and political system.[19] This was no new phenomenon, as we have seen: heavy drinking had been characteristic of Russia/the Soviet Union for centuries. Of course, there were great regional and ethnic variations in such a sprawling, multinational empire. Muslim regions had a much lower level of consumption, as did the Jewish population, while Latvians, whose main drink was vodka, easily outpaced the wine-drinking Georgians in total alcohol consumption. Considered as a whole, however, Soviet citizens had one of the highest alcohol consumption rates in the world, and even more important, it rose more quickly than any other country's from the 1950s to the 1980s. The best estimate of consumption of alcohol (per person over the age of fourteen) from legal and illicit sources suggests that from 7.3 liters of pure alcohol in 1955, consumption rose to 10.2 liters in 1965, 14.6 liters in 1975, and 15.2 liters in 1979.[20]

Every Soviet leader after Stalin's death in 1953 made lukewarm attempts to rein in consumption. In 1958 Nikita Khrushchev called for a campaign against alcoholism, began a program of alcohol education, and limited the sale of alcohol in shops and restaurants. In 1960 the criminal code was amended to provide for compulsory therapy for anyone convicted more than once of being drunk. Under Leonid Brezhnev (Soviet premier from 1964 to 1982 and whose alcohol consumption was notorious), the government intensified penalties for public drunkenness (under the rubric of "hooliganism") and established a chain of rehabilitation camps where convicted persistent drinkers could be sent for therapy that included forced labor. In 1972 the government ordered the reduction of vodka output and the phasing out of stronger vodkas altogether, with an increase in the production of wine, beer, and nonalcoholic drinks to compensate.

The two short-lived governments (1982 to 1985) that followed Brezhnev— one of these premiers, Konstantin Chernenko, probably died of cirrhosis of the liver brought on by chronic heavy drinking—saw the beginnings of a more radical approach to the social problems of high alcohol use. It began as an open discussion of the state of Soviet society and recognition that it had still not, sixty years after the Revolution, sloughed off problems such as gender inequality and alcoholism, issues that Marxists had long associated with capitalist society. A campaign to reduce alcohol abuse included attempts to reduce absenteeism, and a more systematic antialcoholism movement began to emerge. It was none too soon; by the 1980s, alcohol was a major contributor to widespread health problems and to weaknesses in the Soviet economy. Mortality rates actually rose in the Soviet Union, the first time such a thing had happened outside the context of a major catastrophe such as famine or war. The death rates for men over forty increased by 20 to 25 percent between 1965 and 1989, and death rates for women over fifty also rose, though more modestly. Alcohol was not the sole cause of these changes—smoking and poor health services were also implicated—but it is considered to have been a major contributor.

When the Soviet Union's last premier, Mikhail Gorbachev, assumed power in 1985, he inherited an antialcohol campaign that showed some signs of early success—small reductions in consumption and in alcohol-related crime—and he made it one of the priorities of his administration. Fending off occasional radical proposals for total prohibition, Gorbachev supported a complex of policies that both encouraged and coerced. On the educational side, various bodies, such as the Academy of Sciences and the Academy of Pedagogy, were given the task of mounting a campaign to demonstrate the harm that drinking did to health, social order, morality, and the economy. Efforts were made to improve leisure and sports facilities so that young people, in particular, would have more alternatives to drinking. Newspapers, radio, and television were instructed to intensify their antialcohol messages, and filmmakers were forbidden to portray heavy drinking in a positive light.[21]

On the coercive side of the new campaign, new regulations restricted the hours that alcohol could be sold (only after 2:00 PM on workdays), the amount that one person could buy, and the places it could be consumed. Drinking in public was subject to fines, as was drinking in the workplace. Anyone so drunk that they had to be detained overnight was to be charged for the cost of accommodations. A national temperance movement was revived, and by the middle of 1986 it claimed to have 11 million members in 350,000 branches throughout the Soviet Union. The Communist Party set an example by banning alcohol at public functions, including state and diplomatic events, and adopting much sterner measures (including dismissal) against party members and officials who abused alcohol or tolerated abuse. Thousands were expelled from the party as the campaign gathered momentum.[22] Reducing the availability of alcohol was fundamental to this broad-based campaign. A first step, in mid-1985, was a price increase for vodka and other liquors, but not beer or wine, which had a lower alcohol content. Further increases took effect a year later. State production of vodka was cut to 14.2 million liters by 1988, from 23.8 million liters in 1985, and wine production was almost halved.[23]

By the end of 1986 the Soviet government reported impressive results: the consumption of vodka and wine had fallen by a third, as had employee absenteeism, while crime was down by a quarter. But reports throughout the country were mixed. From some regions came descriptions of continued extensive consumption in the face of failed attempts to curb drinking; from other regions came barely credible reports of amazing successes, such as entire bodies of miners who had given up alcohol completely. In such areas, output was said to have improved, and productivity quotas were exceeded. On the demographic front, there were real improvements in the late 1980s. Mortality rates reversed the steady rise they had seen since the 1970s, and deaths resulting from workplace accidents declined. The incidence of fatal heart disease fell, and deaths from alcohol poisoning and from more general alcohol-related causes were halved. The birthrate rose, and there were marked improvements in the health of infants and the proportion that survived the first year of life.[24]

Yet the clandestine production of illicit alcohol undermined the campaign against alcohol. In times when alcohol was freely available, it was estimated that samogon, the illicit liquor widely produced in rural areas, accounted for about a third of the total amount of alcohol consumed in the Soviet Union. By 1988 some estimates set its production at up to 50 percent of the (reduced) state output. As the availability of legal alcohol contracted, illicit production spread to regions (such as Latvia) where it had been virtually unknown and to the cities. This vast underground industry depended on supplies of sugar that was produced in massive quantities in the Soviet Union from beets. It is estimated that by 1987, a tenth of the country's sugar output was being used to make samogon. Desperate citizens who could not obtain illicit liquor turned to commodities that contained alcohol—cologne, hair tonic, and window-washing fluid among them—often with serious or even fatal consequences.

The reports that flowed in to the government must have detailed both real achievements and significant failures. Perhaps they seemed to offset each other, because by 1988 the campaign was judged to have produced "a healthier moral atmosphere in society" while failing to achieve "radical changes." But rather than press forward, the government scaled the campaign back. There was a sense that public support was sagging, and the reduction of alcohol production more than had been envisaged at first had led to increased demand and widespread illicit production. There was, too, the fact that the state had forfeited an estimated 2 billion rubles in revenues from lost alcohol taxes. The campaign would continue but would be rebalanced to stress education and encouragement rather than coercion. Critics likened the repressive measures to the forced collectivization programs of the 1930s and referred to the police crackdown on samogon as a war against the people. Beyond the objections in principle was recognition that the Russian state was, once again, waging a losing battle against alcohol.

The first adjustment to the campaign permitted wine, beer, and brandy to be sold in food stores again, and soon afterward the production of liquor and wines was allowed to rise. Production of vodka and other spirits increased by 50 percent from 1988 to 1990, but although consumption rose, it did not reach its pre-campaign levels. In 1985 Russians had drunk 8.8 liters of alcohol per capita. That had fallen to 3.9 liters in 1987, but it rose to only 5.6 liters in 1990, after restrictions were eased.[25] The health and other gains that had been reported when the full campaign was in place were quickly reversed. The mortality rate rose, the fertility rate fell, and by 1991 the Soviet population was actually in decline.

With the collapse of the Soviet Union in 1991, a freer market in alcohol was introduced to the Russian Federation. The state's monopoly on production ended, and in 1992, home-brewing was decriminalized. Imported alcohol began to appear more regularly, and before long, imported vodka made up as much as 60 percent of the Russian market. Under these conditions, alcohol production and consumption began to rise. From 7 liters of legal pure alcohol in 1991, consumption hit 11 liters in 1995 and hovered above 10 liters through 2006. To the legal alcohol must be added illicit drink, which is calculated to be a third to a half of the legal volume. This would give adult Russians an average consumption of about 16 liters of pure alcohol in the early 2000s, compared with a European average of 12 liters.[26] Another way to put it is that the average Russian citizen consumed a bottle of vodka every two days.[27] But when the abstention rate of 40 percent is taken into account, the average Russian drinker consumed almost a bottle of vodka each day. It was little wonder that alcohol-related crime and marriage breakdown bounced back to earlier rates and traffic accidents attributed to intoxication increased dramatically.

Under the leadership of Vladimir Putin (2000 to 2008 and from 2012), a new campaign against alcohol was undertaken. There was some discussion of banning the production and sale of alcohol; but in the meantime, taxes on it were increased, and alcohol duties almost quadrupled between 2012 and 2014. Showing that he had learned from previous unsuccessful campaigns to reduce alcohol consumption, Putin argued that increasing taxes gradually, rather than radically, would be less likely to produce a growth in illicit alcohol production.[28] In 2012 all alcohol advertising on the Russian internet was forbidden, and as of 2013, newspapers were no longer permitted to carry alcohol advertisements.

The government faced opposition to its campaign from a variety of sources, including small and large retailers. In 2013, sidewalk and roadside kiosks were prohibited from selling beer, which had accounted for about 40 percent of their revenue. In theory, this benefited larger stores, but their sales of alcohol (which accounted for up to a fifth of their total revenues) were also hit because the same law raised the minimum price of a half-liter of vodka by 36 percent and reclassified beer from a food to an alcoholic beverage.[29] This meant that beer could not be sold in any store between 11:00 PM and 8:00 AM.

Such reforms are the latest episodes in the long-running saga of Russian alcohol policies, but it is clear that the Russian authorities are not alone in their concerns about patterns and levels of alcohol consumption. Concern for alcohol-related behavior—whether it is drinking and driving, youth drinking, or the effects of alcohol on economic productivity—crosses national and ideological frontiers. What James Nicholls says of England—that although the "drink question" receded after the 1940s, "by the start of the twenty-first century, drink was back on the political agenda with a vengeance"—is true in a broader geographical sense.[30]

At the same time, arguments for the health benefits of moderate alcohol consumption made a comeback. Alcohol was treated far more suspiciously by the medical profession in the twentieth century than at any time before, and in general it was considered to be more problematic than beneficial for personal health. Far from the days when specific wines and spirits were prescribed for specific maladies, alcohol was recommended, if at all, as a pleasure that might—in carefully measured moderation—ease the stresses of daily life. But doctors were increasingly likely to recommend to their patients that they not drink alcohol.

A major event that transformed medical (and social) attitudes toward alcohol was the discovery of "the French paradox" and its description on American television in 1991. The paradox was that although the diet and lifestyle of French people ought to predispose them to heart disease, French rates of cardiovascular disease were only a third of American levels. The French smoked more than Americans, were physically less active, and ate a diet as rich in fats, from cheese, fried foods, and other products. They also drank more alcohol, but the big difference was the proportion of their alcohol intake that was made up of wine, and specifically red wine. Leading French medical scientists argued that resveratrol, a phenol found in the skin of black grapes and present in varying concentrations in red wine, was the reason for the low incidence of heart disease among populations with higher consumption rates of red wine.

The airing of these findings in the United States in 1991 on the popular television show *Sixty Minutes* produced an increase in sales of red wine: they rose by 40 percent in the United States in the following year. The effect spread to other countries, and many people began to drink red wine on a regular basis as a preventative health measure. For those who did not want to drink alcohol, there was a tablet made from powdered wine that was purported to provide the same benefits as two glasses of red wine.[31]

Because the French paradox ran so counter to trends in medical thinking about alcohol, it proved highly controversial. It was argued that the statistics of heart disease in France were grossly understated and that there really was no paradox: the French had a shorter tradition of eating fried foods, and once the effects were embedded in the populations, their rates of heart disease would rise; it was also impossible to isolate one element, in this case resveratrol, to explain a complex phenomenon. In the United States, the Bureau of Alcohol, Tobacco, and Firearms, the federal agency that regulated alcohol nationally, challenged Serge Renaud, a leading French scientist who had appeared on the television program that aired the French paradox for the first time, to prove his claims for red wine. In 1994 Renaud published research in the *Lancet*, the prestigious British medical journal, showing that 20 to 30 grams (two or three glasses) of wine a day could reduce the risk of dying from a heart attack by about 40 percent. He argued that the wine acts on platelets in the blood and helps prevent clotting. Renaud's later research on a large sample of middle-aged men in France not only reinforced the French paradox but suggested that moderate consumption of red wine also protects against most cancers.

Current medical opinion suggests that drinking moderate amounts of wine on a regular basis does protect many people against heart disease and some cancers. All other variables being constant, moderate alcohol consumption is a healthier option than abstaining from alcohol. Higher than moderate levels of consumption, however, not only neutralize these benefits but actually predispose individuals toward other medical problems. In this light, alcohol—particularly wine—has been restored to the position it had occupied before the nineteenth century, when physicians prescribed it for specific purposes as well as for its perceived benefits as a general tonic.

In many respects, alcohol in the modern world resonates with the issues we can track over the past centuries and millennia. There are the familiar concerns about consumption, expressed more sharply in some places than others, but present almost everywhere. Today the dangers of alcohol are described in much more precise and sometimes different terms: the risks of liver and heart disease are spelled out graphically, as are the dangers of drinking and driving. There is far less worry about women drinking and losing their moral bearings and more stress on men using alcohol as a means of exploiting women sexually. There is far more concern, generally, about alcohol consumption by young people. On the positive side, and after a hiatus of almost a century, alcohol is back in the pharmacy. The French paradox opened a Pandora's box, and soon it was not only red wine that was beneficial but alcohol in general, as long as it was consumed in moderation. Any discourse about abuse or excess implies a level of alcohol consumption that is acceptable. The search for moderation has informed almost all policies that did not ban alcohol altogether, and the search for a definition of "moderation" and the means to persuade people to drink moderately at most lie at the heart of the history of alcohol.

Conclusion

In a survey of alcohol cultures—which embody the ways alcohol is perceived, valued, and consumed—in many regions over hundreds and thousands of years, the one constant that appears to be present, regardless of time and place, is that alcohol was a highly contested commodity. On one hand, it was represented as good—as a beverage sometimes given by a god and often associated positively with religion, and as a beverage that had the potential to be healthy and therapeutic and support sociability and community at all levels. On the other hand, alcohol had the potential to cause individual and social calamities expressed through immorality, impiety, social disruption, poor physical and mental health, and crime.

How these various potentials were realized depended on how alcohol was consumed, and perhaps the most important dimension of the history of alcohol lies in the persistent attempts of authorities to define the point at which moderate and therefore safe drinking crossed over to the excessive and dangerous. In many cases, the point was defined only after the fact, when a drinker had passed it and become intoxicated. Excessive drinking was manifested in speech, physical coordination, and behaviors that were associated with intoxication. At other times, specific maximum volumes have been defined, as public health authorities in many countries now offer guidelines on maximum amounts of alcohol per day. In some cases, authorities have implemented prohibition policies that were universal, as in the case of Muslims and Mormons, or targeted at particular populations, such as indigenous peoples in colonized societies.

These various policies were based on prevailing assessments of the potentials of alcohol for good and bad. Prohibition policies were and are based on the assumption that the dangers presented by those who misuse alcohol outweigh any rights that other consumers might feel they have to be able to consume alcohol. Less rigorous regulatory policies seek to allow people to consume alcohol and derive personal or social benefits from it while trying to mitigate its dangers by restricting access to alcohol by age, gender, or ethnicity and by limiting the occasions on which it may be purchased or consumed.

The general anxieties about alcohol that we have seen expressed in contexts as diverse as ancient Mesopotamia and the British colonies in Africa, or in modern France and nineteenth-century America, were fundamentally broad-based anxieties about social order: if consuming alcohol could lead individuals to lose control of their speech and bodies, then the mass consumption of alcohol could result in loss of discipline in the social body more broadly. These anxieties appear in almost all cultures, but we should be attuned to the variations that exist within persistent themes.

One common anxiety is evident in male attitudes toward women's drinking. Historically, men have been anxious about women's drinking, generally because they believed that women were sexually less restrained or inhibited under the influence of alcohol. This is a reasonable enough assumption, as one of the effects of alcohol is to lower inhibitions of all kinds. But even though women's bodies absorb and metabolize alcohol at a different rate from men's, alcohol does not discriminate between genders in its effects. All things being equal, women are no more given than men to risky behavior, sexual or otherwise, under the influence of alcohol. (It could be argued that cultural influences more often militated against women taking as many sexual risks as men.) Opposition by drinking men to women's drinking is, at base, an expression of the double standard of sexual morality.

Yet although it appears to be a historical constant, male anxiety about the consumption of alcohol by women took different forms at different times. In ancient Rome, the stress was on the consumption of wine by married women, quite likely because of fear than an intoxicated wife would commit adultery and conceive a child that her husband might unknowingly raise as his own. It is notable that the penalties for drinking by a woman—at some times death, at other times divorce—were the same as those imposed on women who committed adultery. In early eighteenth-century England, in contrast, the panic about gin consumption focused on women as mothers rather than as wives. As we have seen, gin was known as Mother Gin and Mother's Folly, and Hogarth's famous print *Gin Lane* depicted a nursing mother as its focal image. Can it be a coincidence that fertility and population growth were among the great concerns of the eighteenth century and that a number of contemporary pamphlets emphasized the harmful effects of gin on children and the birthrate?

A somewhat different emphasis can be located in the anxiety over drinking by young women during and immediately after the First World War. It was widely noted that during the war, women benefiting from new work opportunities and increased incomes began to frequent public houses. This behavior, which until that time was largely associated with men, coincided with changes in women's clothing and hairstyles that were considered masculine. At the end of the war, there were various attempts to refeminize women, not least by firing them from many of the industrial jobs they had performed so as to make room for demobilized soldiers. Anxiety about women's drinking in this period reflected a need to reestablish the gender boundaries that were thought to have been eroded by wartime conditions.

In these and other cases, the fundamental objection was to the consumption of alcohol by women. But the precise formulation of the objection in each period reflected broader cultural anxieties about some aspect of the gendered order that was perceived as threatened by alcohol consumption by women. Although the evidence is patchy and often poor for much of the period covered by this book, it seems that where women were permitted to consume alcohol, they generally consumed less than their male counterparts, no matter which period, region, or class we look at. That is certainly true today, when many more women than men describe themselves as abstainers: 40 percent of women vs. 30 percent of men in the United States; 25 percent vs. 10 percent in Italy; and 45 percent vs. 13 percent in China.[1] Abstention was even more true of children in the past, although we must be aware that definitions of childhood have changed over time. When young people started apprenticeships and full-time work in their early teens in early modern Europe, they might well have started drinking alcohol.

Thus generalizations about historical trends in alcohol consumption are hazardous. But that said, a close reading of materials from many regions and periods might lead us to the conclusion that some important regions of the world have entered what might be thought of as a "post-alcohol" era, in the sense that alcohol consumption has reached historic lows.

For hundreds of years, alcoholic beverages have been part of the daily diet for substantial proportions of the adult populations of Europe, Asia, and the Americas, as well as in Australia, New Zealand, and South Africa. In Europe and North America, as we have seen, regular access to clean drinking water was a challenge that was not addressed until major public water projects were completed in the nineteenth century. Until then, beer and wine were accepted as safer alternatives to the water that was available, and distilled spirits could be added to water to kill some of the bacteria that rendered it harmful to human health. To this extent, alcohol and water have histories that flow together in significant ways.

But although historians have insisted on the importance of alcoholic beverages as safer alternatives to polluted water, we have to recognize that cultural and material considerations seem often to have overridden the imperatives of health. In most of the cultures in most of the periods we are able to study, there was no question that adult men should have access to moderate volumes of alcohol on a regular basis, but as we have seen, there were often acute anxieties about women's drinking and opposition to the consumption of alcohol by children. This raises the question of the priorities in play. It was widely recognized that alcoholic beverages were safer than the water that was available; we should recall the trepidation with which the Puritans faced the prospect of drinking water in America when their supplies of beer and water began to run out. But the males who formulated alcohol policy seemed quite at ease recommending that women and children (boys up to their teens, at any rate) should abstain from alcohol and, by implication, risk sickness and even death.

Alcohol was thought unsuitable for children because, according to the theory that dominated Western medical thinking through the eighteenth century, its warming qualities would act adversely on their already warm bodies. But as we have seen, the argument most commonly advanced against adult women drinking was that alcohol caused them to lose their sexual inhibitions. Men might also become sexually indiscriminate after drinking, but for the most part, they did not consider that nearly as problematic, if problematic at all. It seems that there was a moral calculation that it was better to put women at risk of the illnesses and worse that were believed to ensue from water-drinking than to put them (or their husbands) at moral risk of committing a sexual transgression. From the point of view of a married man, it was preferable to be a widower than a cuckold.

Although women and children were often forbidden to drink alcohol or were rigorously limited in the volumes they could consume, substantial sections of historic populations must have abstained from alcohol because they had no choice. All alcohol—even the poorest quality, such as the watery, sour wine consumed by workers and soldiers in ancient Rome and the adulterated gin fabricated in England in the early 1700s—cost money, whereas water, whether from a public well or a natural source such as a river or lake, was free. Except on rare occasions when wine or beer might have been dispensed gratis at a celebration, the poor did not have access to alcoholic beverages on a regular basis. The absence of alcohol from the diets of the poor and the recourse to low-quality water that followed from it must be added to the generally deficient diets and conditions of life that contributed to their low life expectancy.

These are massive qualifications to the common historical generalization that populations in the past drank alcoholic beverages because they were safer than water. Many of these populations, like those in Europe from the Middle Ages to the nineteenth century, were weighted toward the young, unlike many modern populations where older generations predominate. If we subtract females and poor males from these populations, we are left with only a minority who could drink alcohol on a regular and substantial basis. While it might be true that beer and wine were healthier and safer than existing water supplies, prevailing cultural and financial conditions made it likely that only a minority of the population could avail themselves of the safer options. The notion that alcohol was the common alternative to poor-quality water begins to look very shaky.

Although this scenario reflects what we know of likely practices, we have few reliable statistics on the patterns of consumption to support it. For the most part, we have estimates of per capita consumption in some town for certain years or among specific groups (including nuns, printers, and lawyers) at particular times. Such estimates of historic per capita consumption are almost always based on two statistics that are approximate at best: population numbers, which tend to be unreliable before the mid-nineteenth century, and estimates of alcohol production or distribution, which are also often unreliable and which never account for alcohol that was produced, distributed, or consumed clandestinely or in some manner that escaped the official record. Beyond those weaknesses, figures of per capita consumption conceal what must have been vast variations in consumption by gender, class, age, or region. In cultures where alcohol consumption by women was forbidden or strongly discouraged and where practice might well have followed prescription, it makes more sense to calculate male-only per capita consumption.

In short, there are large gaps in our knowledge of historic patterns of alcohol consumption, and if we are to draw any conclusions about long-term trends, we must speculate to a lesser or greater degree. Doing so suggests that some important regions of the world have entered a post-alcohol era. During the early modern period, from about 1500 to 1800, alcohol consumption in Europe and North America seems to have been robust. We cannot estimate general levels of consumption with any confidence, and we should be wary of taking at face value the many contemporary commentaries that deplored heavy drinking. But the weight of the evidence suggests that alcohol was widely consumed by men and by women (although in greater volumes by men), and that it was consumed throughout the day.

Everything changed in the mid-nineteenth century, when municipal authorities began to provide the inhabitants of cities with reliable supplies of potable water. This was a hinge in the long-term history of alcohol. It initiated a transformation in the cultural meaning of alcohol by removing any need to drink alcohol as an alternative to water. The transformation was buttressed by the increased consumption of other nonalcoholic beverages (such as tea and coffee) by the masses and by the erosion (but not the disappearance) of the positive religious and medicinal associations that alcohol had carried for thousands of years. Alcohol became a discretionary beverage, not one that any person with access to fresh water needed to drink.

But because alcohol consumption was embedded in diets and in cultures—from downing a beer or glass of spirits at the pub or tavern on the way home from work to sipping and toasting with wine at occasions as diverse as weddings and state banquets—alcohol did not disappear, even when it was legislated off the table by prohibition policies. Beyond their value for hydration, alcoholic beverages were popular simply because they were alcoholic, a point we often forget when we talk about the various reasons why consumers historically drank alcohol. Alcohol imparts a pleasant feeling, and it helps many people socialize, unwind, and lose their inhibitions—effects of alcohol that historically have been highly valued and often sought.

Even so, and despite the fact that our knowledge of historic consumption rates is shaky, it seems that alcohol consumption today is lower than ever in many economically developed countries and that it might drop further. There has certainly been a decline in alcohol consumption in a number of Western countries since the early twentieth century, a period when statistical evidence is far more reliable. Despite concerns about youth drinking, the highest alcohol consumption rates in these countries today are generally in the older age groups. That could be a function of financial resources, but it is possible that younger generations have adopted means other than alcohol to achieve the states that alcohol provides. Drugs of many kinds, especially marijuana, are widely popular, and young people also commonly consume beverages fortified with caffeine (sometimes both caffeine and alcohol). Young people also tend to be more respectful of laws regarding drinking and driving than earlier generations were. The overall result is that, unless younger generations start drinking substantially more alcohol as they get older, per capita consumption can be expected to decline even more once the higher-consuming generations die off.

These patterns are most evident in some of the most economically developed societies, but there are societies where there is no evidence of a decline in alcohol consumption. From the global perspective, alcohol is not on the verge of extinction, but its importance as a social issue in many societies might well diminish significantly in the decades to come.

Notes

CHAPTER ONE

1. Robert Dudley, "Evolutionary Origins of Human Alcoholism in Primate Frugivory," *Quarterly Review of Biology* 75, no. 1 (March 2000): 3–15.

2. Ibid., 4.

3. Quoted in John T. Krumpelmann, "Sealsfield's Inebriated Robins," *Monatschefte* 46, no. 4 (1954): 225.

4. Steve Morris, David Humphreys, and Dan Reynolds, "Myth, Marula and Elephant: An Assessment of Voluntary Ethanol Intoxication of the African Elephant (Loxodonta Africana) following Feeding on the Fruit of the Marula Tree (Sclerocarya Birrea)," *Physiological and Biochemical Zoology* 78 (2006), http://www.jstor.org/stable/10.1086/499983 (accessed April 26, 2012).

5. Genesis 9:20.

6. William Younger, *Gods, Men and Wine* (London: Michael Joseph, 1966), 27.

7. Mu-Chou Poo, "The Use and Abuse of Wine in Ancient China," *Journal of the Economic and Social History of the Orient* 42 (1999): 123–24.

8. Carrie Lock, "Original Microbrews: From Egypt to Peru, Archaeologists Are Unearthing Breweries from Long Ago," *Science News* 166 (October 2004): 216–18.

9. F. R. Allchin, "India: The Ancient Home of Distillation?," *Man* 14 (1979): 55–63.

10. Patrick E. McGovern, *Uncorking the Past: The Quest for Wine, Beer and Other Alcoholic Beverages* (Berkeley: University of California Press, 2009), 38–39.

11. Patrick E. McGovern et al., "Chemical Identification and Cultural Implications of a Mixed Fermented Beverage from Late Prehistoric China," *Asian Perspectives* 44 (2005): 251.

12. Patrick E. McGovern et al., "Fermented Beverages of Pre- and Proto-Historic China," *Proceedings of the National Academy of Sciences* 101, no. 51 (December 21, 2004): 17597.

13. Poo, "Use and Abuse of Wine in Ancient China," 127.

14. Patrick E. McGovern, *Ancient Wine: The Search for the Origins of Viticulture* (Princeton: Princeton University Press, 2003), 65–68.

15. http://news.nationalgeographic.com/news/2011/01/110111-oldest-wine-press-making-winery-armenia-science-ucla/ (accessed May 5, 2012).

16. Max Nelson, *The Barbarian's Beverage: A History of Beer in Ancient Europe* (London: Routledge, 2005), 12–13.

17. McGovern, *Uncorking the Past*.

18. Rod Phillips, *A Short History of Wine* (London: Penguin, 2000), 18.

19. Ibid., 22.

20. Tim Unwin, *Wine and the Vine: An Historical Geography of Viticulture and the Wine Trade* (London: Routledge, 1996), 64–66.

21. Nelson, *Barbarian's Beverage*, 21–24.

22. Unwin, *Wine and the Vine*, 71–73.

23. Jean Bottéro, "Le Vin dans une Civilisation de la Bière: la Mésopotamie," in *In Vino Veritas*, ed. Oswyn Murray and Manuela Tecuşan (London: British School at Rome, 1995), 30.

24. M. Civil, "A Hymn to the Beer Goddess and a Drinking Song," in *Studies Presented to Leo Oppenheim* (Chicago: Oriental Institute of the University of Chicago, 1964), 67–89.

25. Phillips, *Short History of Wine*, 26.

26. Quoted in Michael M. Homan, "Beer and Its Drinkers: An Ancient Near Eastern Love Story," *Near Eastern Archaeology* 67 (2004): 85.

27. Patrick M. McGovern, "The Funerary Banquet of 'King Midas,'" *Expedition* 42 (2000): 21–29.

28. Justin Jennings, Kathleen L. Antrobus, Sam J. Antencio, Erin Glavich, Rebecca Johnson, German Loffler, and Christine Luu, "'Drinking Beer in a Blissful Mood': Alcohol Production, Operational Chains, and Feasting in the Ancient World," *Current Anthropology* 46 (2005): 275.

29. Rachel Fulton, "'Taste and see that the Lord is sweet' (Ps. 33:9): The Flavor of God in the Monastic West," *Journal of Religion* 86 (2006): 169–204.

30. Patrick E. McGovern, Armen Mirzoian, and Gretchen R. Hall, "Ancient Egyptian Herbal Wines," *Proceedings of the National Academy of Sciences of the United States of America*, 2009, www.pnas.org/cgi/doi/10.1073/pnas.0811578106 (accessed February 12, 2011).

31. Phillips, *Short History of Wine*, 25.

32. Poo, "Use and Abuse of Wine in Ancient China," 139.

33. Ibid., 139–40.

34. Ibid., 131.

35. Mu-Chou Poo, *Wine and Wine-Offering in the Religion of Ancient Egypt* (London: Kegan Paul International, 1995), 32.

36. Leonard H. Lesko, "Egyptian Wine Production during the New Kingdom," in *Origins and Ancient History of Wine*, ed. Patrick McGovern et al. (London: Routledge, 1996), 217.

CHAPTER TWO

1. Max Nelson, *The Barbarian's Beverage: A History of Beer in Ancient Europe* (London: Routledge, 2005), 13–15.

2. Christian Vandermersch, *Vins et Amphores de Grande Grèce et de Sicile IVe–IIIe Siècles avant J.-C.* (Naples: Centre Jean Bérard, 1994), 37.

3. Patrick E. McGovern et al., "Beginning of Viticulture in France," *Proceedings of the National Academy of Sciences* 110 (2013): 10147–52.

4. Trevor Hodge, *Ancient Greek France* (Philadelphia: University of Pennsylvania Press, 1999), 214–15.

5. Nelson, *Barbarian's Beverage*, 38–39.

6. Quoted in Christopher Hook, Helen Tarbet, and David Ball, "Classically Intoxicated," *British Medical Journal* 335 (December 22–29, 2007): 1303.

7. Ibid.

8. Hugh Johnson, *The Story of Wine* (London: Mitchell Beazley, 1989), 44.

9. Nelson, *Barbarian's Beverage*, 16.

10. Quoted in ibid., 17.

11. Ibid., 33–34.

12. Ibid., 35.

13. Ibid., 42–44.

14. Alison Burford, *Land and Labour in the Greek World* (Baltimore: Johns Hopkins University Press, 1993), 214.

15. Arthur P. McKinlay, "'The Classical World' and 'Non-Classical Peoples,'" in *Drinking and Intoxication: Selected Readings in Social Attitudes and Control*, ed. Raymond McCarthy (Glencoe, Ill.: Free Press, 1959), 51.

16. Nicolas Purcell, "The Way We Used to Eat: Diet, Community, and History at Rome," *American Journal of Philology* 124 (2003): 336–37.

17. Keith Nurse, "The Last of the (Roman) Summer Wine," *History Today* 44 (1993): 4–5.

18. McGovern et al., "Beginning of Viticulture in France," 10147.

19. Thomas Braun, "Emmer Cakes and Emmer Bread," in *Food in Antiquity*, ed. John Wilkins, David Harvey, and Mike Dobson (Exeter: University of Exeter Press, 1995), 34–37.

20. Peter Jones and Keith Sidwell, eds., *The World of Rome: An Introduction to Roman Culture* (Cambridge: Cambridge University Press, 1997), 182.

21. Nicholas F. Hudson, "Changing Places: The Archaeology of the Roman *Convivium*," *American Journal of Archaeology* 114 (2010): 664–65.

22. McKinlay, "'Classical World' and 'Non-Classical Peoples,'" 59.

23. Quoted in Stuart J. Fleming, *Vinum: The Story of Roman Wine* (Glen Mills, Pa.: Art Flair, 2001), 71.

24. Johnson, *Story of Wine*, 64.

25. Rod Phillips, *A Short History of Wine* (London: Penguin, 2000), 57.

26. Marie-Claire Amouretti, "Vin, Vinaigre, Piquette dans l'Antiquité," in *Le Vin des Historiens*, ed. Gilbert Garrier (Suze-la-Rousse: Université du Vin, 1990), 75–87.

27. N. Purcell, "Wine and Wealth in Ancient Italy," *Journal of Roman Studies* 75 (1985): 13.

28. André Tchernia, *Vin de l'Italie Romaine: Essaie d'Histoire Économique d'après les Amphores* (Rome: Ecole Française de Rome, 1986), 16.

29. Quoted in Nelson, *Barbarian's Beverage*, 69.

30. Ibid.

31. Ibid., 70–71.

32. Dan Stanislawski, "Dionysus Westward: Early Religion and the Economic Geography of Wine," *Geographical Review* 65 (1975): 432–34.

33. Simon Hornblower and Anthony Spaworth, eds., *Oxford Classical Dictionary* (Oxford: Oxford University Press, 1996), 229.

34. *Apicius: Cookery and Dining in Imperial Rome*, ed. and trans. Joseph Dommers Vehling (New York: Dover, 1977), 45–47.

35. Marcius Porcius Cato, *On Agriculture* (London: Heineman, 1934), 105.

36. Ulpian, *Digest*, XXXIII:6, 11. Quoted in Phillips, *Short History of Wine*, 51.

37. Tchernia, *Vin de l'Italie Romaine*, 36.

38. Yvon Garlan, *Vin et Amphores de Thasos* (Athens: Ecole Française d'Athènes, 1988), 5.

39. T. J. Santon, "Columnella's Attitude towards Wine Production," *Journal of Wine Research* 7 (1996): 55–59.

40. Tchernia, *Vin de l'Italie Romaine*, 36.

41. Pliny the Elder, *Histoire Naturelle* (Paris: Société d'Edition "Les Belles Lettres," 1958), bk. 4, 20–76.

42. *Hippocrates* (London: Heinemann, 1967), 325–29.

43. Hornblower and Spaworth, *Oxford Classical Dictionary*, 56.

44. Louis E. Grivetti and Elizabeth A. Applegate, "From Olympia to Atlanta: A Cultural-Historical Perspective on Diet and Athletic Training," *Journal of Nutrition* 127 (1997): 863–64.

45. Nelson, *Barbarian's Beverage*, 71–73.

CHAPTER THREE

1. Max Nelson, *The Barbarian's Beverage: A History of Beer in Ancient Europe* (London: Routledge, 2005), 75.

2. Genesis 14:18.

3. Ecclesiastes 9:7.

4. 1 Timothy 5:23.

5. Luke 10:34.

6. Luke 1:15.

7. Proverbs 23:20.

8. 1 Timothy 3:8.

9. Genesis 9:20–27.

10. Devora Steinmetz, "Vineyard, Farm, and Garden: The Drunkenness of Noah in the Context of Primeval History," *Journal of Biblical Literature* 113 (1994): 194–95.

11. Midrash Agadah on Genesis 9:21.

12. Genesis 19:32–35.

13. Deuteronomy 14:26.

14. Leviticus 23:13.

15. Psalms 104:15.

16. Isaiah 24:7, 11.

17. Jeremiah 8:13.

18. Michael D. Horman, "Did the Ancient Israelites Drink Beer?," *Biblical Archaeological Review*, September–October 2010, 23.

19. Proverbs 31:6–7.

20. Randall Heskett and Joel Butler, *Divine Vintage: Following the Wine Trail from Genesis to the Modern Age* (New York: Palgrave, 2012), 88–97.

21. Saint Augustine, *On Christian Doctrine*, bk. 4, chap. 21.

22. The mosaic is reproduced in Hugh Johnson, *The Story of Wine* (London: Mitchell Beazley, 1989), 58.

23. John 2:1–11.

24. Nelson, *Barbarian's Beverage*, 75–76.

25. Ibid., 79.

26. Ibid., 87.

27. Ibid., 89.

28. Edward Gibbon, *The History of the Decline and Fall of the Roman Empire*, ed. David Womersley (London: Penguin, 1994), 238.

29. Tim Unwin, "Continuity in Early Medieval Viticulture: Secular or Ecclesiastical Influences?," in *Viticulture in Geographical Perspective*, ed. Harm de Blij (Miami: Miami Geographical Society, 1992), 37.

30. Ann Hagen, *A Handbook of Anglo-Saxon Food* (Pinner, U.K.: Anglo-Saxon Books, 1992), 94.

31. Kathy L. Pearson, "Nutrition and the Early-Medieval Diet," *Speculum* 72 (1997): 15.

32. Richard W. Unger, *Beer in the Middle Ages and the Renaissance* (Philadelphia: University of Pennsylvania Press, 2004), 26. See pp. 15–36 generally on the early Middle Ages.

33. Nelson, *Barbarian's Beverage*, 104.

34. Eigil, *Life of Sturm*, www.Fordham.edu/halsall/basis/sturm.html (accessed June 13, 2012).

35. Marcel Lachiver, *Vins, Vignes et Vignerons: Histoire du Vignoble Français* (Paris: Fayard, 1988), 46.

36. Desmond Seward, *Monks and Wine* (New York: Crown Books, 1979), 25–35.

37. Lachiver, *Vins, Vignes et Vignerons*, 45–46.

38. Rod Phillips, *A Short History of Wine* (London: Penguin, 2000), 71.

39. See Seward, *Monks and Wine*, 25–35.

40. Kathryn Kueny, *The Rhetoric of Sobriety: Wine in Early Islam* (Albany: State University of New York Press, 2001), 1.

41. Qur'an 5:92.

42. Kueny, *Rhetoric of Sobriety*, 43.

43. Nurdeen Deuraseh, "Is Imbibing *Al-Khamr* (Intoxicating Drink) for Medical Purposes Permissible by Islamic Law?," *Arab Law Quarterly* 18 (2003): 356–60.

44. Ibid., 360–64.

45. *Kitab Al-Ashriba* (*The Book of Drinks*), no. 4977, http://www.usc.edu/org/cmje/religious-texts/hadith/muslim/023-smt.php (accessed April 7, 2013).

46. Kueny, *Rhetoric of Sobriety*, 35–36.

47. Lufti A. Khalil and Fatimi Mayyada al-Nammari, "Two Large Wine Presses at Khirbet Yajuz, Jordan," *Bulletin of the American Schools of Oriental Research* 318 (2000): 41–57.

48. Raymond P. Scheindlin, *Wine, Women and Death: Medieval Hebrew Poems on the Good Life* (Philadelphia: Jewish Publication Society, 1986), 28–29. It is not clear how alcohol content would have been measured at this time.

49. Oleksander Halenko, "Wine Production, Marketing and Consumption in the Ottoman Crimea, 1520–1542," *Journal of the Economic and Social History of the Orient* 47 (2004): 507–47.

50. M. B. Badri, *Islam and Alcoholism* (Plainfield, Ind.: American Trust Publications, 1976), 6.

51. Philip F. Kennedy, *The Wine Song in Classical Arabic Poetry: Abu Nuwas and the Literary Tradition* (Oxford: Clarendon Press, 1997), 105.

52. Thomas A. Glick, *Islamic and Christian Spain in the Early Middle Ages* (Princeton: Princeton University Press, 1979), 80.

53. Scheindlin, *Wine, Women and Death*, 19–25.

54. Omar Khayyam, *The Ruba'iyat of Omar Khayyam*, trans. Peter Avery and John Heath-Stubbs (London: Allen Lane, 1979), 68.

55. John T. McNeill and Helena M. Gamer, *Medieval Handbooks of Penance* (New York: Octagon Books, 1965), 230.

56. Ibid., 286.

57. Itzhak Hen, *Culture and Religion in Merovingian Gaul, AD 481–751* (Leiden: Brill, 1995), 240.

CHAPTER FOUR

1. Ian S. Hornsey, *A History of Beer and Brewing* (Cambridge: Royal Society of Chemistry, 2003), 290.

2. Richard W. Unger, *Beer in the Middle Ages and the Renaissance* (Philadelphia: University of Pennsylvania Press, 2004), 38–42.

3. Ibid., 42.

4. Ibid., 46–48.

5. Hornsey, *History of Beer and Brewing*, 293.

6. Judith M. Bennett, *Ale, Beer and Brewsters in England: Women's Work in a Changing World, 1300–1600* (New York: Oxford University Press, 1996), 18–19.

7. Ibid., 28, fig. 2.3.

8. Ibid., 43–45.

9. Ibid., esp. 145–57.

10. Unger, *Beer in the Middle Ages and the Renaissance*, 59.

11. Christopher Dyer, "The Consumer and the Market in the Later Middle Ages," *Economic History Review* 42 (1989): 309.

12. Unger, *Beer in the Middle Ages and the Renaissance*, 61.

13. *The Exchequer Rolls of Scotland*, ed. George Burnett (Edinburgh: H.M. General Register House, 1883), 6:644.

14. F. W. Carter, "Cracow's Wine Trade (Fourteenth to Eighteenth Centuries)," *Slavonic and East European Review* 65 (1987): 537–78.

15. Ibid.

16. Jan Craeybeckx, *Un Grand Commerce d'Importation: Les Vins de France aux Anciens Pays-Bas (XIIIe–XVIe Siècle)* (Paris: SEVPEN, 1958), 9.

17. Koen Deconinck and Johan Swinnen, "War, Taxes, and Borders: How Beer Created Belgium," *American Association of Wine Economists: Working Paper No. 104 (Economics)*, April 2012.

18. Antoni Riera-Melis, "Society, Food and Feudalism," in *Food: A Culinary History from Antiquity to the Present*, ed. Jean-Louis Flandrin and Massimo Montanari (London: Penguin, 2000), 260–61.

19. Constance Hoffman, *Medieval Agriculture, the Southern French Countryside, and the Early Cistercians: A Study of Forty-Three Monasteries* (Philadelphia: American Philosophical Society, 1986), 93.

20. Béatrice Bourély, *Vignes et Vins de l'Abbaye de Cîteaux en Bourgogne* (Nuits-St-Georges: Editions du Tastevin, 1998), 101.

21. Philip Ziegler, *The Black Death* (New York: John Day, 1969), 96–109.

22. Emmanuel Le Roy Ladurie, *Montaillou: Cathars and Catholics in a French Village, 1234–1324* (London: Penguin, 1980), 9, 15.

23. Martine Maguin, *La Vigne et le Vin en Lorraine, XIV–XVe Siècle* (Nancy: Presses Universitaires de Nancy, 1982), 199–215.

24. P. W. Hammond, *Food and Feast in Medieval England* (Stroud: Allan Sutton, 1993), 13–14.

25. Billy Kay and Caileen MacLean, *Knee-Deep in Claret: A Celebration of Wine and Scotland* (Edinburgh: Mainstream Publishing, 1983), 9.

26. Patricia Labahn, "Feasting in the Fourteenth and Fifteenth Centuries: A Comparison of Manuscript Illumination to Contemporary Written Sources" (Ph.D. diss., St. Louis University, 1975), 60.

27. Georges Duby, *Rural Economy and Country Life in the Medieval West* (London: Hutchinson, 1952), 65.

28. Unger, *Beer in the Middle Ages and the Renaissance*, 129.

29. Christopher Dyer, "Changes in Diet in the Late Middle Ages: The Case of Harvest Workers," *Agricultural Historical Review* 36 (1988): 26, table 2.

30. Yuval Noah Harari, "Strategy and Supply in Fourteenth-Century Western European Invasion Campaigns," *Journal of Military History* 64 (2000): 302.

31. Hornsey, *History of Beer and Brewing*, 291–92.

32. Vernon L. Singleton, "An Enologist's Commentary on Ancient Wine," in *Origins and Ancient History of Wine*, ed. Patrick E. McGovern et al. (London: Routledge, 2004), 75.

33. Hammond, *Food and Feast*, 54.

34. Unger, *Beer in the Middle Ages and the Renaissance*, 127.

35. A. Lynn Martin, *Alcohol, Violence and Disorder in Traditional Europe* (Kirksville, Mo.: Truman State University Press, 2009), 57, table 3.8.

36. A good summary of known wine-consumption statistics is given in Susan Rose, *The Wine Trade in Medieval Europe, 1000–1500* (London: Continuum, 2011), 113–32.

37. Quoted in Emilio Sereni, *History of the Italian Agricultural Landscape* (Princeton: Princeton University Press, 1997), 98.

38. The "Battle of the Wines" is described in Marcel Lachiver, *Vins, Vignes et Vignerons: Histoire du Vignoble Français* (Paris: Fayard, 1988), 102–5.

39. Ibid., 104.

40. Geoffrey Chaucer, *The Canterbury Tales*, trans. Nevill Coghill (Harmondsworth: Penguin, 1951), 271.

41. Hammond, *Food and Feast*, 74.

42. C. Anne Wilson, *Water of Life: A History of Wine-Distilling and Spirits, 500 BC–AD 2000* (Totnes, U.K.: Prospect Books, 2006), 147–48.

43. Hammond, *Food and Feast*, 83.

44. Ibid., 74.

45. Hornsey, *History of Beer and Brewing*, 287.

46. John M. Bowers, "'Dronkenesse is ful of stryvyng': Alcoholism and Ritual Violence in Chaucer's *Pardoner's Tale*," *English Literary History* 57 (1990): 760.

47. Chaucer, *Canterbury Tales*, 269–71.

48. James du Quesnay Adams, *Patterns of Medieval Society* (Englewood Cliffs, N.J.: Prentice Hall, 1969), 111.

49. Jean Dupebe, "La Diététique et l'Alimentation des Pauvres selon Sylvius," in *Pratiques et Discours Alimentaires à la Renaissance*, ed. J.-C. Margolin and R. Sauzet (Paris: G.-P. Maisonneuve et Larose, 1982), 41–56.

50. Quoted in Rose, *Wine Trade in Medieval Europe*, 138.

51. Ibid.

CHAPTER FIVE

1. Mack P. Holt, "Wine, Community and Reformation," *Past and Present* 138 (1993): 58–93.

2. Mack P. Holt, "Europe Divided: Wine, Beer and Reformation in Sixteenth-Century Europe," in *Alcohol: A Social and Cultural History*, ed. Mack P. Holt (Oxford: Berg, 2006), 26–30.

3. Ibid., 33.

4. John Calvin, *Theological Treatises*, ed. J. K. S. Reid (London: SCM Press, 1954), 81.

5. Heinz Schilling, *Civic Calvinism in Northwestern Germany and the Netherlands: Sixteenth to Nineteenth Centuries* (Kirksville: Sixteenth Century Journal Publishers, 1991), 47, 57.

6. Holt, "Europe Divided," 34.

7. Ibid., 35.

8. Jean Calvin, *Institutes of the Christian Religion*, ed. J. T. McNeill (London: SCM Press, 1961), 2:1425.

9. Jim West, "A Sober Assessment of Reformational Drinking," *Modern Reformation* 9 (2000): 38–42.

10. Richard W. Unger, *Beer in the Middle Ages and the Renaissance* (Philadelphia: University of Pennsylvania Press, 2004), 130.

11. Rod Phillips, *A Short History of Wine* (London: Penguin, 2000), 133.

12. *Benjamin Franklin's Autobiography: A Norton Critical Edition*, ed. J. A. Leo Lemay and P. M. Zall (New York: Norton, 1986), 58.

13. The following section on the Arsenal draws mainly on Robert C. Davis, "Venetian Shipbuilders and the Fountain of Wine," *Past and Present* 156 (1997): 55–86.

14. Ibid., 75.

15. Ibid.

16. Ibid., 84.

17. From Unger, *Beer in the Middle Ages and the Renaissance*, 128, table 4.

18. Ibid., 127–29.

19. A. Lynn Martin, *Alcohol, Violence and Disorder in Traditional Europe* (Kirksville, Mo.: Truman State University Press, 2009), 55, table 3.5, and 57, table 3.8.

20. Carl I. Hammer, "A Hearty Meal? The Prison Diets of Cranmer and Latimer," *Sixteenth Century Journal* 30 (1999): 653–80.

21. See, for example, Thomas Brennan, "The Anatomy of Inter-Regional Markets in the Early Modern Wine Trade," *Journal of European Economic History* 23 (1994): 581–607; H. F. Kearney, "The Irish Wine Trade, 1614–15," *Irish Historical Studies* 36 (1955): 400–442; and George F. Steckley, "The Wine Economy of Tenerife in the Seventeenth Century: Anglo-Spanish Partnership in a Luxury Trade," *Economic History Review* 33 (1980): 335–50.

22. Ken Albala, *Eating Right in the Renaissance* (Berkeley: University of California Press, 2002), 8.

23. Daniel Rivière, "Le Thème Alimentaire dans le Discours Proverbial de la Renaissance Française," in *Pratiques et Discours Alimentaires à la Renaissance*, ed. J.-C. Margolin and R. Sauzet (Paris: G.-P. Maisonneuve et Larose, 1982), 201–18.

24. William Harrison, *The Description of England*, quoted in William T. Harper, *Origins and Rise of the British Distillery* (Lewiston: Edwin Mellon, 1999), 38.

25. F. W. Carter, "Cracow's Wine Trade (Fourteenth to Eighteenth Centuries)," *Slavonic and East European Review* 65 (1987): 568–69.

26. Tim Unwin, *Wine and the Vine: An Historical Geography of Viticulture and the Wine Trade* (London: Routledge, 1996), 223–24.

27. William Shakespeare, *Henry IV, Part II*, act 4, pt. 3.

28. Steckley, "Wine Economy of Tenerife," 342, fig. 3.

29. Quoted in ibid., 342.

30. *Englands Triumph; or, The subjects joy* (London, 1675), 1.

31. Fynes Moryson, *An Itinerary containing his Ten Yeeres Travel through the Twelve Dominions of Germany, Bohmerland, Sweitzerland, Netherland, Denmarke, Poland, Italy, Turky, France, England, Scotland, Ireland* (Glasgow: James MacLehose, 1908), 43.

32. Phillips, *Short History of Wine*, 138, 245–46.

33. Carter, "Cracow's Wine Trade," 555.

34. Quoted in Ian S. Hornsey, *A History of Beer and Brewing* (Cambridge: Royal Society of Chemistry, 2003), 324.

35. Judith M. Bennett, *Ale, Beer and Brewsters in England: Women's Work in a Changing World, 1300–1600* (New York: Oxford University Press, 1996), 117.

36. Ibid., 93.

37. Hornsey, *History of Beer and Brewing*, 334. Pipes (Portuguese barrels) used for aging wine varied in size according to region, but the standard shipping pipe was 535 liters.

38. Mendelsohn, *Drinking with Pepys* (London: St. Martin's Press, 1963), 51.

39. Chloe Chard, "The Intensification of Italy: Food, Wine and the Foreign in Seventeenth-Century Travel Writing," in *Food, Culture and History 1*, ed. Gerald Mars and Valerie Mars (London: London Food Seminar, 1993), 96.

40. Mendelsohn, *Drinking with Pepys*, 47.

41. Jean-Louis Flandrin, "Médicine et Habitudes Alimentaires Anciennes," in Margolin and Sauzet, *Pratiques et Discours Alimentaires*, 86–87.

42. Ibid., 87.

43. Piero Camporesi, *The Anatomy of the Senses: National Symbols in Medieval and Early Modern Italy* (Cambridge: Polity Press, 1994), 80.

44. Rudolph M. Bell, *How to Do It: A Guide to Good Living for Renaissance Italians* (Chicago: University of Chicago Press, 1999), 162.

45. Flandrin, "Médicine et Habitudes," 85.

46. Sarah Hand Meacham, "'They Will Be Adjudged by Their Drink, What Kind of Housewives They Are': Gender, Technology, and Household Cidering in England and the Chesapeake, 1690 to 1760," *Virginia Magazine of History and Biography* 111 (2003): 120–21. See also Louise Hill Curth, "The Medicinal Value of Wine in Early Modern England," *Social History of Alcohol and Drugs* 18 (2003): 35–50.

47. Michel Reulos, "Le Premier Traité sur le Cidre: Julien le Paulmier, De Vino et Pomace, traduit par Jacques de Cahaignes (1589)," in Margolin and Sauzet, *Pratiques et Discours Alimentaires*, 97–103.

48. Henri de Buttet, "Le Vin des Invalides au Temps de Louis XIV," in *Les Boissons: Production et Consommation aux XIXe et XXe Siècles* (Paris: Comité des Travaux Historiques et Scientifiques, 1984), 39–51.

49. Holt, "Europe Divided," 35–36.

50. Peter Clark, *The English Alehouse: A Social History, 1200–1830* (London: Longman, 1983), 32–34, 40–44.

51. Ibid., 49.

52. Patricia Funnerton, "Not Home: Alehouses, Ballads, and the Vagrant Husband in Early Modern England," *Journal of Medieval and Early Modern Studies* 32 (2002): 493–518.

53. Thomas E. Brennan, ed., *Public Drinking in the Early Modern World: Voices from the Tavern, 1500–1800* (London: Pickering & Chatto, 2011), 1:51.

54. *A Dreadful Warning for Drunkards* (London, 1678), A2.

55. John Taylor, *The Unnatural Father* (London, 1621), 1.

56. Buckner B. Trawick, *Shakespeare and Alcohol* (Amsterdam: Editions Rodopi, 1978).

57. Beat Kumin, "The Devil's Altar? Crime and the Early Modern Public House," *History Compass* 2 (2005), http://wrap.warwick.ac.uk/289/1/WRAP_Kumin_Devils_altar_History_Compass.pdf (accessed May 27, 2013).

58. Old Bailey records online, April 29, 1674, Oldbaileyonline.org (accessed January 14, 2012). This and other references were collected by my former student Keegan On.

59. The following account is from Beverly Ann Tlusty, "Gender and Alcohol Use in Early Modern Augsburg," in *The Changing Face of Drink: Substance, Imagery and Behaviour*, ed. Jack S. Blocker Jr. and Cheryl Krasnick Warsh (Ottawa: Publications Histoire Sociale/Social History, 1977), 21–42.

60. Hornsey, *History of Beer and Brewing*, 343.

CHAPTER SIX

1. Some scholars think distilling, if not alcohol distilling, was practiced much earlier. See C. Anne Wilson, *Water of Life: A History of Wine-Distilling and Spirits, 500 BC–AD 2000* (Totnes, U.K.: Prospect Books, 2006), 17–34.

2. F. R. Allchin, "India: The Ancient Home of Distillation?" *Man* 14 (1979): 55–63.

3. Fernand Braudel, *Civilisation and Capitalism, 15th–18th Centuries* (New York: Harper & Row, 1985), 1:241.

4. William T. Harper, *Origins and Rise of the British Distillery* (Lewiston: Edwin Mellen, 1999), 11.

5. Allison P. Coudert, "The Sulzbach Jubilee: Old Age in Early Modern Europe and America," in *Old Age in the Middle Ages and the Renaissance: Interdisciplinary Approaches*, ed. Albrecht Classen (Berlin: de Gruyter, 2005), 534.

6. Quoted in Harper, *British Distillery*, 11.

7. Ibid., 13–17.

8. Wilson, *Water of Life*, 149–50.

9. *The Exchequer Rolls of Scotland*, ed. George Burnett (Edinburgh: H.M. General Register House, 1883), 10:487.

10. B. Ann Tlusty, "Water of Life, Water of Death: The Controversy over Brandy and Gin in Early Modern Augsburg," *Central European History* 31, no. 1–2 (1999): 8–11.

11. Walter Ryff, *The New Large Book of Distilling* (1545), quoted in *Public Drinking in the Early Modern World: Voices from the Tavern, 1500–1800*, ed. Thomas E. Brennan (London: Pickering & Chatto, 2011), 2:423.

12. Brunschwig Hieronymus, *Das Buch zu Distilieren* (Strasburg, 1532), fol. 39.

13. Harper, *British Distillery*, 26.

14. Rod Phillips, *A Short History of Wine* (London: Penguin, 2000), 124.

15. Lord Cecil quoted in Harper, *British Distillery*, 42.

16. Ibid., 26–30.

17. Charles MacLean, *Scotch Whisky: A Liquid History* (London: Cassell, 2003), 20 (my translation).

18. Brennan, *Public Drinking in the Early Modern World*, 2:7.

19. Harper, *British Distillery*, 27.

20. Brennan, *Public Drinking in the Early Modern World*, 2:173.

21. Ibid., 2:172.

22. Tlusty, "Water of Life," 17.

23. Ibid., 15.

24. Brennan, *Public Drinking in the Early Modern World*, 2:162.

25. Tlusty, "Water of Life," 18.

26. John Burnett, *Liquid Pleasures: A Social History of Drinks in Modern Britain* (London: Routledge, 1999), 161.

27. A. D. Francis, *The Wine Trade* (London: A & C Black, 1972), 74.

28. Brennan, *Public Drinking in the Early Modern World*, 1:51.

29. Gin got its name from *eau de genièvre* (juniper-water), which was corrupted to "geneva" by English soldiers and then shortened to "gin."

30. MacLean, *Scotch Whisky*, 29.

31. Burnett, *Liquid Pleasures*, 160–61.

32. MacLean, *Scotch Whisky*, 33, 35.

33. Richard Foss, *Rum: A Global History* (London: Reaktion, 2012), 27.

34. Frederick H. Smith, *Caribbean Rum: A Social and Economic History* (Gainesville: University Press of Florida, 2005), 26.

35. Patricia Herlihy, *Vodka: A Global History* (London: Reaktion, 2012), 38–40.

36. William Pokhlebkin, *A History of Vodka* (London: Verso, 1992), 172–74.

37. Herlihy, *Vodka*, 46–47.

38. Dr. Duncan of the Faculty of Montpellier, *Wholesome Advice Against the Abuse of Hot Liquors, Particularly of Coffee, Chocolate, Tea, Brandy, and Strong-Waters* (London, 1706), 12, 16–17, 55.

39. Ibid., 16–17.

40. Richard Short, *Of Drinking Water, Against our Novelists, that Prescribed it in England* (London, 1656), 17–87 passim.

41. *A Proposition for the Serving and Supplying of London, and other Places adjoyning, with a Sufficient Quantity of Good and Cleare Strong Water* (London, [1675]), n.p.

42. *Salt-Water Sweetened; or, A True Account of the Great Advantages of this New Invention both by Sea and Land* (London, 1683), 5–10.

43. *A Dissertation upon Drunkenness . . . Shewing to What an Intolerable Pitch that Vice is arriv'd at in this Kingdom* (London, 1708), 2.

44. Jessica Warner discusses the statistical issues in "Faith in Numbers: Quantifying Gin and Sin in Eighteenth-Century England," *Journal of British Studies* 50 (2011): 76–99.

45. M. Dorothy George, *London Life in the Eighteenth Century* (London, 1925), 51.

46. *An Impartial Inquiry into the Present State of the British Distillery* (London, 1736), 7.

47. Jessica Warner, Minghao Her, and Jürgen Rehm, "Can Legislation Prevent Debauchery? Mother Gin and Public Health in 18th-Century England," *American Journal of Public Health* 91 (2001): 378.

48. Peter Clark, "The 'Mother Gin' Controversy in the Early Eighteenth Century," *Transactions of the Royal Historical Society*, 5th ser., 38 (1988): 64.

49. In the early eighteenth century the English gallon held about 3.76 liters. In 1824 it was standardized at about 4.5 liters.

50. *Distilled Spirituous Liquors the Bane of the Nation* (London, 1736), 35–36.

51. *A Dissertation on Mr. Hogarth's Six Prints Lately Publish'd* (London, 1751), 14.

52. Ibid.

53. Quoted in Jonathan White, "The 'Slow but Sure Poyson': The Representation of Gin and Its Drinkers, 1736–1751," *Journal of British Studies* 42 (2003): 44.

54. Quoted in ibid.

55. Quoted in ibid., 41.

56. Quoted in ibid., 51.

57. Clark, "'Mother Gin' Controversy," 68–70.

58. Ibid., 70.

59. Warner, Her, and Rehm, "Can Legislation Prevent Debauchery?," 381–82.

CHAPTER SEVEN

1. José C. Curto, *Enslaving Spirits: The Portuguese-Brazilian Alcohol Trade at Luanda and Its Hinterland, c. 1550–1830* (Leiden: Brill, 2004), 45.

2. Rod Phillips, *A Short History of Wine* (London: Penguin, 2000), 173–77.

3. B. S. Platt, "Some Traditional Alcoholic Beverages and Their Importance to Indigenous African Communities," *Proceedings of the Nutrition Society* 14 (1955): 115.

4. Curto, *Enslaving Spirits*, 33.

5. Susan Diduk, "European Alcohol, History, and the State in Cameroon," *African Studies Review* 36 (1993): 2–3.

6. Curto, *Enslaving Spirits*, 60–61.

7. Emma Sánchez Montañés, "Las Bebidas Alcohólicas en la América Indígina: Una Visión General," in *El Vino de Jerez y Otras Bebidas Espirituosas en la Historia de España y América* (Madrid: Servicio de Publicaciones del Ayuntamiento de Jerez, 2004), 424.

8. Frederick H. Smith, "European Impressions of the Island Carib's Use of Alcohol in the Early Colonial Period," *Ethnohistory* 53 (2006): 545.

9. Ibid., 545–46.

10. Michael Owen Jones, "What's Disgusting, Why, and What Does It Matter?," *Journal of Folklore Research* 37, no. 1 (2000): 53–71.

11. Smith, "European Impressions," 547–48.

12. Sánchez Montañés, "Las Bebidas Alcohólicas en la América Indígina," 426–28.

13. Peter C. Mancall, *Deadly Medicine: Indians and Alcohol in Early America* (Ithaca: Cornell University Press, 1997), 134.

14. Lidio M. Valdez, "Maize Beer Production in Middle Horizon Peru," *Journal of Anthropological Research* 62 (2006): 53–80.

15. Henry J. Bruman, *Alcohol in Ancient Mexico* (Salt Lake City: University of Utah Press, 2000), 71–72.

16. Ibid., 71.

17. Ibid., 63.

18. Daniel Nemser, "'To Avoid This Mixture': Rethinking *Pulque* in Colonial Mexico City," *Food and Foodways* 19 (2011): 102.

19. José Jesús Hernández Palomo, "El Pulque: Usos Indígenas y Abusos Criollos," in *El Vino de Jerez y Otras Bebidas*, 246.

20. Juan Pedro Viqueira Albán, *Propriety and Permissiveness in Bourbon Mexico* (Wilmington, N.C.: Scholarly Resources, 1999), 131.

21. Ibid., 132.

22. Nemser, "'To Avoid This Mixture.'"

23. Rick Hendricks, "Viticulture in El Paso del Norte during the Colonial Period," *Agricultural History* 78 (2004): 191.

24. Phillips, *Short History of Wine*, 156–58.

25. Ibid., 157–58.

26. Prudence M. Rice, "Wine and Brandy Production in Colonial Peru: A Historical and Archaeological Investigation," *Journal of Interdisciplinary History* 27 (1997): 465.

27. Thomas Pinney, *A History of Wine in America: From the Beginnings to Prohibition* (Berkeley: University of California Press, 1989), 17.

28. Ibid., 31.

29. Robert C. Fuller, *Religion and Wine: A Cultural History of Wine Drinking in the United States* (Knoxville: University of Tennessee Press, 1996), 12.

30. William Wood, *New England's Prospect* (Boston: Prince Society, 1865), 1:16.

31. George Percy quoted in Sarah Hand Meacham, "'They Will Be Adjudged by Their Drink, What Kinde of Housewives They Are': Gender, Technology, and Household Cidering in England and the Chesapeake, 1690 to 1760," *Virginia Magazine of History and Biography* 111 (2003): 123.

32. James E. McWilliams, "Brewing Beer in Massachusetts Bay, 1640–1690," *New England Quarterly* 71, no. 4 (1998): 544.

33. Meacham, "'They Will Be Adjudged by Their Drink,'" 117.

34. Phillips, *Short History of Wine*, 163.

35. Thomas E. Brennan, ed., *Public Drinking in the Early Modern World: Voices from the Tavern, 1500–1800* (London: Pickering & Chatto, 2011), 4:80.

36. Ibid., 4:82.

37. Mark Lender, "Drunkenness as an Offense in Early New England: A Study of 'Puritan' Attitudes," *Quarterly Journal of Studies on Alcohol* 34 (1973): 359–61.

38. Brennan, *Public Drinking in the Early Modern World*, 4:94.

39. Ibid., 4:84.

40. Ibid., 4:100.

41. Gregg Smith, *Beer in America: The Early Years, 1587–1840* (Boulder: Siris Books, 1998), 23.

42. Mancall, *Deadly Medicine*, 64.

43. Mark Edward Lender and James Kirby Martin, *Drinking in America: A History* (New York: Free Press, 1987), 24.

44. Quoted in Mancall, *Deadly Medicine*, 43.

45. Dean Albertson, "Puritan Liquor in the Planting of New England," *New England Quarterly* 23, no. 4 (1950): 483.

46. Ibid., 484.

47. Mancall, *Deadly Medicine*, 44.

48. Brennan, *Public Drinking in the Early Modern World*, 4:297.

49. Mancall, *Deadly Medicine*, 67.

50. Ibid., 67–68.

51. Maia Conrad, "Disorderly Drinking: Reconsidering Seventeenth-Century Iroquois Alcohol Abuse," *American Indian Quarterly* 23, no. 3&4 (1999): 1–11.

52. Ibid., 7.

53. Mancall, *Deadly Medicine*, 68.

54. Ibid., 139–40.

55. D. C. Dailey, "The Role of Alcohol among North American Indian Tribes as Reported in the Jesuit Relations," *Anthropologica* 10 (1968): 54.

56. Gananath Obeyesekere, *Cannibal Talk: The Man-Eating Myth and Human Sacrifice in the South Seas* (Berkeley: University of California Press, 2005). Accounts of cannibalism sometimes associated it with the consumption of alcohol.

57. Mancall, *Deadly Medicine*, 6–8.

58. Quoted in ibid., 2.

59. Quoted in Albertson, "Puritan Liquor," 485.

60. Brennan, *Public Drinking in the Early Modern World*, 4:98.

61. Quoted in Albertson, "Puritan Liquor," 486.

62. C. C. Pearson and J. Edwin Hendricks, *Liquor and Anti-Liquor in Virginia, 1619–1919* (Durham, N.C.: Duke University Press, 1967), 6.

CHAPTER EIGHT

1. The "Moral and Physical Thermometer" is reprinted in several books. See, for example, Mark Edward Lender and James Kirby Martin, *Drinking in America: A History* (New York: Free Press, 1987), 39.

2. Quoted in Dana Rabin, "Drunkenness and Responsibility for Crime in the Eighteenth Century," *Journal of British Studies* 44 (2005): 459.

3. David Hancock, "Commerce and Conversation in the Eighteenth-Century Atlantic: The Invention of Madeira Wine," *Journal of Interdisciplinary History* 29 (1998): 207.

4. Ibid., 215.

5. Ibid.

6. Andrea Stuart, *Sugar in the Blood: A Family's Story of Slavery and Empire* (New York: Knopf, 2013), quoted in *New York Times Book Review*, March 31, 2013, 11.

7. Rod Phillips, *A Short History of Wine* (London: Penguin, 2000), 188.

8. Ibid., 188–89.

9. Hugh Johnson, *The Story of Wine* (London: Mitchell Beazley, 1989), 293–304.

10. Thomas B. Gilmore, "James Boswell's Drinking," *Eighteenth-Century Studies* 24 (1991): 340–41.

11. *Oxford Today* 11, no. 2 (Hilary Term, 1999): 63.

12. Phillips, *Short History of Wine*, 191–92.

13. Vivien E. Dietz, "The Politics of Whisky: Scottish Distillers, the Excise, and the Pittite State," *Journal of British Studies* 36 (1997): 45.

14. Charles MacLean, *Scotch Whisky: A Liquid History* (London: Cassell, 2003), 61–65.

15. J. B. Gough, "Winecraft and Chemistry in Eighteenth-Century France: Chaptal and the Invention of Chaptalization," *Technology and Culture* 39 (1998): 96–97.

16. Barbara Ketcham Wheaton, *Savoring the Past: The French Kitchen and Table from 1300 to 1789* (New York: Touchstone, 1983), 215.

17. Quoted in Charles Ludongton, "'Claret is the liquor for boys; port for men': How Port Became the 'Englishman's Wine,' 1750s to 1800," *Journal of British Studies* 48 (2009): 364–90.

18. Rabin, "Drunkenness and Responsibility," 457–77.

19. Quoted in ibid., 463.

20. Ibid., 458 n 3.

21. This statistic comes from the research of my former student Keegan On.

22. Rabin, "Drunkenness and Responsibility," 473.

23. Roderick Phillips, *Family Breakdown in Late Eighteenth-Century France: Divorces in Rouen, 1792–1804* (Oxford: Clarendon Press, 1980), 116–17. Other references in this section are from this source.

24. On this subject, see Paul E. Kopperman, "'The Cheapest Pay': Alcohol Abuse in the Eighteenth-Century British Army," *Journal of Military History* 60 (1996): 445–70.

25. Ibid., 447–48.

26. Ibid., 450.

27. Ibid., 452.

28. Ibid., 450.

29. Ibid., 453.

30. Ibid., 454.

31. A. J. B. Johnston, "Alcohol Consumption in Eighteenth-Century Louisbourg and the Vain Attempts to Control It," *French Colonial History* 2 (2002): 64.

32. Kopperman, "'Cheapest Pay,'" 464.

33. Ibid., 463.

34. Ibid., 467.

35. Ibid., 460.

36. Benjamin Rush, "An Account of the Disorder occasioned by Drinking Cold Water in Warm Weather, and the Method of Curing it," in Benjamin Rush, *Medical Inquiries and Observations*, 2nd ed. (Philadelphia: Thomas Dobson, 1794), 1:183.

37. Ibid., 186–87.

38. Kopperman, "'Cheapest Pay,'" 467.

39. Lender and Martin, *Drinking in America*, 205–6.

40. *Global Status Report on Alcohol and Health* (Geneva: World Health Organization, 2011), 140.

41. See Dietz, "Politics of Whisky."

42. David O. Whitten, "An Economic Inquiry into the Whiskey Rebellion of 1794," *Agricultural History* 49 (1975): 495–96.

43. Ibid., 493–94.

44. Compare that to 1985, when the total 2.58 gallons was made up of beer (1.34), spirits (0.9) and wine (0.34). See Lender and Martin, *Drinking in America*, 205.

45. Quoted in Whitten, "Economic Inquiry," 497.

46. Ibid., 501.

47. Denis Jeanson, ed., *Cahiers de Doléances, Région Centre: Loire-et-Cher*, 2 vols. (Tours: Denis Jeanson, 1989), 2:480.

48. Phillips, *Short History of Wine*, 208–11.

CHAPTER NINE

1. Scott C. Martin, "Violence, Gender, and Intemperance in Early National Connecticut," *Journal of Social History* 34 (2000): 318–19.

2. James Samuelson, *A History of Drink: A Review, Social, Scientific, and Political* (London, 1880), 170–75, 192–93.

3. Quotes from Daryl Adair, "Respectable, Sober and Industrious? Attitudes to Alcohol in Early Colonial Adelaide," *Labour History* 70 (1996): 131–34.

4. Kevin D. Goldberg, "Acidity and Power: The Politics of Natural Wine in Nineteenth-Century Germany," *Food and Foodways* 19 (2011): 294–313.

5. Thomas Brennan, "Towards a Cultural History of Alcohol in France," *Journal of Social History* 23 (1989): 76.

6. Brian Harrison, *Drink and the Victorians: The Temperance Question in England, 1815–1872* (Pittsburgh: University of Pittsburgh Press, 1971), 66–67.

7. On the 1830 act and its consequences, see Nicholas Mason, "'The Sovereign People Are in a Beastly State': The Beer Act of 1830 and Victorian Discourses on Working-Class Drunkenness," *Victorian Literature and Culture* 29 (2001): 109–27.

8. Quoted in ibid., 115.

9. Quoted in ibid., 118.

10. "Alcoholism in the Upper Classes," *British Medical Journal* 2, no. 716 (September 19, 1874): 373.

11. Edmond Bertrand, *Essai sur l'Intempérance* (Paris: Guillaumin, 1872), 81.

12. On phylloxera, see Rod Phillips, *A Short History of Wine* (London: Penguin, 2000), 281–87.

13. Patricia E. Prestwich, *Drink and the Politics of Social Reform: Antialcoholism in France since 1870* (Palo Alto: Society for the Promotion of Science and Scholarship, 1988), 24–26.

14. Marcel Lachiver, *Vins, Vignes et Vignerons: Histoire du Vignoble Français* (Paris: Fayard, 1988), 617–18.

15. Quoted in Doris Lander, *Absinthe: The Cocaine of the Nineteenth Century* (Jefferson, N.C.: McFarland, 1995), 15.

16. *British Medical Journal* 2, no. 1665 (November 26, 1892), 1187. See also Michael Marrus, "Social Drinking in the Belle Epoque," *Journal of Social History* 7 (1974): 115–41.

17. On the Lanfray case, see Jad Adams, *Hideous Absinthe: A History of the Devil in a Bottle* (London: Tauris Parke, 2008), 205–7.

18. This is based on a widely reproduced table of U.S. alcohol consumption. See Mark Edward Lender and James Kirby Martin, *Drinking in America: A History* (New York: Free Press, 1987), 205–6.

19. Mark A. Vargas, "The Progressive Agent of Mischief: The Whiskey Ration and Temperance in the United States Army," *Historian* 67 (2005): 201–2.

20. Ibid., 204.

21. Harold D. Langley, *Social Reform in the United States Navy, 1798–1862* (Urbana: University of Illinois Press, 1967), 211–12.

22. D. H. Marjot, "Delirium Tremens in the Royal Navy and British Army in the 19th Century," *Journal of Studies on Alcohol* 38 (1977): 1619, table 1.

23. Ibid., 1618.

24. James S. Roberts, *Drink, Temperance and the Working Class in Nineteenth-Century Germany* (Boston: Allen & Unwin, 1984), 43–45.

25. Ibid., 48.

26. James S. Roberts, "Drink and Industrial Work Discipline in 19th-Century Germany," *Journal of Social History* 15 (1981): 28.

27. Louis Chevalier, *Labouring Classes and Dangerous Classes in Paris during the First Half of the Nineteenth Century* (London: Routledge & Kegan Paul, 1973), 360.

28. Peter Mathias, "The Brewing Industry, Temperance, and Politics," *Historical Journal* 1 (1958): 106.

29. *A Transport Voyage to Mauritius and Back* (London: John Murray, 1851), 24.

30. Loammi Baldwin, *Report on the Subject of Introducing Pure Water into the City of Boston* (Boston: John H. Eastburn, 1834), 74.

31. Henry R. Abraham, *A Few Plain but Important Statements upon the Subject of the Scheme for Supplying Leeds with Water* (London: C. Whiting, 1838), 4.

32. Jean-Pierre Goubert, *The Conquest of Water* (Princeton: Princeton University Press, 1986), 41–42.

33. James Salzman, *Drinking Water: A History* (New York: Overlook Duckworth, 2012), 87.

34. John Broich, "Engineering the Empire: British Water Supply Systems and Colonial Societies, 1850–1900," *Journal of British Studies* 46 (2007): 350–51.

35. Goubert, *Conquest of Water*, 196.

36. Theo Engelen, John R. Shepherd, and Yang Wen-shan, eds., *Death at the Opposite Ends of the Eurasian Continent: Mortality Trends in Taiwan and the Netherlands, 1850–1945* (Amsterdam: Aksant, 2011), 158–59.

37. Broich, "Engineering the Empire," 356–61.

38. Ibid., 357.

39. This section on New York draws largely on Gerard T. Koeppel, *Water for Gotham* (Princeton: Princeton University Press, 2000), 141.

40. Ibid., 282.

41. This section on Boston draws on Michael Rawson, "The Nature of Water: Reform and the Antebellum Crusade for Municipal Water in Boston," *Environmental History* 9 (July 2004): 411–35.

42. Quoted in ibid., 420–21.

43. Goubert, *Conquest of Water*, 196.

44. *Thoughts about Water* (n.p., n.d.), 15.

45. *British Medical Journal* 1, no. 492 (June 4, 1870): 580.

CHAPTER TEN

1. I refer to these varied organizations as "antialcohol." Even though some were tolerant of alcohol and more concerned with what they considered its abuse, they were part of a general movement whose aim was to restrict the consumption of alcoholic beverages.

2. Jon Sterngass, "Maine Law," in *Alcohol and Temperance in Modern History: An International Encyclopedia*, ed. Jack S. Blocker Jr., David M. Fahey, and Ian R. Tyrrell (Santa Barbara: ABC-CLIO, 2003), 1:393–94.

3. James D. Ivy, "Woman's Christian Temperance Movement (United States)," in Blocker, Fahey, and Tyrell, *Alcohol and Temperance in Modern History*, 2:679–82.

4. Marni Davis, *Jews and Booze: Becoming American in the Age of Prohibition* (New York: New York University Press, 2012), 41–42.

5. Dierdre M. Moloney, "Combatting 'Whiskey's Work': The Catholic Temperance Movement in Late Nineteenth-Century America," *U.S. Catholic Historian* 16 (1998): 5.

6. Ibid., 8–9.

7. John F. Quinn, "Father Mathew's Disciples: American Catholic Support for Temperance, 1840–1920," *Church History* 65 (1996): 635.

8. K. Austin Kerr, "Anti-Saloon League of America," in Blocker, Fahey, and Tyrell, *Alcohol and Temperance in Modern History*, 2:48–51.

9. Lilian Lewis Shiman, *Crusade against Drink in Victorian England* (New York: St. Martin's Press, 1988), 9–10.

10. Ibid., 18–24.

11. Ibid., 33.

12. Andrew Davidson, "'Try the Alternative': The Built Heritage of the Temperance Movement," *Journal of the Brewery History Society* 123 (2006): 92–109.

13. Edward Cox, *Principles of Punishment* (London, 1877), 99.

14. Roderick Phillips, *Putting Asunder: A History of Divorce in Western Society* (New York: Cambridge University Press, 1988), 497.

15. Shiman, *Crusade against Drink*, 81–82.

16. Neal Dow and Dio Lewis, "Prohibition and Persuasion," *North American Review* 139 (1884): 179.

17. Tim Holt, "Demanding the Right to Drink: The Two Great Hyde Park Demonstrations," *Brewery History* 118 (2005): 26–40.

18. Shiman, *Crusade against Drink*, 107.

19. Richard Cameron, *Total Abstinence versus Alcoholism* (Edinburgh, 1897), 3.

20. *Souvenir of the Essay Competition in the Hull Elementary Schools, on "Physical Deterioration and Alcoholism,"* May 1906 (Hull: Walker's Central Printing, 1906), 11–13.

21. John Charles Bucknill, *Habitual Drunkenness and Insane Drunkards* (London: Macmillan, 1878), 1.

22. Ibid., 69.

23. Mimi Ajzenstadt, "The Changing Image of the State: The Case of Alcohol Regulation in British Columbia, 1871–1925," *Canadian Journal of Sociology* 19 (1994): 441–60.

24. [George Gibbs], *Diprose's Christmas Sketches* (London: Diprose and Bateman, 1859), 1, 4.

25. Patricia E. Prestwich, *Drink and the Politics of Social Reform: Antialcoholism in France since 1870* (Palo Alto: Society for the Promotion of Science and Scholarship, 1988), 37.

26. W. Scott Haine, *The World of the Paris Café: Sociability among the French Working Class, 1789–1914* (Baltimore: Johns Hopkins University Press, 1996), 95–96.

27. Dr. de Vaucleroy, *The Adulteration of Spirituous Liquors* (London: Church of England Temperance Society, 1890), 3.

28. This advertisement is reprinted in Rod Phillips, *A Short History of Wine* (London: Penguin, 2000), between pp. 176 and 177.

29. Prestwich, *Drink and the Politics of Social Reform*, 7–10.

30. Owen White, "Drunken States: Temperance and French Rule in Cote d'Ivoire, 1908–1916," *Journal of Social History* 40 (2007): 663.

31. Quoted in Prestwich, *Drink and the Politics of Social Reform*, 24.

32. James S. Roberts, *Drink, Temperance and the Working Class in Nineteenth-Century Germany* (Boston: Allen & Unwin, 1984), 26–27.

33. Ibid., 114, table 6.1.

34. Susan Diduk, "European Alcohol, History, and the State in Cameroon," *African Studies Review* 36 (1993): 7.

35. Jeffrey W. Alexander, *Brewed in Japan: The Evolution of the Japanese Beer Industry* (Vancouver: University of British Columbia Press, 2013), 44, table 4.

36. Ibid., 49.

37. Elizabeth Dorn Lublin, *Reforming Japan: The Woman's Christian Temperance Union in the Meiji Period* (Honolulu: University of Hawai'i Press, 2010), 134–35.

38. Quoted in Shiman, *Crusade against Drink*, 9.

39. James M. Slade, *An Address Explanatory of the Principles and Objects of the United Brothers of Temperance* [July 3, 1847] (Vergennes, Vt.: E. W. Blaisdell, 1848), 7–9.

40. J. N. Radcliffe, *The Hygiene of the Turkish Army* (London: John Churchill, 1858), 29.

41. *A Plea for the British Soldier in India* (London: William Tweedie, 1867), 19.

42. Quoted in *The Curse of Britain* (n.p., n.d. [1857]), verso.

43. Catherine B. Drummond, *An Outline of the Temperance Question* (London: Church of England Temperance Society, 1906), 10–11.

44. Victor Horsley, *What Women Can Do to Promote Temperance* (London: Church of England Temperance Society, n.d.), 11.

45. *British Medical Journal* 2, no. 1870 (October 31, 1896): 1342.

46. "Alcohol and Mountaineering," *British Medical Journal* 9 (July 1910): 102.

47. Jonathan Zimmerman, "'When the Doctors Disagree': Scientific Temperance and Scientific Authority, 1891–1906," *Journal of the History of Medicine* 48 (1993): 171–97.

48. "Triner's American Elixir of Bitter Wine" (1910) poster in possession of the author.

49. Thomas Graham and A. W. Hofmann, *Report on the Alleged Adulteration of Pale Ales by Strychnine* (London: Schulz and Co., 1852).

50. William Alexander, *The Adulteration of Food and Drinks* (London: Longman, 1856), 30.

51. *The Bordeaux Wine and Liquor Dealers' Guide: A Treatise on the Manufacture and Adulteration of Liquor*, by a Practical Liquor Manufacturer (New York: Dick and Fitzgerald, 1857), vi–ix.

52. *Science* 12 (August 24, 1888): 89.

53. Alessandro Stanziani, "Information, Quality, and Legal Rules: Wine Adulteration in Nineteenth-Century France," *Business History* 51, no. 2 (2009): 282.

54. Walter Johnson, *Alcohol: What It Does; and What It Cannot Do* (London: Simpkin, Marshall, and Co., n.d. [1840s]), 40.

55. Drummond, *Outline of the Temperance Question*, 13.

56. Joseph Harding, *Facts, Relating to Intoxicating Drinks* (London: J. Pasco, 1840), 1–2.

57. *Curse of Britain*, recto.

58. Bucknill, *Habitual Drunkenness*, 5.

59. Patricia E. Prestwich, "Drinkers, Drunkards, and Degenerates: The Alcoholic Population of a Parisian Asylum, 1867–1914," in *The Changing Face of Drink: Substance, Imagery and Behaviour*, ed. Jack S. Blocker Jr. and Cheryl Krasnick Warsh (Ottawa: Publications Histoire Sociale/Social History, 1977), 120–21.

60. Mariana Valverde, "'Slavery from Within': The Invention of Alcoholism and the Question of Free Will," *Social History* 22 (1997): 251–53.

61. Edmond Bertrand, *Essai sur l'Intempérance* (Paris: Guillaumin, 1872).

62. Mark Keller, "The Old and the New in the Treatment of Alcoholism," in *Alcohol Interventions: Historical and Sociocultural Approaches*, ed. David L. Strug et al. (New York: Haworth, 1986), 23–40.

63. See, for example, William Cooke, *The Wine Question* (London: J. Pasco, 1840).

64. Jennifer L. Woodruff Tait, *The Poisoned Chalice: Eucharistic Grape Juice and Common-Sense Realism in Victorian Methodism* (Tuscaloosa: University of Alabama Press, 2010), 102.

65. Phillips, *Short History of Wine*, 275.

66. *British Medical Journal* 2, no. 1960 (July 23, 1898): 222.

CHAPTER ELEVEN

1. Susan Diduk, "European Alcohol, History and the State in Cameroon," *African Studies Review* 36 (1993): 3.

2. John D. Hargreaves, *France and West Africa: An Anthology of Historical Documents* (London: Macmillan, 1959), 74.

3. Lynn Pan, *Alcohol in Colonial Africa* (Uppsala: Scandinavian Institute of African Studies, 1975), 7–8.

4. Diduk, "European Alcohol," 7–8.

5. Raymond E. Dumett, "The Social Impact of the European Liquor Trade on the Akan of Ghana (Gold Coast and Asante), 1875–1910," *Journal of Interdisciplinary History* 5 (1974): 72.

6. Ibid., 71.

7. Quoted in Pan, *Alcohol in Colonial Africa*, 11.

8. Robert G. Carlson, "Banana Beer, Reciprocity, and Ancestor Propitiation among the Haya of Bukoba, Tanzania," *Ethnology* 29 (1990): 297–300.

9. José C. Curto, *Enslaving Spirits: The Portuguese-Brazilian Alcohol Trade at Luanda and Its Hinterland, c. 1550–1830* (Leiden: Brill, 2004), 19–41.

10. Ibid., 155.

11. Simon Heap, "'A Bottle of Gin Is Dangled before the Nose of the Natives': The Economic Uses of Imported Liquor in Southern Nigeria, 1860–1920," *African Economic History* 33 (2005): 75.

12. Quoted in ibid., 71.

13. Ibid., 78.

14. Ibid., 80–81.

15. Owen White, "Drunken States: Temperance and French Rule in Cote d'Ivoire, 1908–1916," *Journal of Social History* 40 (2007): 663–66.

16. Ibid., 668–99.

17. Ibid., 669–70.

18. Dumett, "Social Impact of the European Liquor Trade," 76–77.

19. Ibid., 78–79.

20. Ibid., 88–92.

21. Ayodeji Olukoji, "Prohibition and Paternalism: The State and the Clandestine Liquor Traffic in Northern Nigeria, c.1898–1918," *International Journal of African Historical Studies* 24 (1991): 354.

22. Ibid., 361.

23. White, "Drunken States," 674.

24. Diduk, "European Alcohol," 10.

25. Quoted in Charles van Onselen, "Randlords and Rotgut, 1886–1903: An Essay on the Role of Alcohol in the Development of European Imperialism and Southern African Capitalism, with Special Reference to Black Mineworkers in the Transvaal Republic," *History Workshop* 2 (1976): 50.

26. Ibid., 45–47.

27. Ibid., 52.

28. Pamela Scully, "Liquor and Labor in the Western Cape, 1870–1900," in *Liquor and Labor in Southern Africa*, ed. Jonathan Crush and Charles Ambler (Athens: Ohio University Press, 1992), 69–70.

29. Van Onselen, "Randlords and Rotgut," 81.

30. Kenneth Christmom, "Historical Overview of Alcohol in the African American Community," *Journal of Black Studies* 25 (1995): 326–27.

31. Quoted in William E. Unrau, *White Man's Wicked Water: The Alcohol Trade and Prohibition in Indian Country, 1802–1892* (Lawrence: University of Kansas Press, 1996), 9. Much of the following section on alcohol in the nineteenth-century United States draws on this work.

32. Ibid., 17.

33. Peter Mancall, "Men, Women and Alcohol in Indian Villages in the Great Lakes Region in the Early Republic," *Journal of the Early Republic* 15 (1995): 440.

34. Unrau, *White Man's Wicked Water*, 9.

35. Ibid., 21.

36. Ibid., 35–36.

37. John R. Wunder, *"Retained by the People": A History of American Indians and the Bill of Rights* (New York: Oxford University Press, 1994), 23.

38. Izumi Ishii, "Alcohol and Politics in the Cherokee Nations before Removal," *Ethnohistory* 50 (2003): 670.

39. Unrau, *White Man's Wicked water*, 97.

40. Andrei V. Grinëv, "The Distribution of Alcohol among the Natives of Russian America," *Arctic Anthropology* 47 (2010): 73.

41. Ibid., 75.

42. Nella Lee, "Impossible Mission: A History of the Legal Control of Native Drinking in Alaska," *Wicazo Sa Review* 12 (1997): 99.

43. Ibid., 100.

44. Robert A. Campbell, "Making Sober Citizens: The Legacy of Indigenous Alcohol Regulation in Canada, 1777–1985," *Journal of Canadian Studies* 42 (2008): 106–7.

45. Mimi Ajzenstadt, "The Changing Image of the State: The Case of Alcohol Regulation in British Columbia, 1871–1925," *Canadian Journal of Sociology* 19 (1994): 443–44.

46. Campbell, "Making Sober Citizens," 108; Kathryn A. Abbott, "Alcohol and the Anishinaabeg of Minnesota in the Early Twentieth Century," *Western Historical Quarterly* 30 (1999): 25–43.

47. Erica J. Peters, "Taste, Taxes, and Technologies: Industrializing Rice Alcohol in Northern Vietnam, 1902–1913," *French Historical Studies* 27 (2004): 569.

48. Ibid., 590.

49. Ibid., 594–95.

50. Jeffrey W. Alexander, *Brewed in Japan: The Evolution of the Japanese Beer Industry* (Vancouver: University of British Columbia Press, 2013), 9.

51. Julia Lovell, *The Opium War* (London: Picador, 2011).

52. Neil Gunson, "On the Incidence of Alcoholism and Intemperance in Early Pacific Missions," *Journal of Pacific History* 1 (1966): 50.

53. Ibid., 58.

54. Ibid.

55. Ibid., 60.

56. Charles F. Urbanowicz, "Drinking in the Polynesian Kingdom of Tonga," *Ethnohistory* 22(1975): 40.

57. Mac Marshall and Leslie B. Marshall, "Holy and Unholy Spirits: The Effects of Missionization on Alcohol Use in Eastern Micronesia," *Journal of Pacific History* 15 (1980): 142.

58. Ibid., 152.

59. Ibid., 160.

CHAPTER TWELVE

1. John Stevenson, *British Society, 1914–45* (Harmondsworth: Penguin, 1984), 71.

2. Information provided by Professor Geoffrey Giles, University of Florida.

3. Sir Victor Horsley, *The Rum Ration in the British Army* (London: Richard J. James, 1915), 7.

4. Ibid., 4.

5. *British Medical Journal* 1, no. 2822 (January 30, 1915): 203–6.

6. John Ellis, *Eye Deep in Hell* (Glasgow: Collins, 1976), 95.

7. Henry Carter, *The Control of the Drink Trade: A Contribution to National Efficiency, 1915–1917* (London: Longman, 1918), 282–83.

8. Patricia Herlihy, "'Joy of the Rus': Rites and Rituals of Russian Drinking," *Russian Review* 50 (1991): 141.

9. *British Medical Journal* 1, no. 2825 (February 20, 1915): 344.

10. Horsley, *Rum Ration*, 7.

11. George E. Snow, "Socialism, Alcoholism, and the Russian Working Classes before 1917," in *Drinking: Behavior and Belief in Modern History*, ed. Susanna Barrows and Robin Room (Berkeley: University of California Press, 1991), 257.

12. David Christian, "Prohibition in Russia, 1914–1925," *Australian Slavonic and East European Studies* 9 (1995): 99–100.

13. "Alcohol and the Soldier," *British Medical Journal* 1, no. 2876 (February 12, 1916): 247.

14. *Times* (London), January 11, 1917, quoted in Catherine J. Kudlick, "Fighting the Internal and External Enemies: Alcoholism in World War I France," *Contemporary Drug Problems* 12 (1985): 136.

15. *The Echo of the Trenches*, quoted in *Histoire Sociale et Culturelle du Vin*, ed. Gilbert Garrier (Paris: Larousse, 1998), 366.

16. Ernest Hemingway, *In Our Time* (New York: Scribners, 1986), 13.

17. David Lloyd George, *War Memoirs of David Lloyd George* (London: Nicholson and Watson, 1933), 324–25.

18. L. Margaret Barnett, *British Food Policy during the First World War* (Boston: Allen & Unwin, 1985), 105–6.

19. *British Medical Journal* 1, no. 2833 (April 17, 1915): 687.

20. Ibid., 688.

21. E. M. Jellinek, "Interpretation of Alcohol Consumption Rates with Special Reference to Statistics of Wartime Consumption," *Quarterly Journal of Studies on Alcohol* 3 (1942–43): 277.

22. David W. Gutzke, "Gender, Class, and Public Drinking in Britain during the First World War," in *The Changing Face of Drink: Substance, Imagery and Behaviour*, ed. Jack S. Blocker Jr. and Cheryl Krasnick Warsh (Ottawa: Publications Histoire Sociale/Social History, 1977), 293.

23. Jellinek, "Alcohol Consumption Rates," 277.

24. Gwylmor Prys Williams and George Thompson Brake, *Drink in Great Britain, 1900–1979* (London: Edsall, 1980), 375.

25. Barnett, *British Food Policy*, 179–80.

26. Kudlick, "Fighting the Internal and External Enemies," 147.

27. Ibid., 148.

28. Jean-Jacques Becker, *The Great War and the French People* (Leamington Spa: Berg, 1985), 128.

29. Jellinek, "Alcohol Consumption Rates," 279–80.

30. Shirley E. Woods Jr., *The Molson Saga* (Scarborough, Ontario: Avon, 1983), 232–33.

31. Helena Stone, "The Soviet Government and Moonshine, 1917–1929," *Cahiers du Monde Russe et Soviétique* 27 (1986): 359.

32. Ibid., 362.

33. John Joseph Pershing, *My Experiences in the World War* (New York: Frederick A. Stokes, 1931), 282.

34. Kudlick, "Fighting the Internal and External Enemies," 133–36.

CHAPTER THIRTEEN

1. Nurdeen Deuraseh, "Is Imbibing *Al-Khamr* (Intoxicating Drink) for Medical Purposes Permissible by Islamic Law?," *Arab Law Quarterly* 18 (2003): 355–64.

2. Ricardo Campos Marin, *Socialismo Marxista e Higiene Publica: La Lucha Antialcohólica en la II Internacional (1890–1914/19* (Madrid: Fundación de Investigaciones Marxistas, 1992), 119–39.

3. Laura L. Phillips, "Message in a Bottle: Working-Class Culture and the Struggle for Political Legitimacy, 1900–1929," *Russian Review* 56 (1997): 25–26.

4. Stephen White, *Russia Goes Dry: Alcohol, State and Society* (Cambridge: Cambridge University Press, 1996), 16.

5. Kate Transchel, "Vodka and Drinking in Early Soviet Factories," in *The Human Tradition in Modern Russia*, ed. William B. Husband (Wilmington, N.C.: Scholarly Resources, 2000), 136–37.

6. Carter Elwood, *The Non-Geometric Lenin* (London: Anthem Press, 2011), 133–35.

7. Phillips, "Message in a Bottle," 32.

8. Helena Stone, "The Soviet Government and Moonshine, 1917–1929," *Cahiers du Monde Russe et Soviétique* 27 (1986): 360.

9. White, *Russia Goes Dry*, 21–22.

10. Jack S. Blocker, "Did Prohibition Really Work?," *American Journal of Public Health* 96 (2006): 236.

11. James Temple Kirby, "Alcohol and Irony: The Campaign of Westmoreland Davis for Governor, 1909–1917," *Virginia Magazine of History and Biography* 73 (1965): 267.

12. Ernest R. Forbes, "The East-Coast Rum-Running Economy," in *Drink in Canada: Historical Essays*, ed. Cheryl Krasnick Warsh (Montreal: McGill-Queen's University Press, 1993), 166–67.

13. Gabriela Recio, "Drugs and Alcohol: US Prohibition and the Origin of the Drug Trade in Mexico, 1910–1930," *Journal of Latin American Studies* 34 (2002): 32–33.

14. Alfred G. Hill, "Kansas and Its Prohibition Enforcement," *Annals of the American Academy of Political and Social Science* 109 (1923): 134.

15. John J. Guthrie Jr., "Hard Times, Hard Liquor and Hard Luck: Selective Enforcement of Prohibition in North Florida, 1928–1933," *Florida Historical Quarterly* 72 (1994): 437–38.

16. Joseph K. Willing, "The Profession of Bootlegging," *Annals of the American Academy of Political and Social Science* 125 (1926): 47.

17. Professor W. Dixon of Cambridge University condemned the popularity of cocktails as "particularly pernicious for young people of either sex, who form a large percentage of cocktail drinkers, partly to lose their shyness and partly in a spirit of bravado. . . . [Cocktails

help] to promote the habit of excessive drinking more than any other type of beverage" (*British Medical Journal*, January 5, 1929, 31).

18. Jacob M. Appel, "'Physicians Are Not Bootleggers': The Short, Peculiar Life of the Medicinal Alcohol Movement," *Bulletin of the History of Medicine* 82 (2008): 357.

19. Ibid., 361.

20. Ibid., 361–66.

21. Ambrose Hunsberger, "The Practice of Pharmacy under the Volstead Act," *Annals of the American Academy of Political and Social Science* 109 (1923): 179–92.

22. Blocker, "Did Prohibition Really Work?," 236.

23. Guthrie, "Hard Times, Hard Liquor," 448.

24. Jeffrey A. Miron and Jeffrey Zwiebel, "Alcohol Consumption during Prohibition," *American Economic Review* 81 (1991): 242–47.

25. Ben Fallaw, "Dry Law, Wet Politics: Drinking and Prohibition in Post-Revolutionary Yucatán, 1915–1935," *Latin American Research Review* 37 (2001): 40–41.

26. Ibid., 46.

27. Recio, "Drugs and Alcohol," 29–30.

28. Ibid., 27–28.

29. Craig Heron, *Booze: A Distilled History* (Toronto: Between the Lines, 2003), 179–81.

30. Ibid., 183.

31. Sturla Nordlund, "Norway," in *Alcohol and Temperance in Modern History: An International Encyclopedia*, ed. Jack S. Blocker Jr., David M. Fahey, and Ian R. Tyrrell (Santa Barbara: ABC-CLIO, 2003), 2:459–60.

32. Mark Lawrence Shrad, *The Political Power of Bad Ideas: Networks, Institutions, and the Global Prohibition Wave* (Oxford: Oxford University Press, 2010), 96–97; Halfdan Bengtsson, "The Temperance Movement and Temperance Legislation in Sweden," *Annals of the American Academy of Political and Social Science* 197 (1938): 134–53.

33. Shrad, *Political Power of Bad Ideas*, 97.

34. Ibid., 97–103.

35. "Atreya," *Towards Dry India* (Madras: Dikshit Publishing, 1933), 82–83.

36. Ibid., 143.

37. Thomas Karlsson and Esa Österberg, "Belgium," in Blocker, Fahey, and Tyrell, *Alcohol and Temperance in Modern History*, 1:105.

38. Charlotte Macdonald, "New Zealand," in Blocker, Fahey, and Tyrell, *Alcohol and Temperance in Modern History*, 2:454.

39. Shrad, *Political Power of Bad Ideas*, 9.

CHAPTER FOURTEEN

1. Mark Edward Lender and James Kirby Martin, *Drinking in America: A History* (New York: Free Press, 1987), 135.

2. This discussion draws on John J. Guthrie Jr., "Rekindling the Spirits: From National Prohibition to Local Option in Florida, 1928–1935," *Florida Historical Quarterly* 74 (1995): 23–39.

3. This section draws on Scott Thompson and Gary Genosko, *Punched Drunk: Alcohol, Surveillance and the LCBO, 1927–1975* (Halifax: Fernwood Publishing, 2009).

4. Gwylmor Prys Williams and George Thompson Brake, *Drink in Great Britain, 1900–1979* (London: Edsall, 1980), 83–84.

5. This draws on David W. Gutzke, "Improved Pubs and Road Houses: Rivals for Public Affection in Interwar England," *Brewery History* 119 (2005): 2–9.

6. Ibid., 3.

7. *Alcohol: Its Action on the Human Organism*, 3rd ed. (London: HMSO, 1938).

8. Sylvanus Stall, *What a Young Boy Ought to Know* (Philadelphia: John C. Winston Co., 1936), 135–37.

9. Sarah Howard, "Selling Wine to the French: Official Attempts to Increase French Wine Consumption, 1931–1936," *Food and Foodways* 12 (2004): 197–224.

10. Ibid., 203.

11. John Burnett, *Liquid Pleasures: A Social History of Drinks in Modern Britain* (London: Routledge, 1999), 136.

12. Howard, "Selling Wine to the French," 209 fig. 1.

13. Ibid., 211.

14. Eugene, Ore., *Register-Guardian*, June 15, 1932, 6.

15. B. R. Mitchell, *European Historical Statistics, 1750–1975*, 2nd rev. ed. (London: Macmillan, 1981), 495.

16. Hermann Fahrenkrug, "Alcohol and the State in Nazi Germany, 1933–45," in *Drinking: Behavior and Belief in Modern History*, ed. Susanna Barrows and Robin Room (Berkeley: University of California Press, 1991), 315–34.

17. Ibid., 322.

18. Ibid., 323.

19. Geoffrey J. Giles, "Student Drinking in the Third Reich: Academic Tradition and the Nazi Revolution," in Barrows and Room, *Drinking*, 142.

20. Helena Stone, "The Soviet Government and Moonshine, 1917–1929," *Cahiers du Monde Russe et Soviétique* 27 (1986): 362–63.

21. Ibid., 364.

22. Joseph Barnes, "Liquor Regulation in Russia," *Annals of the American Academy of Political and Social Science* 163 (1932): 230.

23. Stephen White, *Russia Goes Dry: Alcohol, State and Society* (Cambridge: Cambridge University Press, 1996), 26–27.

24. Ibid., 27, 197 n. 133.

25. C. Langhammer, "'A Public House Is for All Classes, Men and Women Alike': Women, Leisure and Drink in Second World War England," *Women's History Review* 12 (2003): 423–43.

26. Tom Harrison, *The Pub and the People* (London, 1943; repr., London: Cresset, 1987), 135.

27. Christopher R. Browning, *Ordinary Men: Reserve Battalion 101 and the Final Solution in Poland* (New York: HarperCollins, 1992), 93, 100.

28. Fahrenkrug, "Alcohol and the State," 331.

29. Quoted in Howard, "Selling Wine to the French," 206.

30. Don Kladstrup and Petie Kladstrup, *Wine and War: The French, the Nazis and the Battle for France's Greatest Treasure* (New York: Broadway Books, 2001), 76–77.

31. Charles K. Warner, *The Winegrowers of France and the Government since 1875* (New York: Columbia University Press, 1960), 158–62.

32. Quoted in Lori Rotskoff, *Love on the Rocks: Men, Women, and Alcohol in Post–World War II America* (Chapel Hill: University of North Carolina Press, 2002), 47–48.

33. Ibid., 49.

CHAPTER FIFTEEN

1. Lori Rotskoff, *Love on the Rocks: Men, Women, and Alcohol in Post–World War II America* (Chapel Hill: University of North Carolina Press, 2002), 194–203.

2. Ibid., 208–9.

3. W. Scott Haine, "Drink, Sociability, and Social Class in France, 1789–1945: The Emergence of a Proletarian Public Sphere," in *Alcohol: A Social and Cultural History*, ed. Mack P. Holt (Oxford: Berg, 2006), 140.

4. Patricia E. Prestwich, *Drink and the Politics of Social Reform: Antialcoholism in France since 1870* (Palo Alto: Society for the Promotion of Science and Scholarship, 1988), 258–60.

5. Kim Munholland, "*Mon docteur le vin*: Wine and Health in France, 1900–1950," in Holt, *Alcohol*, 85–86.

6. Prestwich, *Drink and the Politics of Social Reform*, 300, table F.

7. Gwylmor Prys Williams and George Thompson Brake, *Drink in Great Britain, 1900–1979* (London: Edsall, 1980), 132–33.

8. *Global Status Report on Alcohol and Health* (Geneva: World Health Organization, 2011), 4.

9. Ibid., 188.

10. National Health Service (United Kingdom), *Statistics on Alcohol 2012*, 14,16. https://catalogue.ic.nhs.uk/publications/public-health/alcohol/alco-eng-2012/alco-eng-2012-rep.pdf (accessed February 25, 2013).

11. *Global Status Report on Alcohol and Health*, 140.

12. Haine, "Drink, Sociability, and Social Class in France."

13. http://www.abc.state.va.us/facts/legalage.html (accessed August 11, 2012).

14. *Global Status Report: Alcohol Policy* (Geneva: World Health Organization, 2004), 13–15.

15. Williams and Brake, *Drink in Great Britain*, 387, table III.10; 516, table III.139.

16. *Global Status Report on Alcohol and Health*, 47.

17. Ibid., 11.

18. http://www.espad.org/Uploads/ESPAD_reports/2011/The_2011_ESPAD_Report_SUMMARY.pdf (accessed September 5, 2012).

19. Much of this section on the Soviet Union draws on Stephen White, *Russia Goes Dry: Alcohol, State and Society* (Cambridge: Cambridge University Press, 1996).

20. Vladimir G. Treml, *Alcohol in the USSR: A Statistical Study* (Durham, N.C.: Duke University Press, 1982), 68, table 6.1.

21. White, *Russia Goes Dry*, 70–73.

22. Ibid., 91.

23. Ibid., 103, table 4.1.

24. Ibid., 103.

25. Ibid., 141, table 6.1.

26. *Global Status Report on Alcohol and Health*, 203.

27. White, *Russia Goes Dry*, 165.

28. *Pravda*, April 4, 2011, http://english.pravda.ru/business/finance/04–04–2011/117436-alcohol_tobacco-0/ (accessed August 11, 2012).

29. RiaNovosti, April 5, 2012, http://en.rian.ru/business/20120405/172627949.html (accessed August 11, 2012).

30. James Nicholls, *The Politics of Alcohol: A History of the Drink Question in England* (Manchester: Manchester University Press, 2009), 1.

31. "French Paradox Now Available in Tablets," *Decanter*, June 7, 2001, http://www.decanter.com/news/wine-news/488845/french-paradox-now-available-in-tablets (accessed February 21, 2013).

CONCLUSION

1. *Global Status Report on Alcohol and Health* (Geneva: World Health Organization, 2011), 140, 188, 234.

Select Bibliography

The bibliography on alcohol and alcohol-related subjects is immense and growing, and this bibliography includes only those works that were most useful in the preparation of this book.

REFERENCE WORKS

Blocker, Jack S., Jr., David M. Fahey, and Ian R. Tyrrell, eds. *Alcohol and Temperance in Modern History: An International Encyclopedia*. 2 vols. Santa Barbara: ABC-CLIO, 2003.

Brennan, Thomas E., ed. *Public Drinking in the Early Modern World: Voices from the Tavern, 1500–1800*. 4 vols. London: Pickering & Chatto, 2011.

Fahey, David M., and Jon S. Miller, eds. *Alcohol and Drugs in North America: A Historical Encyclopedia*. Santa Barbara: ABC-CLIO, 2013.

Smith, Andrew F., ed. *Oxford Encyclopedia of Food and Drink in America*. 2nd ed. New York: Oxford University Press, 2013.

BOOKS

Adams, Jad. *Hideous Absinthe: A History of the Devil in a Bottle*. London: Tauris Parke, 2008.

Albala, Ken. *Eating Right in the Renaissance*. Berkeley: University of California Press, 2002.

Alexander, Jeffrey W. *Brewed in Japan: The Evolution of the Japanese Beer Industry*. Vancouver: University of British Columbia Press, 2013.

Apicius: Cookery and Dining in Imperial Rome. Edited and translated by Joseph Dommers Vehling. New York: Dover, 1977.

Badri, M. B. *Islam and Alcoholism*. Plainfield, Ind.: American Trust Publications, 1976.

Bablor, Thomas, et al. *Alcohol: No Ordinary Commodity*. 2nd ed. Oxford: Oxford University Press, 2010.

Barr, Andrew. *Drink: A Social History of America*. New York: Carroll & Graf, 1999.

Bennett, Judith M. *Ale, Beer and Brewsters in England: Women's Work in a Changing World, 1300–1600*. New York: Oxford University Press, 1996.

Blocker, Jack S., Jr., and Cheryl Krasnick Warsh, eds. *The Changing Face of Drink: Substance, Imagery and Behaviour*. Ottawa: Publications Histoire Sociale/Social History, 1977.

Bourély, Béatrice. *Vignes et Vins de l'Abbaye de Cîteaux en Bourgogne*. Nuits-St-Georges: Editions du Tastevin, 1998.

Brennan, Thomas. *Burgundy to Champagne: The Wine Trade in Early Modern France*. Baltimore: Johns Hopkins University Press, 1997.

Bruman, Henry J. *Alcohol in Ancient Mexico*. Salt Lake City: University of Utah Press, 2000.

Brunschwig Hieronymus. *Das Buch zu Distilieren*. Strasburg, 1532.

Bucknill, John Charles. *Habitual Drunkenness and Insane Drunkards*. London: Macmillan, 1878.

Burford, Alison. *Land and Labour in the Greek World*. Baltimore: Johns Hopkins University Press, 1993.

Burnett, John. *Liquid Pleasures: A Social History of Drinks in Modern Britain*. London: Routledge, 1999.

Campos Marin, Ricardo. *Socialismo Marxista e Higiene Publica: La Lucha Antialcoholica en la II Internacional (1890–1914/19)*. Madrid: Fundación de Investigaciones Marxistas, 1992.

Carter, Henry. *The Control of the Drink Trade: A Contribution to National Efficiency, 1915–1917*. London: Longman, 1918.

Cato, Marcius Porcius. *On Agriculture*. London: Heineman, 1934.

Christian, David. *Living Water: Vodka and Russian Society on the Eve of Emancipation*. Oxford: Oxford University Press, 1990.

Clark, Peter. *The English Alehouse: A Social History, 1200–1830*. London: Longman, 1983.

Conroy, David W. *In Public Houses: Drink and the Revolution of Authority in Colonial Massachusetts*. Chapel Hill: University of North Carolina Press, 1995.

Craeybeckx, Jan. *Un Grand Commerce d'Importation: Les Vins de France aux Anciens Pays-Bas (XIIIe–XVIe Siècle)*. Paris: SEVPEN, 1958.

Crush, Jonathan, and Charles Ambler, eds. *Liquor and Labor in Southern Africa*. Athens: Ohio University Press, 1992.

Curto, José C. *Enslaving Spirits: The Portuguese-Brazilian Alcohol Trade at Luanda and Its Hinterland, c. 1550–1830*. Leiden: Brill, 2004.

Dannenbaum, Jed. *Drink and Disorder: Temperance Reform in Cincinnati from the Washington Revival to the WCTU*. Urbana: University of llinois Press, 1984.

Davis, Marni. *Jews and Booze: Becoming American in the Age of Prohibition*. New York: New York University Press, 2012.

de Blij, Harm Jan, ed. *Viticulture in Geographical Perspective*. Miami: Miami Geographical Society, 1992.

de Garine, Igor, and Valerie de Garine, eds. *Drinking: Anthropological Approaches*. New York: Berghahn, 2001.

Dion, Roger. *Histoire de la Vigne et du Vin en France des Origines au XiXe Siècle*. Paris: Flammarion, 1977.

A Dissertation upon Drunkenness . . . Shewing to What an Intolerable Pitch that Vice is arriv'd at in this Kingdom. London, 1708.

Distilled Spirituous Liquors the Bane of the Nation. London, 1736.

Fagan, Brian. *Elixir: A History of Water and Humankind*. New York: Bloomsbury, 2011.

Fenton, Alexander, ed. *Order and Disorder: The Health Implications of Eating and Drinking in the Nineteenth and Twentieth Centuries*. Edinburgh: Tuckwell Press, 2000.

Flandrin, Jean-Louis, and Massimo Montanari, eds. *Food: A Culinary History from Antiquity to the Present*. London: Penguin, 2000.

Fleming, Stuart J. *Vinum: The Story of Roman Wine*. Glen Mills, Pa.: Art Flair, 2001.

Foss, Richard. *Rum: A Global History*. London: Reaktion, 2012.

Francis, A. D. *The Wine Trade*. London: A & C Black, 1972.

Fuller, Robert C. *Religion and Wine: A Cultural History of Wine Drinking in the United States*. Knoxville: University of Tennessee Press, 1996.

Garlan, Yvon. *Vin et Amphores de Thasos*. Athens: Ecole Française d'Athènes, 1988.

Garrier, Gilbert, ed. *Histoire Sociale et Culturelle du Vin*. Paris: Larousse, 1998.

———. *Le Vin des Historiens*. Suze-la-Rousse: Université du Vin, 1990.

Gately, Iain. *Drink: A Cultural History of Alcohol*. New York: Gotham, 2008.

Global Status Report: Alcohol Policy. Geneva: World Health Organization, 2004.

Global Status Report on Alcohol and Health. Geneva: World Health Organization, 2011.

Goubert, Jean-Pierre. *The Conquest of Water*. Princeton: Princeton University Press, 1986.

Gusfield, Joseph R. *Contested Meanings: The Construction of Alcohol Problems*. Madison: University of Wisconsin Press, 1996.

———. *Drinking-Driving and the Symbolic Order*. Chicago: University of Chicago Press, 1981.

Gutzke, David, ed. *Alcohol in the British Isles from Roman Times to 1996: An Annotated Bibliography*. Westport, Conn.: Greenwood, 1996.

Gutzke, David W. *Pubs & Progressives: Reinventing the Public House in England, 1896–1960*. DeKalb: Northern Illinois University Press, 2006.

Guy, Kolleen M. *When Champagne became French: Wine and the Making of a National Identity*. Baltimore: Johns Hopkins University Press, 2003.

Haine, W. Scott. *The World of the Paris Café: Sociability among the French Working Class, 1789–1914*. Baltimore: Johns Hopkins University Press, 1996.

Hames, Gina. *Alcohol in World History*. London: Routledge, 2012.

Hammond, P. W. *Food and Feast in Medieval England*. Stroud: Allan Sutton, 1993.

Hancock, David. *Oceans of Wine: Madeira and the Emergence of American Trade and Taste*. New Haven: Yale University Press, 2009.

Harper, William T. *Origins and Rise of the British Distillery*. Lewiston: Edwin Mellon, 1999.

Harrison, Brian. *Drink and the Victorians: The Temperance Question in England, 1815–1872*. Pittsburgh: University of Pittsburgh Press, 1971.

Harrison, Tom. *The Pub and the People*. London, 1943. Reprint, London: Cresset, 1987.

Herlihy, Patricia. *Vodka: A Global History*. London: Reaktion, 2012.

Heron, Craig. *Booze: A Distilled History*. Toronto: Between the Lines, 2003.

Heskett, Randall, and Joel Butler. *Divine Vintage: Following the Wine Trail from Genesis to the Modern Age*. New York: Palgrave, 2012.

Hippocrates. London: Heinemann, 1967.

Hodge, Trevor. *Ancient Greek France*. Philadelphia: University of Pennsylvania Press, 1999.

Hoffman, Constance. *Medieval Agriculture, the Southern French Countryside, and the Early Cistercians: A Study of Forty-Three Monasteries*. Philadelphia: American Philosophical Society, 1986.

Hornsey, Ian S. *A History of Beer and Brewing*. Cambridge: Royal Society of Chemistry, 2003.

Horsley, Sir Victor. *The Rum Ration in the British Army*. London: Richard J. James, 1915.

Hurley, Jon. *A Matter of Taste: A History of Wine Drinking in Britain*. Stroud: Tempus, 2005.

An Impartial Inquiry into the Present State of the British Distillery. London, 1736.

Johnson, Hugh. *The Story of Wine*. London: Mitchell Beazley, 1989.

Kay, Billy, and Caileen MacLean. *Knee-Deep in Claret: A Celebration of Wine and Scotland*. Edinburgh: Mainstream Publishing, 1983.

Kennedy, Philip F. *The Wine Song in Classical Arabic Poetry: Abu Nuwas and the Literary Tradition*. Oxford: Clarendon Press, 1997.

Kladstrup, Don, and Petie Kladstrup. *Wine and War: The French, the Nazis and the Battle for France's Greatest Treasure*. New York: Broadway Books, 2001.

Koeppel, Gerard T. *Water for Gotham*. Princeton: Princeton University Press, 2000.

Kueny, Kathryn. *The Rhetoric of Sobriety: Wine in Early Islam*. Albany: State University of New York Press, 2001.

Lachiver, Marcel. *Vins, Vignes et Vignerons: Histoire du Vignoble Français*. Paris: Fayard, 1988.

Lanier, Doris. *Absinthe: The Cocaine of the Nineteenth Century*. Jefferson, NC: McFarland, 1995.

Lender, Mark Edward, and James Kirby Martin. *Drinking in America: A History*. New York: Free Press, 1987.

Loubère, Leo. *The Red and the White: The History of Wine in France and Italy in the Nineteenth Century*. Albany: State University of New York Press, 1978.

Lozarno Armendares, Teresa. *El Chinguirito: El Contrabando de Aguardiente de Caña y la Política Colonial*. Mexico: Universidad Nacional Autónima de México, 2005.

Lublin, Elizabeth Dorn. *Reforming Japan: The Woman's Christian Temperance Union in the Meiji Period*. Honolulu: University of Hawai'i Press, 2010.

Lukacs, Paul. *Inventing Wine: A New History of One of the World's Most Ancient Pleasures*. New York: Norton, 2012.

MacLean, Charles. *Scotch Whisky: A Liquid History*. London: Cassell, 2003.

Mager, Anne Kelk. *Beer, Sociability, and Masculinity in South Africa*. Bloomington: University of Indiana Press, 2010.

Maguin, Martine. *La Vigne et le Vin en Lorraine, XIV–XVe Siècle*. Nancy: Presses Universitaires de Nancy, 1982.

Mancall, Peter C. *Deadly Medicine: Indians and Alcohol in Early America*. Ithaca: Cornell University Press, 1997.

Martin, A. Lynn. *Alcohol, Violence and Disorder in Traditional Europe*. Kirksville, Mo.: Truman State University Press, 2009.

Mathias, Peter. *The Brewing Industry in England, 1700–1830*. Cambridge: Cambridge University Press, 1959.

McCarthy, Raymond, ed. *Drinking and Intoxication: Selected Readings in Social Attitudes and Control*. Glencoe, Ill.: Free Press, 1959.

McGovern, Patrick E. *Ancient Wine: The Search for the Origins of Viticulture*. Princeton: Princeton University Press, 2003.

———. *Uncorking the Past: The Quest for Wine, Beer and Other Alcoholic Beverages*. Berkeley: University of California Press, 2009.

McGovern, Patrick E., et al., eds. *Origins and Ancient History of Wine*. London: Routledge, 2004.

Meacham, Sarah Hand. *Every Home a Distillery: Alcohol, Gender, and Technology in the Colonial Chesapeake*. Baltimore: Johns Hopkins University Press, 2009.

Mendelson, Richard. *From Demon to Darling: A Legal History of Wine in America*. Berkeley: University of California Press, 2009.

Mittelman, Amy. *Brewing Battles: A History of American Beer*. New York: Algora, 2008.

National Health Service (United Kingdom). *Statistics on Alcohol 2012*. https://catalogue
.ic.nhs.uk/publications/public-health/alcohol/alco-eng-2012/alco-eng-2012-rep.pdf
. Accessed February 25, 2013.

Nelson, Max. *The Barbarian's Beverage: A History of Beer in Ancient Europe*. London: Routledge, 2005.

Nicholls, James. *The Politics of Alcohol: A History of the Drink Question in England*. Manchester: Manchester University Press, 2009.

Nourrisson, Didier. *Le Buveur du XIXe Siècle*. Paris: Albin Michel, 1990.

Ogle, Maureen. *Ambitious Brew: The Story of American Beer*. Orlando: Harvest, 2006.

Pan, Lynn. *Alcohol in Colonial Africa*. Uppsala: Scandinavian Institute of African Studies,
1975.

Paul, Harry W. *Bacchic Medicine: Wine and Alcohol Therapies from Napoleon to the French
Paradox*. Amsterdam: Rodopi, 2001.

Pearson, C. C., and J. Edwin Hendricks. *Liquor and Anti-Liquor in Virginia, 1619–1919*. Durham, N.C.: Duke University Press, 1967.

Pliny the Elder. *Histoire Naturelle*. Paris: Société d'Edition 'Les Belles Lettres,' 1958.

Phillips, Rod. *A Short History of Wine*. London: Penguin, 2000.

Pinney, Thomas. *A History of Wine in America: From the Beginnings to Prohibition*. Berkeley:
University of California Press, 1989.

———. *A History of Wine in America: From Prohibition to the Present*. Berkeley: University of
California Press, 2005.

Plack, Noelle. *Common Land, Wine and the French Revolution: Rural Society and Economy in
Southern France, c. 1789–1820*. London: Ashgate, 2009.

Pokhlebkin, William. *A History of Vodka*. London: Verso, 1992.

Poo, Mu-Chou. *Wine and Wine-Offering in the Religion of Ancient Egypt*. London: Kegan Paul
International, 1995.

Prestwich, Patricia E. *Drink and the Politics of Social Reform: Antialcoholism in France since
1870*. Palo Alto: Society for the Promotion of Science and Scholarship, 1988.

Roberts, James S. *Drink, Temperance and the Working Class in Nineteenth-Century Germany*.
Boston: Allen & Unwin, 1984.

Rose, Susan. *The Wine Trade in Medieval Europe, 100–1500*. London: Continuum, 2011.

Rotskoff, Lori. *Love on the Rocks: Men, Women, and Alcohol in Post–World War II America*.
Chapel Hill: University of North Carolina Press, 2002.

Rush, Benjamin. *Medical Inquiries and Observations*. 2nd ed. Philadelphia: Thomas Dobson,
1794.

Salzman, James. *Drinking Water: A History*. New York: Overlook Duckworth, 2012.

Scheindlin, Raymond P. *Wine, Women and Death: Medieval Hebrew Poems on the Good Life*.
Philadelphia: Jewish Publication Society, 1986.

Seward, Desmond. *Monks and Wine*. New York: Crown Books, 1979.

Shiman, Lilian Lewis. *Crusade against Drink in Victorian England*. New York: St. Martin's
Press, 1988.

Short, Richard. *Of Drinking Water, Against our Novelists, that Prescribed it in England*. London, 1656.

Shrad, Mark Lawrence. *The Political Power of Bad Ideas: Networks, Institutions, and the
Global Prohibition Wave*. Oxford: Oxford University Press, 2010.

Smith, Andrew. *Drinking History: Fifteen Turning Points in the Making of American Beverages.* New York: Columbia University Press, 2013.

Smith, Frederick H. *Caribbean Rum: A Social and Economic History.* Gainesville: University Press of Florida, 2005.

Smith, Gregg. *Beer in America: The Early Years, 1587–1840.* Boulder, Colo.: Siris Books, 1998.

Smyth, Adam, ed. *A Pleasing Sinne: Drink and Conviviality in 17th-Century England.* Cambridge: D. S. Brewer, 2004.

Stuart, Andrea. *Sugar in the Blood: A Family's Story of Slavery and Empire.* New York: Knopf, 2013.

Tait, Jennifer L. Woodruff. *The Poisoned Chalice: Eucharistic Grape Juice and Common-Sense Realism in Victorian Methodism.* Tuscaloosa: University of Alabama Press, 2010.

Tchernia, André. *Vin de l'Italie Romaine: Essaie d'Histoire Economique d'après les Amphores.* Rome: Ecole Française de Rome, 1986.

Thompson, H. Paul. *A Most Stirring and Significan Episode: Religion and the Rise and Fall of Prohibition in Black Atlanta, 1865–1887.* DeKalb: Northern Illinois University Press, 2013.

Thompson, Scott, and Gary Genosko. *Punched Drunk: Alcohol, Surveillance and the LCBO, 1927–1975.* Halifax: Fernwood Publishing, 2009.

Trawick, Buckner B. *Shakespeare and Alcohol.* Amsterdam: Editions Rodopi, 1978.

Treml, Vladimir G. *Alcohol in the USSR: A Statistical Study.* Durham, N.C.: Duke University Press, 1982.

Trotter, Thomas. *An Essay Medical, Philosophical, and Chemical on Drunkenness and its Effects on the Human Body.* London, 1804.

Unger, Richard W. *Beer in the Middle Ages and the Renaissance.* Philadelphia: University of Pennsylvania Press, 2004.

Unrau, William E. *White Man's Wicked Water: The Alcohol Trade and Prohibition in Indian Country, 1802–1892.* Lawrence: University of Kansas Press, 1996.

Valverde, Mariana. *Diseases of the Will: Alcohol and the Dilemmas of Freedom.* Cambridge: Cambridge University Press, 1998.

Vandermersch, Christian. *Vins et Amphores de Grande Grèce et de Sicile IVe–IIIe Siècles avant J.-C.* Naples: Centre Jean Bérard, 1994.

Vidal, Michel. *Histoire de la Vigne et des Vins dans le Monde, XIXe–XXe Siècles.* Bordeaux: Féret, 2001.

Le Vin à Travers les Ages: Produit de Qualité, Agent Economique. Bordeaux: Feret, 2001.

Viqueira Albán, Juan Pedro. *Propriety and Permissiveness in Bourbon Mexico.* Wilmington, N.C.: Scholarly Resources, 1999.

Warner, Charles K. *The Winegrowers of France and the Government since 1875.* New York: Columbia University Press, 1960.

Warner, Jessica. *Craze: Gin and Debauchery in an Age of Reason.* New York: Random House, 2002.

White, Stephen. *Russia Goes Dry: Alcohol, State and Society.* Cambridge: Cambridge University Press, 1996.

Wilkins, John, David Harvey, and Mike Dobson, eds. *Food in Antiquity.* Exeter: University of Exeter Press, 1995.

Williams, Gwylmor Prys, and George Thompson Brake. *Drink in Great Britain, 1900–1979.* London: Edsall, 1980.

Willis, Justin. *Potent Brews: A Social History of Alcohol in East Africa, 1850–1999*. London: British Institute in Eastern Africa, 2002.

Wilson, C. Anne. *Water of Life: A History of Wine-Distilling and Spirits, 500 BC–AD 2000*. Totnes, U.K.: Prospect Books, 2006.

Younger, William. *Gods, Men and Wine*. London: Michael Joseph, 1966.

Zhenping, Li. *Chinese Wine*. Cambridge: Cambridge University Press, 2010.

Zimmerman, Jonathan. *Distilling Democracy: Alcohol Education in America's Public Schools, 1880–1925*. Lawrence: University Press of Kansas, 1999.

ARTICLES AND ESSAYS

Adair, Daryl. "Respectable, Sober and Industrious? Attitudes to Alcohol in Early Colonial Adelaide." *Labour History* 70 (1996): 131–55.

Ajzenstadt, Mimi. "The Changing Image of the State: The Case of Alcohol Regulation in British Columbia, 1871–1925." *Canadian Journal of Sociology* 19 (1994): 441–60.

Albertson, Dean. "Puritan Liquor in the Planting of New England." *New England Quarterly* 23, no. 4 (1950): 477–90.

Allchin, F. R. "India: The Ancient Home of Distillation?" *Man* 14 (1979): 55–63.

Amouretti, Marie-Claire. "Vin, Vinaigre, Piquette dans l'Antiquité." In *Le Vin des Historiens*, edited by Gilbert Garrier, 75–87. Suze-la-Rousse: Université du Vin, 1990.

Appel, Jacob M. "'Physicians Are Not Bootleggers': The Short, Peculiar Life of the Medicinal Alcohol Movement." *Bulletin of the History of Medicine* 82 (2008): 355–86.

Bennett, Norman R. "The Golden Age of the Port Wine System, 1781–1807." *International History Review* 12 (1990): 221–48.

Blocker, Jack S. "Did Prohibition Really Work?" *American Journal of Public Health* 96 (2006): 233–43.

Bowers, John M. "'Dronkenesse is ful of stryvyng': Alcoholism and Ritual Violence in Chaucer's *Pardoner's Tale*." *English Literary History* 57 (1990): 757–84.

Brennan, Thomas. "The Anatomy of Inter-Regional Markets in the Early Modern Wine Trade." *Journal of European Economic History* 23 (1994): 581–607.

———. "Towards a Cultural History of Alcohol in France." *Journal of Social History* 23 (1989): 71–92.

Broich, John. "Engineering the Empire: British Water Supply Systems and Colonial Societies, 1850–1900." *Journal of British Studies* 46 (2007): 346–65.

Campbell, Robert A. "Making Sober Citizens: The Legacy of Indigenous Alcohol Regulation in Canada, 1777–1985." *Journal of Canadian Studies* 42 (2008): 105–26.

Carter, F. W. "Cracow's Wine Trade (Fourteenth to Eighteenth Centuries)." *Slavonic and East European Review* 65 (1987): 537–78.

Chard, Chloe. "The Intensification of Italy: Food, Wine and the Foreign in Seventeenth-Century Travel Writing." In *Food, Culture and History I*, edited by Gerald Mars and Valerie Mars. London: London Food Seminar, 1993.

Christian, David. "Prohibition in Russia, 1914–1925." *Australian Slavonic and East European Studies* 9 (1995): 89–118.

Christmom, Kenneth. "Historical Overview of Alcohol in the African American Community." *Journal of Black Studies* 25 (1995): 318–30.

Clark, Peter. "The 'Mother Gin' Controversy in the Early Eighteenth Century." *Transactions of the Royal Historical Society*, 5th ser., 38 (1988): 63–84.

Conrad, Maia. "Disorderly Drinking: Reconsidering Seventeenth-Century Iroquois Alcohol Abuse." *American Indian Quarterly* 23, no. 3&4 (1999): 1–11.

Dailey, D. C. "The Role of Alcohol among North American Indian Tribes as Reported in the Jesuit Relations." *Anthropologica* 10 (1968): 45–59.

Davidson, Andrew. "'Try the Alternative': The Built Heritage of the Temperance Movement." *Journal of the Brewery History Society* 123 (2006): 92–109.

Davis, Robert C. "Venetian Shipbuilders and the Fountain of Wine." *Past and Present* 156 (1997): 55–86.

Deuraseh, Nurdeen. "Is Imbibing *Al-Khamr* (Intoxicating Drink) for Medical Purposes Permissible by Islamic Law?" *Arab Law Quarterly* 18 (2003): 355–64.

Diduk, Susan. "European Alcohol, History, and the State in Cameroon." *African Studies Review* 36 (1993): 1–42.

Dietz, Vivien E. "The Politics of Whisky: Scottish Distillers, the Excise, and the Pittite State." *Journal of British Studies* 36 (1997): 35–69.

Dudley, Robert. "Evolutionary Origins of Human Alcoholism in Primate Frugivory." *Quarterly Review of Biology* 75, no. 1 (March 2000): 3–15.

Dumett, Raymond E. "The Social Impact of the European Liquor Trade on the Akan of Ghana (Gold Coast and Asante), 1875–1910." *Journal of Interdisciplinary History* 5 (1974): 69–101.

Dupebe, Jean. "La Diététique et l'Alimentation des Pauvres selon Sylvius." In *Pratiques et Discours Alimentaires à la Renaissance*, edited by J.-C. Margolin and R. Sauzet, 41–56. Paris: G.-P. Maisonneuve et Larose, 1982.

Dyer, Christopher. "Changes in Diet in the Late Middle Ages: The Case of Harvest Workers." *Agricultural Historical Review* 36 (1988): 21–37.

———. "The Consumer and the Market in the Later Middle Ages." *Economic History Review* 42 (1989): 305–27.

Fallaw, Ben. "Dry Law, Wet Politics: Drinking and Prohibition in Post-Revolutionary Yucatán, 1915–1935." *Latin American Research Review* 37 (2001): 37–65.

Funnerton, Patricia. "Not Home: Alehouses, Ballads, and the Vagrant Husband in Early Modern England." *Journal of Medieval and Early Modern Studies* 32 (2002): 493–518.

Gilmore, Thomas B. "James Boswell's Drinking." *Eighteenth-Century Studies* 24 (1991): 337–57.

Gough, J. B. "Winecraft and Chemistry in Eighteenth-Century France: Chaptal and the Invention of Chaptalization." *Technology and Culture* 39 (1998): 74–104.

Grinëv, Andrei V. "The Distribution of Alcohol among the Natives of Russian America." *Arctic Anthropology* 47 (2010): 69–79.

Grivetti, Louis E., and Elizabeth A. Applegate. "From Olympia to Atlanta: A Cultural-Historical Perspective on Diet and Athletic Training." *Journal of Nutrition* 127 (1997): 861–68.

Gunson, Neil. "On the Incidence of Alcoholism and Intemperance in Early Pacific Missions." *Journal of Pacific History* 1 (1966): 43–62.

Guthrie, John J., Jr. "Hard Times, Hard Liquor and Hard Luck: Selective Enforcement of Prohibition in North Florida, 1928–1933." *Florida Historical Quarterly* 72 (1994): 435–52.

————. "Rekindling the Spirits: From National Prohibition to Local Option in Florida, 1928–1935." *Florida Historical Quarterly* 74 (1995): 23–39.

Gutzke, David W. "Improved Pubs and Road Houses: Rivals for Public Affection in Interwar England." *Brewery History* 119 (2005): 2–9.

Halenko, Oleksander. "Wine Production, Marketing and Consumption in the Ottoman Crimea, 1520–1542." *Journal of the Economic and Social History of the Orient* 47 (2004): 507–47.

Hammer, Carl I. "A Hearty Meal? The Prison Diets of Cranmer and Latimer." *Sixteenth Century Journal* 30 (1999): 653–80.

Hancock, David. "Commerce and Conversation in the Eighteenth-Century Atlantic: The Invention of Madeira Wine." *Journal of Interdisciplinary History* 29 (1998): 197–219.

Heap, Simon. "'A Bottle of Gin Is Dangled before the Nose of the Natives': The Economic Uses of Imported Liquor in Southern Nigeria, 1860–1920." *African Economic History* 33 (2005): 69–85.

Hendricks, Rick. "Viticulture in El Paso del Norte during the Colonial Period." *Agricultural History* 78 (2004): 191–200.

Herlihy, Patricia, "'Joy of the Rus': Rites and Rituals of Russian Drinking." *Russian Review* 50 (1991): 131–47.

Hernández Palomo, José Jesús. "El Pulque: Usos Indígenas y Abusos Criollos." In *El Vino de Jerez y Otras Bebidas Espirituosas en la Historia de España y América*. Madrid: Servicio de Publicaciones del Ayuntamiento de Jerez, 2004.

Hill Curth, Louise. "The Medicinal Value of Wine in Early Modern England." *Social History of Alcohol and Drugs* 18 (2003): 35–50.

Holt, James B., et al. "Religious Affiliation and Alcohol Consumption in the United States." *Geographical Review* 96 (2006): 523–42.

Holt, Mack P. "Europe Divided: Wine, Beer and Reformation in Sixteenth-Century Europe." In *Alcohol: A Social and Cultural History*, edited by Mack P. Holt, 25–40. Oxford: Berg, 2006.

————. "Wine, Community and Reformation." *Past and Present* 138 (1993): 58–93.

Holt, Tim. "Demanding the Right to Drink: The Two Great Hyde Park Demonstrations." *Brewery History* 118 (2005): 26–40.

Homan, Michael M. "Beer and Its Drinkers: An Ancient Near Eastern Love Story." *Near Eastern Archaeology* 67 (2004): 84–95.

Hook, Christopher, Helen Tarbet, and David Ball. "Classically Intoxicated." *British Medical Journal* 335 (December 22–29, 2007): 1302–4.

Howard, Sarah. "Selling Wine to the French: Official Attempts to Increase French Wine Consumption, 1931–1936." *Food and Foodways* 12 (2004): 197–224.

Hudson, Nicholas F. "Changing Places: The Archaeology of the Roman *Convivium*." *American Journal of Archaeology* 114 (2010): 663–95.

Hughes, James N., III. "Pine Ridge, Whiteclay, and Indian Liquor Law." University of Nebraska College of Law, Federal Indian Law Seminar, December 13, 2010. http://www.jdsupra.com/documents/4c1267de-b226-4e76-bd8a-4a2548169500.pdf. Accessed April 26, 2012.

Ishii, Izumi. "Alcohol and Politics in the Cherokee Nations before Removal." *Ethnohistory* 50 (2003): 671–95.

Jellinek, E. M. "Interpretation of Alcohol Consumption Rates with Special Reference to Statistics of Wartime Consumption." *Quarterly Journal of Studies on Alcohol* 3 (1942–43): 267–80.

Jennings, Justin, Kathleen L. Antrobus, Sam J. Antencio, Erin Glavich, Rebecca Johnson, German Loffler, and Christine Luu. "'Drinking Beer in a Blissful Mood': Alcohol Production, Operational Chains, and Feasting in the Ancient World." *Current Anthropology* 46 (2005): 275–303.

Joffe, Alexander H. "Alcohol and Social Complexity in Ancient Western Asia." *Current Anthropology* 39 (1998): 297–322.

Johnston, A. J. B. "Alcohol Consumption in Eighteenth-Century Louisbourg and the Vain Attempts to Control It." *French Colonial History* 2 (2002): 61–76.

Kearney, H. F. "The Irish Wine Trade, 1614–15." *Irish Historical Studies* 36 (1955): 400–442.

Keller, Mark. "The Old and the New in the Treatment of Alcoholism." In *Alcohol Interventions: Historical and Sociocultural Approaches*, edited by David L. Strug et al., 23–40. New York: Haworth, 1986.

Khalil, Lufti A., and Fatimi Mayyada al-Nammari. "Two Large Wine Presses at Khirbet Yajuz, Jordan." *Bulletin of the American Schools of Oriental Research* 318 (2000): 41–57.

Kirby, James Temple. "Alcohol and Irony: The Campaign of Westmoreland Davis for Governor, 1909–1917." *Virginia Magazine of History and Biography* 73 (1965): 259–79.

Kopperman, Paul E. "'The Cheapest Pay': Alcohol Abuse in the Eighteenth-Century British Army." *Journal of Military History* 60 (1996): 445–70.

Kudlick, Catherine J. "Fighting the Internal and External Enemies: Alcoholism in World War I France." *Contemporary Drug Problems* 12 (1985): 129–58.

Kumin, Beat. "The Devil's Altar? Crime and the Early Modern Public House." *History Compass* 2 (2005). http://wrap.warwick.ac.uk/289/1/WRAP_Kumin_Devils_altar_History_Compass.pdf. Accessed May 27, 2013.

Lacoste, Pablo. "'Wine and Women': Grape Growers and *Pulperías* in Mendoza, 1561–1852." *Hispanic American Historical Review* 88 (2008): 361–91.

Langhammer, C. "'A Public House Is for All Classes, Men and Women Alike': Women, Leisure and Drink in Second World War England." *Women's History Review* 12 (2003): 423–43.

Larsen, Carlton K. "Relax and Have a Homebrew: Beer, the Public Sphere, and (Re)Invented Traditions." *Food and Foodways* 7 (1997): 265–88.

Lee, Nella. "Impossible Mission: A History of the Legal Control of Native Drinking in Alaska." *Wicazo Sa Review* 12 (1997): 95–109.

Lender, Mark. "Drunkenness as an Offense in Early New England: A Study of 'Puritan' Attitudes." *Quarterly Journal of Studies on Alcohol* 34 (1973): 353–66.

Lock, Carrie. "Original Microbrews: From Egypt to Peru, Archaeologists Are Unearthing Breweries from Long Ago." *Science News* 166 (October 2004): 216–18.

Ludington, Charles. "'Claret Is the Liquor for Boys; Port for Men': How Port Became the 'Englishman's Wine,' 1750s to 1800." *Journal of British Studies* 48 (2009): 364–90.

Lurie, Nancy Oestreich. "The World's Oldest On-Going Protest Demonstration: North American Indian Drinking Patterns." *Pacific Historical Review* 40 (1971): 311–32.

Mäkelä, Klaus, and Matti Viikari. "Notes on Alcohol and the State." *Acta Sociologica* 20 (1977): 155–79.

Mancall, Peter. "Men, Women and Alcohol in Indian Villages in the Great Lakes Region in the Early Republic." *Journal of the Early Republic* 15 (1995): 425–48.

Marjot, D. H. "Delirium Tremens in the Royal Navy and British Army in the 19th Century." *Journal of Studies on Alcohol* 38 (1977): 1613–23.

Marrus, Michael. "Social Drinking in the Belle Epoque." *Journal of Social History* 7 (1974): 115–41.

Marshall, Mac, and Leslie B. Marshall. "Holy and Unholy Spirits: The Effects of Missionization on Alcohol Use in Eastern Micronesia." *Journal of Pacific History* 15 (1980): 135–66.

Martin, Scott C. "Violence, Gender, and Intemperance in Early National Connecticut." *Journal of Social History* 34 (2000): 309–25.

Mason, Nicholas. "'The Sovereign People Are in a Beastly State': The Beer Act of 1830 and Victorian Discourses on Working-Class Drunkenness." *Victorian Literature and Culture* 29 (2001): 109–27.

Mathias, Peter. "Agriculture and the Brewing and Distilling Industries in the Eighteenth Century." *Economic History Review* 5 (1952): 249–57.

———. "The Brewing Industry, Temperance, and Politics." *Historical Journal* 1 (1958): 97–116.

McGahan, A. M. "The Emergence of the National Brewing Oligopoly: Competition in the American Market, 1933–1958." *Business History Review* 65 (1991): 229–84.

McGovern, Patrick E. "The Funerary Banquet of 'King Midas.'" *Expedition* 42 (2000): 21–29.

McGovern, Patrick E., Armen Mirzoian, and Gretchen R. Hall. "Ancient Egyptian Herbal Wines." *Proceedings of the National Academy of Sciences*, 2009. http://www.pnas.org/cgi/doi/10.1073/pnas.0811578106. Accessed February 12, 2011.

McGovern, Patrick E., et al. "Beginning of Viticulture in France." *Proceedings of the National Academy of Sciences* 110 (2013): 10147–52.

———. "Chemical Identification and Cultural Implications of a Mixed Fermented Beverage from Late Prehistoric China." *Asian Perspectives* 44 (2005): 249–70.

———. "Fermented Beverages of Pre- and Proto-Historic China." *Proceedings of the National Academy of Sciences* 101, no. 51 (December 21, 2004): 17593–98.

McKee, W. Arthur. "Sobering Up the Soul of the People: The Politics of Popular Temperance in Late Imperial Russia." *Russian Review* 58 (1999): 212–33.

McWilliams, James E. "Brewing Beer in Massachusetts Bay, 1640–1690." *New England Quarterly* 71, no. 4 (1998): 543–69.

Meacham, Sarah Hand. "'They Will Be Adjudged by Their Drink, What Kinde of Housewives They Are': Gender, Technology, and Household Cidering in England and the Chesapeake, 1690 to 1760." *Virginia Magazine of History and Biography* 111 (2003): 117–50.

Miron, Jeffrey A., and Jeffrey Zwiebel. "Alcohol Consumption during Prohibition." *American Economic Review* 81 (1991): 242–47.

Mitchell, Allan. "The Unsung Villain: Alcoholism and the Emergence of Public Welfare in France, 1870–1914." *Contemporary Drug Problems* 14 (1987): 447–71.

Moffat, Kirstine. "The Demon Drink: Prohibition Novels, 1882–1924." *Journal of New Zealand Literature* 23 (2005): 139–61.

Moloney, Dierdre M. "Combatting 'Whiskey's Work': The Catholic Temperance Movement in Late Nineteenth-Century America." *U.S. Catholic Historian* 16 (1998): 1–23.

Morris, Steve, David Humphreys, and Dan Reynolds. "Myth, Marula and Elephant: An Assessment of Voluntary Ethanol Intoxication of the African Elephant (Loxodonta

Africana) following Feeding on the Fruit of the Marula Tree (Sclerocarya Birrea)." *Physiological and Biochemical Zoology* 78 (2006). http://www.jstor.org/stable/10.1086/499983. Accessed April 26, 2012.

Moseley, Michael E., et al. "Burning Down the Brewery: Establishing and Evacuating an Ancient Imperial Colony at Cerro Baúl, Peru." *Proceedings of the National Academy of Sciences* 102, no. 48 (2005): 17264–71.

Nemser, Daniel. "'To Avoid This Mixture': Rethinking *Pulque* in Colonial Mexico City." *Food and Foodways* 19 (2011): 98–121.

Nurse, Keith. "The Last of the (Roman) Summer Wine." *History Today* 44 (1993): 4–5.

Olukoji, Ayodeji. "Prohibition and Paternalism: The State and the Clandestine Liquor Traffic in Northern Nigeria, c.1898–1918." *International Journal of African Historical Studies* 24 (1991): 349–68.

Osborn, Matthew Warner. "A Detestable Shrine: Alcohol Abuse in Antebellum Philadelphia." *Journal of the Early Republic* 29 (2009): 101–32.

Pearson, Kathy L. "Nutrition and the Early-Medieval Diet." *Speculum* 72 (1997): 1–32.

Peters, Erica J. "Taste, Taxes, and Technologies: Industrializing Rice Alcohol in Northern Vietnam, 1902–1913." *French Historical Studies* 27 (2004): 569–600.

Phillips, Laura L. "In Defense of Their Families: Working-Class Women, Alcohol, and Politics in Revolutionary Russia." *Journal of Women's History* 11 (1999): 97–120.

———. "Message in a Bottle: Working-Class Culture and the Struggle for Political Legitimacy, 1900–1929." *Russian Review* 56 (1997): 25–32.

Platt, B. S. "Some Traditional Alcoholic Beverages and Their Importance to Indigenous African Communities." *Proceedings of the Nutrition Society* 14 (1955): 115–24.

Poo, Mu-Chou. "The Use and Abuse of Wine in Ancient China." *Journal of the Economic and Social History of the Orient* 42 (1999): 123–51.

Purcell, N. "Wine and Wealth in Ancient Italy." *Journal of Roman Studies* 75 (1985): 1–19.

Purcell, Nicolas. "The Way We Used to Eat: Diet, Community, and History at Rome." *American Journal of Philology* 124 (2003): 329–58.

Quinn, John F. "Father Mathew's Disciples: American Catholic Support for Temperance, 1840–1920." *Church History* 65 (1996): 624–40.

Rabin, Dana. "Drunkenness and Responsibility for Crime in the Eighteenth Century." *Journal of British Studies* 44 (2005): 457–77.

Rawson, Michael. "The Nature of Water: Reform and the Antebellum Crusade for Municipal Water in Boston." *Environmental History* 9 (2004): 411–35.

Recio, Gabriela. "Drugs and Alcohol: US Prohibition and the Origin of the Drug Trade in Mexico, 1910–1930." *Journal of Latin American Studies* 34 (2002): 27–33.

Reséndez, Andrés. "Getting Cured and Getting Drunk: State versus Market in Texas and New Mexico, 1800–1850." *Journal of the Early Republic* 22 (2002): 77–103.

Rice, Prudence M. "Wine and Brandy Production in Colonial Peru: A Historical and Archaeological Investigation." *Journal of Interdisciplinary History* 27 (1997): 455–79.

Roberts, James S. "Drink and Industrial Work Discipline in 19th-Century Germany." *Journal of Social History* 15 (1981): 25–38.

Sánchez Montañés, Emma. "Las Bebidas Alcohólicas en la América Indígena: Una Visión General." In *El Vino de Jerez y Otras Bebidas Espirituosas en la Historia de España y América*, 424–28. Madrid: Servicio de Publicaciones del Ayuntamiento de Jerez, 2004.

Santon, T. J. "Columnella's Attitude towards Wine Production." *Journal of Wine Research* 7 (1996): 55–59.

Saracino, Mary E. "Household Production of Alcoholic Beverages in Early-Eighteenth-Century Connecticut." *Journal of Studies on Alcohol* 46 (1985): 244–52.

Smith, Frederic H. "European Impressions of the Island Carib's Use of Alcohol in the Early Colonial Period." *Ethnohistory* 53 (2006): 543–66.

Smith, Michael A. "Social Usages of the Public Drinking House: Changing Aspects of Class and Leisure." *British Journal of Sociology* 34 (1983): 367–85.

Stanislawski, Dan. "Dionysus Westward: Early Religion and the Economic Geography of Wine." *Geographical Review* 65 (1975): 427–44.

Stanziani, Alessandro. "Information, Quality, and Legal Rules: Wine Adulteration in Nineteenth-Century France." *Business History* 51, no. 2 (2009): 268–91.

Steckley, George F. "The Wine Economy of Tenerife in the Seventeenth Century: Anglo-Spanish Partnership in a Luxury Trade." *Economic History Review* 33 (1980): 335–50.

Steinmetz, Devora. "Vineyard, Farm, and Garden: The Drunkenness of Noah in the Context of Primeval History." *Journal of Biblical Literature* 113 (1994): 193–207.

Steel, Louise. "A Goodly Feast . . . A Cup of Mellow Wine: Feasting in Bronze Age Cyprus." *Hesperia* 73 (2004): 281–300.

Stone, Helena. "The Soviet Government and Moonshine, 1917–1929." *Cahiers du Monde Russe et Soviétique* 27 (1986): 359–81.

Tarschys, Daniel. "The Success of a Failure: Gorbachev's Alcohol Policy, 1985–88." *Europe-Asia Studies* 45 (1993): 7–25.

Thorp, Daniel B. "Taverns and Tavern Culture on the Southern Colonial Frontier: Rowan County, North Carolina, 1753–1776." *Journal of Southern History* 62 (1996): 661–88.

Tlusty, B. Ann. "Water of Life, Water of Death: The Controversy over Brandy and Gin in Early Modern Augsburg." *Central European History* 31, no. 1–2 (1999): 1–30.

Transchel, Kate. "Vodka and Drinking in Early Soviet Factories." In *The Human Tradition in Modern Russia*, edited by William B. Husband, 130–37. Wilmington, N.C.: Scholarly Resources, 2000.

Unwin, Tim. "Continuity in Early Medieval Viticulture: Secular or Ecclesiastical Influences?" In *Viticulture in Geographical Perspective*, edited by Harm de Blij, 37. Miami: Miami Geographical Society, 1992.

Urbanowicz, Charles F. "Drinking in the Polynesian Kingdom of Tonga." *Ethnohistory* 22 (1975): 33–50.

Valdez, Lidio M. "Maize Beer Production in Middle Horizon Peru." *Journal of Anthropological Research* 62 (2006): 53–80.

Valverde, Mariana. "'Slavery from Within': The Invention of Alcoholism and the Question of Free Will." *Social History* 22 (1997): 251–68.

van Onselen, Charles. "Randlords and Rotgut, 1886–1903: An Essay on the Role of Alcohol in the Development of European Imperialism and Southern African Capitalism, with Special Reference to Black Mineworkers in the Transvaal Republic." *History Workshop* 2 (1976): 33–89.

Vargas, Mark A. "The Progressive Agent of Mischief: The Whiskey Ration and Temperance in the United States Army." *Historian* 67 (2005): 199–216.

Warner, Jessica. "Faith in Numbers: Quantifying Gin and Sin in Eighteenth-Century England." *Journal of British Studies* 50 (2011): 76–99.

Warner, Jessica, Minghao Her, and Jürgen Rehm. "Can Legislation Prevent Debauchery? Mother Gin and Public Health in 18th-Century England." *American Journal of Public Health* 91 (2001): 375–84.

White, Jonathan. "The 'Slow but Sure Poyson': The Representation of Gin and Its Drinkers, 1736–1751." *Journal of British Studies* 42 (2003): 35–64.

White, Owen. "Drunken States: Temperance and French Rule in Cote d'Ivoire, 1908–1916." *Journal of Social History* 40 (2007): 663–84.

Whitten, David O. "An Economic Inquiry into the Whiskey Rebellion of 1794." *Agricultural History* 49 (1975): 491–504.

Zimmerman, Jonathan. "'One's Total World View Comes into Play': America's Culture War over Alcohol Education, 1945–64." *History of Education Quarterly* 42 (2002): 471–92.

———. "'When the Doctors Disagree': Scientific Temperance and Scientific Authority, 1891–1906." *Journal of the History of Medicine* 48 (1993): 171–97.

Index

126, 129–30; in Caribbean, 135; in First World War, 248–49; during prohibition, 266

Alcoholics Anonymous (AA), 295

Alcoholism, 212, 290, 295, 302

Ale: note on usage of term, 5; production of in Middle Ages, 66–71; in early modern Europe, 100–101. *See also* Beer, production of

Alexander the Great, 32

American Revolution, 167–70

Amphoras, 16–17, 27–28

Angola, 219

Anti-Saloon League of America (ASLA), 196–97

Appellation systems, 157, 178, 289

Aqua vitae, 112, 113, 116. See also Distilled spirits

Assize of Bread and Ale, 68

Australia, 174–75

Bacchus (wine god), 10, 38, 45

"Barbarians": alcohol consumption of, 32; invasions by and alcohol, 52–53

"Battle of the Wines," 80–81

Beer, attitudes toward: in ancient Middle East, 17, 18, 20–21; in ancient Egypt, 19; in ancient Greece, 26, 31, 32; in ancient Rome, 36–37; by early Christians, 51–52; in early modern Europe, 100–101

Beer, consumption of: in ancient Middle East, 18, 36–37; in early Middle Ages, 55; in Middle Ages, 77, 78; in early modern Europe, 92–93, 94, 95, 96; in nineteenth-century Europe, 175–76, 177

Beer, medicinal properties of: in ancient Egypt, 18; in humoral system, 31; in ancient Greece, 41–42; in ancient Rome, 41–42; in twentieth-century United States, 267–68

Beer, production of: in ancient Middle East, 8, 10, 12, 16, 18, 25; in ancient China, 12–13, 14; in early Middle Ages, 55–56; in Middle Ages, 66–68; in early modern Europe, 100–101; in colonial America,

142–43, 145; in nineteenth-century United States, 185–86

Beer Act (1834), 176, 177

Beer fraud, 83

Beer-houses. *See* Public houses

Beer trade, 70, 71

Belgium, 277

Bennett, Judith, 70

Bible, wine in, 46–51, 212–13

Binge-drinking, 23, 308–10

Black Death, 69, 75, 76, 83

Bordeaux, 73, 159–60

Brandy: production of, 113–14, 115, 118, 140, 158–59; health properties of, 113–14, 116; trade in, 118, 159

Brewing. *See* Beer, production of

Brewsters, 69–70, 101, 143

Burgundy, 75, 160

California, 179

Calvin, John, 89, 116

Canada: native peoples in, 234–35; during First World War, 252–53; prohibition in, 273–75; provincial regulations in, 282–83

Canary wine, 97–98

Champagne, 98, 99, 286

Chaptalization, 160, 175

Château Haut-Brion, 102

Chaucer, Geoffrey, 81–82

Chicha (beer), 136

Children and alcohol, 44, 85, 103, 104, 113, 126, 200–201, 285–86, 288. *See also* Binge-drinking; Minimum legal drinking age

China: alcohol in ancient, 11, 12–13, 15, 22–23; opium in, 236–37

Chocolate (beverage), 121

Church, Christian: wine in rituals of, 45–47, 48, 50–51, 52, 212–13; attitudes of toward drinking, 46; wine in Eucharist, 50, 89, 46–48, 212–13; attitudes of toward beer, 51–52; alcohol consumption by clergy, 55–56, 64–65, 84; penitentials on drunkenness, 64. *See also* Monasteries; Reformation, Protestant, and alcohol; "Two-wine" theory

26, 39–40; wine consumption in, 28–31; women and wine in, 30–31. *See also* Symposium

Gruit, 67, 70

Hamburg, 71, 135
Hammurabi, Code of, 17
Hippocrates, 31, 41
Hogarth, William, 126
Honey, 12–13, 19, 22, 38, 39. *See also* Mead
Hops, 70–71, 100
Humoral theory of the body, 31–32, 41, 103–4, 113
Hungary, 100

India, 12, 276–77
Indochina, 235
Inns. *See* Public houses
Ireland, 201
Islam: and prohibition of alcohol, 13–14, 58–64; alcohol in Qur'an, 59–60, 61. *See also* Muslims
Italy: early viticulture in, 27; wine in during Middle Ages, 80; alcohol consumption in, 303. *See also* Rome, ancient

Jamsheed, Persian king, 11
Japan: alcohol in, 205, 236; temperance movement in, 205–6
Jesus Christ, 22, 47, 50, 51
Jews: wine consumption by, 45, 49–50; and wine in Torah, 46, 48, 49; blamed for poisoning water, 76
Judaism. *See* Jews

Lead in alcohol, 38–39
Lenin, Vladimir I., 253, 258
Lloyd George, David, 241, 244

Madeira wine, 155–56
Maine (state), 194, 195
Marx, Karl, 253
Massachusetts (state), 142, 145, 194
Mathias, Peter, 187
Mead, 9, 10, 21, 22, 26, 53, 75

Merrett, Christopher, 98
Mesopotamia: alcohol in, 10, 18–19
Mexico: alcohol in ancient, 15; wine in colonial, 136, 139; pulque in colonial, 136–38; prohibition in, 263, 271–73
Midas, King, funeral feast of, 20–21
Milk, 41, 85
Minimum legal drinking age, 305–6
Monasteries: wine production in, 52, 56–58, 74–75; beer production in, 55–56, 101; consumption of alcohol in, 56, 58, 88; distilling in, 112, 115
Monks. *See* Monasteries
Mormons. *See* Church of Jesus Christ of Latter-day Saints
Mothers Against Drunk Driving (MADD), 307–8
Muhammad, 60, 61
Muslims: in Spain, 61–62; in Africa, 224–25, 289; in France, 304. *See also* Islam

Nahua, 15
Native Americans, alcohol and: in colonial period, 147–52; in nineteenth century, 229–34
Native peoples (Canada), 234–35
Nazis and alcohol, 290–93
Neolithic period, alcohol in, 8
Netherlands, 67, 68
New Zealand, 253, 277, 310
Nicholls, James, 315
Nigeria, 218, 219, 220, 221, 225
Noah, 11, 48
Norway, 275

Pacific Islands, 237–39
Palm wine, 15, 219, 223
Pasteur, Louis, 8
Pepys, Samuel, 102–3
Pérignon, Dom Pierre, 99
Persia, ancient, wine in, 11
Peru, 12, 140
Phylloxera, 178
Poland, 120, 73
Portugal, 99–100, 134–35, 156–58

Port wine, 99–100, 156–57

Prohibition, 45–46, 193, 256–78 passim; in Islam, 58–64; in Reformation, 88–89; in United States, 194–95, 254, 260–71, 279–81; in England, 199–200; in African colonies, 225, 226, 228–29; Native Americans and, 232, 234; native peoples (Canada) and, 235; in Russia, 243–45, 257–60; in Mexico, 271–73; in Canada, 273–75; in Norway, 275; in Sweden, 275–76; in India, 276–77; in Belgium, 277; in New Zealand, 277

Public houses: in ancient Middle East, 17; in Middle Ages, 68, 84–85; in Reformation, 89; in early modern Europe, 106–8, 125; in colonial America, 144, 145; in nineteenth-century Europe, 176–77, 186–87; in temperance campaigns, 193, 196; in First World War, 247–48; speakeasies, 266, 282; in twentieth-century United States, 281–82; in twentieth-century England, 284–85; in postwar France, 301–2. See also Saloons

Pulque, 136–38

Puritans and alcohol, 89, 141–42, 143, 151

Reformation, Protestant, and alcohol, 88–90, 100, 116, 143

Rhine, wine trade down, 54, 73

Rice wine, 9, 12–13

Rome, ancient: wine production in, 32–33, 35–36, 38–39, 52; wine trade in, 33; wine consumption in, 33–36; women and wine in, 34–35; water supply of, 43

Roosevelt, President Franklin D., 279, 280, 289

Rum, 119–20, 146, 242

Rush, Dr. Benjamin, 153–54, 166

Russia: vodka in, 120; in First World War, 243–45; prohibition in, 243–45, 253–54; Revolution in, 244–45, 253–54. See also Soviet Union

Saloons, 196

Second World War, 295–99

Scotland, 112, 116, 119, 201

Shakespeare, William, 97

Sherry wine, 97–98

Short, Dr. Richard, 122–23

Slaves: provided with alcohol, 35, 229; purchased with alcohol, 217, 219

Socialists and alcohol, 272–73

South Africa: wine production in, 134; colonial alcohol policies in, 224, 227–29

Soviet Union: prohibition in, 253–54, 257–60; campaigns against alcohol in, 293–95, 310–14; drinking patterns in, 310–11. See also Russia

Spain: early viticulture in, 27; Islam and alcohol in, 61–62; wine production in, 96–97, 138; American colonies of, 97, 136–40

Sparkling wine. See Champagne; Wine, sparkling

Spirits. See Distillation; Distilled spirits; Absinthe; Brandy; Gin; Vodka; Whiskey

Sugar, 98, 99, 122, 160, 175. See also Chaptalization

Sweden, 275–76

Switzerland, 181

Symposium, 28–31

Tahiti, 237

Taverns. See Public houses

Tea, 43, 121, 214

Teetotalism. See Abstinence from alcohol

Temperance movements, 192–215 passim; in United States, 184, 193, 194–97; in Scotland, 197; in England, 197–98; in France, 202–4, 251; in Germany, 204–5; in Japan, 205–6; in Nigeria, 225; Native Americans and, 232–33

Tithingmen, 144–45

Tokaji aszu, 100

"Two-wine" theory, 46–48, 212–13

United States: wine in, 140–41; nineteenth-century alcohol consumption in, 168–70, 182–84; German immigrants in, 185, 186; Irish immigrants in, 185, 186; national prohibition in, 254, 260–71, 279–82; in First World War, 254–55; twentieth-century drinking patterns in, 281–82. *See also* Native Americans, alcohol and; Prohibition; *and individual states*

Venice, Republic of, 90–92
Vietnam, 235–36
Vikings, 54
Virginia (state), 140–41, 305–6
Vodka, 120, 258–60, 293–95, 312, 313, 314
Volstead Act. *See* Prohibition: in United States

Wales, 201
Water, for hydration, 7–8, 42–44, 54–55, 67, 76, 93–94, 121–23, 133–34, 141, 148, 166–67, 185, 187–91, 214–15, 286, 319–21. *See also* Alcohol, as substitute for water
Whiskey (Whisky): note on usage of term, 5; production of, 119, 159; trade in, 159; consumption of, 182–83
"Whiskey Rebellion," 168–70
Whisky, note on usage of term, 5. *See also* Whiskey
Wine, consumption of: in ancient Middle East, 12–13, 19; in ancient Egypt, 17, 19, 42–44; in ancient Greece, 28–31; in ancient Rome, 33–34; in early Middle Ages, 55; in Middle Ages, 73–74, 76–77; in early modern Europe, 90–92, 94–97
Wine, medicinal properties of, 22–23, 40–41, 49–50, 85, 103–6, 203, 315–16
Wine, production of: in ancient Middle East, 8, 9, 14–16; myths concerning

origins of, 10–11; in ancient China, 11, 12–13; in ancient Egypt, 16–17; in ancient Greece, 26, 38; in ancient Rome, 33, 34, 38–39; in Middle Ages, 71–72, 74–75; in Spain, 96–97, 138; in nineteenth-century France, 178; in twentieth-century France, 286–87
Wine, regulation of: in ancient Greece, 39; in Middle Ages, 81–83
Wine, religion and: in ancient societies, 16, 19–20, 21, 22, 37–38; in Reformation, 89–90
Wine, social status and: in ancient societies, 17, 18, 20, 22, 37; in Middle Ages, 73–74; in early modern Europe, 104–5
Wine, sparkling, 98–99
Wine fraud, 81–83, 157, 160–61, 209–10, 211
Wine trade: in ancient Middle East, 17, 18–19; ancient Greek, 26, 27–28, 33; ancient Roman, 33; in Middle Ages, 72–73; in early modern Europe, 97–98, 157–58
Woman's Christian Temperance Union (WCTU), 195, 296; Catholics in, 195–96, 273; in Japan, 205–6
Women: as brewers, 69–70, 101, 135, 143; as distillers, 115
Women, drinking by, 318–19; in ancient Greece, 30–31; in ancient Rome, 34–35; in early modern Europe, 107–8, 126; during First World War, 248–49; in United States during prohibition, 266; in twentieth-century England, 296; in twentieth-century United States, 302
Women's Organization for National Prohibition Reform (WONPR), 269–70